DESIGN PATTERNS
IN COMMUNICATIONS
SOFTWARE

SIGS Reference Library

DESIGN PATTERNS IN COMMUNICATIONS SOFTWARE

Edited by
Linda Rising

Foreword by
Douglas C. Schmidt

CAMBRIDGE
UNIVERSITY PRESS

PUBLISHED BY THE PRESS SYNDICATE OF THE UNIVERSITY OF CAMBRIDGE
The Pitt Building, Trumpington Street, Cambridge, United Kingdom

CAMBRIDGE UNIVERSITY PRESS
The Edinburgh Building, Cambridge CB2 2RU, UK
40 West 20th Street, New York, NY 10011–4211, USA
10 Stamford Road, Oakleigh, VIC 3166, Australia
Ruiz de Alarcón 13, 28014 Madrid, Spain
Dock House, The Waterfront, Cape Town 8001, South Africa

http://www.cambridge.org

First published in 2001

Typeface Adobe Garamond 11.5/13.5 pt.   *System* Quark XPress®   [GH]

Printed in the United States of America

A catalog record for this book is available from the British Library.

Library of Congress Cataloging in Publication Data

Design patterns in communications software / edited by Linda Rising.
    p. cm. – (SIGS reference library series ; 19)
    Includes bibliographical references and index.
    ISBN 0-521-79040-9
    1. Communications software. 2. Computer software – Development. 3. Software
patterns. I. Rising, Linda. II. Series.

TK5105.9 D48 2001
005.7'13–dc21   00-065094

ISBN 0 521 79040 9

CONTENTS

FOREWORD
THE CONSEQUENCES OF
INFORMATION TECHNOLOGY
COMMODITIZATION

I NFORMATION TECHNOLOGY (IT) is rapidly becoming a commodity, where hardware and software artifacts get faster, cheaper, and better at a predictable pace. For the past decade we've benefited from the commoditization of hardware, such as CPUs and storage devices, and networking elements, such as IP routers. More recently, the maturation of programming languages, such as Java and C++, operating environments, such as POSIX and Java Virtual Machines, and middleware, such as CORBA and Enterprise Java Beans, are helping to commoditize many software layers and components, as well. Historically, however, the quality of commodity software – particularly communication software – has lagged behind hardware. Fortunately, recent improvements have enabled commodity off-the-shelf (COTS) software components to be used in an increasing number of mission-critical applications, ranging from avionics mission computing to hot rolling mills, backbone routers, and high-speed network switches.

The commoditization of IT has a number of consequences:

- *Greater focus on integration rather than programming* – There is an ongoing trend *away from* programming systems from scratch *toward* integrating them by configuring and customizing reusable frameworks and components. While it is possible in theory to program systems from scratch, economic and organizational constraints – as well as increasingly complex requirements and global competitive pressures – are making it infeasible economically to do so in practice. In the future, therefore, most systems will be configured by integrating reusable commodity components implemented by different suppliers.

- *Increased technology convergence and standardization* – To leverage inexpensive commodity hardware and software effectively, application developers are converging toward fewer general-purpose tools, platforms, and methods than they've used in the past. For example, rather than choosing from dozens of programming languages, operating systems, network protocols, and middleware, newer systems are being developed with a relatively small number of common tools and platforms, such as C++, Java, UNIX, Windows NT, TCP/IP, and CORBA, many of which are industry standards. Likewise, there's a general consolidation of development methods and modeling notations away from ad hoc technologies toward industry standards, such as UML.

- *Growing economies of scale for mass market technology and personnel* – Due to technology convergence, there is an increasing abundance of good technology and personnel available at competitive prices for mainstream mass markets, such as e-commerce or consumer electronics built using general-purpose operating systems, languages, networks, and middleware. However, for niche markets – such as real-time embedded systems written using proprietary platforms, languages, and tools – commodity hardware and software artifacts and personnel are much more expensive – if they can be found at all. Thus, the further an industry diverges from the mainstream mass market, (1) the greater the costs it incurs to develop, deploy, and maintain systems and (2) the more its customers must pay for the niche technology.

- *More opportunities for disruptive technologies and global competition* – Another consequence of IT commoditization is that industries long protected by high barriers to entry, such as the telecommunication and aerospace industries, will be much more vulnerable to disruptive technologies and global competition. For example, advances in high-performance COTS hardware and fault-tolerant middleware are making it possible to build dependable network elements ranging from PBXs to high-speed backbone routers using standard hardware and software components that cost much less than today's highly proprietary systems. In turn, the commoditization of network elements will continue to erode the profit margins that market leaders of communication equipment have enjoyed historically.

- *Lower-priced, but potentially lower-quality components* – According to John Chambers, CEO of Cisco Systems, consumers are the big winners of IT commoditization because "everything gets cheaper forever." (Clearly, John must not have purchased a house in Silicon Valley recently.) Nevertheless, global competition and time-to-market pressures are generally increasing productivity and driving commodity IT prices to marginal cost *for low- and middle-end systems.* What's not clear at this point, however, is how well commodity hardware and software can support the dependability and fidelity requirements of *high-end systems,* such as carrier class central office switches or flight-critical avionics control systems. Unfortunately, there will be little incentive to improve the quality of commodity artifacts as long as:

  – Most users emphasize price and features over quality and scalability.
  – Vendors can continue to make money selling lower-quality products inexpensively in mass quantities.
  – There's no credible competition or alternatives.

- *The decline of internally funded R&D* – Shrinking profit margins and increasing shareholder pressure to cut costs are making it hard for companies to invest heavily in long-term research that doesn't yield short-term payoffs. As a result, many companies can no longer afford the luxury of internal R&D organizations that produce proprietary hardware and software components with customized quality-of-service support. To fill this void, therefore, commodity hardware and software researched and developed by third parties is becoming increasingly strategic to many industries. This trend is requiring companies to transition away from proprietary architectures toward more open systems that can reap the benefits of externally funded R&D and open-source development processes.

- *Potential complexity cap for next-generation complex systems* – Over the past five years there has been a steady flow of faculty, staff, and grad students out of the traditional research centers, such as universities and research labs, and into startup companies and other industrial positions. While this migration has helped to fuel a global economic IT boom, it's unclear whether this trend bodes well for long-term technology innovation. In particular, without an investment in fundamental

R&D it will be hard for developers of next-generation systems to master the complexities associated with the move toward large-scale distributed "systems of systems" in many domains. Thus, as the current generation of technology transitions run their course, the systemic reduction in long-term research funding relative to short-term venture capital funding may be limiting the level of complexity of systems that can be developed and integrated using commoditized hardware and software components.

In the face of the relentless drive toward IT commoditization, it has become essential for developers, companies, and even entire countries to reconsider how to remain competitive. As hardware and software components are increasingly being written, fabricated, and deployed as inexpensive commodities via low-cost digital distribution channels over the Internet, traditional market leaders and supply chains are being altered significantly. For example, the ubiquity of the Web and the maturation of operating system and middleware standards are enabling a rapid growth of open-source operating systems, such as Linux, and open-source CORBA middleware, such as MICO, omniORB, ORBacus, and TAO. Moreover, open-source business models based on industrial standards are significantly altering the pricing levels, business strategies, and licensing models for vendors of proprietary "binary-only" solutions.

How Patterns Are Helping Us Succeed in a World of Information Technology Commoditization

In a highly commoditized IT economy, human capital is an increasingly strategic asset. In the future, therefore, I believe that premium value and competitive advantage will accrue to individuals, organizations, and nations that master the patterns and pattern languages necessary to integrate COTS hardware and software to develop complex systems that can't be bought off the shelf. Patterns represent successful solutions to challenges that arise when building software in particular contexts. When related patterns are woven together, they form a language that helps to (1) define a vocabulary for talking about software development and integration challenges and (2) provide a process for the orderly resolution of these challenges.

Identifying, studying, and applying patterns and pattern languages can help us ensure that COTS components are created and integrated into high-quality communication systems by addressing the following system development and evolution challenges:

- *Communication of architectural knowledge among developers* – Patterns help capture essential properties of software architectures, while suppressing certain details that are not relevant at a particular level of abstraction. For example, patterns help to document software architectures by expressing the structure and dynamics of participants at a level higher than (1) source code or (2) object-oriented (OO) design models that focus on individual objects and classes. Patterns also provide software organizations with shared vocabularies and common architectural models, thereby helping to improve communication within and across developers, teams, and projects.

- *Accommodating new design paradigms or architectural styles* – Historically, the adoption of COTS and other technology advances has been limited by the effort required to transition developers trained in traditional techniques to newer paradigms, such as OO analysis, design, and programming. Fortunately, many core patterns have originated in non-OO contexts, such as operating system kernels, I/O subsystems, and databases, that are familiar to developers of legacy systems. Thus, developers who study these patterns can more readily migrate to new paradigms by learning how to leverage and extend domain expertise they gained from their prior experience and express it effectively in newer languages, platforms, methods, and notations.

- *Resolving key nonfunctional forces associated with accidental complexity* – A surprising amount of software complexity is accidental and arises from limitations with development tools and platforms. For instance, the vestiges of legacy hardware and software platform diversity have made it hard to develop portable applications and tools that can run across multiple operating environments, such as POSIX, Win32, and embedded real-time operating systems. These accidental complexities are being addressed today by identifying key patterns and pattern languages and reifying them into reusable middleware, such as CORBA or real-time Java, that shields developers from many tedious, error-prone, and nonportable programming details.

- *Avoiding development traps and pitfalls that were historically learned by costly trial and error* – Developers of communication systems must address many recurring design challenges related to key properties, such as efficiency, scalability, robustness, and extensibility. For decades, successful architects and developers have learned to resolve these challenges by trial and error during a lengthy apprenticeship process. At any point in time, however, the knowledge gained from this process resides largely in the heads of domain experts or buried deep within complex system source code. By externalizing this expertise in the form of patterns and pattern languages, new generations of developers can learn how to avoid common traps and pitfalls in their domains without requiring such an extensive apprenticeship.

MANIFESTING THE MATURATION OF THE PATTERNS COMMUNITY

Over the past seven years an extensive body of literature on patterns and pattern languages has emerged that identifies, documents, and catalogs successful families of solutions to common software challenges. This literature has improved the construction of commercial software significantly by enabling the widespread reuse of software architectures, developer expertise, and OO application framework components. As a consequence, we now have a good collective understanding of how to design and implement certain types of software components using off-the-shelf tools and methods.

Much of the patterns literature has focused on a few well-traveled domains, however, such as graphical user-interface frameworks or business applications. As the scope and criticality of communication system requirements continue to expand, our most pressing need has become elevating the focus from relatively small-scale, stand-alone software mechanisms, protocols, and patterns to large-scale, distributed policies, architectures, and pattern languages. Developers of communication systems face many vexing inherent complexities, such as partial failures, distributed deadlock, and end-to-end QoS enforcement, that contain many interlocking aspects. Therefore, unless the panoply of commodity hardware and software point solutions can be consolidated into integrated frameworks, their value will be diminished and can in fact make matters worse instead of better.

Until now, no single book has focused on patterns and pattern languages for communication systems with mission-critical requirements, such as telecommunications systems with 24 × 7 high-availability requirements or real-time middleware that can provide stringent end-to-end latency and jitter guarantees to applications. The material in this book exemplifies the maturation of the patterns community and is a major contribution to the study of patterns and pattern languages for communication systems. By learning this material you'll be able to better design and implement communication systems that can't be bought off the shelf, thereby improving the productivity and quality of your software solutions and staying ahead of your competition.

We are fortunate that Linda Rising has found time in her busy life to assemble the work of an outstanding group of authors for this book. During the past ten years I've had the honor to meet and work with most of these authors, many of whom are internationally renowned experts in their fields. If you want thorough coverage of the patterns and pattern languages that are shaping next-generation communication software, read this book. I've learned much from it and I'm confident that you will too.

Douglas C. Schmidt
University of California, Irvine

ACKNOWLEDGMENTS

I WAS THE CONFERENCE CHAIR for the first ChiliPLoP in 1998 and was not able to attend the TelePLoP hot topic. This publication was conceived at that gathering, but it was only when the time suddenly became available that I was able to implement it.

I have tried to capture the spirit of the participants' intent even though I'm somewhat removed in time and distance!

Thanks to all the TelePLoPers and all the other contributors of communications patterns. These people are the inspiration for this book and the creators of its content. All I have done is to line 'em up and move 'em out!

Thanks to the good folks at Cambridge University Press, especially Lothlórien Homet, who believed that this book was important and should be published.

Thanks to my husband, Karl Rehmer, for being happy and proud about what I do and supporting and encouraging me along the way.

Linda Rising
Denmark 2001

CONTRIBUTORS

Michael Adams is a telecommunications software engineer with 11 years of experience with AT&T, Lucent Technologies, and Idea Integration. He currently runs Timberway International (www.timberway.com), a company specializing in helping individuals and small businesses market their products on the Internet. He likes to spend his off hours practicing and teaching Wing Tsun Kung Fu. madams@timberway.com

Chris Cleeland graduated with a B.S. in Computer Engineering from Tulane University and currently works for Object Computing, Inc. in St. Louis, Missouri, where he develops and teaches industry courses in CORBA and Design Patterns, consults in the realm of networking and Distributed Computing, and helps support The ACE ORB, an open-source ORB from the Distributed Object Computing (DOC) Center at Washington University, St. Louis, of which he was a founding researcher. His software development experience spans two decades and several areas such as health care, manufacturing automation, and telecommunications. Chris thanks his parents for providing him with a solid foundation, his wife Pat and family for their constant loving support, and the late W. Richard (Rich) Stevens, a close friend whose writings continue to inspire aspirations of greatness. cleeland_c@ociweb.com

James O. Coplien is a member of the Software Production Research Department in Bell Laboratories of Lucent Technologies. He holds a B.S. in Electrical and Computer Engineering and an M.S. in Computer Science, both from the University of Wisconsin at Madison, and a Ph.D. from Vrije Universiteit Brussel. He is currently studying organization communication patterns to help guide process evolution. His other research areas include multiparadigm design and architectural patterns of telecommunication software. He is author of *C++ Programming Styles and Idioms,* the foremost high-end C++ book in the industry, and of *Multi-Paradigm Design for C++.* He was co-editor of two volumes of *Pattern Languages of Program Design,* and he writes a patterns column for the *C++ Report.* He is a Member Emeritus of the Hillside Group. He was program chair of ACM OOPSLA '96 and program co-chair of the First International South Pacific Conference on Pattern Languages of Program Design. cope@research.bell-labs.com

Fernando Das Neves is a Ph.D. candidate at Virginia Tech. He was formerly at Universidad Nacional de La Plata, Argentina, where the *Bodyguard* pattern (included in this publication) was originally written. His research interests include information retrieval and visualization and object-oriented programming. fdasneve@vt.edu

Dennis L. DeBruler is a Distinguished Member of Technical Staff at Bell Laboratories of Lucent Technologies. He received a B.S.E.E. from Northwestern and an M.S. in Computer Science from Purdue University. His work at Bell Laboratories during the 1970s concerned software development tools for the custom processors used in electronic switching systems. In the 1980s and 1990s he helped architect the software and hardware of various telecommunication "boxes" (packet switch, ATM terminal adapter, video server, speech recognition). He has also helped design, implement, and test the software for most of these boxes. Dennis attended the first PLoP conference, for which he submitted a paper, and he has shepherded at least one paper for nearly every PLoP since then. His pattern language on real-time scheduling was workshopped at one of the TelePLoP tracks at ChiliPLoP. debruler@lucent.com

Michael Duell is a software designer at AG Communication Systems in Phoenix, Arizona. He is currently working on the Communications Assistance for Law Enforcement Act feature. He has published papers on software design patterns, including: "Non-Software Examples of Software Design Patterns" in *Object* magazine, July 1997; "Managing Change through Patterns" in *IEEE Communications* magazine, April 1999; and "Non-Software Examples of Patterns of Software Architecture" in *JOOP,* May 2000. He has presented papers at OOPSLA '96 and IEEE COMPSAC '99. He has also organized workshops and poster sessions on non-software pattern examples at OOPSLA '97 and '98. He holds a B.S. in Computer Science and Mathematics from the University of California, Davis, an M.S. in Telecommunications from Southern Methodist University and an M.B.A. from Arizona State University. duellm@agcs.com; http://www.agcs.com/supportv2/techpapers/patterns/papers/tutnotes/index.htm

Robert Gamoke is a Distinguished Member of Technical Staff at Lucent

Technologies in Naperville, Illinois. After joining Western Electric in 1980, he has served as the principal software architect for the 1A and 1B processor used in the 4ESS switch. He continues to develop features and to mine patterns from the designs of that switch. gamoke@lucent.com

Alejandra Garrido has been a graduate student at the University of Illinois at Urbana-Champaign since 1997. She was formerly at Universidad Nacional de La Plata, Argentina, as a member of the research group Lifia. Her research interests include object-oriented frameworks, design patterns, and software refactoring. She obtained an M.S. in Computer Science from UIUC in May 2000. Her M.S. thesis and her current research are in refactoring C programs. garrido@students.uiuc.edu

Christopher D. Gill is a Research Associate in the Computer Science Department at Washington University in St. Louis, Missouri, working in the Center for Distributed Object Computing. He conducts research on quality of service (QoS) patterns and frameworks for distributed object computing. He is a doctoral candidate in the Computer Science Department at Washington University, and is planning to graduate in May 2001. While at the Center for Distributed Object Computing, he has made research contributions in the areas of hybrid static/dynamic processor scheduling strategies, adaptive resource management, and empirical measurement and visualization of dynamic real-time performance. cdgill@cs.wustl.edu http://www.cs.wustl.edu/~cdgill

Robert Hanmer is a Consulting Member of Technical Staff at Lucent Technologies. He is a past Program Chair for the Pattern Languages of Programming Conference held at Allerton Park. He is active in the TelePLoP group, an informal collection of pattern advocates and authors interested in the field of telecommunications. He is a co-author of a collection of patterns in the PLoPD2 book on reliable system design, which has been republished in *The Patterns Handbook: Techniques, Strategies, and Applications.* The Telecommunications Input Output pattern language that he co-authored was published in the PLoPD4 book. Within Lucent, he is active as an advocate and teacher of patterns and designing for reliability. He has been learning the patterns of the 4ESS switch since 1987. He holds B.S. and M.S. degrees in Computer Science from Northwestern University. hanmer@lucent.com

Neil B. Harrison is a Distinguished Member of Technical Staff at Avaya, Inc. He works in telecommunications software, software tools, and software process and organization studies. He was an early advocate of patterns and regularly teaches pattern courses. He has published patterns and articles on patterns in numerous books and was the lead editor of *Pattern Languages of Program Design,* volume 4. His leadership in pattern "shepherding" has been recognized through the "Neil Harrison Shepherding Award," which is awarded at PLoP conferences. He is also a Past Program Chair of ChiliPLoP. Together with Jim Coplien, he has conducted extensive studies on software organizations and has published articles in this field. He received a B.S. from Brigham Young University, with high honors and university scholar designations, and an M.S. from Purdue University, both in computer science. nbharrison@avaya.com

Fred Keeve recently retired from Lucent Technologies after a career of telecomunication system design and development.

Fred Kuhns is a Senior Research Associate in the Applied Research Laboratory at Washington University. He received the M.S.E.E. from Washington University, St. Louis, and the B.S.E.E. from the University of Memphis, Tennessee. His research interests include operating system and network support for high-performance, real-time distributed object computing systems. His recent research projects have focused on the design and implementation of real-time middleware, I/O subsystems, high-performance interfaces, and integrated service routers. His current projects include developing multiservice routers with integrated support for active networking and different QoS models. fredk@arl.wustl.edu; http://www.arl.wustl.edu:/~fredk

David L. Levine is Director of the Center for Distributed Object Computing of the Department of Computer Science, Washington University in St. Louis. Dr. Levine's current research interests include development of efficient object-oriented middleware for embedded systems and testing and performance analysis of real-time systems. In addition, he helps maintain the Adaptive Communications Environment (ACE) framework and The ACE ORB (TAO). levine@cs.wustl.edu; http://www.cs.wustl.edu/~levine

Gerard Meszaros is Chief Architect at Clearstream Consulting, consulting resources in applying advanced software development techniques, such as eXtreme programming to help Clearstream's clients achieve faster and higher quality systems solutions. He helps clients apply business modeling and object and component technology to a variety of problem domains including telecommunication, e-commerce, and gas transportation. Previously, he served as Chief Architect on several major projects at Nortel Networks' R&D

subsidiary, Bell Northern Research. He has had patterns published in each of the first three PLoPD books and has been invited to serve on panels, conduct workshops, and present papers and tutorials at OOPSLA and other conferences. He uses patterns actively in designing software and in mentoring software developers, architects and project managers in good software design practices. He holds a B.Sc. (Honors) in Computer Science from University of Manitoba. gerard.meszaros@acm.org; http://www.clearstreamconsulting.com

Keith Nicodemus received an A.T.&T. Bell Laboratories Fellow award for 1987. He retired from A.T.&T. (now Lucent) in November 1995, and since then he has worked intermittently for Lucent at Bell Laboratories. He holds a B.S.E.E. from the University of Iowa and an M.S.E.E. from Stevens Institute of Technology. knicodemus@lucent.com

Carlos O'Ryan is a Research Assistant of the Distributed Object Computing Laboratory and graduate student of the Department of Computer Engineering, University of California, Irvine. In that position he participates in the development of TAO (The ACE ORB), an Open Source, real-time, high-performance, CORBA-compliant ORB. Before his current position he served as senior developer in GBO, a Chilean company that develops distributed interactive simulation systems for the army and air force of that country. He also participated in the deployment of this system for the armies of Mexico and El Salvador. He obtained his B.S. in Mathematics from the Pontificia Universidad Catolica de Chile in 1992 and an M.S. in Computer Science from Washington University in 1999. coryan@cs.wustl.edu; http://doc.ece.uci.edu/~coryan/

Don S. Olson is a Senior Engineer with AG Communication Systems. With a B.S. in Mathematics from the University of Alabama in Huntsville, Alabama, he has worked in software development for more than 23 years in industries as diverse as CAD/CAM systems, space exploration, commercial flight systems, and telecommunications. He is a Strowger Award recipient for his contributions to a scalable broker-based architecture, and he has received numerous software design awards for his work in automatic call distribution systems, simulators, and real-time database protocols. He is a former Program Chair for ChiliPLoP in Wickenburg, Arizona, contributor to *The Patterns Handbook,* and presented to the plenary session of the Intelligent Networks workshop in Colorado Springs, Colorado, in 1997. He is a frequent visitor and participant in discussions on WikiWikiWeb, a patterns forum, and is currently working on a book about alternative management for software development. olsond@agcs.com

Ossama Othman is a Research Assistant at the Distributed Object Computing Laboratory in the Department of Electrical and Computer Engineering, University of California at Irvine. He is currently pursuing his Ph. D. studies and research in secure, scalable, and high availability CORBA-based middleware. As part of that work, he is one of the core development team members for the open source CORBA ORB TAO (The ACE ORB). Prior to his work in CORBA-based middleware, he served as a computer-imaging specialist at the Center for Radiophysics and Space Research at Cornell University, where he developed software for use in the analysis of NASA Galileo spacecraft images, such as those of the Shoemaker-Levy comet crash on Jupiter. ossama@uci.edu; http://www.ece.uci.edu/~ossama/

Jeff Parsons received his B.S. degree in Computer Science from Washington University in St. Louis, Missouri. He is currently employed as a Research Associate at the Center for Distributed Object Computing, also at Washington University, as a member of the TAO development team, and is pursuing an M.S. degree. His professional interests include object-oriented design patterns and frameworks, distributed object middleware, and CORBA. parsons@cs.wustl.edu; http://siesta.cs.wustl.edu/~parsons/

Nat Pryce is a Senior Software Engineer at Quokka Sports in San Francisco and London. He is part of a team building distributed systems that deliver real-time visualization of sports events over the Web. Previously he worked as a research associate at Imperial College, London, where he obtained a Ph.D. for his research into architectures for component-based, distributed systems. Nat.Pryce@quokka.com

Linda Rising has a Ph.D. from Arizona State University in the area of object-based design metrics. Her background includes university teaching experience as well as work in industry in the areas of telecommunications, avionics, and strategic weapons systems. She has presented a number of tutorials and workshops at OOPSLA and other conferences. She was the Conference Chair for the first Southwestern patterns conference, ChiliPLoP. She is the editor of *A Patterns Handbook.* She was the editor of a special issue of *IEEE Communications* on Design Patterns in Communications Software and the editor of *A Pattern Almanac 2000.* risingl@acm.org

Douglas C. Schmidt is an Associate Professor in the Electrical and Computer Engineering Department at the University of California, Irvine. He is currently serving as a Program Manager at the DARPA Information Technology Office where he leads the national effort on distributed object computing middleware research. His research focuses on design patterns, optimization principles, and empirical analyses of object-oriented techniques that facilitate the development of high-performance, real-time distributed object computing middleware on parallel processing platforms running over high-speed networks and embedded system interconnects. He is an internationally recognized and widely cited expert on distributed object computing patterns, middleware frameworks, and real-time CORBA, and he has published widely in top IEEE, ACM, IFIP, and USENIX technical journals, conferences, and books. His publications cover a range of experimental systems topics including high-performance communication software systems, parallel processing for high-speed networking protocols, real-time distributed object computing with CORBA, and object-oriented design patterns for concurrent and distributed systems. schmidt@uci.edu; http://www.ece.uci.edu./~schmidt/

Greg Stymfal obtained a B.S. in Electrical Engineering from the University of Colorado. Since that time he has developed, tested, and managed software in the embedded telecommunications industry. He has been involved with software and organizational patterns since 1994. The Telecommunications Input Output pattern language that he co-authored was published in the PLoPD4 book. He is currently a Product Manager for VoIP solutions at AG Communication Systems. stymfalg@agcs.com

Junichi Suzuki received B.S., M.S., and Ph.D. degrees in Computer Science from Keio University, Japan. He is currently a research fellow at the Department of Information and Computer Science at University of California, Irvine. Before his current position, he worked for the Object Management Group Japan, Inc. as a technical director. His research interests include object-oriented patterns and frameworks, computational reflection, object-oriented development methodology, distributed object computing, intelligent user interface, agent communication, and computational biology. He is a member of ACM, IEEE-CS, IPSJ, and JSSST. suzuki@yy.cs.keio.ac.jp

Greg Utas obtained an Honors B.Sc. in Computer Science from the University of Western Ontario in 1979. Since joining Nortel Networks in 1981, he has served as the principal architect of the call processing frameworks for DMS-100 Centrex services, the DMS-100 International switch, and Nortel's GSM Mobile Switching Center. He has presented papers at the International Switching Symposium, the International Workshop on Feature Interactions in Telecommunications and Software Systems, and at the TelePLoP track at ChiliPLoP. He is currently Chief Software Architect, Mobility Services Development. utas@nortelnetworks.com

Just A. van den Broecke of Just Objects B.V. (http://www.justobjects.nl) is a freelance software architect/developer/trainer specializing in distributed object technology. Currently he spends most of his time using Java and Web technologies like XML in projects that range from e-commerce banking applications to multiuser-multimedia tools for performing artists (http://www.keyworx.org). At the time of writing the article in this publication, he was working at the Forward Looking Work department within Lucent Technologies in Huizen, The Netherlands. just@justobjects.nl

Yoshikazu Yamamoto received the B.S., M.S., and Ph.D. degrees in Administration Engineering from Keio University, Tokyo, Japan. He is currently an Associate Professor in the Department of Computer and Information Science at Keio University. He worked at Linkoping University, Sweden, as a visiting professor from 1981 to 1983. His current research interests include distributed discrete event simulation and modeling, OOP, agent programming, intelligent interface, and documentation. He is a member of ACM, IEEE-CS, IPSJ, and the director board of JSSST. yama@ics.keio.ac.jp; http://www.yy.ics.keio.ac.jp/

INTRODUCTION
TelePLoP – The Beginning

Linda Rising

PATTERNS CONFERENCES are called PLoP™s[1] – yes, the acronym came first! It represents Pattern Languages of Programs, as defined by Ward Cunningham in preparation for the first PLoP in 1994. There are several PLoPs each year: the original at Allerton Park in Monticello, Illinois, U.S.A., EuroPLoP at Kloster Irsee near Munich, Germany, and ChiliPLoP at the Wickenburg Inn in Arizona, U.S.A. The first KoalaPLoP in Australia was held in May 2000. Originally the primary activity at these conferences was workshopping patterns, but the conferences also provide a place where pattern writers can gather to talk about ideas for patterns, pattern languages, and other pattern topics.

Dick Gabriel introduced the process of a writers' workshop to the patterns community. It's a practice used by authors to get feedback from other authors about their work. Jim Coplien (Cope) has written a pattern language for writers' workshops [Coplien99] and Jim Doble, Gerard Meszaros [Meszaros+98], and I have written about the adventure of pattern writing [Rising98]. In a nutshell, a group of writers will gather to read and comment on their work. The group sits in a circle and one author is chosen for the first session. A facilitator keeps the process on track. The author begins the session by reading a small selection from the work and then leaves the circle to become "a fly on the wall," someone who can hear the comments but make no response. The group then talks about elements of the work that shouldn't be changed – the things they liked. This is followed by suggestions for improvement. During the discussion, the author hears and takes notes but cannot respond. When all comments have been given, the author

---

[1]PLoP is a trademark of The Hillside Group, Inc.

returns and may ask for clarification on any comment but, again, may not respond, explain, or defend any part of the work. The reason for this is simple: If the work cannot stand on its own, the author should hear that and make any needed improvements. This is not a review in the sense of a code review where a list of defects is captured and follow-up reviews are held. The author "owns" the comments and makes adjustments as appropriate.

The PLoPs have been a success. Lots of patterns have been written and published. Lots! The troubling aspect of this success is that now the community is a bit overwhelmed by the number of patterns. I have taken a step to help with this [Rising00], but the real issue is that the focus has been on individual patterns and not on the connections between patterns or on the creation of pattern languages.

Christopher Alexander has been held up as the author of the primae facie pattern language – perhaps the **only** pattern language. For more information on Alexander and his work see http://www.math.utsa.edu/sphere/salingar/Chris.text.html#PHILOSOPHICAL. Alexander's books [Alexander77, Alexander79] describe a collection of patterns for building architecture. These patterns have strong intraconnections. They work together. Patterns depend on other patterns and lead to the use of still other patterns. It is clear when reading these patterns how they work together to build something. The software patterns community has been struggling with the way to apply this technique to our patterns. One solution led to the first ChiliPLoP in 1998. At this "different kind of PLoP" (http://www.agcs.com/patterns/chiliplop) hot topics were announced – for example, telecommunications – and experts in the hot topics attended the conference to plan for a pattern language or pattern languages in the hot topic domain.

Before the first ChiliPLoP, however, a group of telecommunications experts gathered at OOPSLA '96, where Jim Doble, Neil Harrison, and Hans Rohnert jointly proposed TelePLoP: Workshop on Patterns in Telecommunications). Their laudable goals were to:

- Enrich the still small body of publicly available telecommunications patterns.

- Help the participants learn how to write better patterns.

- Clarify costs and benefits of writing and using telecommunications patterns.

- Gain understanding regarding processes for applying patterns in the development of architectures and designs for telecommunications systems.

- Form a group of people interested in telecommunications patterns that will transcend the workshop.

A report on that OOPSLA TelePLoP from Neil Harrison:

> At the end of the day, we talked about telecommunications patterns, and we all agreed that most of the patterns in telecomm were things that will occur in other domains sooner or later. The nature of telecommunications forced these problems on us, and we had to find solutions (the patterns) well before anybody else.
>
> As I look back, I continue to think we were right. We had to deal with high availability and reliability. Today's data networking hardware and software is only now beginning to approach the reliability that the voice networks have had for years. We had to deal with soft real-time constraints. Same thing. We have had to deal with hard memory limits (no virtual memory). James Noble and Charles Weir are just now publishing a book on patterns of limited memory systems [Noble+00], driven in part by the likes of PalmPilots. And so on.

The meeting at OOPSLA led to the hot topic at ChiliPLoP '98 and the birth of a new community. One of the "next steps" identified at ChiliPLoP was to produce a single volume of the already published telecommunications patterns. This book is that volume and can be viewed as a "fat call for papers for future volumes." If you work in the domain of telecommunications (actually this publication has been broadened to communications), please consider becoming a part of this community, participating in future Tele-PLoPs, and writing patterns that enrich the literature that this publication contains. Restructuring of existing patterns and pattern languages is also needed. All contributors are welcome! To subscribe to the TelePLoP mailing list, send e-mail with "subscribe" as the subject to: <u>telecom-patterns-request@cs.uiuc.edu</u> and then start a discussion.

Contributors to the growing collection of patterns in communications come from many different parts of the industry. Since the authors have taken the time to document their expertise, we can still benefit, even if our work is in another area. I remember when I first heard Cope talk about a pattern that the folks working on the 4ESS™ switch had documented called *Leaky Bucket Counters*. When we first heard it was a 4ESS pattern, some of us thought it was something we really wouldn't be interested in or care much about. After all, the 4ESS switch embodies old technology;

development started in the early '70s and its first service was in January 1976. As we listened to the pattern details, however, we realized that this pattern – despite the details of the 4ESS processor and the 4ESS rationale – had a much broader application. Some of us recognized that this pattern had been used on the GTD-5® and others had applied it on products at Honeywell or Motorola. This is a pattern whose context is fault-tolerant systems – bigger than even the 4ESS switch! Let our mistake in judgment help you avoid not hearing and learning from the experience of others. When you read Greg Utas's paper on call processing, for example, don't think that there won't be anything useful for you because you don't work on call processing systems or software at Nortel. Another pattern from Nortel by Gerard Meszaros, *Leaky Bucket of Credits,* used in Nortel's DMS-100, describes the same concept as *Leaky Bucket Counters* for managing distributed system architectures. This pattern is included in Gerard's chapter on reactive systems described later.

STORYTELLING

If Almon Strowger were alive today, he would be astounded at what has happened to the world of communications. Who is Almon Strowger? I was hoping you'd ask! It's amazing how many people working in the wondrous world of communications have never heard his name. Since I helped to write, produce, develop songs, and serve as stagehand for a production of "Strowger the Musical," at AG Communication Systems, I feel I can give you some interesting communications history. Almon Brown Strowger was an undertaker. (No, really, this is a true story.) He was born in New York in 1839. In 1886 he moved to Kansas City, Missouri, to open his own funeral parlor. In those days, when a family needed his services, they would ask the telephone operator (they were called "hello girls") to connect them, but sometimes the calls never reached Strowger. Sometimes it was because of technical difficulties – lines being busy, for example – but Strowger suspected that the operator was (ahem) conspiring with one of his competitors. His suspicions were verified when a dear friend passed away and his final needs were taken care of by the suspected competitor. This was the last straw!

Almon determined to make an "automatic" operator – something that would switch a call to the desired number without the assistance of a human interloper. Luckily his nephew, Walter, was an engineer, and together, Walter and Almon used a collar box (a round wooden box for men's collars, detachable in those days) and pins pushed into the sides. The patent for their invention was granted in 1891. In our musical, we amplified the truth a bit to say that the competitor, Henry Dahlby, had promised to marry Mabel, the operator, when his business got better. She fell for it. When the switch was invented, Mabel was downsized and Henry left her in the lurch. We had to have a happy ending, so we wrote that Walter married Mabel and Henry apologized to Almon – sappy but it made for great songs! The company founded by Almon and Walter became Automatic Electric, and eventually AG Communication Systems, today a subsidiary of Lucent Technologies.

The point of all this is that I'm sharing a good story and you're listening. That's what communication is all about – sharing good stories! Patterns are just one way of doing this. Patterns help us write down good ideas that have solved real problems. The pattern form captures enough information about this solution so that when you read it, you can use the solution to solve your problems. Your implementation of the solution might be different from mine, but the intent will be the same. When I tell you my story, you'll be able to see common threads that overlap our environments and then you can apply my ideas with your own spin. We've been doing this forever. Our brains are story based [Schank90], and a pattern is a one good way to tell a story.

Although the authors of the chapters in this publication use different pattern forms, they all share some key elements. Each pattern has a good name. This is crucial. You'll never forget "The Strowger Story." If someone comes up to you years hence and mentions the name, you'll remember how an undertaker started the communications world we live in. A good pattern with a good name does the same thing for you. The name captures the intent of the solution. Simply using the name is enough to remind the speaker and the listener of the story behind the name. If you know enough patterns and if the patterns are closely related, you can almost speak a language made up of the pattern names. This language will help you work out solutions to complicated problems and you'll be able to develop solutions faster. This works whether you're developing with just one colleague or a team of people, or even when you're talking to yourself. Powerful stuff, patterns!

In addition to the name, the problem you're trying to solve, and the solution, there should be a clear statement of the context. Patterns are proven solutions that work in the specified context. The context helps you understand when you can apply the solution to solve the problem. Changing the context – the setting or the environment – can clearly have an impact on whether the solution will work for you. In addition to the name, problem, solution, and context, the forces tell us why the problem is hard and the trade-offs we might have to make.

Other information that's also helpful includes the resulting context – what will the world be like if you apply the solution? What are possible side effects? The rationale explains why the pattern works and convinces the reader that the solution is a good one. Giving specific known uses also convinces the reader that this is not just a theoretical, pie-in-the-sky, might be a good idea solution – this is real; it's been applied and it works!

PATTERNS IN COMMUNICATIONS

All the chapters in this publication have previously been published. That means they're extra-credible. In addition to being workshopped, they have been reviewed and edited. The chapters describe solutions to problems in the domain of communications. Those who work outside this field might find many of these patterns also to be useful in their domains. Usually when developers read a pattern, they are happiest when they see details that mean something in their area of expertise. As a group, engineers are superb at abstraction. They go "meta" at the drop of a hat! Like the rest of the world, however, they learn best from an example, and the examples that come from their own area of interest mean the most. There are many other published patterns that are used daily in the communications area, but the patterns in this publication are clearly from that domain, use the language from that domain, and have example uses from that domain.

Gerard Meszaros is the author of Chapter 1, "Design Patterns in Telecommunications System Architecture." It appeared in a special issue of *IEEE Communications* on design patterns. This chapter does a good job of setting the stage, especially for those who might be new to patterns. Gerard provides a gentle introduction to the field of telecommunications and distributed environments. Gerard has contributed two other chapters to this publication. One describes a pattern language and the other presents a pattern that has become well known within the pattern community, even among those who do not work in this domain, Half-object + Protocol (HOPP). Gerard introduces this pattern in his first chapter, so it will seem like an old friend when you read about it later.

Large Collections

The authors of the next five chapters share their expertise by introducing collections of patterns. The idea of a pattern language, a set of patterns that work together to yield a product in a particular domain, is really the goal for pattern writers. When we start thinking about patterns and trying our hand at writing one, we think of isolated problems that we've solved successfully. When we've captured that solution, our first inclination is to say, "There! That problem is solved!" In reality, however, the result of applying one pattern is that now we face a set of new problems. These, of course, require new patterns, which, in turn, create new contexts and new problems, and require new patterns. We would like to believe that there's a stopping point, but some would say that as soon as a product is initiated, the maintenance phase begins. Problems are always with us. Related patterns that work together in a pattern language are valuable for others to study, especially newcomers to the field. Wouldn't it be wonderful if we had handbooks of pattern languages for every new person who walked in the door! These patterns would not only help the novice understand the domain but would provide the tools for communication based on the best solutions. Using the pattern names would give a meaningful introduction to ease those initial struggles.

Dennis DeBruler's Chapter 2, "A Generative Pattern Language for Distributed Processing," uses examples from cable television advertising, a video server, and telephony. His patterns address the very early stages of development. The title states that these patterns are for distributed processing, but I think you'll find that they can be useful for any kind of development. Here's what Dennis has to say about his patterns:

> In the fall of 1995, Jim Coplien gave a talk in our auditorium. The topic was a concept he called "pattern languages." The next morning I had one of my 3:00 a.m. "specials." I woke up with an idea dancing over and over in my head – a pattern language for distributed computing. I learned a long time ago, that the easiest way to get back to sleep is to get up and write the idea down. In this case, it was an e-mail to Cope.
>
> In 1996 when Cope learned about the first PLoP conference, he told me that I "had" to submit my pattern language to the conference. He said that the patterns people were "different" enough that an e-mail style would be accepted. He knew that I had not attended conferences for years because they were dominated by academics, who I feel focus on rather artificial problems. I have enough real problems to solve, that I have no need for artificial problems.
>
> Cope edited the e-mail into more traditional English. He also mentioned that

I would not have to present the paper – that all I had to do, in fact, must do, is listen because the conference was going to try a new approach called "writers' workshops." So I decided to attend the conference, and I edited his edit of the e-mail.

After the conference, I made significant revisions to what I submitted. Sometimes, I think the changes were too big.

I have been very grateful that Jim talked me into attending that first PLoP. It had a nice mix of industry, consultants, and academia. The workshop discussions were also very interesting because we discussed content as well as form.

Chapter 3 is the second chapter authored by Gerard Meszaros, "Improving the Capacity of Reactive Systems." These patterns tackle problems in system capacity and throughput. Performance issues are critical in the area of communications and typically include execution time and memory constraints, but this chapter tackles just execution time. I remember when I first read the solution in *Fresh Work before Stale.* Although it makes perfect sense to me now, I can remember being disturbed to hear that service is given to newly arrived customers first, while those who have been waiting, continue to wait. It's like the long line at the supermarket when a new check stand opens and the person at the back of the line jumps over and is served right away, while those of us who have been waiting with melting frozen foods find we're still at the back of the line. The rationale for this solution makes interesting reading.

The next two chapters go well together. The first, Chapter 4 by Mike Adams, Jim Coplien, Robert Gamoke, Bob Hanmer, Fred Keeve, and Keith Nicodemus, "Fault-Tolerant Telecommunication System Patterns," describes a set of patterns that tackles a critical area of importance to communications systems. These were the first to document best practices in communication systems.

I hold these patterns dear because every time I read them I'm reminded of the first time I met Cope and Bob Hanmer. Their visit to AG Communication Systems in the fall of 1995 changed forever the way I look at patterns. In the two-day class Cope and Bob presented, we learned that several veteran developers on the 4ESS™ were due for retirement and folks at AT&T (now Lucent) were uneasy about that loss. The project managers approached Cope with the idea of extracting that expertise and capturing it as patterns. At the time of their visit, Cope and Bob had documented over 100 patterns, "mined" through a process of taping interviews with the experts and extracting patterns from the recorded conversations. A small subset of that collection was presented at the second PLoP Conference in 1995 and is reproduced here. You can read more about the topic of pattern mining in a paper by David DeLano [DeLano98] and in a chapter of a recent collection [Rising99].

Software development at AG Communication Systems falls into one of two arenas. In one is a large central office telecommunications switch, the GTD-5®, developed for GTE and independent telephone companies. It contains over 3 million lines of Pascal and continues to perform well in terms of quality, reliability, and revenue. The other, non-GTD-5 projects are smaller and written, for the most part, in C++. The focus of all the patterns activity up to the time of Cope and Bob's visit had been almost exclusively directed toward the object-oriented projects. After their visit, we expanded our patterns horizon to encompass our entire software development community. Indeed, we began to think about non-software patterns – patterns concerned with the organization of teams, for example. The world is full of patterns!

Chapter 5, a close companion of Chapter 4, was written by Bob Hanmer and Greg Stymfal, "An Input and Output Pattern Language: Lessons from Telecommunications." I asked Bob and Greg how they got together to write this paper and about the name – many patterns have memorable names – *George Washington Is Still Dead!*

From Bob Hanmer:

> During a break in a class I taught about the 4ESS Switch at AG Communication Systems, Greg Stymfal and I started talking. He commented that he had worked on a system that did I/O in the same way. One thing led to another and so we collaborated on the pattern language that we submitted to PLoP.
>
> Pattern naming is important. The name should give the reader some sense of the pattern. *George Washington Is Still Dead* does not satisfy this requirement, unless you are from Phoenix. There it seems to be a regional idiom meaning "nothing has changed, don't ask me again."

From Greg Stymfal:

> The name *George Washington Is Still Dead* actually has a story behind it. On the early "Saturday Night Live" shows, Chevy Chase would have as one of his news items: "General Francisco Franco is still dead." This was the catch phrase for old news.
>
> Because this might be offensive or misunderstood, it was changed to *George Washington Is Still Dead*. If it has now lost all meaning or is not evident from the name, the pattern could be renamed to something like: *Yesterday's News*.

It's a little unusual for people like Bob and Greg, who are from two different companies, to collaborate on a paper about patterns. Since pattern authors are sharing their experience in a domain, that experience is usually company-specific. In fact, many companies regard this information as proprietary – even when that information may be known across the industry. There's something about documenting the details of a solution used in a particular product that ruffles the feathers of those who guard a company's intellectual property. On the one hand, it's easy to sympathize with a company that wants to protect its own best interests; but on the other hand, most patterns are documenting best practices that are probably well known but not necessarily by the pattern name. Greg Utas recalls an example of this from the first TelePLoP:

> At one point someone from Lucent, fearful that he was about to give something away, whispered to a colleague, "Should we mention corrective audits?" I overheard this and interrupted with, "You mean software that recovers resources that are marked in-use but that no longer have valid owners, or software that looks for corrupted queues and fixes them?" It immediately became obvious that both Lucent and Nortel used this technique in the quest for continuous availability.

Maybe this book can help identify the commonality in our business and help us recognize what we share.

Chapter 6 is a coalescence of two papers previously published by Greg Utas. He has done some restructuring and rewriting – we could say, "refactoring" – of the two earlier papers to produce a more complete presentation of his Pattern Language of Call Processing. One of the benefits of this publication is that papers that might have been judged too long for a single publication or conference are appropriate here. This provides Greg and other authors the chance to share an entire collection with us, regardless of its length. Greg's is a very detailed pattern language. Many of the solutions are specific to the area of call processing. Call processing experts and others will benefit from reading this language, even though Greg says that things happened backwards:

> The patterns were written to document an application framework that was developed for a large reengineering project. The feature interaction patterns at the *end* of the paper were workshopped by e-mail and published *first,* since there was a suitable conference to which they could be submitted. The basic patterns were elaborated later and workshopped at the 1999 TelePLoP. A subset of these was published when *IEEE Communications* devoted an issue to patterns in communication systems, so these patterns appeared as a *prequel.*

SMALL COLLECTIONS

Part 2 contains six chapters that present just a single pattern or a few related patterns. Chapter 7, Neil Harrison's "Patterns for Logging Diagnostic Messages," presents three closely related patterns. All systems must report errors, but this task is more difficult when it is a batch system. The error must contain enough information to be useful to the user after the fact. These patterns address this problem for transaction-oriented systems.

Gerard Meszaros's Chapter 8, "Pattern: Half-object + Protocol (HOPP)" is a seminal chapter in the area of telecommunications. It describes a pattern for objects that are a part of more than one address space. This is a short chapter that describes a simple idea, but this pattern has had considerable impact across the pattern community – not just among those who work in communications. I think you'll agree that this is a singularly interesting and important contribution. Here is Gerard's story:

> HOPP was my very first attempt at pattern writing. It was written over the course of a two-day pattern-writing course that Kent Beck gave at Bell Northern Research just before the first PLoP. Kent asked us to try writing a pattern about something we were very familiar with. My group had been debating the merits of restructuring our call processing architecture to be single-ended (like the 5ESS® switch) for quite some time. Our feature processing was already structured this way but concerns about execution time were getting in the way of extending these concepts to the basic 2-party phone call. The original version of the pattern was called "Half-Call plus Protocol."
>
> When PLoP was announced, Kent encouraged me to submit my pattern. I was concerned that the corporate censors, who approve material submitted for publication outside the company, would feel I was giving away vital corporate secrets, so I changed "Half-Call" to "Half-Object" so they wouldn't think I was talking about the company's bread and butter, call processing. *Half-Object Plus Protocol* was born. At PLoP, it was always called by its full name. It was only while preparing the material for submission to the first PLoPD book that I decided it needed a shorter moniker. Since the acronym was pronounceable, I went with HOPP.

In Chapter 9, Nat Pryce describes a single pattern, "Abstract Session: An Object Structural Pattern." Here is Nat's story:

> This pattern made itself known to me in a flash of insight in which the abstractions of context/problem/solution suddenly became clear.
>
> I had used the *Abstract Session* pattern in a framework for building communi-

cation protocol stacks, which inspired the examples in this paper. An implementation of a communication protocol must maintain state for each client that uses the protocol to communicate. I adapted the design of sessions from the University of Arizona's x-kernel to an object-oriented language without thinking very deeply about the design.

Later, when writing a graphical user-interface framework, I found that layout managers also needed to maintain state for each of the widgets that they are laying out. After playing with a number of different designs I realized that, at an abstract level, the context and problem of maintaining state for a widget within a layout manager were the same as for maintaining state for clients of a protocol layer.

Therefore, the solution – the *Abstract Session* pattern – was as applicable to the GUI framework as it was to protocol stacks. I then began finding the pattern in many other designs, including Microsoft's OLE2 and the Java AWT, so I wrote it up and presented it at EuroPLoP.

Chapter 10, by Fernando Das Neves and Alejandra Garrido, describes the *Bodyguard* pattern. This pattern allows controlled access to shared objects in a distributed environment where there may not be system-level support for distributed objects. The pattern provides an intuitively appealing solution in a small framework that includes several other well-known patterns.

In Chapter 11, "Worth a Thousand Words," Jim Coplien talks about the relationship between patterns and geometry. Alexander's long-awaited work on the Nature of Order is concerned with his theory of centers. I'm not an expert on this theory, but I'm one of those anxiously awaiting the publication of this work. Since Cope's paper follows Gerard's "Half-Object + Protocol," you'll be able to appreciate the discussion of HOPP in the context of geometry and the pattern *Three-Part Call Processing* written by Bob Hanmer.

I'm sure you'll enjoy reading Don Olson's Chapter 12, "A Pocket-Sized Broker." Don not only has a wonderful sense of humor, but he also has the ability to make us see the world in interesting ways. The pattern names are wonderfully reflective of the different variations on the theme of the *Broker* pattern. Don's experience with the *Broker* pattern derives from a framework developed at AG Communication Systems. Don's team was part of the training in Design Patterns [GoF] that led to another of Don's patterns, *Train Hard, Fight Easy* [Olson99]. Here is Don's story:

It sure was easy to think of the patterns movement as the end-all and be-all to our problems. Now, some five years since we had a workshop with Jim Coplien and Bob Hanmer, I've tempered my evangelical enthusiasm so that it burns perhaps less brightly, but still pretty damned hot. Despite the confusion on what really constitutes patterns and pattern languages, or how best to express them, or that Christopher Alexander himself thinks that perhaps his original ideas were too static as he begins delivery of his new masterwork, *The Nature of Order,* I still believe that there is a lot of benefit to be had from the *attempt* to understand and develop patterns wherever we happen to dwell in the software world. Organizationally, technically, from a managerial perspective, none of it really matters. You see, right about the time I was thinking about a new career, the patterns movement gave me something that was sorely needed – hope.

The best part of that early experience was the fact that being wacky was almost a requisite part of the discovery process – the first lesson to learn was *loosen up!* Not that I didn't first stumble into the idea of patterns like so many other people, via *Design Patterns* [GoF]. In late 1994 someone handed me a copy of a draft pattern called *Observer.* It just happened to be the right prescription for a particular problem we were grappling with at the time. I got my hands on the book first chance I got, and slowly worked my way through it. It was useful. It was timely. It was something different from anything I had seen before. Of course, that was before Cope and Bob showed up.

The problem was, for me, that during our workshop I couldn't think of a single pattern that had to do with my work. Brilliant engineers surrounded me and here I was drawing a complete blank. I dug and dug and thought and thought and in the morning I was still completely stymied. As I drove to work I toyed with avoiding the last session altogether to save myself the embarrassment that was inevitable.

Though it was August in Phoenix, my mind drifted to thoughts of skiing up in the Wasatch region of Utah. For years I used a visualization exercise to calm myself that involved imagining that I was standing atop a place at Snowbird called Peruvian Cirque, looking down the steep face through my ski tips. A light snow was falling and it was perfectly silent except for the soft ticking of the flakes against my jacket. I would stay suspended in that moment just before pushing off, when one finds the very center and then, in the heart of silence, pitches into the void. I saw my hands before me as I made the first critical turn and then began the rhythmic dance down the slope. In this vision, my hands were always consciously in view, though I hadn't much thought of that before.

Hands in View. I drove on, formulating the context, forces, solution, and rationale for why this was so critical to successfully negotiating the cirque. Cope's pattern form became a framework for examining something I had been taught long ago but hadn't much thought about until now. Why did keeping my hands in view always seem to be the key to skiing like a champ rather than crashing like a chump in a huge "yard sale" with my gear spread over the south 40?

When I got to work, I scribbled my sorry skiing pattern onto a piece of paper in longhand, and feeling pretty sheepish, shuffled to my doom in the workshop.

As I had thought, the others had come up with good technical stuff and here I was gripping my humiliation in hand, hoping we'd run out of time, hoping there would be a fire drill, hoping that I could somehow in these final minutes come up with something that wouldn't seem so lame.

Alas, my turn came. I passed out my pattern with mumbled words of apology. Then came the first big lesson that made all the difference. Cope looked up and started to talk about generativity. All of a sudden, the product of my commuting unconscious revealed to me what this pattern stuff might really be all about. It wasn't about nailing down some phenomenon, but rather creating a state in which the desired outcomes could produce themselves. Keeping your hands in view didn't in and of itself help you turn or float or keep from doing the human groom on steep slopes, but it did set in motion a chain of events that indirectly made things happen. Now I saw the problem I had been having envisioning things in the technical realm. You couldn't stare directly at something and then draw some schematic of its being with the ability to replicate it wherever you needed. Rather, you had to understand the preconditions, the subtler elements, the spirit of the thing. Yeah, it was nebulous and kind of weird. And I dug it. I *really* dug it.

So now five years later, I feel as though I'm still trying to get a handle on this thing called patterns, and that tells me I'm right where I ought to be. I've taught them, used them, written them, collected them, workshopped them, shepherded them, and debated them, and I'm just as uncertain now as I was then, but with this one extra fillip – certainty isn't required. Only a little faith is needed, a little hope, some unfocused time musing about things, and the desire to understand rather than solve.

Simple.

EXPERIENCE REPORTS

It's difficult to read about a pattern and easily turn to the work at hand and apply the new solution. I hope this book will help you if you are solving problems in the domain of communications. What helps most of us is a concrete example where the implementation details are meaningful in our current context. It is also extremely useful if someone can tell us a story about how the pattern was used to solve a real problem. We need more experience papers in our respective domains. Experience papers will help us understand how to apply the solutions in our own work. Each of the following chapters has a story to tell. The authors will relate their struggle with a problem and then show you how one or more patterns helped them reach a successful solution. Some of these chapters also introduce new patterns but when they do, it's in the context of the problem where they're also applying other, known patterns.

In Chapter 13, Mike Duell describes the use of *Mediator* and *Layers* in his description of an intelligent peripheral. Mike has also collected real-world, non-software examples for all of the patterns in the *Design Patterns* [GoF] and the *POSA1* [POSA1] book. These examples are not only entertaining but also useful. First of all, it's easier to learn the patterns and then it's easier to remember them. Here is Mike's story:

In 1995, I attended a class on software design patterns at AG Communication Systems. After sitting in a classroom for a week while 23 patterns were "introduced" to me, I did not see the relevance of patterns. Most of the examples were from applications that were unfamiliar. All of the examples used a programming language other than the one that I was using. As a "coping mechanism" I tried to relate the patterns to something that I already knew. As the instructor was talking about station monitors and sensor networks, I was thinking about McDonald's Happy Meals™. No I wasn't hungry at the time!

Not long after completing the class, my team was working on a design in which several objects interacted with one another. Our requirements specified the constraints placed upon the object interactions. I was tasked with finding a pattern to help manage these constraints. After consulting the Gang of Four book [GoF], I was confident that the *Mediator* would work nicely in our application. The *Mediator* did work well for us and I wrote an experience report that was accepted for OOPSLA '96.

Before I left for OOPSLA '96, I went through a dry run of my presentation before a group of 30 designers from different projects. When I had finished, one of my colleagues made the statement that the mediator object in my example was nothing more than a manager object. He went on to say that in his OO training, the presence of a manager object was an indication that the object decomposition is wrong. Great! Two days before I leave for OOPSLA and the whole premise of my presentation may be wrong! I tried to no avail to convince him that I did have the decomposition right. In desperation I began to search for an analogy. "The air traffic control tower at an airport is like a mediator object. The tower manages constraints between aircraft in the terminal area." With this example, my colleague could see how a management object in the real world was analogous to my mediator object. He now agreed that the object decomposition in my example was correct. I also felt better about speaking at OOPSLA!

While at OOPSLA, I reflected on the experience. My colleague had a hard time accepting patterns based on an unfamiliar example. My initial reaction was much the same. When I used an analogy, we began discussing an example that was common to both of us. We didn't need code snippets or specialized knowledge to relate to the example. The analogy proved to be a very useful tool. Unfortunately, the *Mediator* pattern is not the only pattern used in software! I began to think about other examples for patterns in the Gang of Four book. I was able to enlist the help of Linda Rising and John Goodsen of Saguaro Software to organize a workshop for OOPSLA '97 where participants submitted their own examples from the Gang of Four. We discussed the examples and refined them and then presented them in a poster session at OOPSLA to gain more feedback. When it was all said and done, we had a catalog of examples for the Gang of Four patterns.

The following year, Linda and I were able to enlist Peter Sommerlad and Michael Stal to workshop examples from the POSA1 book. Again a catalog of examples was developed.

Today the catalog is on the AG Communication Systems web site: http://www.agcs.com/patterns/papers/index.htm. If you've read about patterns and just don't get it, take a look at these examples. After all, I went through a weeklong class and didn't "get it" and even when I finally "got it," I had a hard time explaining it to someone else. Maybe these examples will help you as they have helped me.

Chapter 14, by Jim Coplien and Just van den Broecke, "Using Design Patterns to Build a Framework for Multimedia Networking," describes the authors' experience in building a framework. Patterns are useful for capturing good ideas and enabling their use by others, but the real power of reuse comes into play with frameworks. As Ralph Johnson has said [Johnson00], "Patterns tell you what to do. Frameworks do it for you." A framework is a reusable design expressed as a set of cooperating abstract classes (implementations of collections of patterns). That means code! A framework represents a family of solutions for a given domain. Frameworks have "cold spots" where behavior is fixed and "hot spots" where behavior can be varied. This behavior is determined by the patterns within. The Old Reuse Model was based on a library of small components. When I reach an appropriate point in coding I look for something in the library that might meet my needs. My code then calls the reusable code (usually a small module). The New Reuse Model is based on a reusable framework. I alter the hot spots to meet the needs of my application. My code is called by the reusable code (usually a large system or subsystem). This is called The Hollywood Principle – Don't call us; we'll call you! You can see the difference. In the new model the amount of code that is reused is considerable, which leads to greater savings. I have seen this principle at work. I have seen a series of related products produced in a very short time. This is the way to improved productivity.

The main message in this chapter, however, is not so much the usefulness of frameworks, but (1) the use of patterns as building blocks for a specific middleware framework (MediaBuilder) and (2) the introduction of a possible extension to UML to include, extend, and combine patterns graphically within a class design. According to Just, Platinum, the framework described in the chapter, has also been applied in a follow-on project, called MESH (Multimedia services on the Electronic Super Highway).

Chapter 15, by Junichi Suzuki and Yoshikazu Yamamoto, "OpenWebServer: An Adaptive Web Server Using Software Patterns," was part of the special issue of *IEEE Communications* on design patterns. One thing I like about this chapter is the opportunity to read about an application of a pattern I struggle to understand, *Reflection*. I think you'll find that if you've had trouble understanding this pattern – perhaps, like me, you've never actually used it – this chapter will help you!

Chapters 16–20 are by a collection of authors who have worked with Doug Schmidt, who has led research groups at Washington University in St. Louis, Missouri, and at the University of California, Irvine (UCI), over the past decade. Here is Doug's story of how he became convinced of the importance of communication patterns in his research on ACE and TAO, which are middleware frameworks that reify many core communication software and network programming patterns, and why he was motivated to write experience papers on patterns and pattern languages:

> I was fortunate to have learned about the patterns movement in 1993 as a reviewer for early drafts of the "Gang of Four" book [GoF] during my doctoral research at UCI on parallel communication protocol architectures and optimizations. Toward the end of my graduate student apprenticeship, I realized that interest in transport-level communication protocol research was waning. Luckily, many of the same patterns I'd identified in that domain were applicable to my middleware research and development on ACE and TAO. By refocusing my protocol software skills, and combining them with my knowledge of OO design and programming, I was able to capitalize on the surge of interest in distributed object computing middleware that began in the mid-1990s.
>
> I joined the faculty at Washington University, St. Louis, in the fall of 1994. I quickly realized that documenting the patterns and pattern languages we'd identified in ACE and TAO was a useful research contribution, which is always an important asset for an assistant professor! Over the next six years, the patterns we documented also provided a solid foundation for training and mentoring our thirty or so grad students and staff, as well as thousands of members of the ACE and TAO community, who worked on our open-source software. When I returned to UCI as a tenured professor in the fall of 1999, patterns were once again important to help educate the members of my new research group. I'm

firmly convinced that without focusing on patterns, we never could have developed, maintained, and optimized the millions of lines of highly portable C++ and Java code in ACE and TAO as quickly or as inexpensively.

From my earliest days in graduate school, I've been convinced that the best way to showcase the power of advanced software research and development techniques, such as patterns, frameworks, components, and middleware, is to apply them to develop reusable software that can be deployed in real-world systems. My experience over the past decade has confirmed that the transition of research and development into the commercial market-place will be limited until researchers actually demonstrate the benefits of their work in operational systems. At Washington University and UCI we've worked hard to ensure the ACE and TAO middleware frameworks are of sufficient quality to be used to build mission-critical distributed and embedded systems with stringent quality of service requirements. We've found that experience papers centered around patterns and pattern languages help to explain and generalize the techniques we've used to develop, optimize, and evolve our research and development activities.

Chapters 16 and 17 have Doug as the sole author. "Applying a Pattern Language to Develop Application-Level Gateways" introduces the *Reactor, Acceptor-Connector, Non-blocking Buffered I/O, Component Configurator,* and *Active Object* patterns and describes the ADAPTIVE Communication Environment (ACE), which is a widely used communication framework designed using patterns and written in C++. "Applying Design Patterns to Flexibly Configure Network Services in Distributed Systems" focuses on how the *Acceptor-Connector* pattern has been implemented flexibly in the ACE framework by applying other patterns, such as *Bridge, Factory Method, Strategy,* and *Wrapper Facade.* The next chapter, "Applying a Pattern Language to Develop Extensible ORB Middleware," was co-authored by Doug and Chris Cleeland. A shorter version of this chapter appeared in the special issue of *IEEE Communications* on design patterns, so once again this book includes a complete version of a paper that was shortened to meet publication requirements. This chapter describes the pattern language used to develop another communication framework, The ACE ORB (TAO), which is a widely used high-performance, real-time CORBA-compliant object request broker built on top of ACE. Here is a story from Chris:

> When we got sponsorship to work on a real-time ORB, given that a subinterest of our group was patterns, we looked for opportunities to apply them in the creation of the ORB. We started from a simple code base (the SunSoft reference IIOP 1.0 implementation) that had just enough of an ORB around it to prove that the IIOP implementation was sound. The reality was that few of us really

knew (well, at least I didn't!) how to architect a CORBA-compliant ORB, much less a real-time ORB!

As we started to fold the IIOP implementation into our own code, we found that we applied the same patterns repeatedly and that some were more useful than others. We captured these insights in our experience report. There are really no earth-shattering new patterns in the paper, but I believe that taken together, these patterns represent the basis of a pattern language for ORB architectures, as well as many other communication systems.

One of the most interesting aspects of the paper is the section at the end that offers empirical evidence that applying patterns to the TAO ORB development made things quantitatively "better." I'm not trying to toot my own horn, but I think that kind of evidence is crucial and often overlooked in the patterns community. It's the type of metrics that managers can sink their teeth into and use to justify the actions of their group to their higher-ups.

Chapter 19 was co-authored by Doug, Carlos O'Ryan, Fred Kuhns, Ossama Othman, and Jeff Parsons, "Applying Patterns to Develop a Pluggable Protocols Framework for ORB Middleware." This chapter provides more information about the use of patterns that were used to develop and configure a wide range of protocols into TAO. Finally, the last chapter in this group, Chapter 20, "Object Lifetime Manager," was co-authored by Doug, David Levine, and Christopher Gill. This chapter addresses the topic of object lifecycle management and destruction, which is clearly as important as object creation, particularly in long-lived embedded telecommunication systems that must manage their resources carefully to avoid resource leaks.

All five of these chapters have been extensively updated and improved by Doug just for this book publication. The chapters appear in his suggested order, so that if you read the chapters in sequence all the terms and patterns should be defined before they are used. The chapter rewrites have been done in light of the POSA2 book [POSA2], which includes enhanced versions of patterns previously documented by Doug and his colleagues. POSA1 [POSA1] has become a classic in the domain of software architecture, and I'm sure the second book in this series will be as significant for communication software developers as the first was for software architects. Doug and his research group have been major contributors of patterns to the domain of communication software, particularly distributed object computing middleware. If you are interested in this area, please see his web site listed in the list of contributors at the front of the book. It has a wealth of information, including handouts, assignments, and other supporting material from courses he has taught at Washington University in St. Louis, Missouri, the University of California,

Irvine, the University of California, Los Angeles, and the University of California, Berkeley, U.S.A.

REFERENCES

[Alexander77] Alexander, C.A., *A Pattern Language*, Oxford University Press, 1977.

[Alexander79] Alexander, C.A., et al., *The Timeless Way of Building*, Oxford University Press, 1979.

[Coplien97] Coplien, J.O., "A Pattern Language for Writers' Workshops," *C++ Report*, Apr. 1997, 51–60.

[Coplien00] Coplien, J.O., "A Pattern Language for Writers' Workshops," PLoPD4, Addison-Wesley, 2000, 557–580.

[DeLano98] DeLano, D., "Pattern Mining," PHand, 87–95.

[GoF] Gamma, E., R. Helm, R. Johnson, J. Vlissides, *Design Patterns: Elements of Reusable Object-Oriented Software*, Addison-Wesley, 1995.

[Johnson00] Johnson, R.E., private e-mail, June 00.

[Meszaros+98] Meszaros, G., J. Doble, "A Pattern Language for Pattern Writing," PLoPD3, 529–570.

[Noble+00] Noble, J., C. Weir, *Small Memory Software*, Addison-Wesley, 2000.

[Olson98] Olson, D., "Patterns on the Fly," PHand, 141–170.

[PHand98] Rising, L., ed., *The Pattern Handbook: Techniques, Strategies, and Applications*, Cambridge University Press, 1998.

[PLoPD3] Martin, R., D. Riehle, F. Buschmann, eds., *Pattern Languages of Program Design 3*, Addison-Wesley, 1998.

[PLoPD4] Harrison, N.B., B. Foote, H. Rohnert, eds., *Pattern Languages of Program Design 4*, Addison-Wesley, 2000.

[POSA1] Buschmann, F., R. Meunier, H. Rohnert, P. Sommerlad, M. Stal, *Pattern-Oriented Software Architecture: A System of Patterns*, John Wiley & Sons, 1996.

[POSA2] D.C. Schmidt, M. Stal, H. Rohnert, F. Buschmann, *Pattern-Oriented Software Architecture: Patterns for Concurrent and Networked Objects*, John Wiley & Sons, 2000.

[Rising98] Rising, L., "Pattern Writing," PHand, 69–82.

[Rising99] Rising, L., "Pattern Mining," *Handbook of Object Technology*, CRC Press, Inc., Boca Raton, FL, 1999, Chap. 38, 1–39.

[Rising00] Rising, L., ed., *The Pattern Almanac 2000*, Addison-Wesley, 2000.

[Schank90] Schank, R.C., *Tell Me a Story*, Charles Scribner's Sons, 1990.

1

DESIGN PATTERNS IN TELECOMMUNICATIONS SYSTEM ARCHITECTURE

Gerard Meszaros

ABSTRACT

The telephone network could be called the world's first distributed computing network. People in telecommunications treat as second nature many of the issues just surfacing in other problem domains. This article describes some of the techniques used in the telecommunications industry to deal with highly distributed high-reliability systems. A number of recurring patterns are identified and used to describe the design of the telecommunications network and its components.

> *Telephony has even more acronyms than computing, because we've had 50 more years to come up with them.*
> Telephone pioneer to young turk, 1981

SINCE ALEXANDER GRAHAM BELL made the first phone call, the telecommunications industry has been constantly striving to produce a more reliable and feature-rich telecommunications network. As evidence of their success, telephone service is something we all take pretty much for granted. Even when disaster strikes, such as the big San Francisco earthquake of 1989, the phone system continues to work when all other utilities are knocked out.

Being a well-established industry, the telecommunications industry has a rich set of patterns that are used to solve commonly occurring problems. It is through the use of these patterns that the highly stringent requirements of the network are met. Many of these patterns are visible to the operators of the telecom network, while others are only visible to those building the equipment from which the telecom network is assembled. This chapter focuses on the use of design patterns, as exemplified in the book *Design Patterns* [1], in the architecture and construction of the telephone network and its elements.

THE TELEPHONY BACKGROUND

Telephone networks are complex distributed systems with a long and colorful heritage. The domain has a number of inherent challenges. These include the physical distribution of the network and the need for reliability and high capacity. To meet the reliability and capacity challenges, the designers of the telephone network and its components have introduced even more distributed processing. The resulting system is distributed in many dimensions, and this distribution must be handled to ensure that reliability is increased rather than decreased.

OBJECTS

Telephone switching systems do not have a "main" program: there are many different activities going on inside the system at any time. As a result, these systems have always had to be decomposed into smaller components. The protocols used in communication between such components usually contain an identifier of the object being affected, typically the call or the facility the call is using. This, and specification techniques such as Systems Description Language (SDL), have naturally led to switching systems being implemented using object-based techniques long before object orientation was fashionable.

INHERENT DISTRIBUTION

At the simplest end of the scale, a typical basic telephone call requires coordination of resources and actions across many telephone switching systems (aka switches) and other network elements. The coordination is carried out through the use of protocols between the switches. In the early days, this signaling was done using electrical pulses that told electromechanical "steppers," a hardware implementation of a 10-ary tree, which outgoing circuit to select.

As the network evolved, steppers were replaced by electromechanical logic boards, and ultimately by stored-program-controlled switching mechanisms. As the capabilities of the switches improved, it was possible to upgrade the signaling, first with the addition of multifrequency tones and later with digital messaging. Originally, only digits representing the called party were signaled. Using tones instead of pulses decreased the time required to communicate the information about the desired call, thus allowing more information to be sent, such as call type and billing indicators. Later, information about the calling party was added to the protocols. A key factor driving the richness of the signaling protocols was the desire to support features across the network.

After the basic call, the first significant networked feature was Inward Wire Area Telephone Service (INWATS). This service, now called 800, Toll-free, or Freephone, necessitated the signaling of the whereabouts of the calling party relative to the final destination of the call to give the terminating switching office enough information to generate the appropriate billing records. The details of the protocols (using fancy called-number manipulation) are beyond the scope of this article; suffice it to say that this was truly a case of trying to make a single call "object" appear simultaneously in several telephone switches.

REDUNDANCY

A key requirement of the telephone industry is fault tolerance. This is achieved through massive redundancy; anything critical to the operation of the network is duplicated. This is seen at all levels of granularity, from duplicated processors in peripheral modules of switching systems to "mated pairs" of the network databases known as service control points (SCPs). In between, we find duplicated signaling links between network elements, alternate speech paths through connection modules, and alternate routes to reach the same destination, just to name a few.

This rampant redundancy comes at the price of increased complexity. Whenever functionality is duplicated to improve reliability, a need for synchronization is introduced. This is just one of the reasons why telecommunication systems typically contain many millions of lines of code.

KEY DESIGN AND DISTRIBUTION PATTERNS

To facilitate the description of the design of the telephone network in a succinct fashion, it is necessary to introduce a higher-level vocabulary than that traditionally used to describe computer programs. *Design Patterns* [1] introduced such a vocabulary by naming the recurring solutions to common design problems. Patterns are a way to capture the best practices of software design so that other designers can easily reuse them. The patterns community has a unique culture that values stating the obvious and recording known practices over inventing novel, possibly untried, solutions. Therefore, it should come as no surprise that many of the patterns can be found in systems built long before the patterns were "discovered" and named.

DESIGN PATTERNS

Design patterns, such as Observer, Event Object, and Memento, are commonly used in the detailed design of object-oriented software systems. They can also be used to describe how architecture-level components of a system or network interact with each other.

Observer. *Observer* allows an object, known as the observer, to request notification of published events of another object, known as the subject. When the event actually occurs, the subject notifies all observers without caring about what they are or why they want to be notified.

A key design decision when using Observer is whether the subject should send (push) information about the event occurrence to the observer. The alternative is to force the observer to ask for ("pull") the information it cares about once it has been notified on the event occurrence.

When implemented in a distributed environment, the cost of callbacks across the network can be avoided by using the push model. The subject creates an event object to describe the event and pass it to the observer. This ensures that all relevant information about the event is available to the observer when it is notified. If the observer is in a different address space, the event object should be passed by value (recreated in the observer's address space) since it won't change once created.

Event Object. An event object is created to notify an object that has expressed interest in the occurrence of an event. Typically, the interested objects will have either registered the notification of such events (as described for *Observer*), or the notifying system assumes they are interested (a form of implicit registration).

Each event object belongs to an event class, and its instance data describes details about the particular event occurrence. In windowing systems, a common event is Mouse Down, and the attributes of it would include things like the X-Y coordinates of where and when it occurred. An instance of the Mouse Down event object class would be passed to any objects that had requested notification of this type of event. They could ask the event object where and when it had occurred, and use this information to determine what, if anything, they should do in response to the event.

Memento. When an object must be recreated at a later time or another location, we can create a memento of the object and save it or send it to its new location. When we want to recreate the object, the memento can be reconstituted.

Self-extracting archives and ZIP files are examples of mementos of the files from which they were created. Object distribution mechanisms use mementos to turn objects and requests into messages and back again. The messages of many communication protocols are mementos of event objects. In Common Object Request Broker Architecture (CORBA), the process of turning an object into a memento is called *marshalling*, while in the Java programming language it is called *serialization*.

DISTRIBUTION PATTERNS

Distribution patterns deal with the placement and replication of objects in a distributed computing environment. They are typically used when mapping components of the logical (undistributed) architecture onto a physical (deployment) architecture consisting of multiple processing contexts. They describe several alternative ways to allow objects to be used from different processing contexts.

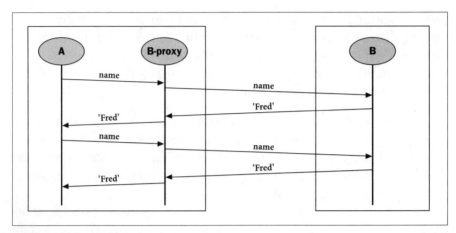

Figure 1.1. Remote Proxy.

Objects that implement *Remote Proxy* (Fig. 1.1), *Caching Proxy* (Fig. 1.2), or *Half Object Plus Protocol* (HOPP) Fig. 1.3) all present the same interface to the client object (object A in these examples), making it possible to select the appropriate distribution pattern at runtime when a reference to an object is passed from one processing context to another.

Remote Procedure Call. Remote procedure calls (RPCs) allow an object or a program to invoke procedures in a remote processing context. The RPC is the basic building block of most distributed systems. Each RPC is translated into a message that is sent to the remote system. The arguments of the RPC

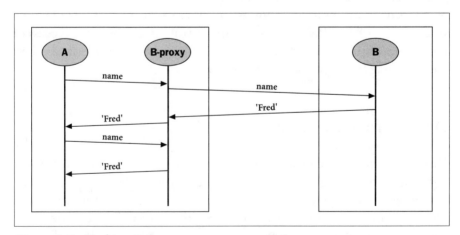

Figure 1.2. Caching Proxy.

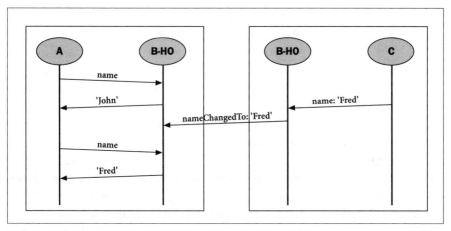

Figure 1.3. Half Object Plus Protocol.

are copied into the message and reconstituted at the receiving end before the target procedure is invoked.

Other than the obvious performance impact, the main problem with RPCs is that they usually need to be done programmatically. That is, the RPC looks different in the source code than a "normal" procedure call. In object-oriented programming languages, the RPC can be hidden behind a Remote Proxy object.

Remote Proxy. Remote Proxy [2] is the pattern at the heart of the *Broker Architecture* [2] implemented by the Object Management Group's (OMG's) CORBA. It hides the fact that an object is remote by substituting a proxy object with the same signature as the remote object. Method calls are passed to the remote object using an RPC-like mechanism. The remote object responds to the proxy, which then returns control to the caller. The proxy object isolates the client object from the location and asynchronous nature of the server object, as illustrated in Fig. 1.1.

One of the drawbacks of using a Remote Proxy is that performance suffers because all method calls involve messaging to a remote context. Caching commonly used information can mitigate the performance impact. This version of the solution is known as Caching Proxy [2].

When an object is passed from one network element to another as a Remote Proxy, it has *pass by reference* semantics. All method calls on it will result in the methods being delegated back to the object the proxy object represents (in the real object's processing context).

Half Object Plus Protocol. HOPP [3] is found in many time-critical distributed systems. It allows distributed objects to be accessed in real time without incurring the cost of messaging to a remote system. This is achieved by creating a copy of the object, known as a *half-object* or *replicate,* in each processing context that requires real-time access to the object. The half-objects are kept consistent with each other by using asynchronous change notifications (events or messages). This synchronization protocol is completely independent of the public interface of the object.

HOPP hides processor boundaries from the other objects in the system by making an object appear to exist locally in more than one context. Thus, HOPP allows processor boundaries to pass *through* objects rather than between them. It is a more appropriate model than RPC for real-time applications that cannot afford to wait or block while the data is retrieved. Not all attributes of the object need always be kept synchronized between the half-objects.

In Fig. 1.3, object B has close ties with A and C, which live in different processing contexts. Performance considerations do not allow either A or C to access it remotely, so it must be replicated (designated B-HO for B-Half Object). The set of B-HOs in all processing contexts collectively acts as though it was a single unique object. They each coordinate their actions with their counterpart(s) in the other processing contexts.

A common example of applying *HOPP* is a database that is replicated onto several servers.

DESIGN AND DISTRIBUTION PATTERNS IN TELECOMMUNICATION NETWORKS

The design and distribution patterns described thus far are found to occur throughout the design of the telephone network and its components. They appear at many levels of granularity, ranging from deep within the detailed implementations of network components to the way those network components interact with each other. This section describes examples of some of the more common occurrences of these patterns. It is not a comprehensive description of telephone network design, but does illustrate typical problems and how their solutions can be described succinctly using design patterns. In Chapter 6, Greg Utas describes the more detailed patterns used to implement some of these interactions.

Each section describes a problem encountered in the design of the telephone network. It then describes, at a very high level, how the problem is solved. Finally, the solution is described in terms of this small set of design patterns. In all cases, we emphasize the architecture-level interaction between significant system components. The exact implementation mechanisms may or may not correspond to the object-oriented designs described in the patterns literature.

PROPAGATING CALL INFORMATION THROUGH THE NETWORK

As a call is established, information about the call may be needed for connection control, billing, and features running on behalf of either the calling or called party. Figure 1.4 shows a simplified model of a telephone call. An event received from a facility causes a call to be originated. A calling party is created to represent the facility in the call. Based on the number dialed (and possibly other information), the destination facility is determined, and a called party is added to the call to represent it. Once this facility accepts the call, a connection is created between the facilities.

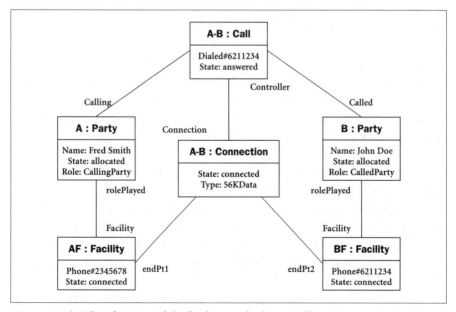

Figure 1.4. The object model of a basic telephone call.

When a call must pass through several switches in the network, information about the calling party (and the requested call) is first passed forward from switch to switch, and later, information discovered about the called party (name, number, capabilities, status) may be passed back toward the originating switch. Thus, the call exists in some form in every switch involved in the call. Changes in the state of the call in one switch must be propagated to the other switch(es).

Figure 1.5 shows the model when a call is made across two switches in the network: billing must record the answer and disconnect times of a call; it uses them to determine call duration. Features such as call transfer are interested in whether a call has been answered to determine whether they should be enabled.

For a basic call, the originating switch is informed when the called party answers or hangs up, and the terminating switch is informed when the calling party hangs up. Modern protocols have introduced signaling of other intermediate state changes, including:

- Having sufficient information to route the call

- Ringing the called party

- Leaving the network

- Routing via less capable facilities

Patterns Applied. This is an example of HOPP. The call object needs to exist locally in every switch because events may be received from either user. The changes in call state required to process the call signaling and billing are propagated through the network using protocols such as integrated services digital network (ISDN) user part (ISUP) or primary rate interface (PRI). The first protocol message creates the object in the new switch, and each subsequent protocol message corresponds to a *Memento* of an *Event Object* signaling a change in the state of the call. Each event message includes the relevant event parameters, namely the attributes of the call that have changed. The key call events of interest to features are CalledPartyAnswer, CalledPartyDisconnect, and CallingPartyDisconnect. As an example, the change in state from Alerting (Ringing) to Answered initiates the sending of a Connected event. In the PRI protocol, the Connected event is signaled via the Connect message, which includes the relevant connected party information (including both the name and telephone number of the connected party). Features may register as *Observers* of the call to be notified of changes

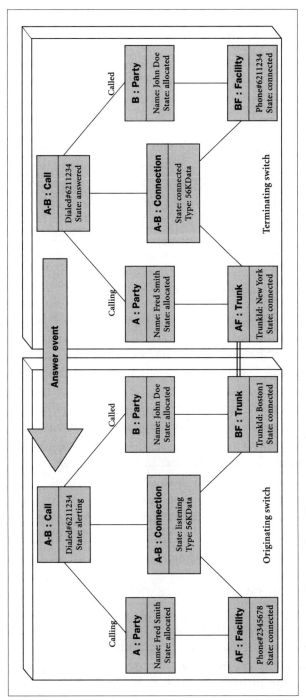

Figure 1.5. Distributing the call across switches.

party). Features may register as *Observers* of the call to be notified of changes important to them.

NETWORKING FEATURED CALLS

When additional features are added to a call, the call and its constituent objects may acquire additional attributes primarily of interest to the feature. Often, the feature has something to do during the origination phase of the call, and something else to do during the termination phase; the attributes hold the necessary information. The feature is attached to the call, watching for certain call events, waiting for the right time to take action. If the call traverses several switches, the attributes required by the feature must be passed along so that they will be available when the terminating switch component of the feature attempts to use them.

Patterns Applied. This is another example of HOPP being used to keep multiple copies of the call and feature objects synchronized across several network elements. The feature itself has a component in both the originating and terminating switches. Feature-specific call attributes must be replicated or at least passed through all switches involved in the call. HOPP is used to keep the various parts of the call (in the switches) in sync by sending any changes to the information. Sometimes, a special message is sent containing the information (a change event), but some protocols require that the information be sent with the next protocol message. In the latter case, the attribute has to ask to be notified of the imminent sending of the next compatible message; this can be done using *Observer.* For a more detailed description of how call processing features are implemented, refer to Chapter 6 by Utas in this book.

INTELLIGENT NETWORK PROCESSING

Operating companies are increasing their use of IN, where the switches inform the SCP when predefined trigger points are encountered on a predefined call model that presents a common view of call processing across the many switch implementations. The SCP may initiate feature processing on either the SCP or the switch as a result of these triggers. To facilitate this processing, the switch and SCP exchange a fair amount of data about the call.

Patterns Applied. There are several patterns utilized here. First, the SCP registers with the switch for notification of certain events on certain calls. This is an example of Observer. When one of these events occurs, information about the call is packaged up and send to the SCP. This message is an example of Event Object and Memento. The SCP recreates a partial copy of the call to which features on the SCP may attach themselves as observers. This is another example of HOPP with one half-object on the switch, the other on the SCP. This SCP may use Observer and Chain of Responsibility to allow features to interact with the call. Subsequent triggers on the call are events that keep the half-objects synchronized.

CONCURRENCE OF MATED SCPs

The introduction of the SCP has created a potential single point of failure in the telephone network. Naturally, SCPs must be made very reliable by having full redundancy; but even this is not enough. Thus, SCPs are deployed in mated pairs. Half of the pair might be in Chicago, the mate in Dallas. This ensures that an event that cripples one SCP is unlikely to cripple both. All the switches in the network have access to both SCPs in the pair, and may send requests to either SCP and expect the same response.

Since SCPs hold subscriber profile information, it is essential that any change to the information on one SCP be reflected on its mate. These changes are initiated by "call processing" (e.g., call forward number programming, speed-call list programming, or a user moving about the network) and by the provisioning system. As a result, the pair of SCPs must be in constant communication, updating each other with any changes.

Patterns Applied. Once again, this is an example of HOPP, this time applied to the subscriber objects, which must each exist on both SCPs of an SCP pair. This way it doesn't matter which SCP is asked to respond to a request for a particular subscriber's profile. Any change to the subscriber half-object on one SCP causes an object concurrence message to be sent to the mate. Note that the message need not have any similarity to the message that initiated the original change. The notification of the mate is an example of an implicit Observer where the mate is registered for the Any Change in

Subscriber Data event. The concurrence messages are examples of Mementos of Event Objects.

DISTRIBUTING CALLS AMONG PERIPHERALS OF A SWITCH

Most switching systems employ hierarchical multiprocessing architectures to achieve the very high capacity objectives. This typically requires a large number of (possibly duplicated) peripheral processing modules plus one or more (duplicated) central or administration modules. To effectively process calls and features, the peripheral modules must have some common view of the call being processed (as shown in Fig. 1.6). Each may have a subset of the total information in the call; however, each must also have a common subset of information. Whenever this common core information is modified in one module, all the other modules holding this information must be notified. As a bare minimum, the state of the call and its connection must be shared, but typically, additional information is required about the call and the parties.

Patterns Applied. Once again, the HOPP pattern shows up. Changes in core call information in one processor trigger the sending of synchronization messages (Mementos of Event Objects) to the affected processor(s). This protocol may or may not resemble the external protocols used to set up the call. (Greg Utas describes this in more detail in Chapter 6.)

SYNCHRONIZING THE PROCESSORS OF A SWITCH

Telephone switches must be highly reliable. A common availability target was two hours downtime in 40 years of service. This did not allow for many half-hour outages for upgrading the software from one release to another! System upgrades are often compared to changing the engine in a car driving down the freeway. The only concession is that you can slow down slightly, but you cannot get off the freeway or stop!

To meet the reliability requirements, almost every part of a switch is duplicated, including the processing modules, their memory, and the links between the modules. For most modules a pair of redundant CPUs process events. During a software upgrade, one CPU is made inactive, forcing the full load to be carried by the other processor (typically called the *active unit*).

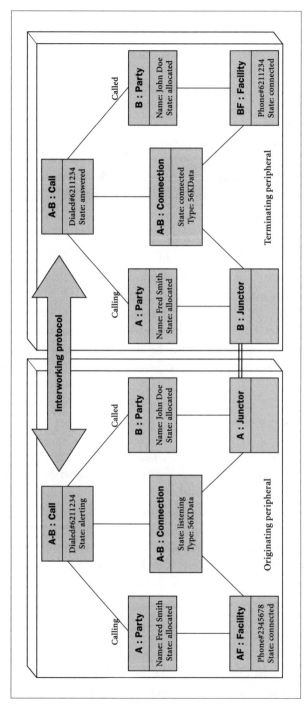

Figure 1.6. Interworking of originating and terminating peripheral modules.

After the new software is installed in the inactive unit, control is transferred to it. However, to prevent calls from being dropped, the two units must be resynchronized. This requires that each call in the active unit be packaged, sent to the inactive unit, and recreated there. Because the software in the two units may be different and may expect different memory layouts, it is not sufficient to just copy call memory.

Until the inactive unit has fully come up to speed and taken on active status, all relevant changes to calls on the active unit must be sent to the inactive unit. In effect, each call exists twice, once in each unit, but only the active unit is handling the external signaling. The synchronization protocol may be completely independent of the protocols used to set up the calls; the only requirement is that state changes in one unit be reflected in the other.

Patterns Applied. Packaging up a call to be sent to the other unit is an example of Memento. The existence of the call in each unit (often with different software implementations) is an example of HOPP.

The protocol used by HOPP to keep the calls synchronized can be implemented using Observer. The synchronization messages are Mementos of Event Objects, passed from one unit to another using a transport mechanism and carrying the changed call attributes.

CONCLUSIONS

The telecommunications industry is well established. As a result, it has a rich set of patterns that are used to solve commonly occurring problems. It is through the use of these patterns that the highly stringent requirements of the network are met. The fact that a common set of patterns occurs in the product lines of competing equipment vendors confirms that the common solutions discovered independently are indeed the most appropriate. More examples of such common solutions can be found in [4] and Chapter 3 of this book.

ACKNOWLEDGMENTS

I'd like to thank David DeLano, Bill Haney, and Greg Stymfal of AG Communication Systems, who gave me many useful comments on drafts of this article.

References

[1] E. Gamma et al., *Design Patterns: Elements of Reusable Object-Oriented Software*, Addison-Wesley, 1995.

[2] F. Buschmann et al., *Pattern-Oriented Software Architecture*, Wiley, 1996.

[3] G. Meszaros, "Half Object Plus Protocol," *Pattern Languages of Program Design*, Addison-Wesley, 1995.

[4] G. Meszaros, "Improving the Capacity of Reactive Systems," *Pattern Languages of Program Design 2*, Addison-Wesley, 1996.

Part 1
Large Collections

2

A GENERATIVE
PATTERN LANGUAGE FOR
DISTRIBUTED PROCESSING

Dennis L. DeBruler

This chapter consists of three sections. The first section is a "meta" section containing some thoughts about patterns and their use. The second section fulfills the charter of these proceedings with an edited version of the conference patterns. I learned a lot at the conference, and thus the editing was actually a rewrite. Consequently, I have been unable to change all of the patterns, and the third section records the conference patterns I have not been able to revisit. In short, this chapter is like the patterns movement in general – it is only a beginning.

SOME THOUGHTS ON PATTERNS AND THEIR USAGE

Our experience at the conference indicated that even a very cryptic description is sufficient among experienced practitioners. In this form, patterns can be used as a tool to identify and solidify experience. However, we also

©1995 Lucent Technologies. Originally published in *Pattern Languages of Program Design*, vol 1., J.O. Coplien and D.C. Schmidt, eds. (Reading, MA: Addison-Wesley, 1995), pp. 69–89. Used with permission from the editor.

learned that a much better description and some examples are needed to use patterns as a teaching tool.

I have become comfortable with formally labeled sections of a pattern – such as name, context, problem, solution, rationale, and so on – as long as the solution section immediately follows the problem section. The reason the problem and solution sections should be adjacent is that I have tried to follow the advice that the problem section should build up a tension for which the solution section provides a catharsis.

The "forces" section is currently rather weak because the many missing patterns of this "distributed computing" pattern language need to be identified before one can properly begin to identify and sort out the forces. Working with patterns has given me additional insight as to why I have such a difficult time with the waterfall "*myth*odology." I generate programs by tackling different levels of abstraction in parallel. For example, at the beginning of a development I'll discuss both high-level structural issues such as the boundary between the application and the platform, low-level issues such as what kind of protocol to use over a fiber link, and a myriad of miscellaneous issues such as source code control strategy and tools. However, there are other topics, such as measurement collection, that I don't even want to start designing until after most of the code has been implemented. I can envision a methodology based on generative pattern languages that allows the design of some aspects of the system to precede by a considerable interval the design of other parts of the system. For several years I have thought of the software-development cycle as a pail of water freezing into ice. It doesn't freeze top-down or bottom-up, it starts crystallizing throughout the pail around loci of impurities. In the case of software design, I prefer to think of loci of understanding or insight rather than loci of impurities.

One lesson I learned at the writers' workshop was the conflict between the initial reading of the patterns as expository material and reading them later as reference material. In the expository mode many examples should be included. But in the reference mode many examples make it more difficult to find the nuggets of information. Ultimately we may be able to use hypertext to resolve this conflict. While we are constrained to the printed page, I'm experimenting with using a smaller font for the examples so that they may be easily skipped during subsequent references to the pattern.

My experience with these patterns ranges from having used a pattern systematically since the early 1970s to having just learned about one. Like Alexander contends, each pattern's utility will eventually have to be graded.

However, I have yet to undertake a project in which all of these patterns are systematically utilized. One reason is that until this documentation effort many of these patterns were the result of intuition rather than knowledge. Another reason is that some of my colleagues think object-based programming means coding in C++, rather than my meaning, "understand your data." Culture clash is a force I haven't even begun to consider how to resolve. Another reason I haven't systematically practiced this pattern language is that there are many patterns still missing.

TOWARD A PATTERN LANGUAGE FOR DISTRIBUTED COMPUTING

To provide continuity one would like all of the examples in the paper to be drawn from the same application. However, to explore the scope of a pattern language it is useful to draw examples from several different applications. I compromise here by choosing several rather distinct applications – the data processing–oriented application of cable television advertising and the hardware-intensive, real time-flavored problem domain of a video server.[1] I also draw examples from telephony, because that is the application I am most familiar with. Each example will begin with a header that indicates which of these applications the example draws from. The examples also assume that the paper is being read sequentially and that the previous examples will have been read.

NAME: DEFINE THE DATA STRUCTURE

Context. The beginning of a software design project has a seed team consisting of at least two areas of expertise: marketing and software. Some projects also have a hardware subteam. The marketing subteam provides a "vision,"

---

[1] The video server is a "box" that has many disk-drive interfaces (SCSI standard) and many fiber interfaces (ATM SONET standard). The job of the video server is to play out movies stored in a digital format on the disks onto the appropriate fiber interface. In a typical application, the fiber interface carries 155 million bits per second (Mbps) and each movie plays out at a rate of 3 Mbps on a Virtual Channel.

but they are a long way from providing specific requirements. Performance and availability[2] requirements are not yet well understood.

Forces. Forces are to be determined, as mentioned in metacomments in the first section.

Problem. For a large, distributed programming problem, how do you begin the architecture/design?

Solution. Ignoring anything that is known about the distributed nature of the hardware architecture, do a data structure analysis.

Resulting Context. After the data structure analysis, the state data and the relationships that model the "real world" of interest will be well understood. Note that I have avoided the word *done.* If an application is successful, this activity continues for years, if not decades. However, for any one release cycle, it will settle down. Several of the lower-level patterns have the property of reducing the risk of getting the data model "just right," which helps reduce the time to market.

In addition to the patterns discussion here concerning the data structure, other patterns, concerning aspects of architecture and design such as identifying application programming interfaces [Rubel94], are also needed.

Design Rationale. A data analysis exercise is complex enough without the problems of distributed computing, so do a first phase of the analysis while ignoring processor boundaries.

Name: Identify the Nouns

Context. This is the beginning of the Describe the Data Structure phase.

Forces. Everybody is frozen by the immensity of the job that lies ahead [Cunningham94].

Problem. For a large programming problem, how do you begin the architecture/design? Note, it is not a large *distributed* programming problem.

Solution. Brainstorm the values, attributes, and roles of the system, and give them precise names.

---

[2]I design for applications where unavailability is specified in terms of a few (1–3) minutes a year.

It continues to amaze me how simply naming things helps the brain go from the "vision" stage to the "reality" stage. Don't worry at this point whether a noun is an attribute or a role. It should be easy to identify values and their associated enumerated types, however. These should be recorded directly in the project's programming language. That is, it is OK to produce some code during the architecture and design phases concerning details. Furthermore, producing some code early in the waterfall helps force the project to address topics such as source code control before they become critical path issues.

Some enumerated types are easy to identify, but the identification of the values for those types will continue throughout the development of the code – including, unfortunately, system testing. Nonetheless, whenever a new value is identified, it should be recorded directly in the programming language. Any other medium, such as a design document, is simply a waste of keyboarding effort. (One can always include selected code files into a design document, if such detail is desired.)

Telephony Example. The attribute Cause Value [Bellcore92] is defined as the result code in a call disconnect report. It contains values such as normal clearing, destination out of service, invalid call reference, and message unimplemented. It has been interesting to watch this list of values grow over the years.

Resulting Context. The resulting context includes enumerated value definitions under source code control and the beginnings of a glossary of roles and their attributes.

Design Rationale. This is essentially the first stage of any data analysis or object-oriented analysis, except that we introduce an intermediate notion between attributes and objects/entities, called roles. The notion of role will be defined later as we describe additional patterns.

NAME: FACTOR OUT COMMON ATTRIBUTES

Context. A first cut at a list of things and their attributes has been developed by the **Identify the Nouns** pattern.

Forces. Reuse of software must be maximized.

Problem. During the coding phase of a project there is sometimes a need to copy code and edit it because basically the same operation needs to be done but there are small differences that preclude the use of procedures. Copying code is great for getting your Non-Commentary Source Line (NCSL) count up; but it creates a maintenance nightmare, because whenever a change is needed it must be made in all of the copies.

Cable TV Advertising Business Example. There are a remarkable number of companies involved in getting a local advertisement to appear on a cable TV show. We define a record for each of these companies. The name of the record is indicated in parentheses.

- *The cable networks (Network), which schedule programming and identify periods of time that are available for the insertion of advertisements by affiliates.*

- *The cable system advertising business units (CSABU), which are responsible for selling the advertising slots for all of the channels for all of the neighborhoods they serve.*

- *The advertising agencies (Agent), which buy advertising slots for their client companies.*

- *The advertising sales representatives (ASR), who function as brokers between the CSABUs and the advertising agencies.*

- *The video preparation facilities (Preparer), which produce and prepare the spot for each of the CSABUs that will run the ad.*

- *The ad insertion locations (Inserter), which accept, store, retrieve, and insert the spots at the appropriate times into the appropriate channels.*

- *The verification locations (Verifier), which independently verify that a video spot has run.*

All of these companies have an Address attribute. Three years after the software is deployed, all seven records have to be changed because the existing address becomes the Mailing Address and an optional Shipping Address must be added.

Video Server Hardware Example. Let us assume that four board designs are used – Clock, Disk, Fiber3, and Fiber12. The Clock board derives a clock from one of the fiber terminations or from a local oscillator and distributes that clock to the other boards. The Disk design implements two Small Computer System Interfaces (SCSI). The Fiber3 design implements four OC3 (155 Mbps SONET) interfaces, and the Fiber12 design implements one OC12 (620 Mbps SONET) interface. The design of the Disk and Fiber boards includes a powerful RISC processor with several million bytes of memory. These "smart" boards share methods to diagnose the processor and the memory. Later in the design cycle, an Ethernet chip is added to the processor core to facilitate program development. Thus an additional method must be added to each of the smart board types to diagnose the Ethernet chip.

Each of the board types also contains attributes that record the hardware's Current and Goal states. The Current state indicates if the hardware is currently in service (ACTIVE), out of service because it is being tested (OOS-TEST), out of service because the hardware has failed (OOS), out of service because the board has yet to be connected to equipment and turned up for service (INACTIVE), or out of service because a user has removed it from service (OOS-RMV). The Goal state indicates which current state's values. For example, being OOS because of a failure would never be a goal. Later, while implementing diagnostics,[3] one discovers that when the test is completed it is unknown if the goal should be changed from OOS-TEST to ACTIVE or from OOS-TEST to INACTIVE. Thus each board type definition must be modified to add a Policy state attribute that records the long-term goal of ACTIVE versus INACTIVE.

Solution. Identify the attribute inheritance structure. The reader will recognize this pattern as one of the basic tenets of object-oriented design. However, we use the term *role* instead of *object* because object programming not only implies attribute inheritance, it also implies a specific way of animating data. As we will see later, there are other ways to animate data, but the notion of attribute inheritance makes sense for these other techniques as well. Factoring out shared attributes will introduce new roles of a more general nature that are inherited by the more specialized roles. An object-oriented programming language supports this structure directly. A more traditional language must resort to unions or a field that points to another structure containing the specialized attributes.

Cable TV Advertising Business Example. We note that all of the different types of companies listed in the previous example are specializations of a more fundamental entity type: Company. Thus a Company role should be defined that has the Mailing Address and optional Shipping Address attributes. The more specialized roles should inherit the Company role and define their own attributes, such as Media Format[4] for the Inserter role. Even if a role currently does not have any additional attributes, it should still have a distinct name because it may acquire additional attributes later in the program's life cycle.

---

[3]We use the term *diagnostics* for hardware tests that affect service. That is, the equipment must be taken OOS while they run.

[4]We assume that this attribute indicates the transmittal format used by its video equipment, such as Betamax analog tape, Betamax digital tape, MPEG 28mm digital tape, and MPEG-2 delivered over an ATM SONET interface.

Video Server Hardware Example. To avoid having to edit multiple board defini-tions whenever another attribute or method is identified that applies to several board types, we introduce the more general role of Board. Furthermore, the processor-related attributes such as Type – for example, 80960 versus 68360, RAM size, and diagnostic methods – are factored out into a Processor mix-in. Note that the mainte-nance states of Current, Goal, and Policy also apply to each of the interfaces on the Disk and Fiber interfaces. Thus we introduce the role Port to model the common aspects of these hardware interfaces. Noticing that both boards and ports share the maintenance states, we introduce an even more general role of Hardware. Further investigation discovers that some Software roles, such as protocols, also have the notion of a maintenance state. For example, it makes sense to talk about a TCP con-nection being ACTIVE or OOS. Thus we introduce the role Resource as a general-ization across Software and Hardware roles. Figure 2.1 summarizes this inheritance structure.

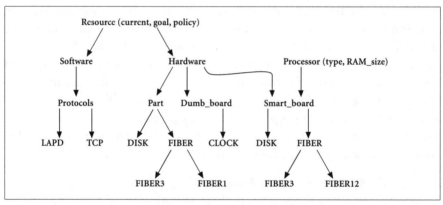

Figure 2.1. Part of the role inheritance structure of the video server.

Resulting Context. The resulting context is a graph recording the inheri-tance structure among the roles.

To facilitate software reuse, we try very hard during the design phase to make our inheritance rather deep. That is, we strive for more and more gen-eralization. I like to use the term *entity* for the most fundamental base objects discovered by this generalization process and use the term *role* for the "typical" objects of the problem domain used in the data-structure diagrams.

Design Rationale. The utility of inheritance is discussed extensively in the existing literature.

NAME: NORMALIZE THE ROLES

Context. A diagram of the program's inheritance structure exists.

Forces. Programming languages provide good support for aggregating attributes into records, but they do not provide good support for recording relationships between records.

Problem. Attributes are defined for one large role that instead should be defined for multiple related roles.

> *Cable TV Advertising Business Example. In addition to the company roles of Agent and ASR defined previously, the Identify the Nouns exercise defined a role, Sale, to record the sale of ad time from an ASR to an Agent. The attributes of the Sale role are contract number, ASR, broker, commission, agent, account manager, date of sale, ad ID, start date, end date, slot ID. The broker is an employee of the ASR, and the account manager is an employee of the agent. The ad ID keys another role that records such things as the name of the ad, the client company for which it was made, and the media formats that are available. The slot ID keys a role that records the play time and channel number of the time being sold. Assume that an ASR employee, Jane, has several active contracts. If we assume that her commission has changed, we have the update problem of consistently changing the Commission attribute of all the role instances associated with her contracts. This is an example of the "update anomaly" [Date81]. Now assume that while she is on vacation all of her contracts expire. We can no longer determine her commission. This is an example of the "deletion anomaly."*
>
> *By including the address attributes in the company role, we can't accommodate companies that have multiple locations without the risk of repeating information that is unique for a company, such as its legal and common names.*

Solution. Apply the normalization techniques developed for relational database models. Descriptions of these normalization techniques can be found in Tsichritzis and Lochovsky [TL77] and Ullman [Ullman82]. Notice that there is a one-to-many relationship between a role with a key of $<k_1, \ldots, k_{n-1}>$ and a role with a key of $<k1, \ldots, k_{n-1}>$. These one-to-many key-subset relationships should be diagrammed using Bachman's data structure diagram [Bachman69]; however, we use the diagrams in the spirit of his later thinking, when he introduced the notion of roles. Specifically, we don't interpret a node in a data structure graph as a record; instead we interpret it simply as a set of attributes with a strong logical cohesion. How to map roles to storage concepts such as records or objects comes later, when we consider how to animate the data.

To summarize the conventions of a data structure diagram, the role with the $<k_1, \ldots, k_{n-1}>$ is said to be the owner and the role with the key i$<k_1, \ldots, k_n>$ is said to be the member. Boxes are drawn to represent each of the roles, and the name of the role is placed in the box. An arrow is drawn from the owner to the member role, and the name of the relationship is placed near the arrow.

Alternatively, one can view each arrow of a data structure diagram as a functional mapping. Specifically, the role at the arrow's tail is the range and the role at the arrow's head is the domain. The arrow's name becomes the name of the functional mapping.

Cable TV Advertising Business Example. The original roles are diagrammed in Figure 2.2. The ">" symbol is used to indicate the inheritance ancestry of a role. We convert the roles ASR, Agent, and Sale to third-normal form by introducing roles for each of the employees. We also notice that several different time slots may be sold at the same time between the same two people. Thus we add another role that records the time slot–specific data. To accommodate multiple locations, we introduce a Location role between an employee and a company. The normalized roles are diagrammed in Figure 2.3.

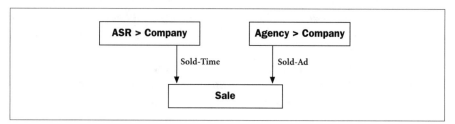

Figure 2.2. Initial data structure diagram of ad sales.

Resulting Context. As a result of using this pattern, additional roles have been introduced and several one-to-many relationships have been identified. But there remain additional relationships to identify using the pattern: Identify Problem Domain Relationships.

Design Rationale. The relational-model objectives of normalization [TL77] that apply to programming are (1) the removal of undesirable insertion, update, and deletion dependencies, and (2) the reduction of the need to

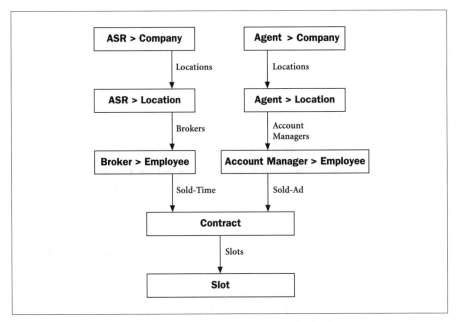

Figure 2.3. Normalized data structure diagram of ad sales.

restructure relations as additional information is added to the model. Documenting a relational model using a data structure diagram helps me formulate the equijoins that are needed to access attributes during implementation.

NAME: IDENTIFY PROBLEM DOMAIN RELATIONSHIPS

Context. The inheritance structure has been diagrammed by **Factor Out Command Attributes,** and the one-to-many mappings that result from mechanically decomposing compound keys have been diagrammed by **Normalize the Roles.**

Forces. The application has relationships that have not yet been diagrammed.

Problem. Many relationships, such as Sale, are implicitly identified as compound roles during the Identify the Nouns brainstorming. But "pure" relationships may need additional effort to capture.

Video Server Hardware Example. *While developing the maintenance-state model of resources, it quickly becomes evident that there are dependencies between resources. In fact, there are two types of dependencies: Supporting/Supported and Composite [Bellcore93]. The Supporting/Supported relationship is many-to-many, and it records the fact that some resources cannot be ACTIVE if a resource it depends upon is not ACTIVE. For example, if a Fiber3 port fails, then all of the TCP/IP and video stream connections that it was carrying become OOS. Furthermore, the TCP/IP connections not only need the port, they also need the Fiber3's RISC processor to be ACTIVE. The Composite relationship is one-to-many, and it records physical containment (for example, the four OC3 ports contained by a Fiber3 printed circuit board). Other examples of the Composite relationship are the 24 DS0 (64000 bps) circuits that are carried on a single DS1 (1.544 Mbps) facility and the 2048 DS0 circuits that are carried by an OC3 fiber facility.*

Solution. Convert many-to-many relationships to two functional mappings and a new role.

Video Server Hardware Example. *The Supporting/Supported relationship is very general and thus is associated with the most general role – resource. As the Bellcore name implies, this relationship consists of two functional mappings: those resources that this resource supports (Supporting in their terminology and* Sponsors *in our terminology) and those resources needed by this resource (Supported and* Dependent). *The new role is Dependency.*

The Composite relationship can be modeled with an arrow labeled Contains that has the Resource role for both its range and domain roles. However, other roles, such as Connections, can also have this relationship. So we define a new role, Node, that can be inherited by both resources and connections. The Contains arrow now points from and to the Node role instead of the Resource role. Figure 2.4 summarizes the pattern. We use overlapping rectangles to model the inheritance of the same mix-in by different roles.

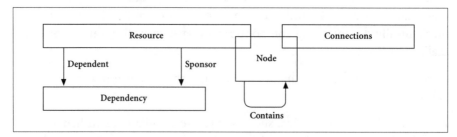

Figure 2.4. Data structure diagram of resource relationships.

Resulting Context. The result is the end of the **Define the Data Structure** effort.

Design Rationale. There are several reasons why I convert many-to-many relationships to two functional mappings and a new role. One is that the new role is needed by both relational- and network-implemented database-management systems. In the case of the network implementation, the two functional mappings are required. In the case of the relational implementation, the two functional mappings will appear on the data structure diagram because of the pattern **Normalize the Roles.** Another reason is that it is not uncommon for additional attributes to be associated with the relationship. If a double arrow is used for many-to-many relationships, then how does one depict a many-to-many-to-many relationship? In the case of functional mappings, it just requires adding another arrow with a third range role. Finally, a double-ended arrow tends to get lost in the diagram. I find it very easy to spot the boxes that have more than one arrow pointing to them. Since much of the complexity and dynamics of a system is associated with these low-level roles that model many-to-many mappings, I like them to be very visible in the diagrams.

Name: Introduce Virtual Attributes

Context. The context is that every functional mapping has been identified.

Forces. Forces are to be determined, as mentioned in a metacomment in the first section.

Problem. A network implementation of the data model introduces the need for tedious navigation code, which breaks easily if the model must be changed. The relational model also has this problem for non-key attributes.

> *Cable TV Advertising Business Example. Consider the Broker role in the example for the pattern **Normalize the Roles.** To obtain the attribute Company Name, one must traverse two functional mappings. Worse yet, if the Location role was not identified during the original design, all code that obtained the Company Name of a Broker (and an Account Manager) must be changed.*

Solution. Access all attributes with accessor functions, and post-process a data-definition language to automatically generate accessor functions to attributes defined by range roles. Apply the range role analysis recursively.

That is, as long as there is a unique path to an ancestor node, all of the attributes of all of the roles in the path are propagated down as virtual attributes of the role under consideration. In practice it is sufficient to provide virtual access functions for reading an attribute but not for creating or updating an attribute. One reason for this is that there are typically few places in the code that create or change an attribute, compared to the many places that use an attribute. Another reason is that code that changes data should "know what it is doing." In general, I feel that subschemas should be read-only.

> *Cable TV Advertising Business Example. All of the attributes of the Company and the Location roles can be accessed from a Broker instance using the same mechanism that accesses the "native" attributes such as broker name.*

Resulting Context. For code that uses, as opposed to changes, a role, the role appears to have many attributes.

Design Rationale. Virtual attributes minimize the impact on existing code of adding additional roles to the data structure. This reduces the need to get the data model "just right" early in the program-development process.

NAME: ANIMATE THE DATA

Context. The Define the Data Structure phase of the software-development cycle has reached the point of diminishing returns.

Forces. Forces are to be determined, as mentioned in the metacomments.

Problem. Any application uses a data model to model the relevant aspects of the real world. Thus the essence of the application's actions becomes updating data based on events and transactions from the real world, making decisions based on those events and transactions, sending controls and transactions back to the real world, and generating various views of what is happening in the real world by interrogating the data and/or generating reports. Also, the data itself becomes an issue, because the accuracy of the data must be maintained in spite of challenges such as computer failures.

Solution. See the following patterns, which decompose this pattern.

Resulting Context. Each role has been mapped onto an actor, and each actor has been mapped onto a processor. The paradigm of communicating finite-state machines has been chosen instead of the paradigm of remote function calls.

Design Rationale. Roles provide a layer of indirection between determining *what* must be done and *how* it is done [Lea94]. For example, the mapping of actors to processors can be changed from a design decision to a run-time decision and can be used to help solve problems such as load balancing and processor fault recovery.

NAME: TIME THREAD ANALYSIS

Context. The beginning of the **Animate the Data** phase.

Forces. Forces are to be determined as mentioned in a metacomment in the first section.

Problem. How are the data created and changed?

Solution. Use time-thread analysis [BC93]. First, list the problem domain events and transactions that the real world generates. Then, for each event, trade the causality flow through the roles of the data structure and note the actions performed by each role.

> ***Cable TV Advertising Business Example.*** *The following are examples of external events that need to be traced:*
>
> - *Joe Ford's advertising executive calls his account manager to request that his current advertisement be played during each of the local high school football games aired this fall on the local cable channel.*
>
> - *A sports event has a commercial opportunity, such as a time-out or a change of innings.*
>
> - *Programming determines that a particular movie is going to be aired during a 7:00 p.m. time slot; a promotional spot for that movie needs to be scheduled for earlier that day and for sometime during the previous day.*
>
> - *A commercial features a star who has just committed an unsavory act; all showings of that commercial must be yanked.*
>
> - *A tornado has been spotted, and the graphics overlay feature of the commercial-insertion equipment is used to display a warning on all cable channels.*

- *A display of unsold time for the next week is requested.*

- *An invoice is prepared by an advertising sales representative for an advertising agent.*

Resulting Context. The result is that the actions needed by roles to animate the data have been identified.

Design Rationale. As Buhr and Casselman note [BC93], this type of analysis has typically been done already informally. We might as well capture the insights it provides.

NAME: DETERMINE THE ACTORS

Context. The actions that each role needs to perform in response to outside events have been identified.

Forces. The forces are to be determined, as mentioned in a metacomment at the beginning of this chapter.

Problem. How to determine what lines of code get executed when an event happens.

Solution. Use objects, callbacks, and Finite-State Machines (FSM). One technique is to view each role as an object and add methods to its definitions, along with the attributes that have already been identified. This works fine for role-specific actions that are not state-dependent. For example, it is quite appropriate to define an Alert method for a specific phone type to cause a phone of that type to ring. At this phase of the design process, assume that each role has a dedicated actor that runs on its own computer. That is, each role is implemented as an object within its own computer.

However, for actions that are not role-specific, such as removing a piece of equipment from service, the object-oriented paradigm requires that the bulk of the code be implemented as before and/or after methods. For these generic types of actions I prefer the callback paradigm exemplified by the X Window System.[5]

Video Server Hardware Example. *To remove a resource requires changing the Goal attribute to OOS-RMV and recording the identity of the user entering the* remove

---

[5]This is a trademark of the Massachusetts Institute of Technology.

request as the cause code. The program must also recursively change the Goal of all the resources the removed resource sponsors. Furthermore, the program recursively changes the state of all the resources the removed resource contains. When the current state of all the sponsored and contained resources have transitioned to OOS-RMV, the "down" handler of the requested resources is called to transition it to OOS-RMV. If a sponsored resource does not transition to OOS-RMV within a generous time-out value, such as a minute, an error is logged and the resource is removed anyhow. To implement a new hardware role, only a few (typically simple) handlers need to be defined. The typical handlers are Init, Up, and Down. With these handlers defined for each resource type, several rather complex actions such as Remove, Restore, Diagnose, Error Detection, and Fault Recovery can be handled by centralized, generic code.

Resulting Context. The result is a massively distributed design because each object is assumed to be running on its own computer.

Design Rationale. A reason to assume during this phase that each actor runs on its own computer is that "with each object residing on its own computer, you cannot afford to ignore interference problems that are at the heart of most distributed system design errors" [Lea93].

RAW CONFERENCE PATTERNS

This section contains some "rules of thumb" as they appeared in the conference draft. They should become patterns in the more detailed part of a distributed pattern language.

Process Considered Harmful. "Real-time operating system" is an oxymoron: use finite-state machines instead of processes.

Processes were invented to implement time-sharing systems to give each user a virtual machine. Nowadays, if an application calls for the emulation of a machine, just give it a real machine. For other types of applications, three problems with processes are context switching overhead, wasted stack space, and unnecessary message buffering.

Consider the structure of a typical process in a distributed system:

```
main()
  while (1) {
    select(. . .);
    recvfrom(. . .);
    switch (message_opcode) {
```

```
      case SETUP: /* setup code */
      case FLASH: /* call feature code */
      case HANGUP: /* call teardown code */
      etc.
      }
    }
  }
```

There may be many processes of this nature – each roadblocked until an event happens. While each is roadblocked, its nearly empty stack represents wasted memory. Memory is cheap, but it is not free. For embedded system coding, I prefer an infrastructure that understands the event structure of "the box" under development and that dispatches the event handlers directly, rather than using classical operating system models.

In many event handlers there will be calls to the operating system's "send message" primitive. Unfortunately, in every operating system I am aware of (UNIX plus about five so-called real-time operating systems), the message is queued, even if the target process is resident in the same processor. If the program counter were to follow the message rather than fall through to the statement following the "send message" statement, I would have less concern with a process structure. This would allow the system to finish current work before beginning new work, and it would remove the headache of trying to engineer message buffer utilization. (The engineering headache in this case is not so much memory consumption as it is additional processing delay.)

Time Granularities. There is no such thing as immediate. First, determine the order of the magnitudes of the event processing times. The granularities I have experience with are microseconds, a few milliseconds, tenths of a second, and fractions of an hour. Fortunately I haven't had all of these granularities in one system! For the tight granularities (a few milliseconds or less), determine if the short processing time is required because of latency/delay requirements or because of total throughput requirements. If you have requirements of a few microseconds due to throughput (such as for ATM cell processing), dedicate a microprocessor to the problem and support the other granularities with another microprocessor. Otherwise, these granularities can be handled using interrupts.

Queues should be used only when an event handler discovers work that should be handled at a slower granularity of time. For example, if an Ethernet interrupt handler discovers that an incoming UDP packet contains an SNMP command rather than a call-processing command, it will put that packet on the tenths-of-a-second queue. The SNMP handler may discover that the command requests a diagnostic that will take several minutes to run. The SNMP handler will add the diagnostic request to the fractions-of-an-hour queue.

Run to Completion. Minimize the use of interrupts. If the smallest granularity of time is around a hundredth of a tenth of a second, interrupts can be avoided altogether.

We do not use time-slice interrupts to force an event handler to give up control for another event handler. Instead, we require that each event handler periodically call a special scheduling primitive that allows handlers with a finer granularity to run. That is, a handler is allowed to run to completion or until it voluntarily gives up control. (We do have a sanity timer interrupt, but it is considered a very serious error if it fires.) For embedded software, giving up control is usually a simple matter of placing the scheduler call at the end of each loop in the code. Avoiding preemptive scheduling greatly simplifies critical regional programming.

We avoid error handler interrupts by designing hardware with error counters that can be periodically polled.

Alarm Triage. The importance of an alarm is relative. A lesson from Three Mile Island is that there should be no more than seven red lights on a display. Normally, if a line to a customer fails it is a major alarm. However, if an OC12 fiber link (which can carry 8064 connections) fails, a failed customer line is no longer major compared to the OC12 break. The alarms for lines whose calls were being carried by the failed fiber are of especially low priority. Unfortunately, we have yet to develop a system architecture that successfully implements relative alarm priority.

Invent System-wide "Pressure Gauges." Put some of the "computing" into the message transport subsystem. If the job of a software module is to sum the contents of many messages together, then whatever processor that module is assigned to will become the focal point of a large set of messages. Instead, if we design the message transport nodes to recognize whenever there is more than one message in its buffer that is destined to the same "summing" module to replace the messages with one message that contains an intermediate sum, then only one message is delivered to the systemwide summing module, and the total message traffic in the network is significantly reduced.

One of the big differences between a real-time system and a time-sharing system is shedding load. If a system has the capacity to do *n* jobs satisfactorily but *n* + *m* jobs are submitted to the system, a time-sharing system will do *n* + *m* jobs poorly, whereas a real-time system will kill (or ignore) *m* jobs so that it can continue to do *n* jobs satisfactorily.

It is rather easy for distributed elements to shed work if they can detect that the system is overloaded. The real problem is determining a systemwide load factor. To do this we define a centralized software module to compute the needed systemwide load parameters and "broadcast" the computed parameters back to each element. (Broadcast is in quotes because in a WAN, broadcasting usually has to be implemented using many point-to-point connections or a spanning tree.) These centralized software modules are also useful for driving interfaces that allow humans to see the "big picture." The "intelligent message nodes" technique can be used so that these centralized modules don't become a bottleneck as the size of the system is scaled up.

The same technique can be used to help implement alarm triage. In this case the "pressure gauge" is measuring system alarm severity rather than traffic load, and the intelligent nodes are computing a maximum rather than a sum. Also, if a new alarm is of less severity than the current severity level of the system, it would not be reported in the first place. This helps to lower message traffic when the system is in trouble.

Strategy versus Tactics. Use the messaging capability of the distributed system to centralize strategy. Traditionally, algorithms have been either centralized or distributed. In many cases a hybrid approach would be beneficial. Pressure gauges are a simple example of a hybrid approach. The load- or alarm-shedding logic is distributed, but the determination of the current state of the system is centralized. Another example of a hybrid algorithm is in the realm of network routing. The network design algorithm that I use takes about ten hours to run on a Sun 3 for a 100-node network. On a Sparc 10, this algorithm takes ten minutes. Telephony networks gather and log traffic measurement data every fifteen minutes. Thus processing power has become cheap enough that one can now redesign the entire network during each traffic collection period. The tables that are distributed to each network element can be simplified, because they don't have to cover as many contingencies. This, in turn, simplifies the routing algorithms in the network elements that use these tables.

Don't Retransmit at the Link Level. You can add increased reliability at the application layer, but you can't decrease delays. Most Layer 2 protocols are a legacy from the 1970s, when modems struggled to deliver 300 baud. Nowadays, especially with fiber optics, messages are lost due to internal congestion rather than bit errors. Thus link level retransmission is not going to compensate for most lost message problems. You have to accommodate for lost messages at the application level anyhow. Furthermore, for some applications, such as process control, it is easier to send "fresh" data than it is to store and retransmit stale data. In fact, a retransmitting frame delaying a frame with newer information simply adds even more delay. The upper layers of the protocol stack can always add more reliability; however, no layer can reduce a delay after it has been introduced. So it is important that the lower layers be "lean and mean."

References

[Bachman69] Bachman, C.W. "Data Structure Diagrams." *Data Base* 1,2 (1969):4–10.

[BC93] Buhr, J.A., and Casselman, R.S. *Designing with Timethreads*. SCE-93-05. Ottawa: Carleton University.

[Bellcore92] Bellcore Technical Reference: TR-NWT-000303, Issue 2, December 1992, pp. 12-34 to 12-35.

[Bellcore93] Bellcore Technical Reference: TR-NWT-001093, Issue 1 *(Generic State Requirements for Network Elements)*, September, pp. 2-7 to 2-8.

[Cunningham94] Personal conversation with Ward Cunningham, PLoP Conference, August 4, 1994.

[Date81] Date, C. *An Introduction to Database Systems*. Reading, MA: Addison-Wesley, 1981.

[Lea93] Email from Doug Lea, September 12, 1993.

[Lea94] Personal conversation with Doug Lea, PLoP Conference, August 5, 1994.

[Rubel94] Rubel, B. "A Pattern for Generating a Layered Architecture." In J.O. Coplien and D.C. Schmidt, eds., *Pattern Languages of Program Design*. Reading, MA: Addison-Wesley, 1995, Chapter 7.

[TL77] Tsichritzis, D.C., and Lochovsky, F.H. *Data Base Management Systems,* Section 2.5. New York: Academic Press, 1977.

[Ullman82] Ullman, J.D. *Principles of Database Systems*. Rockville, MD: Computer Science Press, 1982, Chapter 7.

3

IMPROVING THE CAPACITY OF
REACTIVE SYSTEMS

Gerard Meszaros

ABSTRACT

This chapter describes a set of patterns related to improving the capacity and reliability of real-time reactive systems such as telephone switching exchanges. While these patterns are commonly found in telecommunications systems, they can be applied to any reactive system with peak-capacity issues.

INTRODUCTION

A common problem related to increasing the supply of well-documented patterns is the time required to capture them. The people with the most patterns in their heads also have the least time to document them. *"Pareto's Law,"* also known as the 80/20 rule, states that 80 percent of the value is attributable to 20 percent of the effort; with this in mind, this pattern languages uses the "Coplien form." Jim Coplien has shown us that it is possible to capture very important knowledge with significantly less effort by using a more compact pattern format.

This language refers to a number of patterns that are known to exist but have not yet (to my knowledge) been documented. I invite others to "flesh out" these patterns based on their own experience, and perhaps submit the expanded forms for discussion at future PLoP conferences.

PROBLEM DOMAIN HISTORY

Reactive systems are those whose primary function is to respond to requests from users outside the system. These users may be people or machines. Reactive systems must typically be able to handle a wide range of loads (the number of requests received in a given unit of time) with a high expected rate of request completion.

Examples of reactive systems include

- Time-sharing computer systems

- Telephone switching exchanges (or "switches") and Service Control Points (SCPs)

- Servers (as in client-server architectures)

- On-line transaction processing (such as banking ATM networks, etc.)

These systems all share a need for high capacity at a reasonable cost and high reliability in the face of high or extreme loads, which can lead to system overload.

THE PATTERN LANGUAGE

Capacity Bottleneck (Pattern 1) deals with identifying the limiting factor in a system's capacity. This leads to **Processing Capacity (Pattern 2)**, which describes how to deal with system capacity. Expanding on Pattern 2, three basic strategies for improving system throughput in processing-bound systems are presented: **Optimize High-Runner Cases (Pattern 3)**, which reduces the cost of frequently occurring requests; and **Share the Load (Pattern 8)**, which increases the amount of processing available.

Shed Load is supported by **Finish Work in Progress (Pattern 5)**, **Fresh Work Before Stale (Pattern 6)**, and **Match Progress Work with New (Pattern 7)**. When **Share the Load** is used in combination with **Shed Load**, it is further supported by several patterns relating to efficient implementation of load shedding in a distributed processing environment: **Work Shed at Periphery (Pattern 9)** and **Leaky Bucket of Credits (Pattern 10)**.

For patterns that are referenced but not presented here, a "fat reference"[1] is included in the footnotes. Figure 3.1 shows the structure of the pattern language graphically. Several patterns referenced but not presented here are also shown, within dashed borders.

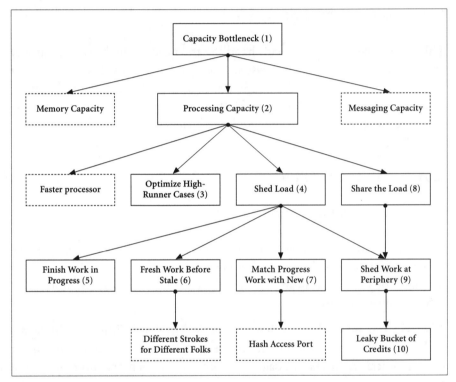

Figure 3.1. The structure of the pattern language presented graphically.

All the patterns contained herein come from the DMS-100 family of telephone switching products manufactured by NorTel (formerly known as Northern Telecom). These products share a common operating system and core processing hardware. They also share a need for very high reliability and

---

[1] At "fat reference" is a short summary of the item referred to, beyond its name and location. It is one of a number of patterns discovered during PLoP '95 that describe factors that make patterns and pattern languages easy to read and digest.

availability, even in the face of natural disasters, "mass calling" marketing campaigns, radio station contests, and the like. These natural and man-made events can cause extreme fluctuations in the arrival rates of "service requests" from the phone-calling public; the system must be able to react gracefully in the face of such periods of extreme demand.

RELATED PATTERN LANGUAGES

This pattern language deals with handling the need for high system capacity and survivability in the face of system overload conditions. For patterns that describe how to increase the reliability of underlying hardware platforms, refer to Adams et al. [Adams+95]. For patterns related to optimizing Smalltalk programs, refer to Auer and Beck [Auer+95].

CAPACITY PATTERNS

PATTERN 1: CAPACITY BOTTLENECK

Problem. Customers always want the system to handle the largest possible numbers of users, terminals, requests per hour, and so on, preferably without having to buy more hardware. What is the most effective way to improve the capacity of the system?

Context. You are working with a reactive system that is limited in its capacity by available processing power, number of access ports, connections, other finite physical resources, message reception limits, memory limitations, and so on.

Forces. Adding memory, processors, or other resources increases the customer's hardware costs and may reduce available processing time due to extra refreshing, auditing, interprocessor messaging, and the like. Optimizing data structures to reduce memory requirements may increase the processing cost of accessing the data. Optimizing algorithms to reduce processing cost may increase the data structures' memory requirements and result in duplicated logic. Most optimizations increase development effort and system complexity. Increased complexity could result in reduced flexibility and reliability as well as increased maintenance cost.

Solution. Understand what determines your system capacity and the circumstances that affect it. Determine both the nature of capacity limits (memory, processing, messaging, etc.) and their location (i.e., in which processing context – core, peripherals, clients, servers, the network, etc.). Only optimize those elements that truly limit the system's capacity. Engineer the system in such a way that these limits can be avoided automatically, or ensure that the system can withstand circumstances in which the demands on its resources are exceeded.

Apply **Processing Capacity (Pattern 2)** if the limiting factor is the processing cost of the necessary number of transactions. Use **Memory Capacity**[2] if the limiting factor is the amount of memory required to handle the load. Use **Messaging Capacity**[3] if the limiting factor is the messaging system's inability to deliver messages between processors in a timely manner.

Related Patterns. **Processing Capacity (Pattern 2)** is the entry point for a set of patterns used to increase available processing capacity and reduce the cost per transaction.

PATTERN 2: PROCESSING CAPACITY

Problem. The throughput of a system is limited by the capacity of its processor(s). How can you increase the capacity without installing a faster processor?[4]

Context. You are working with a reactive system in which the capacity is limited by the available processing power, and work arrives from external sources in a stochastic fashion. There are predictable peaks and valleys in the arrival rates. As the number of requests received exceeds the system's process-

---

[2] Not included here. This is the first pattern in a yet-unwritten pattern language describing techniques for reducing the amount of memory required by a system. Sample patterns include **Overlay Spare Bits** and **Allocate Only What You Use** (a.k.a. Waste Not, Want Not).

[3] Not included here. This is the first pattern in a yet-unwritten pattern language describing techniques for reducing the amount of messages passed between processors. Sample patterns include **Message Bundling** and **Message Compression.**

[4] The use of a faster processor may seem like an obvious alternative. However, many systems are already using the fastest processors available to them, and they must therefore seek alternative means of addressing this problem.

ing capacity, the number of requests successfully handled actually decreases because of the effort wasted attempting to handle all the requests.

The system's available processing capacity can be summarized as follows:
Total number of cycles per second – reserved headroom.[5]

The average cost per request (in seconds) of any particular mix of requests can be computed as follows:

Sum over request type:
Cost per request * Number of such requests per second.[6]

The capacity (the "rated capacity"), in requests per second, for any particular mix of requests can be expressed as follows:
Available processing/Average cost per request.

Forces. The available share of the processing capacity within the existing processor(s) can be increased by reducing reserved processing, but this will reduce the safety margin when too many requests arrive at once. One can make do with a reduced margin if the system is designed to shed excess load reliably, but this increases the complexity of the system and the development cost. And system latency (response time) increases as the size of the buffer is reduced.

The total processing capacity can be increased by adding more processors to the system. This does not provide linear growth in available processing power, however, due to the increased cost of communication between the processors. And, unless the system design already supports distributed processing, extensive redesign may be required, at considerable additional development cost and increased system complexity.

The cost of frequently occurring requests can be reduced by optimizing them, but this requires additional design and may add complexity. Optimizations typically come at a loss of flexibility, which will make future extension of the system more difficult. And there is a cost associated with measuring and analyzing the cost of each type of request.

Solution. Determine the cost-to-benefit ratio of increasing capacity by reducing the average cost per request vs. increasing the available processing horsepower vs. reducing the size of the safety buffer needed in case of surges

---

[5]"Headroom" includes any reserve processing capacity required to ensure that system responses are within specifications.

[6]Another way of calculating this is as follows: Sum over request type: Cost per request * % of this request type (of total requests).

in requests. Based on the amount of increase required, one or more of these approaches may prove to be insufficient; in the most extreme cases, they may all need to be applied.

If a small number of request types constitute a large part of the processing cost, use **Optimize High-Runner Cases (Pattern 3)** to reduce the cost of these request types. If a large amount of processing capacity has to be kept in reserve to handle peak loads, use **Shed Load (Pattern 4)** to reduce the necessary size of this buffer. (In extreme cases this can double the available processing power, from 40 percent to over 80 percent.) You can then further tune the system capacity at the expense of latency, using **Max Headroom.**[7] If the necessary increase in processing capacity exceeds what can be recovered through these techniques (or if you have other reasons to distribute your system), you will have no choice but to use **Share the Load (Pattern 8)** to increase the amount of processing that can be made available to your system.

Related Patterns

Shed Load (Pattern 4) reduces the number of requests accepted during overload, thus reducing the necessary processing headroom.

Optimize High-Runner Cases (Pattern 3) reduces the cost of frequently occurring requests, thus increasing capacity.

Share the Load (Pattern 8) can reduce the cost of requests by delegating work to other processors, and it may reduce the number of requests any one processor must handle (this can also be viewed as increasing the number of cycles available per second).

Max Headroom describes how to increase the available processing by tailoring the responsiveness of the system to maximize the rated capacity.

PATTERN 3: OPTIMIZE HIGH-RUNNER CASES

Problem. The average processing cost of service requests is too high to allow the required capacity target to be met. How can we reduce the cost of individual requests?

---

[7]Not included here. Headroom is required to ensure that system responses are within acceptable levels and that work load peaks do not push the system "over the edge." The more fully loaded a system becomes, the longer the average delays become – hence the need to engineer the headroom.

Context. You are working with a reactive system in which the required capacity has not yet been achieved. Available processing power may have already been maximized, and all possible extraneous work may have already been shed.

For example, consider a telephone switch using the fastest available processors, with overload handling mechanisms already in place; the capacity must be increased by 4 percent.

Forces. We need to ensure that the system performs adequately and meets its performance (capacity) targets, but we don't want (or can't afford) to optimize every transaction type. The development cost of optimizations is high (often more expensive than providing the basic functionality). Optimizations typically increase the complexity of the implementation or reduce the flexibility of the system when it comes time to handle new requirements. Optimizing the wrong parts of a system will contribute little to capacity but greatly increases project cost and system complexity.

Solution. The solution lies in "Pareto's Law" (also known as the 80/20 rule); in most systems, 80 percent (or more) of the processing power is consumed by 20 percent of the use cases (transaction types).

Measure or project the high-runner transactions and optimize only those parts of the system that contribute significantly to their cost. This can be done by characterizing exactly what code each high-runner transaction executes (using "profiling" tools) and ensuring that all this code executes efficiently. Optimize only as much of the code as necessary to meet the capacity targets; optimizing more than is necessary just creates extra maintenance cost and increases the likelihood of having to "undo" the optimizations when greater flexibility is required in the future.

For example, suppose that for a telephone switch in a residential area, 80 percent of all calls are basic "line-to-line" calls with no features involved. You need to recover 4 percent of the switch's call-handling capacity. You can either reduce the cost of these "line-to-line" calls by 5 percent or reduce the cost of all the other types of calls by 25 percent! It takes much less development effort to create a special, "fast" version of parts of the "line-to-line" call software than to save a similar amount of processing on a diverse set of call types.

Related Patterns. The following is a list of patterns that may be used to support this pattern; they are all pretty standard techniques, so they are not discussed here. Refer also to [Auer+95] for similar patterns relating to Smalltalk development.

Instructions Cached. Make instructions execute faster by keeping them in a processor cache. This is typically done entirely under hardware control, during program execution.

Faster RAM for Higher-Runners. Make frequently used sequences of instructions (procedures or methods) execute faster by keeping them in faster memory (such as SRAM). The decision as to what code to put into faster memory is typically made by the system developer at system design or configuration time.

Method Calls Inlined. Reduces procedure/method call overhead by "inlining" (copying) the code that would otherwise have been called into the source or object code of the calling procedure. This may result in many copies of the object code for a single fragment of source code, but better that than many *clones* of the source code.

Polymorphism Precluded (a.k.a. Fixed Methods). Reduces method call overhead by making methods fixed; this allows the compiler to generate jumps to an address rather than having to look up that address at runtime.

Hardware Traps Exceptions. Move checking for exceptions like bad pointer contents, divides by zero, and so on, into the hardware, to eliminate the need to check in software at runtime. (Less "defensive coding" also makes the program logic easier to read and understand.)

PATTERN 4: SHED LOAD

Problem. Large numbers of requests arriving from outside systems can easily cause your system to bog down or "thrash." The amount of real work actually getting done can decrease as the thrashing increases. This results in users' experiencing degraded (or complete loss of) service, which is neither appreciated by the users nor compliant with many communication protocol standards. In extreme cases, the entire system could crash. How can a system best react to such "overload" conditions to ensure that it continues to function?

Context. You are working on a processing-bound, reactive system faced with more requests than it can handle. Overloads of the system must not allow it to become unavailable.

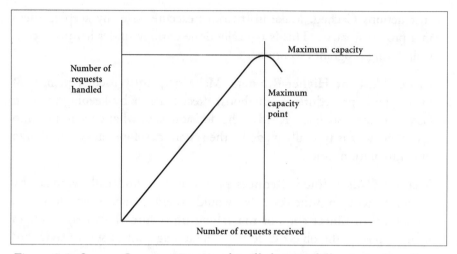

Figure 3.2. System Capacity. Requests handled successfully as number of requests increase.

Forces. Efforts to keep the system functioning can use up all its available capacity. Adding more software to handle possible overload situations adds complexity to the system. The cost of trying to shed work could exceed the processing it saves. The cost of determining the overload status of the system may itself reduce the system's capacity. How does the external system behave when work is rejected? (Does the work quietly go away, or does it repeat the requests and hence increase the load on the system?)

Solution. To ensure that the amount of work accepted by the system does not exceed its capacity, shed some requests so that others can be served properly. This is a variation on the system of triage used in hospital emergency rooms[8]: Let the dying die, let those who will heal by themselves heal, and treat only those who really need assistance. In this case, service requests that cannot be properly handled should be shed as early as possible, before a lot of processing is expended on them. By doing this, one can actually decrease the amount of processing power that needs to be reserved for unexpected peaks, thus increasing the available processing and, with it, system capacity. At first glance this seems like "something for nothing," but in fact it carries a very real cost in terms of the increase in system complexity required to handle the peaks with reduced impact.

---

[8]Triage is a technique used in medical emergencies to decide how the services of an overwhelmed group of doctors should be deployed when the number of patients exceeds the number of doctors. It determines which patients should be treated first.

When the protocols to the outside world have explicit time-outs within which a response must be provided, any received request that is predicted to be delayed longer than the specified time-out can safely be discarded without any change in the visible behavior of the system, and with potentially large savings in processing cost.

Interfaces to humans are a bit more difficult to predict, because human behavior may be affected by the local culture. For example, in some countries people will wait patiently for a dial tone, while in others, if a dial tone is not presented within 2 to 4 seconds, they will hang up and try again or "rattle" the switchhook impatiently. This can require significantly different handling under overload conditions. The Strategy pattern [Gamma+95] is a good way to deal with this required variation.

Related Patterns

Finish Work in Process (Pattern 5) maximizes the return on investment of processing cycles by ensuring work already in progress gets completed before new work is taken on.

Match Progress Work with New (Pattern 7) prevents the deadlock that could be caused by throwing away the wrong work.

Fresh Work Before Stale (Pattern 6) maximizes the number of customers who get acceptable service.

Work Shed at Periphery (Pattern 9) maximizes system throughput by reducing or eliminating the cost of shedding work in a bottleneck processor.

PATTERN 5: FINISH WORK IN PROGRESS

Alias. Finish What You Start

Problem. What requests should be accepted, and which should be rejected to improve system throughput?

Context. You are working with a reactive or transaction-oriented system in which use requests are in some way dependent upon one another. A request may build on an earlier request, provide additional information in response to (or in anticipation of) another request, or cancel or undo a previous request.

Forces. Understanding the interdependencies among requests is crucial to shedding working in a productive fashion. Rejecting the wrong work could negate considerable prior investments, or even worse, result in deadlock by "hanging" some transactions along with all the resources they are using. Failing to identify any work that can be rejected prevents improvement of system capacity through the application of **Shed Load (Pattern 4)**.

Solution. Requests that are continuations of work in progress must be recognized as such and given priority over entirely new requests. Clearly categorize all requests into New and Progress categories, and ensure that all Progress requests are processed before serving any New requests. The only exception to this rule is when the time between original requests and follow-up requests is fixed and predictable (e.g., t seconds). In this situation, completely shutting off all new requests will result in a "load dip" t seconds after the system starts shedding new work. This creates an oscillation between an overloaded and underloaded condition; the result is reduced average capacity. This can be countered by "bleeding" a small amount of new work in during the overloaded period to reduce the depth of the dip.

Related Patterns. This pattern supports the application of **Shed Load (Pattern 4)**.

PATTERN 6: FRESH WORK BEFORE STALE

Alias. Good Service for Some, No Service for Others

Problem. How can you maximize the number of customers who get good service?

Context. You are working on a reactive system that cannot possibly satisfy all the requests it receives. The grade of service (GOS), or performance standard, may be based upon the percentage of requests serviced beneath some threshold (e.g., GOS = percentage of callers receiving a dial tone within 2 seconds).

Forces. When a system is overloaded, users may give up waiting. The system will then have to do extra work to clean up. If the delays are long enough, users may have already given up before the system starts processing their initial request. This can result in a great deal of wasted system resources. But how can you tell whether uses are likely to give up, negating all your efforts to serve them?

Keeping track of the age of every request adds memory and complexity to the system. Sorting them could add processing cost to the task of choosing the next request to process. Some requests cannot be ignored and must be given priority handling (e.g., 911 calls and calls from hospitals and police stations).

Solution. If some users get served immediately while others wait a long time, at least some users receive good service; if everyone waits an equally long time, however, everyone gets poor service. So it is better to give good service to as many people as possible and give the remainder poor or no service. This may not seem "fair,"[9] but it is an example of putting the common good before individuals' good.

To maximize the number of users who get good service, put all new requests in a last-in-first-out queue: serve the most recently received requests first. These requests are the least likely to be abandoned. Only after the "fresh" requests have been exhausted will you get around to serving the "stale" ones. If users have been patient and are still there, they will be served. If they've given up, there should already be an "undo" (a cancellation of the request) somewhere in the queue with which we can cancel their request entirely.

For example, suppose you are swamped with e-mail and haven't been able to read it for a week. When you finally have an hour to read your mail, you must ask yourself, "How can I spend my time most effectively?" Start with the most recently received mail and work backward. What about the ones you never get to? Many requests will have been responded to by someone else. Some will be invitations to meetings long since over. Many of the messages weren't really important; those that were were probably re-sent when you failed to response promptly.

Related Patterns

Match Progress Work with New (Pattern 7) describes how to eliminate some work entirely when the user "cancels" a request.

"Different Strokes for Different Folks"[10] describes how to guarantee good service for access ports or requests designated as requiring priority handling.

---

[9]Since the selection process is random, based on when a request happens to arrive, it actually is equally fair to everybody.

[10]Not included here. For each access port, designate the queue to which new work requests are to be added when the requests arrive. High-priority access ports can use a different queue, which is served before the "normal" priority "new work" queue. Of course, if too many ports use the high-priority queue, its value is diluted.

Pattern 7: Match Progress Work with New

Problem. A lot of processing may go completely to waste if a user's actions cancel previous ones. How can the system avoid wasting its limited processing capacity handling requests that will be "undone"?

Context. You are working with a processing-bound, reactive system that is under a heavy load and is trying to shed work. Some users are giving up because their requests are not served immediately; this forces the system to "undo" work it just did, at an expense it cannot really afford.

For example, consider the work performed by a telephone network when a user lifts his handset off its hook to initiate a call and then, after waiting several seconds for a dial tone, hangs up the phone before a tone is delivered.

Forces. In many systems, the external actor – be it a live user or another machine – will eventually "time out" on a request and either re-send it or cancel it. It is especially important to detect such duplication or cancellation during periods of peak load, to prevent further degradation of service. Detecting related requests adds complexity to the system. The cost of detecting duplicated or canceled requests must be significantly lower than the processing cost; otherwise the system will have been made more complex without achieving much capacity improvement.

Solution. When "progress" requests are received, pair them up with the appropriate "new work" requests. If the second is a "cancel," the "new work" item can be removed from the queue without having been processed at all! If the "progress" work is something other than a cancel, it should be kept matched with the "new" work in case the "new" work must later be shed. This prevents the system from having to try to figure out what the "progress" work means in the absence of the "new" work.

For example, "threaded" e-mail and news-reading programs collect all the items related to a topic and present them as a bundle to the user. The user can then decide whether to pay attention to a bundle of messages, saving the cost of making this decision on a message-by-message basis.

Related Patterns

Work Shed at Periphery (Pattern 9) describes how to avoid the cost of matching the "new" and "progress" work in the bottleneck processor.

Hash Access Port[11] is an efficient way to match "progress" requests with previous requests.

PATTERN 8: SHARE THE LOAD

Move Function Out of Processor

Problem. The cost of processing all the requests may exceed the available capacity of a single processor at a specified system capacity. How can the available processing power be increased?

Context. You are working on a processing-bound, reactive system that falls short of meeting its target capacity. All other means of increasing the available processing capacity have been exhausted.

Forces. Adding additional processors increases the amount of processing power available, but it also makes the system more complex because of the increased messages required to synchronize the work being done. It also increases the amount of memory required. Many of the processors will have the same programs, and they may have common data as well; these will have to be synchronized, requiring further interprocessor messaging. Unless the amount of processing being delegated is significant, the increased interprocessor communications could cost more than they save.

Solution. Given the circumstances, you have no choice but to shift some of the processing to another processor. Select the functions to be moved based on those that are clearly partitioned from what is being left behind, to reduce the amount of synchronization (number of messages which need to be exchanged) required.

Related Pattern. A process for determining suitable partitioning is described in the pattern **Context Mapping.**[12]

---

[11]Not included here. Assuming that requests from the same (logical) access port are related in some way, one can hash the access port id and detect related requests via "hashing collisions."

[12]From Allen Hopley's unpublished pattern language called "Levels of Abstraction." In each processing context, start with the entire model, plus objects representing each of the other contexts. Then, optimize out those parts of the model that are completely unnecessary in this context, based on which function has been assigned to it.

Pattern 9: Work Shed at Periphery

Problem. How does one shed work, at a minimum additional cost, that is beyond the system's capacity?

Context. You are working on a multiprocessor, reactive system that is shedding work to minimize the impact on its capacity of an overload condition (for example, a telephone switch during a rock concert ticket giveaway call-in contest).

Forces. As a request is processed by the system, increased effort is invested in it, contributing to the system's overload condition. But the information needed to determine whether the system is overloaded may only be available in the "central processor" (the "bottleneck" processor). Thus by the time the system determines that a request should be shed, it may be substantially complete.

Solution. Detect new work and shed it at minimum cost by moving the detection of new work as close to the periphery of the system as possible. Provide this part of the system with information regarding the available processing capacity of the most limiting part of the system.

Related Pattern. Leaky Bucket of Credits (**Pattern 10**) describes how to communicate the status of the system's "bottleneck processor" to its periphery.

Pattern 10: Leaky Bucket of Credits

Problem. How can one processor know whether another processor is capable of handling more work?

Context. You are working with a reactive system in which one processor needs to be aware of the overload state of another processor.

Forces. For a peripheral to be able to reject new work when the system is overloaded, it must be able to recognize this condition. But having the bottleneck processor take up valuable processing cycles to inform a potentially large number of other processors of its state would further reduce its capacity. And what happens if it gets so bogged down that it can't send out a "Stop sending me work!" message?

Solution. The bottleneck processor tells the other processors (the peripherals) when it is capable of accepting *more* work. It does so by sending them "credits." Each peripheral holds a "leaky bucket" of these credits. The buckets gradually "leak" until they are empty. When the system is not at capacity, the buckets are continuously refilled with new credits sent from the bottleneck processor until they are full; however, when the system is at capacity, the bottleneck processor will not send out credits, and the peripherals will therefore soon start to hold back new work. When a peripheral sends work to several different and independent processors, it can and must track the credits from each processor separately.

Related Patterns. This pattern is a specialized usage of **Leaky Bucket.**[13] The amount of work forwarded to the bottleneck processor can be fine-tuned by sending a variable number of credits, based on the remaining headroom.

This is also an example of applying the **Context Mapping;** each processor keeps a model of "its world," which includes a description of the state of the other processors in the system (i.e., overloaded or not). The credits provide a means of keeping the distributed views of any one processor synchronized, in something near real time but at a reasonable cost (especially when the processor is overloaded). This, in turn, is an example of **Half-Object Plus Protocol,** as described in an earlier paper [Meszaros95] and also in Chapter 8 of this book; in this case, the "object" that needs to appear in more than one context is the bottleneck processor itself!

Acknowledgments

I would like to thank all the people who developed the many solutions described in these patterns, and especially Gord Adamyk and Pierre Johnson, who first described them to me.

Special thanks go to Erich Gamma, who was the PLoP '95 shepherd for this pattern language.

References

[Adams+95] M. Adams et al. "Fault-Tolerant Telecommunication System Patterns." Chapter 4, this volume and *Pattern Languages of Program Design 2*, eds., J.M Vlissides, J.O. Coplien, N.L. Kerth, Addison-Wesley, 1996.

---

[13]Not included here. The concept of a bucket that leaks until empty and is then refilled (or a bucket that is leaked into until it overflows or is manually emptied) is used throughout high-availability systems to detect all kinds of transient problems. Refer to the pattern by the same name described by Adams et al. [Adams+95].

[Auer+95] K. Auer and K. Beck. "Lazy Optimization: Patterns for Efficient Smalltalk Programming." Chapter 2, see previous citation.

[Gamma+95] E. Gamma, R. Helm, R. Johnson, and J. Vlissides. *Design Patterns: Elements of Reusable Object-Oriented Software.* Reading, MA: Addison-Wesley, 1995.

[Meszaros95] G. Meszaros. "Half-Object Plus Protocol." In J.O. Coplien and D.C. Schmidt (eds.), *Pattern Languages of Program Design.* Reading, MA: Addison-Wesley, 1995, pp. 129–132 and Chapter 8 of this book.

4

FAULT-TOLERANT TELECOMMUNICATION SYSTEM PATTERNS

Michael Adams, James Coplien, Robert Gamoke, Robert Hanmer,
Fred Keeve, and Keith Nicodemus

INTRODUCTION

THE PATTERNS PRESENTED HERE form a small, partial pattern language within the larger collection of patterns in use at AT&T. We chose them because of their interconnectedness and the diversity of their authorship, and because they are probably well known to the telecommunications programming community. Many of these patterns work in other domains, but for this chapter we expect telecommunications designers to be our primary audience.

Two of the unique characteristics of telecommunications software are its reliability and human factors. Many switching systems, including the ones referred to in these patterns, are designed to be in virtually continuous operation – they may be out of service no more than two hours in forty years. In many cases this requirement limits design choices.

The systems must also be designed so that maintenance personnel efforts are optimized. This can lead to largely automated systems or systems in which remote computers monitor and control the switching equipment.

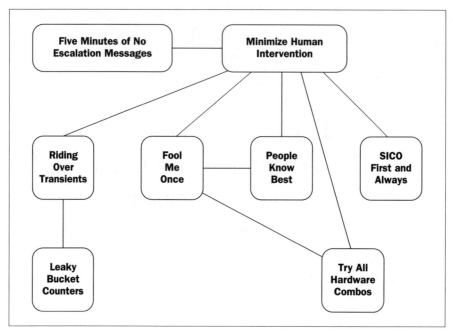

Figure 4.1. Pattern map.

Glossary

1A: A central processor for telecommunications systems.

1: A second-generation central processor based on the 1A architecture.

4ESS Switch, 5ESS Switch: Members of the AT&T Electronic Switching System product line.

Application: The portion of systems software that relates to its call processing function.

Call Store: The system's memory store, used for static or dynamic data.

CC: Central Control (the central processor complex), either a 1A or a 1B processor.

FIT: Failures in a Trillion, a measurement of the failure rate of hardware components (one FIT equals one component failure in 10^9 hours).

PC: Processor Configuration, the initialization and recovery mechanisms (independent of the application) that deal with the common underlying hardware/software platform. *PC* is also used as a verb, to indicate a certain level of system reboot.

Phase: A level of system recovery escalation.

Program Store: The memory stores used for program text.

SICO: System Integrity Control.

Stored Program Control: A term used to differentiate between central control-based switching and the older relay- and crossbar-based systems.

Transient: A condition that is transitory in nature. It appears and disappears. Lightning might produce transient errors.

PATTERN: MINIMIZE HUMAN INTERVENTION

Problem. History has shown that people cause the majority of problems in continuously running systems (wrong actions, wrong systems, wrong button).

Context. Highly reliable, continuously running digital systems for which downtime, human-induced or otherwise, must be minimized.

Forces. Humans are truly intelligent; machines aren't. Humans are better at detecting patterns of system behavior, especially among seemingly random occurrences separated by time. (See the pattern People Know Best.)

Machines are good at orchestrating a well thought out, global strategy; humans aren't.

Humans are fallible; computers are often less fallible.

Humans feel a need to intervene if they can't see that the system is making serious attempts at restoration: A quiet system is a dead system. Human reaction and decision times are very slow (by orders of magnitude) compared to computer processors.

Human operators get bored with ongoing surveillance and may ignore or miss critical events.

Normal processing (and failure) events happen so quickly that it is infeasible to include the human operator.

Solution. Let the machine try to do everything itself, deferring to the human only as an act of desperation and a last resort.

Resulting Context. The result is a system less susceptible to human error. This will make the system's customers happier. In many organizations, the system operator's compensation is based on system availability, so this strategy actually improves the operator's lot.

Application of this pattern leads to a system in which patterns such as Riding Over Transients, SICO First and Always, and Try All Hardware Combos apply as well, providing a system with the ability to proceed automatically.

Rationale. A disproportionate number of failures in high-availability systems are due to operator errors, not primary system errors. By minimizing human intervention, overall system availability can be improved. Human intervention can be reduced by building in strategies that counter human tendencies to act rashly; see patterns like Fool Me Once, Leaky Bucket Counters, and Five Minutes of No Escalation Messages.

Notice the tension between this pattern and People Know Best.

Authors. Robert Hanmer and Mike Adams

PATTERN: PEOPLE KNOW BEST

Problem. How do you balance automation with human authority and responsibility?

Context. A highly reliable, continuously operating system that tries to recover from all error conditions on its own.

Forces. People have a good subjective sense of the passage of time, how it relates to the probability of a serious failure, and how outages will be perceived by the customer.

The system is set up to recover from failure cases. (See the pattern Minimize Human Intervention.)

People feel a need to intervene.

Most system errors can be traced to human error.

Solution. Assume that people know best, particularly the maintenance folks. Design the system to allow knowledgeable users to override automatic controls.

Example: As you escalate through the 64 states of processor configuration (see Try All Hardware Combos), a human who understands what's going on can intervene and stop it, if necessary.

Resulting Context. People feel empowered; however, they are also held accountable for their actions.

This is an absolute rule: people feel a need to intervene. There is no perfect solution to this problem, and the pattern cannot resolve all the forces well. Fool Me Once provides a partial solution in that it doesn't give humans a chance to intervene.

Rationale. Consider the input command to unconditionally restore a unit: what does "unconditional" mean? Let's say the system thinks the unit is powered down; what should happen when the operator asks for the unit to be restored unconditionally? Answer: Try to restore it anyhow, no excuses allowed; the fault detection hardware can always detect the powered-down condition and generate an interrupt for the unit out of service. Why might the operator want to do this? Because the problem may be not with the power but with the sensor that wrongly reports that the power is off.

Notice the tension between this pattern and Minimize Human Intervention.

Author. Robert Gamoke

PATTERN: FIVE MINUTES OF NO ESCALATION MESSAGES

Problem. Rolling in console messages: The human-machine interface is saturated with error reports rolling off the screen, or the system is consuming extreme computational resources just to display error messages.

Context. Any continuously operating, fault-tolerant system with escalation and where transient conditions may be present.

Forces. There is no sense in wasting time or reducing the level of service trying to solve a problem that will go away by itself.

Many problems work themselves out, given time.

You don't want the switch to use all of its resources displaying messages.

You don't want to panic users by making them think the switch is out of control (see Minimize Human Intervention).

The only user action related to the escalation messages may be inappropriate to the goal of preserving system sanity.

There are other computer systems monitoring the actions taken. These systems can deal with a great volume of messages.

Solution. When taking the first action in a series that could lead to an excess number of messages, display a message. Periodically display an update message. If the abnormal condition ends, display a message that everything is back to normal. Do not display a message for every change in state (see Riding Over Transients).

Continue to communicate trouble status and actions taken to the downstream monitoring computer system throughout this period.

For example, when the 4ESS switch enters the first level of system overload, post a user message. Post no more messages for five minutes, even if there is additional escalation. At the end of five minutes, display a status message indicating the current status. When the condition clears, display an appropriate message.

Resulting Context. The system operator won't panic from seeing too many messages. Machine-to-machine messages and measurement provide a record for later evaluation and make the system's actions visible to people who can deal with them. In the 4ESS switch overload example, measurement counters continue to track overload dynamics; some downstream support systems track these counters.

Other messages, not related to the escalating situation that is producing too many messages, will be displayed as though the system were normal. Thus the normal functioning of the system is not adversely affected by the volume of escalation messages.

Note the conflict with People Know Best.

Rationale. Don't freak out the user. The only solution to 4ESS switch overload for an on-site user is to resort to the command "Cancel Overload Controls," which tells the system to ignore its overload indicators and behave as though there were no overload.

This is a special case of Aggressive versus Tentative.

Authors. Robert Hanmer and Mike Adams

PATTERN: RIDING OVER TRANSIENTS

Alias. Make Sure Problem Really Exists

Problem. How do you know whether or not a problem will work itself out?

Context. You are working with a fault-tolerant application in which some errors, overload conditions, and so on may be transient. The system can escalate through recovery strategies, taking more drastic action at each step. A typical example is a fault-tolerant telecommunications system using static traffic engineering, for which you want to check for overload or transient faults.

Forces. You want to catch faults and problems.

There is no sense in wasting time or reducing the level of service while trying to solve a problem that will go away by itself.

Many problems work themselves out, given time.

Solution. Don't react immediately to detected conditions. Make sure a condition really exists by checking it several times, or use Leaky Bucket Counters to detect a critical number of occurrences in a specific time interval. For example, by averaging over time or just waiting awhile, you can give transient faults a chance to pass.

Resulting Context. Errors can be resolved with truly minimal effort, because the effort is expended only if the problem really exists. This pattern allows the system to roll through problems without its users noticing them and without bothering the machine operator to intervene (like Minimize Human Intervention).

Rationale. This pattern detects "temporally dense" events. Think of such events as spikes on a time line. If a small number of spikes (specified by a threshold) occur together (where "together" is specified by the interval), then the error is a transient. This pattern is used by Leaky Bucket Counters, Five Minutes of No Escalation Messages, and many others.

Author. James O. Coplien

PATTERN: LEAKY BUCKET COUNTERS

Problem. How do you deal with transient faults?

Context. You are working with fault-tolerant system software that must deal with failure events. Failures are tied to episode counts and frequencies.

For example, in 1A/1B processor systems used in AT&T telecommunications products, as memory words (dynamic RAM) get weak, the memory module generates a parity error trap. Examples include both 1A processor dynamic RAM and 1B processor static RAM.

Forces. You want a hardware module to exhibit hard failures before taking drastic action. Some failures come from the environment and thus should not be blamed on the device.

Solution. A failure group has a counter that is initialized to a predetermined value when the group is initialized. The counter is decremented for each fault or event (usually faults) and incremented on a periodic basis; however, the count is never incremented beyond its initial value. There are different initial values and different leak rates for different subsystems (for example, the leak interval is a half hour for the 1A memory (store) subsystem). The strategy for 1A dynamic RAM specifies that for the first failure in a store (within the timing window), you must take the store out of service, diagnose it, and then automatically restore it to service. On the second, third, and fourth failures (within the window), you just leave it in service. On the fifth failure (again, within the window), you must take the unit out of service, diagnose it, and leave it out.

If the episode transcends the interval, it's not transient: the leak rate is faster than the refill rate, and the pattern indicates an error condition. If the burst is more intense than expected (i.e., it exceeds the error threshold), then it represents unusual behavior not associated with a transient burst, and the pattern indicates an error condition.

Resulting Context. A system in which errors are isolated and handled (by taking devices out of service), but transient errors (e.g., errors caused by excessive humidity) don't cause unnecessary loss of service.

Rationale. The history is instructive: in old call stores (1A memories that contained dynamic data), why did we collect data? For old call stores, the field replaceable unit (FRU) was a circuit pack, while the failure group was a store composed of 12 or 13 packs. We needed to determine which pack was bad. Memory may have been spread across seven circuit packs; the transient bit was only one bit, not enough to isolate the failure. By recording data from four events, we were better able to pinpoint (with 90 percent accuracy) which pack was bad, so the machine operator didn't have to change seven packs.

Why go five failures before taking a unit out of service? By collecting data on the second, third, and fourth failures, you can make absolutely sure you know the characteristics of the error; thus you reduce your uncertainty about the FRU. By the fifth time, you know it's sick and you need to take it out of service.

Periodically increasing the count on the store creates a sliding time window. The resource is considered sane when the counter (re)attains its initialized value. Humidity, heat, and other environmental problems cause transient errors, which should be treated differently (i.e., pulling the card does no good).

See, for example, Fool Me Once, which uses simple leaky bucket counters. This is a special case of the pattern Riding over Transients. The strategy is alluded to by Downing et al. [Downing+64].

Author. Robert Gamoke

PATTERN: SICO FIRST AND ALWAYS

Problem. You are trying to make a system highly available and resilient in the face of hardware and software faults and transient errors.

Context. You are working with a system in which the ability to do meaningful work is of the utmost importance, but rare periods of partial application functionality can be tolerated (for example, the 1A/1B processor-based 4ESS switch from AT&T).

Forces. Bootstrapping is initialization.

A high-availability system might require (re)initialization at any time to ensure system sanity.

The System Integrity Control program (SICO) coordinates system integrity.

The SICO program must be in control during bootstrapping.

The focus of operational control changes from bootstrapping to executive control during normal call processing.

Application functioning is very important.

The System Integrity Program takes processor time, but that is acceptable in this context.

The system is composed of proprietary elements, for which design criteria may be imposed on all the software in the system.

Hardware designed to be fault-tolerant reduces hardware errors.

Solution. Give the SICO program the ability and power to reinitialize the system whenever system sanity is threatened by error conditions. The same System Integrity Program should oversee both the initialization process and the normal application functions so that initialization can be restarted if it runs into errors.

Resulting Context. In short, System Integrity Control plays a major role during bootstrapping, after which it hands control over to the executive scheduler, which in turn lets System Integrity Control regain control for short periods of time on a scheduled basis.

See also Audit Derivable Constants after Recovery.

Rationale. During a recovery event (phase or bootstrap), SICO calls processor initialization software first, peripheral initialization software second, then application initialization software; finally it transfers to executive control. Unlike a classic computer program in which initialization takes place first and "normal execution" second, the SICO architecture does not make software initialization the highest-level function. System integrity is at an even higher level than system initialization.

The architecture is based on a base level cycle in the executive control. After bootstrapping, the first item in the base cycle is SICO (though this is different code than that run during bootstrapping). So, after the SICO part of bootstrapping is done, the base level part of SICO is entered into each base level cycle to monitor the system on a periodic basis.

The System Integrity Control program must be alert to watch for failures during both bootstrapping and normal base-level operation. There is a system integrity monitor in the base level that watches timers. Overload control and audit control check in with SICO to report software and hardware failures and (potentially) request initialization, while watching for errors within their own realms.

During bootstrapping and initialization, system integrity employs a number of similar mechanisms to monitor the system (for example, Analog Timers, Boot Timers, Try All Hardware Combos, and others).

Much of the rationale for this pattern comes from AUTOVON, Safeguard, missile guidance systems, and other high-reliability real-time projects from early AT&T stored program control experience. See [Meyers+77].

Author. Robert Hanmer

PATTERN: TRY ALL HARDWARE COMBOS

Problem. The central controller (CC) has several configurations. There are many possible paths through CC subsystems, depending on the configuration. How do you select a workable configuration when there is a faulty subsystem?

Context. You are working with highly fault-tolerant computing complexes, such as the 1B processor.

The processing complex has a number of duplicated subsystems. Each one consists of a CC, a set of call stores, a call store bus, a set of program stores, a program store bus, and an interface bus. Major subsystems are duplicated with standby units to increase system reliability rather than to provide distributed processing capabilities. There are 64 possible configurations of these subsystems, given fully duplicated spacing. Each configuration is said to represent a configuration state.

The system is brought up in stages. First, you need to have the memory units working. Second, you need to talk to the disk, so you can pump stuff into memory (which allows you to run programs to pump the rest of the stores, so code can recover other units). Third, after the base system is configured and refreshed from disk, you can bring up the application.

Forces. You want to catch and remedy single, isolated errors.

You also want to catch errors that aren't easily detected in isolation but result from interaction between modules.

You sometimes must catch multiple, concurrent errors.

The CC can't sequence subsystems through configurations, since it may be faulty itself.

The machine should recover by itself without human intervention (see Minimize Human Intervention).

Solution. Maintain a 64-state counter in hardware. We call this the configuration counter. There is a table that maps from that counter onto a configuration state: in the 1A, it's in the hardware; in the 1B, it's in the boot ROM. Every time the system fails to get through a PC to a predetermined level of stability, it restarts the system with a successive value of the configuration counter.

In the 5ESS switch there is a similar 16-state counter. It first tries all side zero units (a complete failure group), then all side one units (the other failure group), hoping to find a single failure. The subsequent counting states look for more insidious problems, such as those that come from interactions between members of these coarse failure groups.

Resulting Context. The system can deal with any number of concurrent faults, provided there is at most one fault per subsystem.

Table 4.1. Configurations Established by Emergency Action Switching (Status of Units after a Switch Performed by the Indicated State) [Downing+64, p. 2006]

PC State	CC0	CC1	PS0	PS1	Bus0	Bus1	Other Stores
X000	U	U	U	U	U	U	U
X001	C	C	U	U	U	U	U
X010	U	U	U	U	C	C	U
X011	U	U	A	S	A	S	T
X100	U	U	A	S	S	A	T
X101	U	U	S	A	S	A	T
X110	U	U	S	A	A	S	T
X111	U	U	S	A	A	S	T

X: Don't care; A: Active; S: Standby; U: Unchanged; C: Complemented; T: Marked as having trouble.

The state will increment when a reboot (PC) fails.

Sometimes the fault won't be detected right after the reboot sequence (i.e., not until more than 30 seconds after the resumption of normal activities). This problem is addressed in Fool Me Once.

Sometimes, going through all 64 states isn't enough; see Don't Trust Anyone and Analog Timer.

Rationale. This design is based on the FIT rates of the original hardware – and on the extreme caution of first-generation developers of stored program control switching systems.

Note that the pattern Blind Search apparently violates this pattern, because it uses a store to hold the identity of the out-of-service module; this is addressed in the pattern Multiple Copies of Base Store.

Authors. Robert Gamoke; 5ESS switch information, Fred Keeve. See [Downing+64, pp. 2005–2009].

PATTERN: FOOL ME ONCE

Problem. Sometimes the fault causing a processor configuration (PC) is intermittent (usually triggered by software, such as diagnostics). After a PC is complete, users expect the configuration state display to disappear from the system's human control interface and the system to be sane. If the configuration display state continues to be displayed for more than 30 seconds, users may become concerned that the system still has a problem. But if the system in fact trips on another fault, it may reboot itself (take a phase) and reinitiate the initialization sequence using the same configuration as before (or, worse, start the configuration sequence at the beginning), which raises the probability that the system will loop in reboots ("roll in recovery") and never attempt different configurations.

Context. You are working with a highly available system using redundancy, and you are employing the pattern Try All Hardware Combos.

You're going through Try All Hardware Combos. The system finds an ostensibly sane state and progresses 30 seconds into initialization, beyond boot and into the application. The application "knows" that the hardware is sane if it can go for 30 seconds (using Leaky Bucket Counters). When the system reaches this state, it resets the configuration counter. However, a latent error can cause a system fault after the configuration counter has been reset. The system no longer "knows" that it is in PC escalation, and it retries the same configuration that has already failed.

Forces. It's hard to set a universally correct interval for a Leaky Bucket Counter; sometimes 30 seconds is too short. The application (and customer) would be upset if the Leaky Bucket Counter were set too long (for example, a customer doesn't want to wait a half hour for a highly reliable system to clear its fault status). Some errors take a long time to appear, even though they are fundamental hardware errors (e.g., an error in program store that isn't accessed until very late in the initialization cycle or until a hardware fault is triggered by a diagnostic run out of the scheduler). People's expectations are among the most important forces at work here. In spite of the potential for some classes of faults to be latent, the application and user feel assured that the system must be sane if it's been exercised for 30 seconds.

Solution. The first time the application tells PC that "all is well," believe it and reset the configuration counter. The second and subsequent times, within a longer time window, ignore the request.

The first request to reset the configuration counter indicates that the application's 30-second Leaky Bucket Counter says that everything is fine. Set up a half-hour Leaky Bucket Counter to avoid being fooled. If the application tries to reset the 64-state configuration counter twice in a half hour, ignore it. This indicates recurring failures that would result in reboots.

Resulting Context. Any subsequent failures will cause the configuration counter to advance, guaranteeing that the next PC will use a fresh configuration. For a single subsystem error that is taking the system down, this strategy will eventually reach a workable configuration. Once the system is up, schedule diagnostics to isolate the faulty unit (see People Know Best). The system will be able to handle repetitive failures outside the shorter window, thereby reinforcing Minimize Human Intervention.

Rationale. See the forces. It's better to escalate to exceptionally extravagant strategies like this, no matter how late, if it eventually brings the system back on line. The pattern has been found to be empirically sound.

Author. Robert Gamoke

ACKNOWLEDGMENTS

Many thanks to Gerard Meszaros of BNR, who served as the PLoP '95 shepherd for these patterns, and to all those who reviewed these patterns in the writers' workshops at PLoP.

REFERENCES

[Downing+64] R.W. Downing, J.S. Nowak, and L.S. Tuomenoska. *Bell System Technical Journal, 43* (September 1964), Part 1, "No. 1 Electronic Switching System": 1961–2019.

[Meyers+77] M.N. Meyers, W.A. Routt, and K.W. Yoder. *Bell System Technical Journal, 56,* 2 (September 1977): 1139–1167.

5

AN INPUT AND OUTPUT PATTERN LANGUAGE: LESSONS FROM TELECOMMUNICATIONS

Robert Hanmer and Greg Stymfal

A SPECIALIZED SET OF PATTERNS for defining the human-machine interface has come into use within the world of telecommunications switching products. The patterns presented here provide an essential interface between a system and its human masters. Several of the patterns discuss concepts specific to a telecommunications system, but most are general enough to provide insight for anyone designing the input/output (IO) interface for a large system.

This chapter begins by discussing the environment within which these patterns are applicable. Two different methods of visualizing the overall structure of this language are then presented, one graphical and the other in the form of topical pattern groupings. The patterns are then introduced. Supplemental material includes thumbnail sketches of the patterns.

BACKGROUND

The environment within which telecommunications switching equipment is installed is different from that of a traditional computing center. This section describes some of the differences that constitute the common context for these patterns.

A key difference between the IO of a telecommunications system and a general computer is that the IO of a telephone switching system is purely secondary to its main purpose. A general computer might be specialized to a special function, such as processing mathematical equations quickly, but the results still must proceed through the IO channel. This is not the case in a switching system. These systems manage specialized hardware to connect (switch) different telephone lines. This function does not require CRTs, paper printers, keyboards, mice, or magnetic tape.

Another significant difference is that a telecommunications system has a multitude of workers who are responsible for system maintenance and administration. This workforce can be grouped into several different communities of interest ([Huttenhoff+1977], [Green+1977], [Giunta+1977]):

- **Those concerned with the maintenance of the machine.** This community has a work center called the Maintenance Operations Center.

- **Those concerned with administrating the machine.** Their work center is called the Maintenance Administration Center.

- **Those concerned with the telephone lines and trunks connected to the switching machine.** They have two work centers in addition to the Maintenance Administration Center, called the Trunk Operations Center and the Terminal Equipment Center.

In many computing environments a console terminal is the primary channel for the operator to communicate with the system. Most users are not authorized to send and receive administrative commands. In telecommunications systems there are many terminals within each work center that are each as powerful as a traditional console.

Telephone switching systems are large. A switching office serving a city center might occupy several thousand square feet and have tens of thousands of telephone lines and trunks connected to it. As a result, the workers are a long physical distance from the primary input/output devices when they are working inside the system. It also means that the workforce has many pieces of equipment to operate and maintain.

Reliability is a very important system capability. Reliability engineers calculate the expected availability of the system based upon some predicted

Mean Time to Repair. This is the time it takes for maintenance personnel to respond to and repair a component. It is therefore very important that the maintenance people be informed quickly of any problems. Reliability, usually expressed in terms of a few minutes of downtime per office per year, also leads the designers towards using custom hardware and software especially designated to facilitate reliable systems. In order to maintain this availability, telephone switching systems are typically monitored around the clock by personnel trained and ready to respond to any emergency.

Using custom hardware and software usually results in the system being behind the leading edge of computer technology. When the systems from which these patterns were mined were being created in the 1970s their IO channels were capable of being operated at either 110 or 1200 baud [Budlong+1977, pp. 169–170]. In some cases these primitive IO devices are still used because they are well-known to the system designers and are more reliable.

Even as telephone networks get more complicated, the desire to remotely monitor and maintain them has increased. The ability to remotely monitor system operations adds an additional level of complexity. Handling this additional complexity wasn't always provided for in the initial designs.

KNOWN USES

The patterns contained here are the proven practices of a number of telephone switching systems such as the Lucent Technologies 1A ESS local switch, the 4ESS toll and tandem switch also from Lucent Technologies, and the AG Communication Systems GTD-5 local switch.

LANGUAGE MAP

Figure 5.1 shows the relationships among the patterns in this language.

The diagram shows patterns that enhance the solutions of other patterns, resolve previously unresolved forces in a pattern, or take advantage of an earlier pattern to provide some new system capability. In Figure 5.2, pattern *B* refines pattern *A,* helping to solve unresolved forces or new problems that *A* introduced.

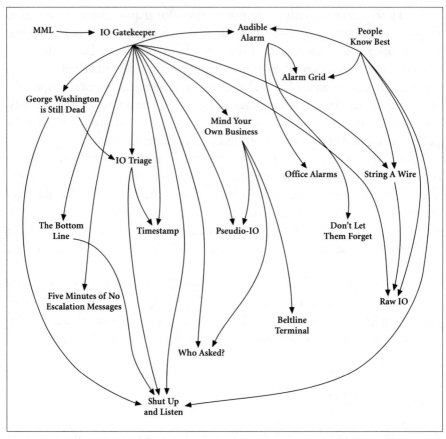

Figure 5.1. The relationship among patterns in this language.

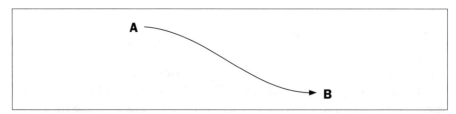

Figure 5.2. Pattern B refines Pattern A.

CATEGORIES OF PATTERNS

Four functional categories can be used to categorize these patterns. Both MML and IO Gatekeeper deal with all four of these topics. The categories are physical location, the relative importance of input, the quantity of messages, and periods of emergency interaction.

1. *Physical* **location.** Switching offices are large in physical terms. These patterns present measures to be taken to mitigate the effects of large size.

    Mind Your Own Business

    Beltline Terminal

    Pseudo-IO

    Audible Alarms

    Alarm Grid

    Office Alarms

    Who Asked?

2. *Relative* **importance** *of input.* Some interactions with the system are more important than others. These patterns present the measures that need to be taken to ensure that the important interactions happen in a timely fashion.

    IO Triage

    Timestamp

    Shut Up and Listen

    Don't Let Them Forget

3. **Quantity** *of messages.* Switching systems are large in terms of lines of code and numbers of subsystems; many will have things to say at the same time. These patterns help to manage the sheer quantity of messages.

    George Washington Is Still Dead

    The Bottom Line

    IO Triage

    5 Minutes of No Escalation Messages

    Shut Up and Listen

4. *Periods of* **emergency** *interaction.* During crisis times special rules should apply. These patterns discuss some of these special rules as they impact IO.

> Audible Alarms
>
> Alarm Grid
>
> Office Alarms
>
> String A Wire
>
> Raw IO
>
> Don't Let Them Forget

THE PATTERNS

MML (ALSO KNOWN AS HUMAN-MACHINE LANGUAGE)

Problem. How can communications with a large and complex machine be made easier for humans and more reliable?

Context. There are many different subsystems that will need to communication with human operators and administrators. A large volume of IO with many varied user needs and functions is expected.

Forces
- Switching system software development will be easier if each software subsystem defines and implements its own IO specifications. It is easier to develop alone than to coordinate with others.

- Development expense and system architecture will be more streamlined if the different subsystems define the system languages to a common specification.

- At least one-third of errors during system operation are due to mistakes made by the human operator. (The other two-thirds are hardware faults and software faults.) Any steps that can be taken to reduce the contribution of the human-machine interface to this statistic will be beneficial.

Solution. Use a standard message format. This allows the system to be consistent when reporting problems in different parts of the system. It also allows humans to become familiar with the format of messages and thus simplifies learning. This reduces the amount of documentation that is required because there can be commonality between subsystems. (See Figure 5.3.)

Figure 5.3. Reduced documentation with MML.

Resulting Context. A large volume of IO with many varied users' needs and functions using a standard language/format will be given a consistency that helps users. Mechanisms to deal with the large volume of input and output are needed, such as Bottom Line and George Washington Is Still Dead.

In addition, since the system is quite large, there might be many different users, each trying to interact with the system. To keep things straight, patterns such as Mind Your Own Business, Who Asked?, and IO Triage are useful.

Sometimes, especially to save human resources, a computer system might be created to monitor the system. In many cases, a custom interface can be created to facilitate computer-to-computer communications. Sometimes this is too much overhead and a pattern such as Pseudo-IO helps by having the monitoring computer use the MML messages intended for humans.

Examples. MML (huMan-Machine Language, an international standard) and PDS (Program Documentation Standard) are two examples.

Rationale. Imagine if all application/user programs on a general computing system used the same standard message language. That is the scope of this pattern. This is accomplished in the world of telecommunications as described in the Background section. Doing so lowers the rate of procedural (human-caused) errors and hence increases the system availability. It also simplifies development by allowing the creation of shared, reusable command parsers.

Reference. [Clement+1977, pp. 245–246].

IO GATEKEEPER

Problem. How can a large system support the existence of a single MML for a large community of authorized users?

Context. IO is secondary to the system's primary purpose. There may be many different subsystems that need some sort of interface with the human world.

Forces
- Allowing each subsystem to send messages to the terminals independently produces anarchy. Obtaining a cohesive view of the system's status is impossible due to the disordered presentation.

- Creating a centralized subsystem introduces a bottleneck into the IO processing.

Solution. Design a centralized point to conduct all communication between humans and the system (see Figure 5.4). Design and then use an internal interface language that supports the use of MML towards the human interfaces. This will function as a gatekeeper or doorway through which all IO must pass. Use a Singleton [Gamma+1995] to enforce a single occurrence of the Gatekeeper.

Resulting Context. By defining the interfacing language for the Gatekeeper, development and use of the system is made easier.

The Gatekeeper function allows many useful features to be created. These include timestamping, identifying important messages (IO Triage), sorting messages to internal or external recipients (Pseudo-IO and Who Asked?), throttling the output of messages (The Bottom Line and George Washington Is Still Dead). The Gatekeeper can also tie the IO system together with the alarm system (Audible Alarm), using a tag associated with the message (such as its priority tag, see IO Triage) to indicate if an alarm should be sounded. The Gatekeeper also can be made responsible for privileges and only allow privileged people or terminal groups to execute the most potentially destructive commands.

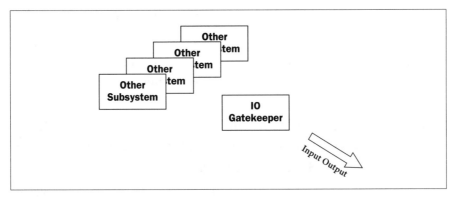

Figure 5.4. System IO must pass through the IO gatekeeper.

The Gatekeeper by definition will consolidate IO together into a single stream. The resulting output stream can be torrential. The patterns Mind Your Own Business and Who Asked? are employed to sort it out.

Rationale. Since IO is not essential to the primary system processing of telephone calls, the impacts of this bottleneck are mitigated.

If the IO Gatekeeper is not a Singleton [Gamma+1995], few benefits arise from having a gatekeeper at all since the result is as if every subsystem communicated directly with humans.

Mind Your Own Business

Problem. If all the output comes through the IO Gatekeeper, who should see it?

Context. There is a standard input and output messaging language (MML) defined for the whole system. This implies that there will be some framework within the system that supports all IO, consolidating messages from every part of the system into a single unified output.

Forces
- Only a few workers need to see any particular output. For example, the people in the Maintenance Operations Center don't need to see messages about the progress of a Recent Change (database update) transaction.

- The system shouldn't confuse the workers by presenting information they don't know how to use.

- The volume of messages that are possible from a large system is enormous. If it were all to be dumped to one terminal it would be impossible for workers to find the information they need.

- Access control is enhanced if the type of information a particular terminal receives is changed through simple wiring configurations rather than complicated programming changes.

- Frequently the entities watching the outputs are not human, but are other computer systems. Output stream specialization is useful because these systems are only interested in a small part of the possible output.

- Much of the information in the system is routine and not related to any particular user.

- The primary output devices in a maintenance center should always receive output, even if no one is logged on.

Solution. Define different output classifications. The IO Gatekeeper should mark different terminal/console connections to receive output only for some classifications. These are called *logical channels.* The system sends messages only to the community of users interested in them. Some example of logical channels are Maintenance, Secondary Record, Recent Change, and Network Management (see Figure 5.5). A receive-only printer is used within maintenance communities to provide for a continual record of activity even if no one is logged on.

Resulting Context. The large volume of IO is reduced on any one channel when it is distributed by function. This results in labor savings – workers don't need to wade through the output to find the messages in which they are interested. And the reduction in IO helps computer systems monitoring this system by reducing the volume of output they must digest.

Some users move around within an office and might still need to see the output. Beltline Terminals addresses this by providing the ability to redirect output to a different output device.

By centralizing output processing (see IO Triage), the categories and logical channels can be used to send output to the right place as in Who Asked?

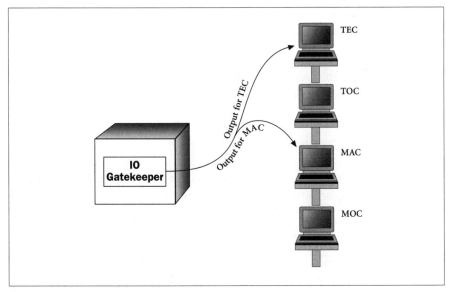

Figure 5.5. IO Gatekeeper sends messages only to interested users.

Example. In a general-purpose computing system the operator console receives some messages that user terminals do not receive. In telecommunications systems there are many different operator consoles for different communities of interest.

Reference. [Clement+1977, pp. 245–246].

IO TRIAGE

Problem. Important information is hidden or delayed by less important information.

Context. The IO Gatekeeper coordinates the IO message stream. A large volume of IO is still presented to the workers even after applying the message reduction patterns George Washington Is Still Dead and The Bottom Line.

Forces
- Too much information deadens the workers.

- Information about a critical situation – for example, all the telephone lines going out of service, or a critical piece of the system hardware fail-ing – needs to be issued as soon as it is detected to allow the workers to repair it.

- Information that reports trivial things can be deferred to display after the important information is presented.

- Workers might not be looking at the screen when there is something important happening.

Solution. Tag messages with a priority classification. Design IO software to display a higher priority message on the output device before a message of a lower priority (see Figure 5.6). Use a consistent definition of the different priorities. One definition used by the 4ESS Switch is shown in Table 5.1.

Resulting Context. The most important information will be displayed first, followed by less important and possibly quite old information. This requires the IO Gatekeeper to prepare messages for display in the desired order. Use a

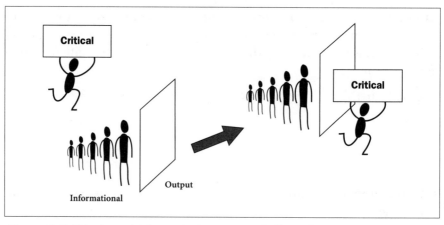

Figure 5.6. Display a higher priority message before a lower priority one.

message sequence tag to facilitate a complete understanding of the system state (see Timestamp).

Output messages tagged critical, major, or minor are sometimes referred to as action messages because they require some action on the part of the local workforce.

Table 5.1. 4ESS Switch Message Priorities

Priority Tag	Meaning
Critical	The office cannot perform its required actions to process telephone calls.
Major	The system is in a state that one more failure will result in a critical loss of service.
Minor	A small portion of the system is in trouble. The system is more than one failure away from a total lack of service.
Manual	The system is responding to a human input message.
Information	The system is behaving normally.

The issue of people not watching their terminal when something important is being reported will be addressed by the Audible Alarm pattern. The priority tag provided by IO Triage should be used as an input into the alarm system to sound the appropriate alarm.

TIMESTAMP

Problem. How can workers provide some sense to a seemingly random order of output?

Context. IO Triage has been applied. Messages may not come out in the strict order requested by subsystems.

Forces

- Some problems reported in the IO stream are difficult to analyze. Little clues might be important, even the order in which things happen, especially when trying to decipher near-coincident failures. The informational message printed fifteen minutes ago might contain the essential clue to help with the critical message printed five minutes ago.

- Time within a computer system is different from time to humans. A timestamp with just the minutes and seconds hides millisecond time period details.

- The IO Gatekeeper can perform a little extra processing and tag messages with some helpful information.

Solution. Apply a sequence number to all messages when the IO Gate-keeper receives them (see Figure 5.7). That will help identify message ordering. Since humans like to work with a time base, the current time can be used as the sequence number. The current time is when the message was received by the IO subsystem and should contain meaningful time units such as seconds or milliseconds.

Resulting Context. If the message printing time also is displayed, the difference in times can provide a valuable clue to the analyst.

```
#135/0957 am/Critical: εαιϖεεαιϖε
#134/0956 am/Minor: αρειρεαιϖεα
#120/0952 am/Information: ερυερυ
#121/0953 am/Information: νϖιναϭπιν3
#136/0958 am/Information: εφϖειϖαλ
#140/1002 am/Major: α4εραϖα
#137/0958 am/Information: φεφιαυβε
#138/0959 am/Information: ϖϖειαυβεπ
#139/1000 am/Information: αρευιβπυαεβι
```

Figure 5.7. A sequence number is applied to all messages.

WHO ASKED?

Problem. What logical channel receives the results of a specific manual input request?

Context. A worker usually only uses one terminal at a time. Mind Your Own Business has resulted in the IO stream being divided into different logical channels. The IO Gatekeeper centralizes output with a prioritization scheme.

Forces
- Lots of terminals, lots of terminal classifications, many users – do they all see my messages?

- Broadcasting the answer to everyone would confuse the workers who have no idea about that function (i.e., maintenance workers seeing database change output). It also pollutes the output channels with extraneous information, resulting in desired information being lost in reams of paper.

- There is a class of workers that has primary responsibility for the correct functioning of the system. These workers should be kept informed, to some degree, of what the other communities of workers are doing.

Solution. The IO Gatekeeper should display the output related to a specific input request to the logical channel that made the request. Send it to all terminals monitoring a particular logical channel. You might want to put it on additional channels to allow for logging or oversight by a superuser (see Figure 5.8). Give the message a Manual tag to indicate that it is a direct response to an input message (see IO Triage), so the message won't be misinterpreted as a spontaneous system output.

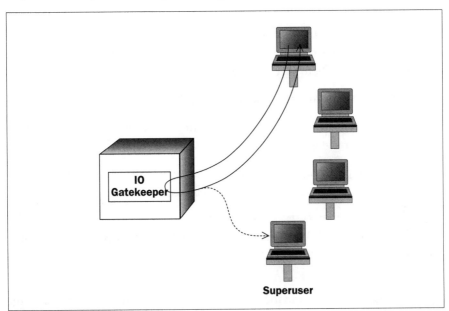

Figure 5.8. IO Gatekeeper displays output to the channel that made the request and to a Superuser.

Resulting Context. Sometimes important information is displayed at the primary maintenance terminal, so that people responsible for the correct functioning of the system see it.

Reference. [Clement+1997, pp. 245–246].

George Washington Is Still Dead (also known as Show Changes)

Problem. How can the output be kept free from too many messages saying the same thing?

Context. Sometimes the system needs to output reports about the state of the machine. While a particular problem might be detected hundreds of times (as in The Bottom Line), if the state isn't changing frequently the messages might be overkill. For example, if hundreds of trunks go out of service, the office condition might change when the first trunk goes out of service, and then not change again until the 101st trunk goes out of service.

Forces

- Displaying the status of the office condition for each new trunk out of service report from the second to the hundredth trunk is too much information. There isn't really enough to require a new report.

- Too much information deadens the workers.

- The fact that the office state or condition has changed is the real information that the workers need to know.

- Just display messages that report a change in state. Don't display a message each time the alarmed state is detected.

Solution. Have the IO Gatekeeper keep track of messages and send only changed state announcements that represent a real change of state (see Figure 5.9).

Resulting Context. Redundancies will be removed from an otherwise large volume of IO.

The reports of state changes are important, so some method of reporting them is required. IO Triage is needed to keep the important information coming out even when the output channels are flooded.

Related Patterns. Sometimes there are no actions that the workers can perform in response to a change in system state. It is in these circumstances that the Five Minutes of No Escalation Messages pattern applies.

Even given the reduction in messages that results from applying this pat-

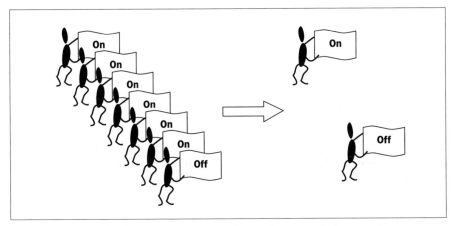

Figure 5.9. Send only announcements that reflect a real change of state.

tern, a mechanism to ensure that humans are able to input a message against a flood of output is required. Shut Up and Listen addresses this problem.

The Bottom Line is similar to this pattern but deals with multiples of the same report. It summarizes a given report with the number of occurrences. This leads to delay in reporting the event, however, because of the need for aggregation.

THE BOTTOM LINE

Problem. Many messages are about the same type of event (such as a trunk going out of service), and they flood the output message stream.

Context. Some situations produce many, many reports. For example, if a part of the system interfacing to many trunks has just gone out of service, a message reporting that a trunk is out of service might display hundreds of reports, one for each trunk. This pattern applies to the places where a report should be generated because some condition has just been detected.

Forces
- Outputting a report whenever an event happens pollutes the output channels, diverting attention from other activities. Even with a priority output system in place (IO Triage), the channel can become full, and important output or input (see Shut Up and Listen) can be missed.

- Sometimes reporting many events gives the workers an idea of a trend, but this information can be given many times or as a single message reporting many events. Reports are not of critical importance and can be delayed slightly during the aggregation period.

Solution. The IO Gatekeeper should group messages about a common event and only display a summary message that includes a tally of the number of occurrences (see Figure 5.10). The system should also supply a way to provide the entire output upon human request, as it may be essential to identify problems.

Figure 5.10. Group messages about a common event and display a summary.

Resulting Context. Even with the reduction in messages from applying this pattern, a mechanism to ensure that humans are able to input a message against a flood of output is required. Shut Up and Listen addresses this problem.

Related Patterns. George Washington Is Still Dead deals with state change reports while The Bottom Line deals with aggregation of nearly identical messages.

Five Minutes of No Escalation Messages helps those cases in which aggregation delays can only partly be tolerated. It causes messages to be printed out periodically as well as in summary form.

Five Minutes of No Escalation Messages

Problem. The human-machine interface is saturated with error reports for which humans can't do much except worry.

Context. Any continuous-running, fault-tolerant system, where transient conditions may be present, can produce too many messages, even with summary and priority filters (The Bottom Line, George Washington Is Still Dead, IO Triage).

Some system reports describe events that humans cannot help resolve.

Forces
- Many problems work themselves out, given time. There is no sense in wasting time or reducing level of service trying to solve a problem that will go away by itself (Riding over Transients [Adams+1966]).

- The switch can use all of its resources displaying messages.

- Humans panic when they think the switch is out of control (Minimize Human Intervention [Adams+1996]).

- If the only human action might be detrimental to the system, the best action might be for the system to delay reporting information.

Solution. When taking the first action in a scenario that could lead to an excess number of messages, display a message. Then periodically display an update message (see Figure 5.11). If the abnormal condition ends, display a message that everything is back to normal. Do not display a message for every change in state.

Continue nonstop machine-to-machine communication of status and actions throughout this period (see String A Wire).

If something is so important that it can't wait five minutes, an Audible Alarm should report it.

Resulting Context. This solution will keep the system operator from panicking from seeing too many messages. Machine-to-machine messages and measurements will keep a record for later evaluation as well as keep the system's actions visible to people who can deal with it. There are other computer systems monitoring the actions taken. These systems can deal with a great volume of messages.

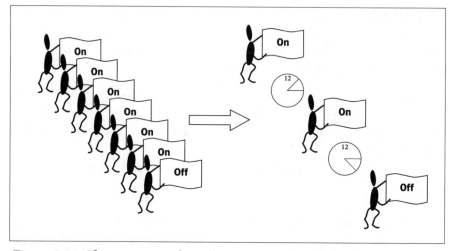

Figure 5.11. If an excess number of messages is expected, display an initial message then periodically display an update.

Other messages that are not related to the escalating situation that is producing too many messages will be displayed as though the system were normal. Thus the volume of escalation messages does not adversely affect the normal functioning of the system.

Of course the five-minute time period alluded to in the title is only a suggestion. It is based upon the situations from which this pattern is mined.

Related Patterns. Note the conflict with People Know Best [Adams+1996] in which humans should be kept thoroughly informed of system progress. Five Minutes of No Escalation Messages applies when no helpful human actions are possible. This can occur when the system is reporting traffic-induced system overloads.

This pattern also applies to those cases in which the delay to aggregate messages (see The Bottom Line) is too long and some intermediate report is necessary.

SHUT UP AND LISTEN

Problem. Humans need to be heard by the system. Users need a way to shut the output stream off.

Context. The IO Gatekeeper is flooding the system output stream with both priority messages reporting abnormal events and informational messages. A priority scheme for message output is in place (see IO Triage). This will get the most important information out to the workers first. It doesn't address humans taking control and altering system behavior. People Know Best [Adams+1996] states that even when the system is designed to correct problems automatically, experts will sometimes be able to help the system through stressful incidents.

Sometimes, even though George Washington Is Still Dead and The Bottom Line are applied, the output stream is still flooded.

Forces

- If the output is shut off, important information might be missed.

- If users wait until the outputting is completed, the system might be in a degraded service mode. Then again, in some circumstances the output stream may be perpetually flooded.

- Full-duplex IO might help, but makes message interpretation more difficult. If half-duplex is chosen, some way of interrupting the output is necessary.

Solution. The IO Gatekeeper should give human input a higher priority than displaying output information. Make sure that input messages are processed even when the output system is operating at full capacity.

Provide a way to interrupt the output stream long enough for a human to get a request into the system. Design this so that no output messages are lost.

Mark the output related to human input messages at priority level comparable with Critical output messages (see IO Triage) so that responses to human input are not stuck at the end of the output message queue (see Figure 5.12).

Resulting Context. Human requests (input messages) will be heard even though the output buffer is full. All human input messages are treated at the same priority level. A separate input mechanism (such as a Master Control Console [Budlong+1977]) that bypasses the IO subsystem can be provided for high priority input.

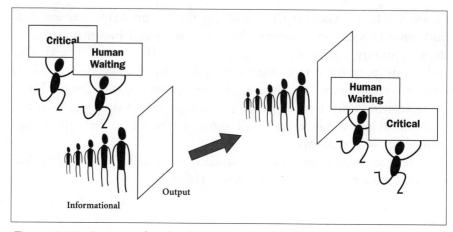

Figure 5.12. Output related to human input should be comparable to critical output.

PSEUDO-IO

Context. The system is large and has several subsystems. The IO Gatekeeper processes individually buffered messages and distributes them to the appropriate subsystem for handling. IO that previously went only from machine to human now must also go between subsystems inside the system.

The system has many logical IO channels (see Mind Your Own Business).

Forces

- Adding a machine-to-machine interface increases the complexity of the system.

- Adding in a powerful new interface or interface protocol is difficult once the system architecture is set.

- Perturbing a working subsystem to add a new interface to a new subsystem risks introducing new faults and breaking the working subsystem.

Solution. Allow one subsystem to insert a message into the input message stream. In other words, allow the system itself to create a message that is processed just like any other input message received from outside the system (see Figure 5.13).

Resulting Context. This provides a system that makes it easy to add new

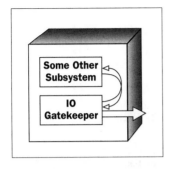

Figure 5.13. The system can create an input message.

switch feature capabilities and to connect them to already present IO services.

BELTLINE TERMINAL

Problem. The terminal isn't where the worker needs to be to do his or her work.

Context. The system produces a large volume of IO that is distributed by function (see Mind Your Own Business). Certain terminals are dedicated for specific workers. Some workers move around in the office. Because of the size of the system, they might be a long way from their maintenance terminal when they want to enter or see some messages related to what they are doing (e.g., they might be changing circuit packs).

For many years within a telephone office there have been jacks to plug in audio headsets to allow workers to talk with other workers.

Forces

- Reduced labor costs/higher productivity if the worker doesn't need to continually go for long walks to use a terminal.

- Reduced possibility of accidentally damaging something by frequent traversals of the office to reach the terminal.

- Increased system availability if workers can attend to their work quickly. Long walks to the terminal area increase the Mean Time to Repair.

Solution. Provide remote terminal connections so that workers can plug in a terminal IO device anywhere they want (see Figure 5.14). This is called a *Beltline Terminal.* Allow the worker to redirect (copy) the output of the desired logical channel to the Beltline Terminal.

Resulting Context. Workers can move around the office and can take their terminal with them. This increases productivity and system availability and reduces Mean Time to Repair. The typical configuration of a Beltline Terminal is an ordinary display device, such as a VT100 terminal, on a cart.

Rationale. The system is already physically large, with many wires. The sys-

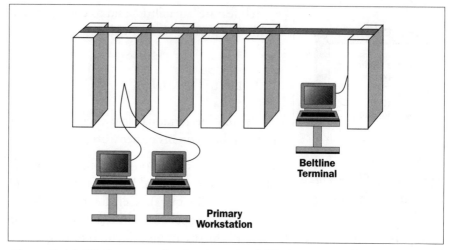

Figure 5.14. Workers can plug in a terminal IO device anywhere.

tem is mounted in custom cabinets with custom wiring. Adding a few additional wires around the office to allow the workers to plug in a terminal (in addition to audio headsets) is a minor expense.

Reference. [Huttenhoff+1977, p. 1050].

AUDIBLE ALARM

Problem. How can the system get information to workers immediately when a significant problem has occurred?

Context. Some things are too important to wait for a potentially slow IO Gatekeeper to process and to wait for some human to notice and read. Even with messages receiving a priority tag (IO Triage) the IO Gatekeeper must still queue the message for output. People Know Best [Adams+1996] requires that the support systems and humans that monitor the system have full information about its state. Due to the complexity of the IO system the overhead to perform the standard IO cannot be afforded in all circumstances, so MML does not apply.

Forces
- In a large office a simple message on one or several terminals might be unnoticed by the office personnel who are needed to handle the prob-

lem. This can lead to service being impacted longer than is absolutely necessary.

- The IO system has a lower processing priority than the systems that ensure that the system is sane and functioning normally. We cannot count on the IO system being executed in a timely manner during times of crisis. This can delay processing for a long time in a system that is trying to recover from catastrophes.

- During crisis situations the humans may be looking elsewhere and will not see a report on a terminal.

Solution. Provide a method of reporting alarms audibly in the office. This will reach out and alert humans that there is some problem that they should identify and resolve to reduce telephone service impacts. Remote visual indicators also should be provided, such as colored lights spread throughout the office.

The audible alarm system should be driven by the IO protocol defined within the system. Messages being passed to the IO Gatekeeper should have a special tag to indicate that an alarm should be sounded and which alarm. The priority tag defined by IO Triage can be used for this. There are a multitude of sounds

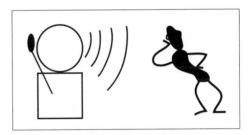

Figure 5.15. Provide audible alarms.

that can be used to indicate different alarm severities, including sirens, bells, gongs, and the like (see Figure 5.15).

Resulting Context. The time to begin the correct remedial action has a contribution towards the Mean Time to Repair, which in turn has an impact on the system's overall availability.

Priority messages will be presented to personnel in a way that stimulates several senses.

The specification of the alarmed items is usually done at design time. Since these are big systems that may vary subtly from office to office some method of customizing to a specific customer site is desirable (see Office Alarms).

A method of silencing the alarms by a manual action needs to be implemented. This allows the staff to have some peace and quiet while they try to isolate the problem. This method needs to rely upon as little software as possible, since the operators might want to retire the alarm while the software system is insane. A push button driving a hardware circuit is the best solution. Now that they have a method to silence the alarms, Don't Let Them Forget that the alarm happened and that there is something needing their attention.

Rationale. Audible Alarms provide an interface to the human operators that parallels the interface provided by the IO system. Since it is parallel, it will provide the operators with information that they might not get in a timely manner through the IO system.

The alarm system should have a low probability of failure. The hardware should have few failure points and use reliable components. Another consideration in the hardware design is to make the system "toothpick proof." This refers to the ease with which office personnel can disable a part of the system by inserting a toothpick into the appropriate relay contact to prevent closure.

If the alarm system itself is to fail, having it report its own failure is a desirable event. In the area of alarms the usual principle of "failing silently" may not apply.

Reference. [Huttenhoff+1977, p. 1051].

ALARM GRID

Problem. Workers need to know where to look for the problems, especially hardware problems.

Context. Audible Alarms and IO messages report emergency situations. People Know Best [Adams+1996] requires that support systems monitoring the system have full information about the system's state. The time required to begin the correct remedial action has a contribution towards the Mean Time to Repair, which in turn has an impact on the system's overall availability. There might be many alarms asserted simultaneously. For example, when a piece of hardware that terminates the trunks fails, the system will want to report the hardware failure as well as the failures of all of the trunks that it contains.

Forces
- Simultaneous alarms confuse workers and create uncertainty on where to look first.
- The IO system has a lower processing priority than the subsystems that

ensure that the system is sane and functioning normally. We cannot count on the IO system to quickly report routine messages during times of crisis. This can delay processing for a long time in a system that is trying to recover from catastrophes.

- Audible Alarms are presented by the IO Gatekeeper as soon as they are detected.

Solution. Divide the office into smaller grids that point to the location of the error. Tie alarm circuits together to report to the main office alarm panel. When an alarmable situation occurs within this alarm grid, alert all concerned personnel via Audible Alarms that there is a problem. Also provide visual indicators in the form of colored lights on the ends of frames within a grid to show that abnormal conditions exist somewhere in the grid (see Figure 5.16).

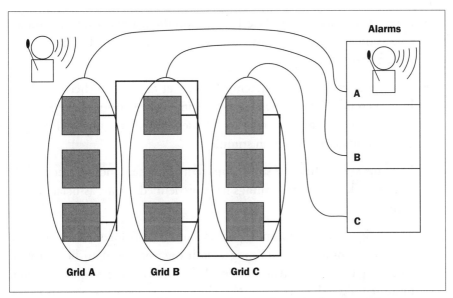

Figure 5.16. Divide the office into grids that show the location of an error.

Resulting Context. Alarm grids allow problem reports to selected communities of interest. This is similar to the logical channel concept of Mind Your Own Business.

Alarm grids can be arranged hierarchically within an office. This allows refinement of reporting and the potential to tie together several grids to report larger summary events during off-hours when fewer people are watching the system.

Reference. [Huttenhoff+1977, p. 1051].

OFFICE ALARMS

Problem. How can problems that are unique to a particular field site be integrated into the predefined classification of messages?

Context. Both visual and audio alarms show emergency information organized by Alarm Grid. Different sites might have custom alarming requirements, such as door locks, specialized A/C, coffeepots, related systems, and so forth.

Forces

- A separate, parallel interface for site-specific alarms would introduce confusion, since its user interface would probably not be identical to the standard interface.

- The actual interface and system actions that take place when the alarm is fired could be transparent and indistinguishable from the predefined system alarms. This will help avoid user errors and potential outages based upon failure to act on stimuli.

- Humans are confused if some important things are not alarmed while seemingly less important things have predefined alarms associated with them.

- The designers and equipment manufacturers can't foresee every unique office configuration containing conditions that need to be alarmed. The switch-owning customers probably don't want to pay for such thoroughness either.

- Good user interface design requires that similar things behave in similar manners.

Solution. Design the alarm system to allow easy insertion of new office-specific alarms (see Figure 5.17). This is an example of the Decorator pattern [Gamma+1995].

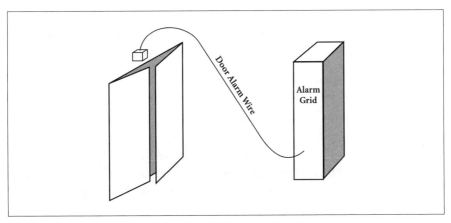

Figure 5.17. Allow easy insertion of office-specific alarms.

Resulting Context. Both generic priority messages and site-specific events have visual and audio alarms. This provides a measure of customer programmability to the office. Switch owners may tailor this part of the system to their own corporate operating policies.

Switch owners should be able to change the priority (IO Triage) of the messages so that they fit the situation.

DON'T LET THEM FORGET

Problem. For how long should the system honor a human's request to silence the alarms?

Context. Audible Alarms can be very annoying, leading workers to want to silence and ignore them. A system in trouble can have many alarms asserted simultaneously. Sometimes the noise can be overwhelming and distracting to the workers, so a method of silencing, or retiring, the alarm is provided.

Forces

- The choices include reasserting alarms immediately, or keeping them quiet for some predetermined length of time.

- Some mechanism to silence the alarms is desirable to provide some quiet for thought.

- If the system is in trouble the ability to function properly may be compromised if alarms aren't reported promptly. This can lengthen Mean Time to Repair.

- Ignoring the manual action to silence alarms will be annoying and distracting to the workers. They might spend time trying to silence them, instead of resolving the problem that is trying to be reported.

Solution. Act on all requests to retire an alarm. But don't remember a request to silence alarms. The next time that the system detects an alarmed condition, sound the alarm, regardless of how recently it was retired (see Figure 5.18).

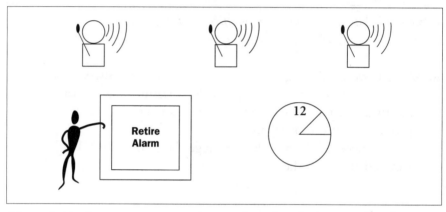

Figure 5.18. Act on requests to retire an alarm but don't remember them.

Resulting Context. The system will report alarms whenever they are appropriate. The worker will have to repeatedly silence them, until the problem is corrected and the system no longer reasserts the alarm. The worker will have until the next alarm detection period before hearing the alarms again.

Related Pattern. This pattern deals with alarmed situations, whereas George Washington Is Still Dead is about slightly less critical information.

STRING A WIRE

Problem. Critically important information must get to other computer systems.

Context. Sometimes the IO Gatekeeper is too slow, or is in a partial capability mode, or the system can't afford the resources to send a message to a nearby system.

An interface specification document has probably been written that outlines how the two systems should communicate, or at least that the need to communicate exists and what information should be exchanged.

Forces

- Standard MML messages could be used between two systems, but both systems will have to spend resources (memory, time) to encode and decode the message in the other system's language.

Solution. Provide a hardwired messaging connection (e.g., Dynamic Overload Controls, E2A telemetry channels, etc.). Use the interface specification document to describe the interface so that both systems can be developed towards a common interface view (see Figure 5.19).

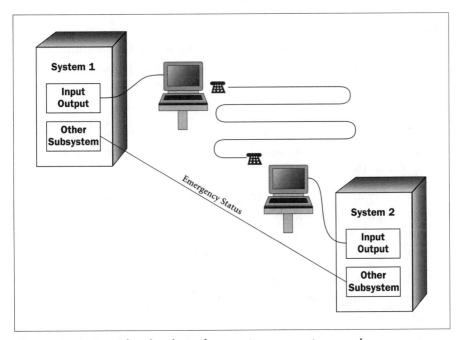

Figure 5.19. Provide a hardwired messaging connection to other computer systems.

Resulting Context. The system will present information to monitoring systems even when the ordinary IO methods cannot be afforded due to emergency or resource utilization priorities.

If more information is needed than a simple hardwired messaging connection can provide, consider adding Raw IO.

Reference. [Green+1977, pp. 1174–1175].

RAW IO

Problem. How do we provide IO during those times when the IO system is unavailable, for example, during system initialization or times of emergency?

Context. Sometime the IO Gatekeeper is too slow, or is in a partial capability mode, or the system can't afford the resources to do IO. These might be just the situations in which people need to be informed about system state. String A Wire cannot provide enough information in these circumstances.

Forces

• Humans watching a system that has no ability to communicate are tempted to do something drastic – like manually requesting an initialization. This is rarely the right thing to do (see Minimize Human Intervention [Adams+1996]).

• If the system doesn't communicate during times of crisis, there is nothing to help an expert user help the system (see People Know Best [Adams+1996]).

• Recovery and initialization programs are in total control of the system and typically have the ability to look inside other subsystems and perform their work. In fact, this is probably safer than allowing the IO subsystem loose during periods of system recovery.

• The IO system is large with many more interfaces than the recovery system, so a large amount of code must be available during recovery for IO to work.

Solution. Display the output via brute force mechanisms such as writing directly to a logical channel and avoiding the IO system. This should be limited to recovery periods only (see Figure 5.20).

The periods during which this raw IO mechanism operates should be

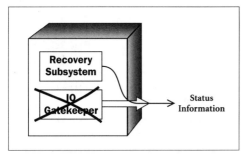

Figure 5.20. Display output using brute force.

limited. The system should try to restore the IO system as soon as possible.

Resulting Context. During critical periods, the safe course is chosen and the recovery programs administer IO rather than rely on the IO system.

Table 5.2. Input Output Patterns

Pattern Name	Pattern Intent
Alarm Grid	Group alarms into grids to help the workers identify problems.
Audible Alarms	Sound audible alarms to alert office personnel of problems.
Beltline Terminal	Allow workers to take their terminals with them.
Don't Let Them Forget	Reasserts alarms when necessary, purposely forgetting requests to retire the alarms.
Five Minutes of No Escalation Messages	Don't confuse workers with too frequent messages.
George Washington Is Still Dead	Issue state change messages only when the state changes, not to remind about the current state.
IO Triage	Add a priority tag to each output message and sort the output using them.
Mind Your Own Business	Only send output to concerned terminal groups (logical channels).
MML	Use a standardized IO language.
Office Alarms	Allow the alarm system to be customized with site-specific alarms.
Pseudo-IO	Provide for internal subsystems to add IO to the stream.
Raw IO	Provide a way for recovery systems to bypass the IO Gatekeeper.
Shut Up and Listen	Give human input/output messages a high priority.
String A Wire	Provide a system-to-system emergency information channel.
The Bottom Line	Issue messages to summarize a number of events rather than for each of many events.
Timestamp	Add a timestamp and/or a sequence number to each output message.
Who Asked?	Return output only to the logical channel/terminal that requested it.

Table 5.3. Referenced Patterns

Pattern Name	Pattern Intent	Page References to [Adams+1996]
Minimize Human Intervention	Give machine enough intelligence to not require human intervention	551–552
People Know Best	Assume humans know more than the machine.	552–553
Riding Over Transients	Give transients time to clear up on their own	554–555

ACKNOWLEDGMENTS

The authors would like to acknowledge the following people for their help in preparing this pattern language: Ralph Jones (1937–1998) – inventor of the Alarm Grid concept and of the concept of using message tags as the key to sound an Audible Alarm. Reviewers within Lucent Technologies: Rick Rockershousen who reviewed 1A ESS content; Glen Moore who was one of the original developers of the 4ESS Switch IO system; Chuck Borcher and Deatrice Childs who participated in a review of Alarm Grid and Office Alarms; and Juel Ulven for reviewing the alarm patterns.

David DeLano, our PLoP '98 shepherd, provided invaluable comments to improve these patterns, and the participants in a TelePLoP sponsored workshop and the Zen View Writers' Workshop group at PLoP '98 provided invaluable assistance.

Five Minutes of No Escalation Messages is co-authored by Mike Adams, and a previous version was published in [Adams+1996].

REFERENCES

[Adams+1996] M. Adams, J. Coplien, R. Gamoke, R. Hanmer, F. Keeve, and K. Nicodemus. "Fault-Tolerant Telecommunication System Patterns." In J.M. Vlissides, J.O. Coplien, and N.L. Kerth (eds.), *Pattern Languages of Program Design* 2. Reading, MA: Addison-Wesley, 1996.

[Budlong+1977] A.H. Budlong, B.G. DeLugish, S.M. Neville, J.S. Nowak, J.L. Quinn, and F.W. Wendland. "1A Processor: Control System." *Bell System Technical Journal*, 56(2): 135–179, 1977.

[Clement+1977] G.F. Clement, P.S. Fuss, R.J. Griffith, R.C. Lee, and R.D. Royer. "1A Processor: Control, Administrative, and Utility Software." *Bell System Technical Journal*, 56(2): 237–254, 1977.

[Gamma+1995] E. Gamma, R. Helm, R. Johnson, and J. Vlissides. *Design Patterns Elements of Reusable Object-Oriented Software*. Reading, MA: Addison-Wesley, 1995.

[Green+1977] T.V. Green, D.G. Haenschke, B.H. Hornbach, and C.E. Johnson. "No 4 ESS: Network Management and Traffic Administration." *Bell System Technical Journal*, 56(7): 1169–1202, 1977.

[Giunta+1977] J.A. Giunta, S.F. Heath III, J.T. Raleigh, and M.T. Smith Jr. "No 4 ESS: Data/trunk Administration and Maintenance." *Bell System Technical Journal*, 56(7): 1203–1237, 1977.

[Huttenhoff+1977] J.H. Huttenhoff, J. Janik Jr., G.D. Johnson, W.R. Schleicher, M.F. Slana, and F.H. Tendrick Jr. "No 4 ESS: Peripheral System." *Bell System Technical Journal*, 56(7): 1029–1055, 1977.

6

A PATTERN LANGUAGE OF CALL PROCESSING

Greg Utas

INTRODUCTION

The call processing component of a switching system is responsible for setting up basic calls between external interfaces and for providing a broad range of features such as call forwarding, conference calling, and call waiting. This article discusses design concepts that address some of the challenges faced when developing a call processing system. Each design concept is presented in the form of a *pattern*, a term recently adopted by the software design community [1,2,3,4,5]. A group of related patterns constitutes a *pattern language* for its domain, which in this case is the domain of call processing. This chapter develops a pattern language for call processing by using a number of examples. Each pattern within the language is presented using an outline that has become fairly standard within the design pattern community:

- **Context:** the situation in which the pattern applies

- **Problem:** the challenge to be addressed

Based on "An Overview of Selected Call Processing Patterns," by Greg Utas, which appeared in *IEEE Communications* 37(4), pp. 64–69, April 1999, ©1999 IEEE; and from, "A Pattern Language of Feature Interaction" by Greg Utas, which appeared in *Feature Interactions in Telecommunications and Software Systems*, K. Kimbler and L.G. Bouma, eds. (Amsterdam: IOS Press, 1996), pp. 98–114. Used with permission from the author.

- **Forces:** factors that contribute to the problem and/or its solution

- **Solution:** how to address the problem

- **Rationale:** the reasoning behind the solution

- **Resulting context:** any interesting side effects or problems that the solution creates

- **Examples:** examples of how the pattern is applied

- **Related patterns:** any patterns that are closely related to the one just described

Although the patterns focus on call processing systems, a number of them are applicable to transactional, real-time systems in general. Some of the patterns are also instances or refinements of patterns described elsewhere. They are included because of their importance to the overall pattern language and to illustrate how previously published patterns can be applied to the call processing domain.

Because this chapter deals with software implementation, it discusses base classes that are defined by a call processing framework that uses the chapter's patterns. This involves the development of some terminology. To assist the reader, a glossary is provided at the end of the chapter, and Figure 6.2 illustrates relationships between the framework classes discussed in the article.

SUMMARY OF THE PATTERN LANGUAGE

The language (see Figure 6.1) begins by advocating the use of *State Machine* to implement basic calls and features. This pattern is somewhat prescriptive in terms of implementation details because it seeks to avoid disadvantages associated with double-dispatching. *Separation of Call Halves* splits basic calls into originating and terminating state machines in order to enable scalable distributed processing and avoid an $O(n^2)$ explosion when interworking the protocols of originating and terminating interfaces. In each half-call, *Separation of Protocols* provides a separate PSM (Protocol State Machine) for each protocol involves in the call. *Run to Completion* minimizes critical section bugs by making each call processing transaction an indivisible operation. *Agent Factory* describes how to instantiate the appropriate subclasses of the dynamic objects used in a call. Finally, *Message Preservation* describes how

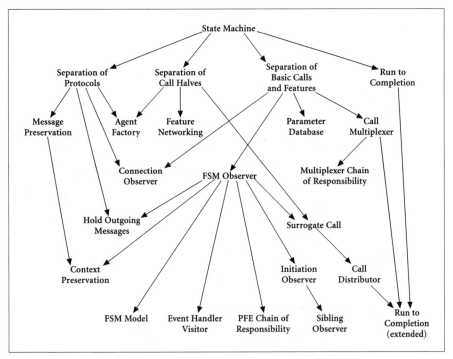

Figure 6.1. A map of the pattern language. Arrows indicate dependencies. For example, Separation of Call Halves and FSM Observer are prerequisites for Surrogate Call.

saving entire messages, so that they can be referenced during subsequent transactions, makes it easier to handle certain scenarios.

The patterns described thus far are used in basic calls. However, the introduction of features gives rise to additional patterns. *Separation of Basic Calls and Features* is a metapattern that discusses the importance of keeping basic call and feature state machines completely separated. This is largely achieved by *FSM Observer*, which allows features to observe the behavior of basic call state machines and augment or override this behavior as required. Some features, however, need to modify many basic call subclasses, and so *FSM Model* is introduced to provide a common abstract state machine for all basic calls. This frequently allows a single version of a feature to modify all of the necessary basic call subclasses. A feature may also need to modify messages built by basic call software; this is addressed by *Hold Outgoing Messages*, which allows a feature to access an outgoing message and modify it before it is sent.

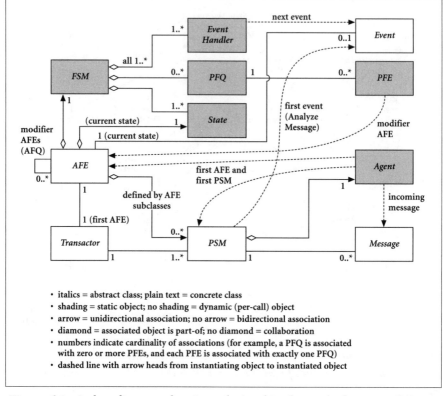

Figure 6.2. A class diagram showing relationships between the types of objects discussed in this article. The Transactor class is not discussed elsewhere but is shown here because it is involved in scheduling a call process. An incoming message is temporarily assigned to a Transactor, which is then queued to run. When the call runs, its Transactor passes the message to the PSM associated with the I/O address on which the message arrived. This PSM subsequently raises the Analyze Message event to pass the message to the first AFE.

The next group of patterns addresses situations in which a feature affects more than one half-call. When a feature affects both halves of a call, *Feature Networking* splits it into two state machines; this is just an elaboration of *Separation of Call Halves*. When a feature allows more than one call to be presented to the same interface, *Call Multiplexer* provides it with a separate context that subtends those calls, which makes it easier to coordinate actions that affect more than one call. Other features redirect a call to a new interface. Here *Surrogate Call* allows the redirected leg of the call to be set up on behalf of the redirecting user, who is logically – but not physically – involved in the call. Finally, when a feature simultaneously redirects a call to multiple interfaces, *Call Distributor* – essentially the reverse of *Call Multiplexer* – provides the feature with a separate context for managing the resulting fan-out.

Run to Completion, as described for basic calls, is inadequate for handling certain scenarios involving features. When *Call Multiplexer* or *Call Distributor* is applied, a user's processing context no longer consists of a single half-call. The transaction initiated by an incoming message must now ripple through multiplexers and distributors as well as half-calls; all of these are peer processing contexts that communicate using asynchronous messages. *Run to Completion (extended)* therefore broadens the definition of a transaction so that all processing within a user's context is performed as an extended critical section. This eliminates state-space explosions and race conditions that would occur if pure asynchronous messaging were used between the user's half-calls and multiplexers or distributors. However, some features must interrupt a transaction to interact with other nodes in the network. For various reasons, it is undesirable to use synchronous messaging (blocking sends) in these situations. *Context Preservation* allows a feature to save the current processing context so that it can transparently resume an interrupted transaction when it receives an asynchronous response from another node.

The final set of patterns handles interactions between features. In many of these situations, features must cooperate even though their state machines are completely decoupled from one another. *Parameter Database* allows call setup information to be modified by one feature and subsequently retrieved by another. *Connection Observer* allows a feature to monitor precisely what a user is receiving and transmitting, even as other features modify the connection topology. *Multiplexer Chain of Responsibility* sorts out signaling and connection interactions when more than one multiplexer is running in a user's context. When an observable basic call event might trigger more than one feature, *PFE Chain of Responsibility* arranges the features so that the most desirable one is able to trigger first. If a feature is already running on the call and an incompatible feature is triggered, *Initiation Observer* allows the active feature to deny the initiation of the new feature. When more than one feature is modifying the same half-call, *Event Handler Visitor* allows one feature to effect a basic call state transition without hiding it from the others, so that all features have the chance to react appropriately. And if two features must interact in some peculiar manner, *Sibling Observer* allows them to define a private protocol for this purpose.

Patterns for Basic Calls

State Machine

Context. You are developing a call processing application.

Problem. When the application receives a message, how can it decide what work to perform?

Forces. When a message arrives from an external interface, the work to be performed is determined by the application's current state. As work is performed, the application's state must be updated so that it can correctly react to the next message.

Solution. Provide a framework for implementing applications as state machines. Define the abstract classes **FSM** (finite state machine), **state, event,** and **event handler.** Each application has its own FSM subclass, which is a *Flyweight* [1] that is shared by all run-time (per-call) instances of the application. The FSM subclass registers the *Flyweight* state and event handler subclasses that implement the application. The FSM's two registries, for states and event handlers, are implemented as simple arrays by assigning a unique integer identifier to each state and event handler subclass. Registration then simply consists of indexing into the appropriate array and saving a reference to the state or event handler subclass.

At run time, events are instantiated ("raised") to perform work on behalf of an FSM, which is assigned an **active FSM element** (AFE) to house its per-call data. The AFE contains a reference to its corresponding FSM, its current state, and the event that it is processing. This allows the correct event handler to be invoked. This event handler sets the next state and returns the next event to be processed if another event handler must perform additional work.

Event subclasses are also assigned unique integer identifiers to index an array belonging to state subclasses. The entries in this array are event handler identifiers. Given an FSM, state, and an event, a two-step procedure invokes the correct event handler:

```
eh_id = current_fsm->states[current_state_id][cur-
    rent_event_id];
next_event = current_fsm->event_handlers[eh_id](cur-
    rent_event);
```

Rationale. Standards often use Specification and Description Language (SDL) to describe the behavior of call processing applications. SDL is based on state machines, so the use of state machines makes the relationship between specifications and implementations clear. And if all call processing applications are implemented using a common framework, it is much easier for one designer to support applications developed by other designers.

Object-oriented designs frequently use double-dispatching to invoke event handlers. The approach just described improves on double-dispatching in many ways. First, indexing by state and event identifiers to find event handlers is more intuitive. Second, the decoupling of states, events, and event handlers allows state machines to be modified with far less recompilation. Third, any new or modified subclasses can easily register in a running system, which is critical because switches must be continuously available. Finally, the framework performs all event handler dispatching, which prevents designers from adding inappropriate "hooks" to such software.

Related Patterns. This pattern extends *Three-Level FSM* [6], *State Objects* [7], and *Owner-Driven Transitions* [8] by decoupling states, events, and event handlers. The importance of using a common state machine framework will be further reinforced when we see how the patterns *FSM Observer* and *FSM Model* add features to basic calls.

RUN TO COMPLETION

Context. You are using *State Machine* to develop call processing applications

Problem. How do you prevent state machines from interfering with each other?

Forces. Call processing applications contend for resources among themselves and with other parts of the system, such as hardware maintenance and provisioning applications. These applications share resources such as inter-switch trunks, service circuits, and memory for objects. Under round-robin, preemptive scheduling, critical sections must be used when obtaining and releasing shared resources.

Solution. When a call begins to process a message, let it run until it has completed all of its work. At that point, the call takes a real-time break to wait for its next input. The scheduler is not allowed to preempt one call to run another. This pattern is also described in [9].

Rationale. Running one call at a time eliminates most critical sections in call processing applications, which simplifies their design and makes them less prone to error. It also improves the system's call-handling capacity by reducing the amount of time spent on process swapping.

Resulting Context. If a call runs to completion, how does it wait for its next input? Call processing is a transactional, real-time system that must react to asynchronous inputs (messages) that arrive from external interfaces. The solution is *Half-Sync/Half-Async* [10], which decouples the handling of I/O from applications. I/O interrupts are allowed when a call is running, but incoming messages are simply queued against a call. No call processing occurs until the call runs, so resource contention between calls does not increase. Finally, a sanity timeout is required on each transaction so that a call cannot hang the switch by running forever!

SEPARATION OF CALL HALVES

Context. You are using *State Machine* to develop call processing applications.

Problem. How do you implement state machines for basic calls?

Forces. Many calls are set up between external interfaces that use different protocols. There are hundreds of inter-switch trunk protocols in use around the world. A switch intended for global markets must support calls between many combinations of these protocols.

Solution. Separate each basic call into two halves – an originating basic call (OBC) and a terminating basic call (TBC) – which are implemented as separate state machines. Define a call interworking protocol for all communication between OBC and TBC subclasses. This is an example of *Half-Object + Protocol* [11].

Rationale. There are many reasons for this pattern. First, software that deals directly with both originating and terminating external protocols becomes $O(n^2)$ in size, where n is the number of protocols. The standard call interworking protocol reduces the amount of software to $O(n)$. Second, Intelligent Network standards [12,13] are based on originating and terminating call halves. A switch supports Intelligent Network capabilities more easily if its internal design is based on a similar model. Third, the pattern allows distribution because OBC and TBC can run on separate processors. A multi-processor system based on such distribution will have a higher call-handling capacity than a single-processor system. In a multi-processor system, it is unclear where a central call object, as opposed to half-call objects, should run. A half-call, however, can run in the processor that owns the external interface where the call originated or terminated. Once call halves are separated, an intermediate call object is not needed.

Example. Figure 6.3a shows a typical OBC-TBC configuration. Figure 6.3b shows the messages that establish a call. The call interworking protocol (CIP) is based on ISUP [14], the most comprehensive protocol for setting up calls between switches, but it also adds parameters that support internal switch capabilities such as call recording and connection control.

SEPARATION OF PROTOCOLS

Context. You are using *State Machine* to develop call processing applications

Problem. How do you support protocols?

Forces. Protocols are fundamental to call processing. All external interfaces supported by a switch are specified in terms of protocols. Protocols are also used to communicate with service circuits that are internal to the switch. A call often uses a number of protocols simultaneously, and each protocol dialogue begins and ends independently.

Solution. Define the abstract class **protocol state machine** (PSM) to support protocols. Each protocol will have its own PSM subclass. Implement each per-call usage of a protocol using a separate PSM, and pass all messages sent or received by call processing applications through PSMs. Each PSM is associated with an I/O address where it receives messages, and it knows the I/O address of its conjugate (peer) PSM, with which it communicates using asynchronous messages. PSMs closely resemble the Port objects described in [15].

Rationale. This pattern allows each protocol's PSM to be created (destroyed) when an initial (final) message in the protocol is sent or received. Because it is the first object to process an incoming message, and the last one to process an outgoing message, a PSM can enforce its protocol. And because PSMs are distinct objects, they are easily reused by different applications. Reuse is most common for service circuit PSMs, which AFEs create as required.

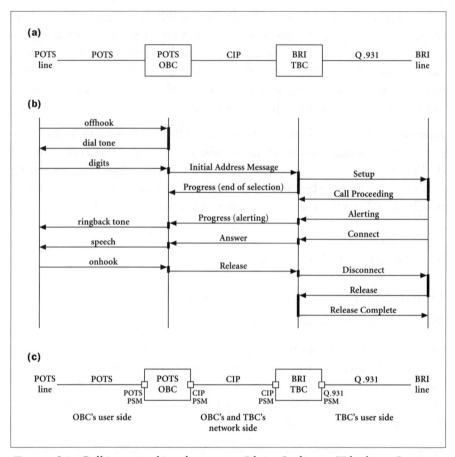

Figure 6.3. Call interworking between a Plain Ordinary Telephone Service (POTS) line OBC and an ISDN Basic Rate Interface (BRI) line TBC. The diagrams show (a) the basic call AFEs and protocols used in the call, (b) the sequence of messages that set up and take down the call, and (c) basic call PSMs (the small squares) in addition to the AFEs. Each AFE and its PSMs comprise a context that runs to completion.

Resulting Context. FMSs and PSMs are decoupled, so their states are independent. This is important in allowing call phases to be repeated. During call reorigination, for example, a user logs into a calling card account, usually over an ISUP trunk, makes a call, and then makes another call after dialing "#." This can cause answer to occur more than once. For each call, OBC creates a billing record and records the time of answer and disconnect. However, an ISUP Answer Message cannot be sent when a subsequent answer occurs because the ISUP protocol does not allow this. So although OBC enters its Active (talking) state more than once, it must consult its ISUP PSM before telling it to send an Answer Message, because one might already have been sent during a previous call.

Examples. Both OBC and TBC use two primary PSMs. One PSM appears on the OBC or TBC *network side* and uses the call interworking protocol (CIP) to communicate with its conjugate PSM on the other half-call. The other PSM appears on the OBC or TBC *user side* and uses a standard call control protocol to communicate with an external interface, such as a subscriber line or inter-switch trunk. Figure 6.3c shows the PSMs in a basic call.

There are also other types of PSMs. Some communicate with service circuits such as tone generators and receivers, announcements, and conference bridges. Others communicate with Service Control Points to provide Intelligent Network protocols such as CS-2 [12] and AIN 0.2 [13], which allow call processing applications to run outside of the switch.

AGENT FACTORY

Context. A message arrives to create a call. You are using *Separation of Call Halves* and *Separation of Protocols* to implement calls.

Problem. How do you create the objects that will handle the message?

Forces. When a call's first message arrives, a PSM and AFE must be created. In addition, a message object must be created as a wrapper for each incoming message (byte stream). However, all of these objects are subclassed based on the protocol they support. How do you instantiate the correct subclasses?

Solution. Define the abstract class **agent**, each of whose *Singleton* subclasses acts as an *Abstract Factory* [1] for creating AFEs, PSMs, and incoming messages. When provisioning an external interface, assign it an I/O address on which its messages will be received and sent. The interface will use this address for as long as it remains provisioned. Associate the I/O address with the agent subclass that supports the type of external interface being provisioned. When a message arrives on an I/O address, delegate creation of the message object to the agent that is associated with the address. If the I/O address is not yet associated with a PSM, the message is the first one for a new call, in which case the agent must also "bootstrap" the call by creating a PSM and an AFE. The creation of objects by an agent subclass is shown in Figure 6.2.

Rationale. I/O addresses are used by different types of interfaces. The types of messages received on an I/O address are determined by the interface associated with the I/O address. The creation of message objects, PSMs, and AFEs should therefore be delegated to an object that is subclassed based on the type of interface that owns the I/O address. The abstract agent superclass allows the I/O interrupt handler to delegate instantiation in a uniform manner.

Examples. In Figure 6.3c, the POTS agent subclass creates the POTS PSM and the POTS OBC; it also wraps each message arriving from the POTS line. The creation of the BRI TBC is interesting because the first message received by a TBC is always a CIP Initial Address Message. This message arrives on an I/O address associated with the CIP agent subclass, so it creates a CIP PSM and CIP message wrapper. However, AFEs are subclassed according to the user-side protocol that they support. The TBC to be created must be based on the terminating interface, in this case a BRI line. The CIP agent knows this because OBC includes, in the CIP Initial Address Message, a parameter that identifies the type of agent that will receive the call. OBC obtains this parameter from the switch's translation and routing database, which it uses to analyze the dialed number and determine the call's destination.

MESSAGE PRESERVATION

Context. A message arrives at a call, or a call sends a message. Messages are first-class objects, as shown in Figure 6.2, and are received and sent through PSMs, as described in *Separation of Protocols.*

Problem. How do you reference parameters in the message during transactions?

Forces. The parameters in an incoming message are used to set up a call, but call setup is not always completed within a single transaction. And when an outgoing message is sent, a PSM often starts a timer. If a reply to the message is not received before the timer expires, the PSM may have to retransmit the message. Specifications may require this behavior even if message delivery is guaranteed, as a way to handle race conditions or errors in terminal equipment.

Solution. Define `save` and `unsave` methods on an abstract **message** class from which all messages are subclassed. The default behavior is for an incoming message to be destroyed when the transaction ends, and for an outgoing message to be destroyed after it is sent. However, invoking the `save` method increments a counter within the message, in which case the message is not destroyed until the call ends or an `unsave` operation drops the count to zero. A saved message is owned by the PSM through which the message was received or sent.

Rationale. It is inefficient to copy parameters to "permanent" locations when they need to be referenced during a subsequent transaction. It is also inefficient, and difficult, to reconstruct an outgoing message when it must be retransmitted. Not only does a message object allow a message to be saved, but it also allows details such as message building and parsing to be hidden from applications. Finally, preserving only parts of a message churns software because the list of parameters to be preserved grows as new applications are added. The easiest solution is to simply preserve the entire message. The memory cost of doing so is usually outweighed by improved performance and reduced software churn.

Examples. A call saves its first incoming message, such as Q.931 Setup or a CIP Initial Address Message, until answer occurs; this allows the message's parameters to be referenced during call setup. A PSM saves an outgoing message, such as a Q.931 Release, when it must retransmit it if an expected response (a Release Complete, in this case) is not received.

PATTERNS FOR FEATURES

This section extends the pattern language for basic call processing with patterns that support features such as call forwarding, call waiting, and conference calls.

SEPARATION OF BASIC CALLS AND FEATURES

Context. You have developed a call processing system whose basic calls use *State Machine.*

Problem. How do you add features to the system?

Forces. The system will support dozens of features. Many features will be developed in each software release, so their designers must be able to work in parallel. Some features are as complex as basic calls, being comprised of many states and dozens of events. Features must also interact with basic call and each other. Features need to override basic call behavior, augment it, or reuse it. There are also cases in which multiple features might run on a call, either sequentially or in parallel. In such cases the features must interact harmoniously or, at the very least, avoid interfering with each other. This problem is known as *feature interaction.*

Solution. Implement each feature as a separate state machine.

Rationale. Separating state machines avoids the drawbacks of *One Big State Machine,* which quickly becomes a morass of convoluted, error-prone software that designers are constantly waiting in line to modify. A call-processing system that does not separate state machines will resemble a *Big Ball of Mud* [16].

Resulting Context. This pattern is a metapattern because it says nothing about *how* to separate basic calls and features. Achieving such a separation is difficult because features must seamlessly interact with both basic calls and each other. The remaining patterns in this section focus on how features can interact with basic calls even though their state machines are separated. The topic of feature interaction – how multiple features on the same call can interact even when they all run as separate state machines – is discussed later in this chapter.

FSM OBSERVER

Context. You are using *Separation of Basic Calls and Features* and are developing a feature that affects the behavior of basic calls.

Problem. How can you keep feature logic out of basic call but allow the feature to reuse basic call software whenever possible?

Forces. When a basic call event is raised, a feature must be able to override, augment, or reuse basic call behavior, depending on feature requirements.

Solution. Allow features to observe the behavior of the basic call FSM. Before basic call processes an event, allow a feature to override basic call behavior by intercepting the event. After basic call processes an event, inform each feature of the state transition that just occurred, in case some features need to perform additional actions. Features that react to a state transition can only augment, not override, basic call behavior.

Features register interest in basic call events in two ways. Here it is necessary to distinguish *active* features, which have already been initiated, from *passive* features, which are waiting to be triggered. Just like basic call, each active feature has its own AFE. When a feature is initiated, its AFE is created and placed in an active FSM queue (AFQ) owned by basic call.

In the same way that active features have AFEs, passive features have **passive FSM elements** (PFEs). Each PFE is registered in a passive feature queue (PFQ) owned by a basic call FSM. Basic call defines a PFQ for each of its observable events and state transitions.

Just before a basic call event handler finishes executing, it specifies the PFQ that should be informed of the state transition that just occurred, as well as the PFQ that should be given an opportunity to react to the next event, if any. Features in basic call's AFQ are automatically informed of each observable event and state transition. To put it another way, a PFE registers with a basic call *class* (an FSM) so that it is notified when *any* basic call in that class signals the event or state transition in which it is interested. The PFE may then create an AFE, which registers with a basic call *object* (an AFE) so that it is notified of events and state transitions signaled only by that *specific* basic call instance.

After a feature processes an event, it returns the next event to be processed, and an instruction that specifies how this event should be routed. **Continue** indicates that the feature will process the next event as well; this allows work to be split among a series of event handlers. **Consume** indicates that there is no next event, and so the transaction ends. **Pass** returns the same event. If no other feature is interested in the event, it returns to basic call, which processes it. **Reenter** is used after raising a new basic call event, which then overrides any event that basic call had planned to process. This allows a feature to reuse basic call software after it has altered the normal call flow.

Rationale. This pattern allows basic calls and features to be implemented as separate state machines while maximizing reuse of basic call software through the use of the event routing instructions **pass** and **reenter.**

Resulting Context. This pattern can be applied recursively, to allow one feature to modify the behavior of another feature. Because the framework provides the abstract classes that support all state machines, it is easy to support such recursion.

Active features (in the AFQ) observe events before passive features (in the PFQ). The reason for this is that active features are already modifying basic call behavior and therefore have priority when overriding basic call events, so as to ensure that their overrides take effect. The same approach is used during state transitions, although here the order is not important: all features in the AFQ and PFQ are notified because they can only augment basic call behavior.

The AFQ actually behaves as a stack so that the most recently triggered feature will be in the foreground, where it has the first opportunity to react to events. The ordering of features in the PFQ is discussed later, in *PFE Chain of Responsibility*.

Examples. Call waiting (CWT) has a PFE that reacts to the basic call event that is raised when a user is busy. If the user subscribes to CWT, the PFE asks for CWT to be initiated, in which case a CWT AFE is created and placed in basic call's AFQ. Control then transfers to CWT's AFE, which attempts to present the call to the user instead of allowing basic call to release it because the subscriber is busy.

Figure 6.4 shows the Intelligent Network service switching function (SSF) running in the context of an originating basic call and communicating with a Service Control Point (SCP). The SSF feature allows features implemented in the SCP to observe basic call events and state transitions so that they can override and augment basic call's behavior in the same way as switch-based features.

Related Patterns. This pattern extends *State Machine* with *Recursive Control* [17] and *Orthogonal Behavior* and *Broadcasting* [18]. The overall behavior is guided by event routing instructions and is *dynamically defined* by whatever features are currently modifying basic call.

FSM MODEL

Context. You are developing a feature that is required on many types of basic calls. Each basic call supports *FSM Observer*.

Problem. How can you avoid developing a different version of the feature for each basic call?

146

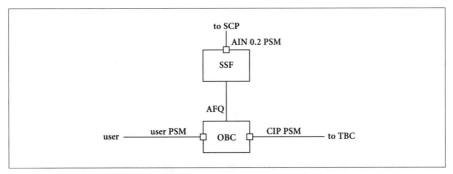

*Figure 6.4. The Intelligent Network service switching function (SSF) running as a feature that modifies the behavior of a basic call OBC. SSF has created a PSM in order to communicate with a Service Control Point (SCP) using the AIN 0.2 protocol. The "protocol" between OBC and SSF is synchronous and is shown using an object association. In the OBC to SSF direction, the protocol consists of basic call events and state transitions. In the SSF to OBC direction, it consists of the event routing instructions (**consume, pass,** and **reenter**) associated with basic call events. OBC, SSF, and their three PSMs comprise a context that runs to completion.*

Forces. There are many similarities between the basic call state machines that support different external interfaces. Each OBC, for example, must collect digits, analyze the digits to find a route over which the call can be completed, send a call setup request to TBC, wait for an acknowledgment from TBC, then wait for TBC to answer, and finally wait for the user or TBC to release the call. However, the ways in which different OBCs implement these actions depend on the user-side protocol.

Solution. Define a generic call model that is based on all basic call state machines. In fact, Intelligent Network standards already define a basic call model that is split into two parts, one for OBC and one for TBC. This call model is a good starting point for use within a switch.

A call model specifies a standard set of states, events, and state transitions used by all basic calls. Each basic call maps its actions to the state-event space defined by the call model. This allows a feature to use *FSM Observer* to monitor the behavior of *any* basic call, without regard to the underlying user-side protocol. Differences among user-side protocols are hidden by basic call event handlers, which are subclassed (when necessary) according to the user-side protocol.

Rationale. This pattern allows features to be reused on different types of basic calls. Basing the call model on Intelligent Network standards makes it easier for the Intelligent Network service switching function to support those standards.

Resulting Context. This is only a partial solution to reusing features on different basic calls. In the same way that basic calls are subclassed according to the user-side protocol that they support, so too are features. Thus, if a feature must directly interact with a user-side protocol, it must still be subclassed. In many of these cases, however, much of the feature's software will be protocol-independent and thus reusable on all call types. To make the feature totally generic, it would be necessary to create an abstract superclass user-side PSM that hides the differences among all user-side PSMs. The CIP PSM is a start in this direction, but its scope is limited to the setup and takedown of basic calls between different interfaces. Extending the CIP PSM to act as a superset of all line (access) protocols is very difficult. A detailed discussion of this topic is beyond the scope of this chapter. Suffice it to say that CIP exists to reduce the amount of call software from $O(n^2)$ to $O(n)$, as described in *Separation of Call Halves*. An abstract user-side PSM is then an attempt to reduce the amount of feature software from $O(n)$ to $O(k)$, where k=1. This attempt will be futile, however, because each feature's protocol-specific components will simply move from its FSM's event handlers to user-side PSMs. This will also increase system complexity by significantly increasing the collaboration required between event handlers and PSMs.

Examples. Features that need to be used by many different types of basic calls include toll-free (for example, 800 numbers in North America), local number portability, and the Intelligent Network service switching function.

Related Patterns. The use of a *call model* is central to Intelligent Network standards. The name *FSM Model* reflects the fact that the pattern can be applied to any feature, not just basic calls. However, this usage is rare because most features observe basic calls, not other features.

HOLD OUTGOING MESSAGES

Context. A feature needs to alter a message that is built by basic call, which uses *Separation of Protocols* and supports *FSM Observer.*

Problem. How can the feature alter the message?

Forces. The feature may need to add a parameter to the message or modify a parameter that was already added to the message by basic call.

Solution. Queue each outgoing message on the appropriate PSM and send it only when the transaction ends.

Rationale. Basic call remains free of feature-specific messaging logic. A feature can locate a queued message and alter it, usually when it is informed of a basic call state transition. A feature can also be given the option of being notified when the transaction ends, so that it can modify any message before it is sent.

Example. If a user is forwarding incoming calls, the call forward notification feature reminds the user that call forwarding is activated whenever the user originates a call. The feature does this by including a parameter in the Q.931 Call Proceeding message sent to the user. The feature triggers after basic call has processed the Send Call event, finds the Call Proceeding message built by OBC's Send Call event handler, and modifies it by adding the call forward notification parameter.

FEATURE NETWORKING

Context. You are developing a feature that must perform actions on both users in a call. Basic calls use *Separation of Call Halves,* so the feature's actions affect more than one processing context.

Problem. How can the feature coordinate its actions across both user contexts?

Forces. Each user could reside on a different switch. Even if the users reside on the same switch, their features run in separate contexts: OBC and TBC. Because OBC and TBC may be running on separate processors, they can only communicate by exchanging CIP messages.

Solution. Split the feature in half, just like basic call. Run one half on OBC and the conjugate half on TBC. To support communication between the two halves, define a generic feature parameter that can be added to any message in the call interworking protocol. Each feature parameter has an identifier to specify the feature associated with the parameter. The rest of the parameter's contents are feature-specific. The two halves of the feature can then communicate by exchanging feature parameters that are appended to standard CIP messages.

Rational. This pattern extends *Separation of Call Halves* to apply to features as well as basic calls. Reasons for this separation are given in *Separation of*

Call Halves. Moreover, the only way that a feature can affect a user *on another switch* is to add a parameter to an inter-switch trunk protocol such as ISUP. Because the feature must be designed in this way when it operates *between* switches, it is reasonable to use the same design *within* a switch. Otherwise the feature will be implemented in two ways, which will increase development costs.

Resulting Context. A networked feature usually triggers on OBC, after which *Hold Outgoing Messages* allows it to add a feature parameter to a CIP message. This parameter can cause the feature's conjugate AFE to be created on the remote half-call, in this case TBC.

Example. Call waiting originating (CWO) allows an originating user to impose call waiting on a busy user, even if the busy user does not subscribe to call waiting. After OBC builds the CIP Initial Address Message (IAM), CWO adds its feature parameter to this message. If the called user is busy, CWO's conjugate (on TBC) triggers if it finds CWO's parameter in the IAM. If TBC is a trunk, the parameter has no effect. However, let us say that ISUP was enhanced to support a CWO parameter. In this case, CWO's conjugate would wait for ISUP TBC to build the outgoing ISUP Initial Address Message. It would then include the CWO parameter in the ISUP IAM if that parameter was also present in the CIP IAM.

CALL MULTIPLEXER

Context. You are using *Separation of Basic Calls and Features* and are developing a feature that affects more than one of a user's calls. A conference call is an example of such a feature.

Problem. How can the feature coordinate its action across more than one of the user's calls?

Forces. If a feature affects only one of a user's calls, it runs in the context of that call. But if a feature affects many calls, it cannot run within a single call because that call can disappear while other calls remain active. This occurs, for example, if one member of a conference drops out. Moreover, calls only communicate using asynchronous messages sent and received by PSMs, and so the feature would have to run on all of the calls to coordinate its actions between them. This would be unwieldy because each instance of the feature would need a separate PSM to communicate with every other instance. Only in this way, for example, could all conference members be notified when one member dropped out.

Solution. Allow a feature to run as a *peer* of the calls that it affects. Insert the feature between the user interface and those calls. The feature will have one user-side PSM to communicate with the user interface, and also a number of network-side PSMs, each of which will communicate with one of the user's calls.

Rationale. This simplifies coordination of multiple calls by allowing them to be associated. The association is provided by the feature that requires it. The feature runs in a separate context that subtends precisely those calls that the feature affects.

Resulting Context. Asynchronous messaging between a multiplexer and the calls that it subtends introduces race conditions that complicate the design of multiplexers. This issue is addressed in *Run to Completion (extended)*.

Examples. Three-way calling and call waiting use this pattern to coordinate the actions of two calls. Thus, when three-way calling receives a hookflash from a POTS line, it can easily coordinate the actions required by both of its calls, either by conferencing them or by releasing the second call and returning to the simple configuration where only the original call remains.

A terminal that supports independent calls uses a *terminal multiplexer* to manage those calls. This is the case for BRI lines and GSM mobiles. BRI lines also use an *interface multiplexer* to manage the terminals on a BRI interface. When a BRI interface multiplexer receives a message on its user side, it relays the message to the correct terminal multiplexer by looking at the message's terminal endpoint identifier. Similarly, a BRI terminal multiplexer relays incoming user-side messages to the correct call (OBC, TBC, or a three-way calling multiplexer) by looking at the message's call reference. Figure 6.5 shows various multiplexers that are serving a BRI interface.

SURROGATE CALL

Context. Basic calls use *Separation of Call Halves* and support *FSM Observer*. You are developing a feature that redirects a call to a new destination.

Problem. How do you implement the feature?

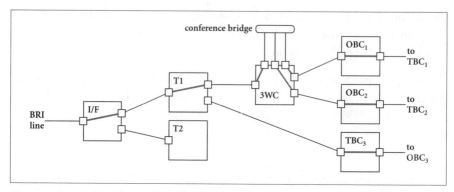

Figure 6.5. A BRI line, showing its interface multiplexer, I/F, which is serving two terminal multiplexes, T_1 and T_2. T_2 is idle, whereas T_1 has three calls, OBC_1, OBC_2, and TBC_3. OBC_1 and OBC_2 have been conferenced by the three-way calling (3WC) multiplexer. Speech connections are shown as internal lines that connect PSMs belonging to the same multiplexer or basic call. TBC_3 is on hold, which is illustrated by the absence of a speech connection within T_1 that leads from I/F to TBC_3. The diagram also shows, for the first time, the use of PSMs to interact with a service circuit that is internal to the switch, in this case a conference bridge.

Forces. When a call from user *A* to user *B* is redirected to user *C*, the redirection feature runs on behalf of user *B*. The redirected part of the call, from *B* to *C*, is set up using *B*'s dial plan, is subject to *B*'s restrictions, such as not being allowed to make toll calls, and is charged to *B*.

Solution. Allow a half-call to be set up on a user's behalf even if the user is not connected to the call. To support this, each half-call must be able to run in surrogate mode, in which it only performs logical actions on behalf of a user. It also relays CIP messages between the calls that have been joined (redirected) together instead of interworking those messages to the user's PSM, which does not exist in the call. The relaying of CIP messages occurs between two PSMs that replace the user-side PSMs that exist when the user is connected to the call.

Rationale. This pattern directly follows from requirements that user *B*'s features remain part of the call. When *B* redirects a call from *A* to *C*, the result is *not* a direct call from *A* to *C*. The *connection* is from *A* to *C*, but there are two *calls*: *A* to *B*, and *B* to *C*. This is reflected in the fact that *B* pays for the *B* to *C* call, so *B*'s billing software must run on that call.

Resulting Context. Although a redirection feature usually relays an entire CIP message, this is not true for the Initial Address Message (IAM). Some IAM parameters describe end-to-end call characteristics, such as the need for echo suppression, whereas others describe leg-by-leg characteristics, such as the billing number and long distance service provider for a call leg. All CIP IAM parameters must be partitioned into those relayed during call redirection (end-to-end parameters) and those deleted and provided afresh (leg-by-leg parameters).

Examples. Features such as call forwarding, call transfer, and call pickup use this pattern. Figure 6.6 shows the configuration that results after call forwarding on no reply redirects a call.

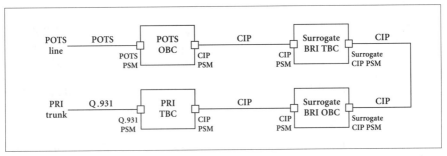

Figure 6.6. The configuration after a BRI line's call forwarding on no reply (CFNRy) feature has forwarded a call from a POTS line to a PRI trunk. The surrogate BRI TBC was originally a standard BRI TBC whose user-side PSM communicated with a terminal multiplexer. However, the BRI line was idled when the call was forwarded, so this multiplexer has disappeared. The forwarded leg was set up by the surrogate BRI OBC, and the two surrogate half-calls are now relaying CIP messages between the POTS line and PRI trunk. The initial message from the surrogate TBC to the surrogate OBC was a CIP Initial Address Message created by the CFNRy feature. It contained the information necessary to set up the forwarded leg, as well as an encapsulated Q.931 Setup message. The Setup message allows the surrogate OBC to reuse standard BRI OBC event handlers, which expect to see a Q.931 Setup message on the user-side PSM.

CALL DISTRIBUTOR

Context. You are developing a feature that presents a call to multiple destinations. *Surrogate Call* is available for redirecting a call to a single destination.

Problem. How can the feature set up a separate call to each destination?

Forces. Each destination has its own phone number but may be served by a different switch.

Solution. Use a variant of *Call Multiplexer.* A multiplexer maps multiple calls onto a single *user-side* PSM. Here, however, it is necessary to map multiple calls, one to each destination, onto a single *network-side* PSM.

Rationale. This pattern reuses OBC, which is capable of setting up a call to any destination. Because there are multiple destinations, a separate OBC instance is required to reach each one. The distributor runs as a surrogate TBC that hides the existence of these multiple OBCs from the original OBC that originated the call.

Resulting Context. Asynchronous messaging between a distributor and the calls that it subtends introduces race conditions that complicate the design of distributors. This issue is addressed in *Run to Completion (extended).*

Examples. The flexible alerting feature simultaneously forwards a call to multiple locations. The call is awarded to the first destination that answers, and other destinations are released. The preset conference feature is similar, except that any destination that answers is conferenced into the call. Figure 6.7 shows how preset conference presents a call to multiple destinations. The Session Initial Protocol (SIP) defined for Internet telephony uses the term *forking proxy* to describe simultaneous forwarding.

Run to Completion (extended)

Context. You are using *Run to Completion* and developing a feature that uses *Call Multiplexer* or *Call Distributor.*

Problem. Race conditions occur between the feature and the calls that it subtends.

Forces. Peer features (namely OBCs, TBCs, multiplexers, and distributors) communicate with asynchronous messages.

Solution. Extend *Run to Completion* so that all features running *on behalf of the same user* run to completion. When one feature sends another feature a message, and both features are running on behalf of the same user, place the

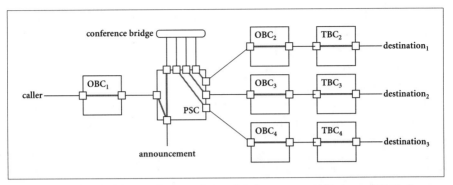

Figure 6.7. The use of Call Distributor by the preset conference (PSC) feature to present a call to three locations. PSC runs on a surrogate TBC and uses three surrogate PSMs to originate calls (OBC_2, OBC_3, and OBC_4) for the purpose of reaching the target destinations (TBC_2, TBC_3, and TBC_4). This is equivalent to simultaneous call forwarding: OBC_2, OBC_3, and OBC_4 are all surrogate OBCs associated with the user who subscribes to the PSC feature. Some destinations have not yet answered, and so PSC is playing an announcement to both the originator of OBC_1 and the conference, informing them that the conference will be established after all destinations have been given time to answer.

message in a priority queue that is emptied prior to accepting any messages from outside the user's processing context.

Rationale. This eliminates race conditions that make multiplexers and distributors that much more difficult to implement.

Examples. All of the AFEs in Figure 6.5 run as an unpreemptable cluster. And in Figure 6.7, preset conference, OBC_2, OBC_3, and OBC_4 run as an unpreemptable cluster.

GSM standards specify that when a mobile has more than one call, its active call may not be held until a message to retrieve another call arrives. Three peer features therefore cooperate to hold a call: a GSM terminal multiplexer and two basic calls, as shown in Figure 6.8. When the terminal multiplexer receives a Hold message, it relays this message to the call to be held. If the reply is a Hold Ack, it saves this message and waits for a Retrieve from the user. When the Retrieve arrives, the terminal multiplexer relays it to the call to be retrieved. If the reply is a Retrieve Ack, the terminal multiplexer sends the saved Hold Ack to the user and then relays the Retrieve Ack to the user as well. The message sequence that begins with receiving the Hold and that ends with saving the Hold Ack, as well as the one that begins with receiving the Retrieve and that ends with sending the final Retrieve Ack, occurs within a single user context and therefore runs unpreemptably. Messages from outside this context remain queued. This allows the three features to focus on the task at hand, without worrying about race conditions that would occur if messages from the user or the two remote parties were processed during this time.

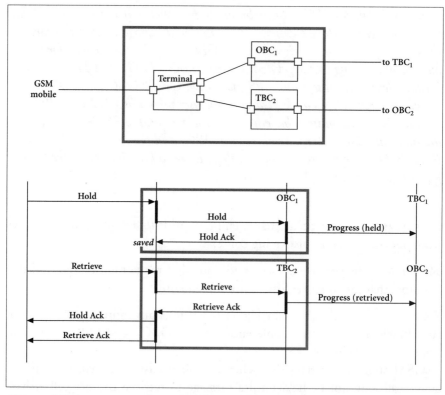

Figure 6.8. Run-to-completion with a single user context. The GSM terminal multiplexer and basic calls are running on behalf of the same user, so all messages between them are processed to completion before any external message (from the user or the two remote call halves) are accepted. Only outgoing messages can cross the boundary of a shaded box while any message inside the box remains unprocessed.

CONTEXT PRESERVATION

Context. You are using *FSM Observer* and *Message Preservation* and are developing a feature that needs to interrupt a basic call transaction by sending a message to another processor and waiting for a response. The response will either cause the feature to change the call's default behavior or cause it to resume the interrupted transaction.

Problem. How do you implement this requirement?

Forces. When a feature interrupts a transaction, the current basic call event goes unprocessed. When the feature receives a response, this event must either be processed or be discarded.

An interruption always occurs before processing an event, but there are two scenarios to consider. If the feature is already active, the interruption occurs while traversing the basic call AFQ. But if the feature was just triggered by the event, the interruption occurs while traversing a PFQ. The interruption leaves the current message and event unprocessed.

Solution. Extend *Message Preservation* so that the feature can save the current context. This consists of not only the context message, but also the current basic call event and the position in the AFQ or PFQ. When the response arrives, the feature can either discard or restore this context. In the former case, the feature usually reenters basic call with a new event. In the latter case, the feature uses a new event routing instruction, **resume,** which transparently resumes processing of the interrupted transaction. The feature's query-response operation is therefore performed asynchronously.

Rationale. Asynchronous messaging is used because hardened real-time systems should avoid synchronous messaging. Synchronous messaging can cause deadlocks, as well as unacceptable latencies when timeouts occur. It is also inefficient from a scheduling perspective.

The feature cannot use the **reenter** instruction to resume processing of the saved event because the AFQ or PFQ would then be traversed again, which could cause other features to retrigger. The feature cannot use the **pass** instruction because the saved message and event are no longer in context when the feature is processing the response to its query.

Examples. The Intelligent Network service switching function often uses this pattern. It may, for example, query a Service Control Point (SCP) during call setup to determine if the call should be blocked. If the SCP responds with a Continue instruction, the pending event and message are restored so that call setup can resume. But if the SCP indicates that the call should be barred, the pending event and message are discarded prior to releasing the call.

When a GSM mobile answers a waiting data call on which data inter-working is required, the AFQ already contains the call waiting (CWT) and data interworking (IWF) features. CWT must react to the Local Answer event by ensuring that the radio channel is encoded for data, and IWF must prepare its rate adaption circuit. Before basic call can process the Local Answer event, CWT must receive confirmation that the radio channel is properly encoded, and IWF must receive confirmation that its rate adaption circuit is ready. Both CWT and IWF use *Context Preservation* when they interrupt processing of the Local Answer event. After CWT receives its con-firmation, it returns the **resume** instruction, and IWF runs next. After IWF receives its confirmation, it also returns **resume**, and basic call finally processes the Local Answer event by enabling the connection and sending a CIP Answer Message to the originator.

Patterns for Feature Interactions

The patterns presented thus far allow basic calls and features to run as sepa-rate state machines. *FSM Observer, FSM Model,* and *Hold Outgoing Messages* allow features to modify basic call without changing its software. *Call Multi-plexer, Call Distributor,* and *Feature Networking* allow features to coordinate their actions across more than one call. But how can features interact when more than one is running? To keep features partitioned, generic techniques are required so that features do not constantly have to check for the presence of other features before deciding what to do. This is the topic of the patterns in this section.

Parameter Database

Context. You are implementing two features. The first feature changes a basic call parameter that must subsequently be accessed by the second fea-ture. The two features and basic call conform to *Separation of Basic Calls and Features.*

Problem. How do you implement this interaction while keeping basic call and the two features unaware of each other?

Forces. Features must sometimes read and/or write basic call parameters, and some parameters can be read/written by multiple features running on the same call. If a feature changes a parameter, other features may later need to use the new value. A feature cannot always use *Hold Outgoing Messages* because another one may need to access a modified parameter *before* the feature publishes it by adding it to a message.

Solution. Store the parameter in a database that is associated with basic call.

Resulting Context. Basic call also uses the database, typically when it builds the CIP Initial Address Message. The database also allows a feature to place a parameter in the database and remove itself from the call if it has nothing to do except wait to modify a message that is not built until much later.

Rationale. Associating the parameter with basic call ensures that it is accessible to basic call and all of its features.

Examples. Calling number delivery blocking uses *Parameter Database* when it sets the presentation indicator in the calling address, which is one of the parameters in the database. If the Intelligent Network service switching function is subsequently triggered, it will include the correct presentation indicator when it sends the calling address to the Service Control Point. The database also contains a stack of all analyzed called addresses, such as those that triggered the local number portability or toll-free features. This allows OBC to include them as generic addresses when it builds the CIP Initial Address Message. In most cases, however, parameter history need not be retained: usually only the most recent version of a parameter is required.

CONNECTION OBSERVER

Context. You are implementing a feature that must monitor what a user's bearer channel is transmitting and receiving. Other features, however, can modify the user's connection. The system uses both *Separation of Basic Calls and Features* and *Separation of Protocols*.

Problem. How can the feature monitor the user's connection without being aware of other features that affect the connection?

Forces. Connections can be modeled as associations between PSMs, in the manner of Figure 6.5. When a PSM's signaling channel is also associated with a bearer channel, the PSM acts as an endpoint or relay point for connections to and from its underlying bearer channel. Basic call creates a connection association between its user-side and network-side PSMs. Other features, however, may cause either of these PSMs to receive from another PSM instead.

Solution. To monitor what the user is transmitting, the feature listens to the user-side PSM. This PSM must also allow the feature to register as a connection observer, which means that the feature will be informed whenever the PSM's incoming connection disappears or changes to another PSM. The feature can then listen to the conjugate PSM on the new incoming connection, if any, which allows the feature to monitor precisely what the user is receiving.

Rationale. Connection events should not be added to the basic call model because event handlers become unnecessarily complicated if they are split up to factor out connection work. Moreover, connection events are orthogonal to basic call events: in GSM, for example, bearer channel allocation can occur in one of three different OBC states. It is therefore necessary to provide an observable connection model in addition to the basic call model.

Example. GSM's call intercept feature provides wiretaps of GSM calls, and its data interworking feature inserts a rate adaption circuit in the basic call connection. When the circuit is inserted, the user-side PSM receives from the circuit, not from the network-side PSM. *Connection Observer* allows call intercept to monitor precisely what the user is receiving, even when the data interworking feature is running on the call.

Related Patterns. The *Observer* pattern is described in [1].

EVENT HANDLER VISITOR

Context. You are using *FSM Observer* and are implementing a feature that must perform some work that cannot be accomplished by raising a basic call event and reentering basic call to reuse one of its event handlers. Logically, however, the work should change the basic call state.

Problem. How can the feature change the basic call state?

Forces. A feature is not allowed to change the basic call state directly because this would prevent other features from observing the basic call state transition. When the basic call state changes, other features may need to perform additional work associated with the state transition.

Solution. Have the feature raise a generic "Force Transition" event and reenter basic call. The parameter to this event is an event handler that is supplied by the feature but executed in basic call's processing context. If the event handler updates the basic call state, the state machine framework informs features of the state transition, just as if basic call had updated the state itself.

Rationale. Basic call cannot anticipate all of the state transitions that future features may require. The work associated with a new state transition is feature-specific, so it should be performed by the feature that requires it. However, other features must be able to observe the work as if it had been performed by basic call.

Example. POTS TBC presents a call by applying power ringing to the subscriber's line. Call waiting, however, presents a call by injecting a tone into the speech path, so it cannot use TBC's Present Call event handler to present the waiting call. Call waiting must present the call using one of its own event handlers. However, call waiting should use *Event Handler Visitor* to do this so that the Call Presented state transition is processed after the call is presented. This state transition must be observable because it triggers the no-answer timer for call forwarding on no reply. If the state transition is hidden, this timer will not be started, and the waiting call will not be forwarded if the subscriber ignores it.

Related Patterns. The *Visitor* pattern is described in [1].

MULTIPLEXER CHAIN OF RESPONSIBILITY

Context. You are using *Call Multiplexer* to design multiplexer features that can simultaneously run on behalf of the same user.

Problem. How do you resolve interactions between the multiplexers?

Forces. The order in which multiplexers are arranged determines their signaling and connection interactions. If multiplexer *A* is closer to the user interface than multiplexer *B,* then *A* reacts to user-to-network messages before *B*, and *B* reacts to network-to-user messages before *A*. Since *A* subtends *B*, *A* can hold all of the calls subtended by *B*, whereas *B* can only hold a subset of the calls subtended by *A*.

Solution. Assign a priority to each peer AFE (multiplexers and basic call) that can run within a user's processing context. A higher priority means that the AFE is placed closer to the user interface. An interface multiplexer has the highest priority when processing user-to-network messages, and OBC and TBC have the lowest priority.

Rationale. Priorities cause peer AFEs to be configured in a consistent order, regardless of the order in which they are created. This is important because it produces consistent behavior. Ideally the behavior is what is required by the specifications!

Examples. *Multiplexer Chain of Responsibility* resolves the interaction – prohibited by most specifications – that arises when a waiting call arrives after a user has initiated three-way calling. If the call waiting multiplexer is given priority over the three-way calling multiplexer, as shown in Figure 6.9, call waiting will process user messages first. A hookflash will switch between the three-way call and the waiting call, and an onhook will release the active call and cause the remaining call (even if it is a three-way call) to re-alert the user. *Multiplexer Chain of Responsibility* also trivially resolves the situation in which call waiting occurs at both ends of a call. Here, the two call-waiting features run in separate user contexts and therefore do not interfere with one another. Although this can lead to interesting interactions, such as two lines re-alerting each other, this is a natural outcome when features are distributed, whether between switches or within a switch.

Related Patterns. The *Chain of Responsibility* pattern is described in [1].

PFE CHAIN OF RESPONSIBILITY

Context. You are using *FSM Observer.* More than one feature can trigger on the same event.

Problem. How do you ensure that the proper feature triggers in reaction to the event?

Forces. If more than one feature can trigger, the specifications will state

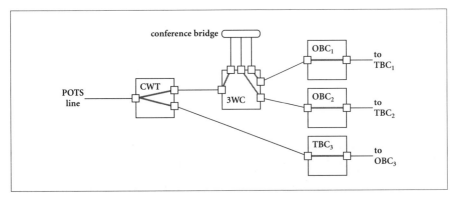

Figure 6.9. Resolving the hookflash contention between call waiting (CWT) and three-way calling (3WC) by giving CWT a higher priority than 3WC. Once CWT's multiplexer is inserted, it intercepts hookflashes, which no longer control 3WC. If the user goes onhook, CWT re-alerts the user, and so 3WC (if it has already conferenced its calls, as shown here) must be prepared for an offhook (re-answer), an event that it would not normally see.

which feature is more desirable. In most cases, the features will also be mutually incompatible.

Solution. Assign a priority to each PFE that registers in the same PFQ. Arrange the PFEs in order of their priority. After a PFE triggers its feature, it can prevent further traversal of the PFQ by returning the **consume** event routing instruction, which ends the current transaction.

Rationale. Priorities allow features to trigger in the order required by specifications. When a feature overrides basic call behavior, it should be able to prevent other features from triggering if the call is no longer in the state that those features would expect.

Examples. *PFE Chain of Responsibility* allows call waiting to have priority over call forwarding on busy at the Local Busy event. If call waiting is possible, call forwarding on busy does not occur. *PFE Chain of Responsibility* also allows terminating call screening to have priority over the component of automatic recall that remembers the last calling address. This prevents automatic recall from returning a call to an address from which the user rejects calls. However, terminating call screening should probably react to the Authorize Termination event, and automatic recall to the Termination

Authorized state transition. They would then appear in separate PFQs, and automatic recall would never have the opportunity to remember the address of a rejected caller.

INITIATION OBSERVER

Context. You are using *FSM Observer.* A feature is active when an incompatible feature is triggered. Both features are associated with the same user.

Problem. How do you prevent the incompatible features from running together?

Forces. Specifications often state that two features are incompatible, so that one cannot be used in the presence of the other. There are various reasons for this. Perhaps the features would react to an event in ways that would interfere with each other, as in the infamous hookflash contention between call waiting and three-way calling. Or perhaps one feature would violate a policy associated with the other, such as call waiting holding an emergency call to answer the waiting call.

Solution. When feature initiation is requested, notify any active features and allow them to deny the initiation request.

Rationale. This maximizes the simultaneous use of compatible features while preventing the simultaneous use of incompatible features. Knowledge of feature incompatibilities must exist *somewhere* in the software. *Initiation Observer* distributes it among the features, in much the same way that it is distributed among many feature specification documents. Each feature knows which features it must deny.

Examples. Initiation Observer is used frequently. It allows emergency calling to deny call hold. More broadly, it allows the active feature to follow up in any appropriate manner. For example, call forward programming can reenter OBC to collect and analyze the forward-to address. It can then reject the programming attempt if it observes the initiation of originating call screening, abbreviated dialing, or emergency calling. Similarly, automatic callback can determine if the target user is idle by reentering TBC to perform a trial termination. Automatic callback monitors TBC's progress, hoping to eventually observe the Facility Selected state transition. If automatic callback instead observes the initiation of call forwarding unconditional, it can deny the automatic callback request. If it observes the initiation of call waiting, it can treat the user as busy or idle, depending on what is required by the specifications.

Initiation Observer is also used when inserting a multiplexer. The multiplexers and half-calls running on behalf of user A form a tree whose root is A and whose leaves are A's half-calls. To insert a new multiplexer, M, permission is required from (a) the half-calls and multiplexers that appear in the subtree below M and (b) the multiplexers that appear on the path between M and A. This allows call waiting to be denied by emergency calling and three-way calling.

SIBLING OBSERVER

Context. You are implementing two features. Specifications call for a certain behavior when both features are active. The first feature can use *Initiation Observer* to detect the creation of the second feature.

Problem. How can the features interact to satisfy the specifications?

Forces. Compatible features should run independently. However, specifications sometimes violate this principle. If possible, such specifications should be ignored. But this is not always feasible.

Solution. Support event-based communication between features when it is needed. Implement the interaction between the features with a protocol that is specific to the features involved. If feature A must observe feature B, then B raises an event for A whenever B does something that A needs to observe. The event contains any information required by A, and the framework delivers the event to A if A is active. After A processes the event, it has the option of returning a new event as a response to B.

Rationale. The time required to define an inter-feature protocol discourages designers from creating arbitrary couplings to handle interactions. However, the mechanism is generic enough to handle situations in which features truly need to communicate.

Example. GSM's call intercept (CI) feature uses *FSM Model* and *Connection Observer* to monitor basic call and the user's connection. However, specifications also require CI to monitor other features, such as the Intelligent Network service switching function (SSF). CI and SSF use *Sibling Observer* to define a protocol that allows SSF to inform CI of each trigger that results in a query to an Intelligent Network Service Control Point (SCP), as well as the SCP's response.

FEATURE NETWORKING (REUSED)

Context. You are implementing two features that need to interact when they are running on behalf of different users. *Feature Networking* is available when one feature needs to perform actions on both users in a call.

Problem. How can the interaction be supported across the two user contexts?

Solution. Use the previously described *Feature Networking* pattern. The first feature places a feature-specific parameter in a CIP message and the second feature reacts to this parameter.

Examples. CIP defines a presentation indicator in its calling address parameter so that a terminator's calling number delivery feature can avoid displaying a number that was marked private by the originator's calling number delivery blocking feature. CIP also defines a redirection counter that limits the number of times that a call can be forwarded, to prevent infinite call forwarding loops or excessively long call forwarding chains. Each call forwarding feature also sends a CIP Progress Message to the originator, to indicate that forwarding has occurred and to provide the address to which the call was forwarded. If the originating call screening feature reacts to the Remote Progress event, it can look for this parameter to prevent the originator from being forwarded to an address that would have been blocked by his originating call screening feature if he had dialed directly.

Feature Networking can also resolve a very annoying interaction. If a conferee subscribes to music on hold, music disrupts the conference when the conferee puts it on hold. A conference feature should therefore use a CIP Progress Message to inform each conferee that he is part of a conference, and music on hold should not trigger when the user is a conferee.

EXPERIENCES WITH THE PATTERN LANGUAGE

All the patterns in this article are currently used in Nortel Networks' GSM Mobile Switching Center (MSC). A framework that supports these patterns was used to reengineer this MSC's call processing software over a period of

18 months. During that time, 550K lines of software were developed at a cost of 55 designer-years, a significant improvement in productivity. The MSC's features are completely decoupled from basic calls and from each other. Other Nortel design groups have also adopted the pattern language described in this chapter.

Some of the patterns in this chapter are also used in other products. Nortel's DMS-100 uses *Run to Completion, Separation of Basic Calls and Features,* and *Call Multiplexer.* Lucent's 5ESS uses *Separation of Call Halves* [19], which is also important in Intelligent Network standards, as are *FSM Observer* and *FSM Model.* There are undoubtedly many other cases where these and other patterns described in this chapter are used, but they are difficult to uncover because of the lack of substantive literature on call processing software architectures.

Acknowledgments

Much of this chapter is taken from "An Overview of Selected Call Processing Patterns" [20] and "A Pattern Language of Feature Interaction" [21]. Tony Blake, Sam Christie, Dennis Debruler, Jim Doble, Bob Hanmer, Neil Harrison, Allen Hopley, Gerard Meszaros, Martin Nair, Linda Rising, and the anonymous reviewers from the 1998 Feature Interaction Workshop all offered comments that helped to improve the original articles on which this chapter was based.

Glossary

AFE: Active FSM Element: an object that contains an FSM's per-call data.

AFQ: Active FSM Queue: the queue containing the AFEs that are modifying basic call behavior.

BRI: Basic Rate Interface: an ISDN line that uses the Q.931 call control protocol.

CIP: Call Interworking Protocol: the call control protocol used between OBC and TBC.

FSM: Finite State Machine.

GSM: Global System for Mobile Communications.

ISUP: ISDN User Part: a call control protocol used by CCS7 trunks.

network side: the direction towards the network.

OBC: Originating Basic Call: an AFE used to originate a call.

PFE: Passive FSM Element: an object that observes a basic call event or state transition to trigger the creation of its feature's AFE.

PFQ: Passive FSM Queue: a queue containing the PFEs that are interested in the same event or state transition.

POTS: Plain Old Telephone Service.

PRI: Primary Rate Interface: an ISDN trunk that uses the Q.931 call control protocol.

protocol: a set of signals (message types), parameters, and rules that specify the order in which signals may be sent and received and the parameters that are mandatory or optional for each signal.

PSM: Protocol State Machine: an object that implements an instance of a protocol dialogue.

Q.931: the ISDN call control protocol.

TBC: Terminating Basic Call: an AFE used to receive a call.

user side: the direction towards the user.

REFERENCES

1. E. Gamma, R. Helm, R. Johnson, and J. Vlissides. *Design Patterns*. Reading, MA: Addison-Wesley, 1995.

2. J. Coplien and D. Schmidt, eds. *Pattern Languages of Program Design*. Reading, MA: Addison-Wesley, 1995.

3. J. Vlissides, J. Coplien, and N. Kerth, eds. *Pattern Languages of Program Design 2*. Reading, MA: Addison-Wesley, 1996.

4. R. Martin, D. Riehle, and F. Buschmann, eds. *Pattern Languages of Program Design 3*. Reading, MA: Addison-Wesley, 1998.

5. N. Harrison, B. Foote, and H. Rohnert, eds. *Pattern Languages of Program Design 4*. Reading, MA: Addison-Wesley, 1999.

6. R. Martin. "Discovering Patterns in Existing Applications." In [2], pages 383–389.

7. A. Ran. "MOODS: Models for Object-Oriented Design of State." In [3], pages 129–131.

8. P. Dyson and B. Anderson. "State Patterns." In [4], pages 138–140.

9. D. DeBruler. "A Generative Pattern Language for Distributed Computing." In [2], pages 69–89, and this volume, Chapter 2.

10. D. Schmidt and C. Cranor. "Half-Sync/Half-Async: An Architectural Pattern for Efficient and Well-Structured Concurrent I/O." In [3], pages 437–459.

11. G. Meszaros. "Pattern: Half-object + Protocol (HOPP)." In [2], pages 129–132, and this volume, Chapter 8.

12. *Distributed Functional Plane for IN CS-2.* Recommendation Q.1224, ITU-T, September 1997.

13. *AIN 0.2 Switching Systems Generic Requirements.* GR-1298-CORE, Bellcore, September 1997.

14. *Specifications of Signalling System No. 7.* Recommendations Q.761 and Q.763, ITU-T, September 1997.

15. B. Selic, G. Gullekson, and P. Ward. *Real-Time Object-Oriented Modeling.* New York: John Wiley and Sons, 1994.

16. B. Foote and J. Yoder. "Big Ball of Mud." In [5], pages 653–692.

17. B. Selic. "Recursive Control." In [4], pages 147–161.

18. S. Yacoub and H. Ammar. "A Pattern Language of Statecharts." Presented at the 1998 Pattern Languages of Programs Conference, Monticello, Illinois, August 1998. http://jerry.cs.uiuc.edu/~plop/plop98/final_submissions/P22.pdf.

19. L.G. Anderson, C.H. Bowers, D.L. Carney, J.J. Kulzer, and W.W. Parker. "Distributed Systems Tradeoffs." In *Proceedings of the 12th International Switching Symposium.* Piscataway, NJ: IEEE Service Center, 1987, pages 26–33.

20. G. Utas. "An Overview of Selected Call Processing Patterns." In *IEEE Communications,* April 1999, pages 64–69.

21. G. Utas. "A Pattern Language of Feature Interaction." In K. Kimbler and W. Bouma, eds., *Feature Interactions in Telecommunications and Software Systems V,* Amsterdam: IO Press, September 1998, pages 98–114.

PART 2
SMALL COLLECTIONS

7

PATTERNS FOR LOGGING DIAGNOSTIC MESSAGES

Neil B. Harrison

ABSTRACT

EVERY SOFTWARE SYSTEM must deal with errors. Most systems report errors to the user in some manner, and many provide additional diagnostic information to assist the user in tracking down the problem. Transaction-oriented systems lend themselves to common approaches to logging diagnostic messages. These approaches are embodied in three general software patterns. The first pattern, Diagnostic Logger, separates logging from the rest of the software, and lays the groundwork for the other patterns. The second pattern, Diagnostic Context, provides association of diagnostics with the correct transactions. The third pattern, Typed Diagnostics, helps ensure uniformity of presentation for all diagnostics. It also allows the software to handle various diagnostics differently, depending on characteristics such as severity.

INTRODUCTION

Many software systems are transaction-oriented; that is, they take discrete, sometimes independent inputs, perform some operations, and generate some output. In business applications, programs deal with payroll or other personnel functions. Most database applications are query-response based. And in software development, compilers and other translators take input such as programs and produce output such as object code.

All these systems must be able to handle error conditions. These may come about from bugs in the software, but often simply arise from erroneous input. In interactive systems, the system can give immediate feedback to the user that an input error has occurred. Ward Cunningham's CHECKS [Cunn95] pattern language is useful in this situation. However, if the input is batched (for example, source code for a program is a batch of lines of code), the problem becomes one of producing diagnostic messages with sufficient context. Imagine trying to compile a program if the only message the compiler gives is "syntax error," with no line number!

A related issue is that although transactions themselves may be somewhat independent, processing a transaction may impact the processing of later transactions. At the very least, many programs keep track of the number of errors encountered, and give up when a certain threshold is reached. In some systems, certain errors may happen repeatedly, such as when a system keeps trying to re-establish a connection to another machine. So the message is given once, with periodic status messages (e.g., "The above message repeated 10 times"). So it is necessary for many systems to remember information about errors after they happen.

These issues are addressed in three following patterns. They are Diagnostic Logger, Diagnostic Context, and Typed Diagnostics. Each builds on the previous pattern.

THE PATTERNS

DIAGNOSTIC LOGGER

Problem. How do you report diagnostic information in a consistent manner?

Context. Software systems all have the need to provide feedback information to the user in case of errors or other difficulty. This pattern applies specifically to systems where users do not actively interact on a per-transaction basis (e.g., batch mode processing, compiling, and other types of translation systems).

Forces

1. Any part of a system might have need to create a diagnostic message; therefore, any approach must be available to all parts of the system.

2. Diagnostic messages are very important to the users; they should have a consistent look and feel.

3. In most projects, error handling is largely ignored until coding is under way, and programmers realize that errors will happen. At this point, the programmers are most interested in simple, easy-to-use error reporting strategies. There is a strong temptation to throw something together without regard for other programmers.

4. The user may wish to specify the destination of diagnostic messages.

5. The order of messages may be significant.

6. Diagnostic messages almost always have specific information; for example, a compiler may report the line number and suspected offending token where a syntax error occurs.

7. It may be important to retain information from one message to the next. For example, it is common to keep track of total errors, and exit when a threshold is crossed.

Solution. Use a Diagnostic Logger object to handle all the details of diagnostics. Create it as a Singleton [Gamma+95], so that there is a single point for all messages to flow through.

The Diagnostic Logger has two types of functions. The first type is for control of logging in general, such as specifying the output destination, error thresholds, or debugging levels. These are used chiefly by some main controlling objects. The other type of function provides the rest of the software the ability to output the diagnostic messages. These message types may be as general as passing a message, but are usually broken down by type of message or event. In most cases, the Diagnostic Logger will provide an individual function for each type of message, such as errors and warnings.

In order to handle different methods of output, it may be desirable to derive different types of Diagnostic Loggers. In such a case, the program specifies the destination of the output. The correct type of Diagnostic Logger is created either at that time or at the first time the `instance()` function is called. This is somewhat in the flavor of the Abstract Factory

[Gamma+95] pattern. In this case, the message functions may be implemented using the Template Method [Gamma+95] pattern.

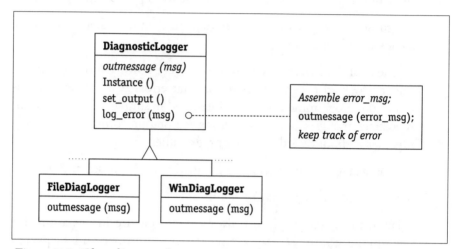

Figure 7.1. Class diagram for Diagnostic Logger, showing two derived Diagnostic Loggers.

Example. Simulation systems are often used for automated testing. A telephone simulator, for example, can instruct a telephone switching system to place a call and answer it, and can verify the connection. A person may run the simulator interactively, in which case the WinDiagLogger will be used. Often, though, the simulator is run unattended overnight, and messages are logged to a file via the FileDiagLogger.

At startup, if a file is designated as the output destination, that information is remembered. When the `Instance()` function is first called, the correct type of DiagnosticLogger is created. Here is how the DiagnosticLogger class might be declared, and how the `Instance()` function might be written:

```
class DiagnosticLogger
{
public:
    virtual void outmessage (Message) = 0;
    // Set the output destination
    static void set_output (String f) { _fname = f;
    }

    // Access function for the Singleton instance
    static DiagnosticLogger* Instance ();
```

```
private:
    static DiagnosticLogger* _instance;
    static String _fname;
};

//  The Instance() function is an Abstract Factory

DiagnosticLogger*
DiagnosticLogger::Instance()
{
    if (_instance)
        return _instance;

    if (_fname)
    {
        _instance = new FileDiagLogger(_fname);

// if creation fails, create a default DiagLogger,
// in this case, WinDiagLogger (not shown)
        .
        .
        .
    }
    else
        _instance = new WinDiagLogger ();

    return _instance;
}
```

Resulting Context. The Diagnostic Logger pattern provides consistency in diagnostic messages, with the details of outputting the messages encapsulated and hidden from the rest of the program. Because it is a Singleton, it easily preserves the order of the messages. The messaging functions are readily accessible to all parts of the system and are easy to use. In fact, the interface can be determined early in design, without worrying about the details of format or destination of messages. Developers may start out with rudimentary functionality in the Diagnostic Logger, such as dumping all messages to stderr.

On the other hand, Diagnostic Logger is slightly more complex to implement, and is slightly slower than simple writes to stderr, for example. But in all but the very simplest programs, it is expected that the advantages far outweigh the cost.

Rationale. This pattern began in a program that translated test cases to automatically executable test scripts. The program later was easily modified to generate a different test language, with the changes made inside the Diagnostic Logger. The Diagnostic Logger also sent diagnostic messages to a designated destination, while creating a different file for every test script it generated. This brings us to the next pattern, Diagnostic Context.

Variations. In client-server systems, a log server often handles the logging of diagnostic messages. In such cases, the Diagnostic Logger might be implemented as a Proxy [Gamm+95]. In distributed applications, Remote Proxy [Buschmann+96] may be useful for implementing Diagnostic Loggers.

Related Patterns. Logging diagnostic messages is an activity that is particularly important in highly reliable systems. Diagnostic Loggers are compatible with the Fault-Tolerant Telecommunication System Patterns [Adams+96], particularly Five Minutes of No Escalation Messages and Leaky Bucket Counters.

DIAGNOSTIC CONTEXTS

Problem. If an error occurs in processing a set of discrete inputs, how do you associate error messages with the correct input?

Context. The system is transaction-oriented; that is, it processes a set of discrete inputs. Examples include compilers, interpreters, database systems, or network servers.
You are using Diagnostic Logger to handle diagnostic messages.

Forces
1. The inputs to the system are somewhat autonomous, and may even be entirely independent of each other. In addition, the input may be processed in batches, so it is often not obvious how the output corresponds to the input.
2. However, the user wants to know which output was produced by which input. This is very important, and is absolutely critical with error or other diagnostic messages.
3. A single input may produce multiple output messages.
4. The results of the inputs are not necessarily independent, such as total error count. In some cases, such as compiling a program, the inputs

are highly dependent on each other, but the diagnostic messages are linked to specific inputs.

5. Internally, the place where an error occurs may be many function calls away from the information that identifies the input. For example, a syntax error of an input statement may be caught deep in the parser, far from the input line number.

6. The information that identifies the input may be complex; for example, an input may be identified by the line number, file name, and directory name. It would be undesirable to pass such information through multiple functions in order to enable error reporting. Think what would happen if it becomes necessary to report machine name as well as the above information; many functions would have to change.

Solution. Use the Diagnostic Logger pattern, and augment it with Diagnostic Context objects. A Diagnostic Context is an object that exists for the life of processing a particular transaction, and provides unique identification of that transaction. Its birth marks the beginning of processing a transaction, and its death marks the end.

Obviously, the easiest approach to this is to take advantage of scoping to create and destroy Diagnostic Context objects. For example, when processing a set of lines:

```
for (int i = 1; i < num_lines; i++)
{
    DiagContext        dc (i);
// Process the input line, generating diagnostic
// messages as appropriate

}

// The Diagnostic Context is automatically destroyed.
```

The constructor for the Diagnostic Context registers with the Diagnostic Logger, and its destructor unregisters.

```
DiagContext::DiagContext (int line_no) :
                    _curr_line_no (line_no)
{
        DiagLogger::Instance()->sign_on (this);
}

DiagContext::~DiagContext ()
```

```
    {
            DiagLogger::Instance ()->sign_off ();
    }
```

Likewise, the DiagLogger ensures that there is only one transaction processed at a time:

```
void
DiagLogger::sign_on (DiagContext* dc)
{
    if (_curr_diag_context != NULL)
    {
        // Bad; take appropriate action
    }

    _curr_diag_context = dc;

    // Write a message indicating the start of a
    // transaction
}

void
DiagLogger::sign_off ()
{
    _curr_diag_context = NULL;
}
```

With Diagnostic Context, the software still continues to log messages directly to the Logger. The Logger will associate the message with context information in the Diagnostic Context. Note that this presents a slight problem at startup; there may be errors to be logged before the first transaction is processed. One approach to this is, until the first time a Diagnostic Context object registers with the Logger, the Logger simply outputs the messages, indicating that no context has been given because the program is in startup mode.

Example. The telephone simulator described earlier can process batches of test scripts. Not only is it necessary to associate output with the correct script, but it is often helpful to remember the state of the system under test (SUT) when a scripts starts. Therefore, at the start of each script, create a DiagnosticContext object, capturing the state of the SUT. Assume that there is a function that returns the current state of the SUT. Then the execution loop might look like this:

```
Script s;

while (s = get_next_script())
{
    DiagContext dc (s, get_sut_status());

    // execute the test script
    execute_script (s);
}
```

Resulting Context. The Logger can mark the start and end of transactions, and provide context to messages. The context includes not only information that comes as part of the message (i.e., immediate information), but also surrounding information, such as file name, line number, earlier state of the system, etc. New context objects can easily be added wherever needed.

Diagnostic Context objects provide an easy way to implement leaky bucket counters. Because the Logger hears about every transaction, it can count successful or unsuccessful processing of transactions. On the other hand, Diagnostic Contexts can handle errors on a per-transaction basis. For example, a Diagnostic Context may limit the number of errors from a single transaction, without aborting the entire session.

Note that Diagnostic Context objects incur a slight performance penalty through the creation and deletion of Diagnostic Context objects. This happens regardless of whether any messages are logged. As long as Diagnostic Context objects are not abused (e.g., creating one for every character of input), the performance price is minimal.

Variations. It may be convenient to use a single Diagnostic Logger and Diagnostic Context to implement diagnostic message handling in a multithreaded environment. In such a case, the DiagLogger would keep track of a Diagnostic Context for each thread. Each Diagnostic Context would be created with some information that would uniquely identify its thread. This is similar to the registry of singletons discussed in the Singleton pattern description.

In other cases, it may be desirable to allow nested Diagnostic Context to provide layers of contextual information. The DiagLogger would manage the stack of Diagnostic Contexts. This makes adding messages and new context easy; simply create a new Diagnostic Transaction to capture the desired context.

Diagnostic Context may be implemented much like the Command Processor pattern [Somm96]. The Diagnostic Context object is much like the Command object, with the Diagnostic Logger playing the role of the Command Processor. Of course, a Diagnostic Context object is not executed, as Command objects are.

Rationale. The Diagnostic Context came about as a result of trying other, inferior approaches to associating messages with the transactions from which they came. Originally, it was necessary to register explicitly at the beginning and end of processing each transaction. The Diagnostic Context is a more automatic and safer approach to this problem.

TYPED DIAGNOSTICS

Problem. If you are logging many different messages (such as errors, warnings, debugging messages, etc.), how do you ensure that these messages are handled consistently?

Context. The system uses the Diagnostic Logger to handle diagnostic messages. There are several different types of events that must be handled consistently, but with enough variation to allow the essential information to be trapped and passed to the user. The system is a transaction-oriented system, and you are using the Diagnostic Context to associate messages with each other on a per-transaction basis.

Forces
1. Once again, it is necessary to keep the details of handling messages out of the main program.
2. For each event you want to log, you want to capture the important information of the moment. Depending on the nature of the event, what is important may vary.
3. Handling diagnostic or debug messages can be troublesome. It is desirable to be able to simply call a diagnostic message handler member function of the Diagnostic Logger. However, diagnostics are usually turned off, but the user would still incur the cost of calling the message handler function. If character strings are created and passed as arguments to the function (which is likely), repeated calls to the function could create a noticeable performance impact.
4. In some cases, it may be desirable to handle messages differently depending on a later event. For example, an error report may include a record of previous events, but they would not normally be reported.

Solution. Create an inheritance hierarchy of Diagnostic Message Types. Each type encapsulates the characteristics of that category of diagnostics, and parameterizes the specific variations. In particular, details of diagnostic messages are embedded in the classes, so as not to incur overhead when creating the Diagnostic Message objects. In fact, the data in these classes should be pretty sparse to minimize the overhead of creation and destruction.

It is necessary to send Diagnostic Messages to the Logger; this usually happens when the object is created. The standard interface to the Logger for messages becomes a simple function for all types of diagnostics:

```
// For an error
DiagLogger::Instance()->message
          (new DiagMsg_Error(err_type, etc));
// For a debug message at debug level 2
DiagLogger::Instance()->message
          (new DiagMsg_Debug (2, etc));
```

The Logger hands the Diagnostic Message to the Diagnostic Context, which then assumes the responsibility for managing them, including destruction of the Diagnostic Messages at the proper time.

Typed Diagnostic Messages combine with Diagnostic Contexts to handle conditional output of messages. Message handling can be quite flexible. For example, debugging messages may or may not be output, depending on the current debugging level. On the other hand, context messages can be stored, and output in the event that an error message arrives.

Note that Typed Diagnostics are different from the previously discussed subclasses of Diagnostic Logger. Diagnostic Logger subclasses designate approaches to handling of all messages, such as output style or destination. Typed Diagnostics differentiate handling of different types of messages, such as error messages versus levels of debugging messages.

Example. The telephone simulator described earlier has two major types of errors. The most obvious errors are when the system under test does not do what is expected; these may indicate that the software being tested has an error. But the test script may have syntax errors, which should be handled differently from the "real" errors. This can be done by having two DiagMsg types, DiagMsg_ParseError, and DiagMsg_RunError. The parsing and execution functions create the type of Diagnostic Message that corresponds to the error encountered.

Error handling and reporting is now more intelligent. If Diagnostic-Logger keeps track of execution errors, it simply asks DiagMsg to report

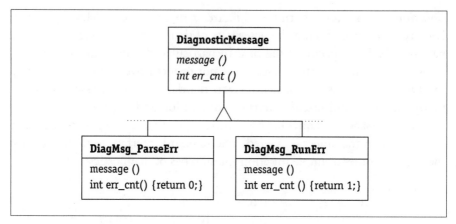

Figure 7.2. Class diagram for Diagnostic Message, showing two derived Diagnostic Message classes.

the number of execution errors it represents. `DiagMsg_RunError` reports one, and `DiagMsg_ParseError` reports zero. Output of error messages can be similarly customized. The code for the Diagnostic Logger `log_err()` function is as follows:

```
void
DiagnosticLogger::log_error (DiagMsg* dm)
{
    // Assume we track total running errors

    _err_count += dm->err_cnt ();

    // Now output the message
    outmessage (dm->message ());
}
```

Resulting Context. With the application of Typed Diagnostics, a program can output several different types of meaningful diagnostic messages while still maintaining a consistent output style. It also retains the characteristics of Diagnostic Logger, such as ease in changing output destination and adaptation to different output types.

Note that Typed Diagnostics does incur a performance cost. Objects may be created and later destroyed, even though they do not create output. For example, debugging Typed Diagnostic Messages are created and destroyed, but only used when debugging is turned on. In addition, if they are passed to the Diagnostic Logger, they may implicitly invoke a copy constructor. Therefore, the classes should be designed so that creation and destruction are inexpensive. In practice, this has not been a problem. For message text, one might consider using a standard set of messages and message numbers. This can be useful in dealing with message sets in different languages.

The user of Typed Diagnostics may also wish to explore alternatives to passing them by value to the Diagnostic Logger.

Rationale. This pattern grew out of various attempts to create a way to handle different types of messages. In some cases, the output was automatically processed, so the messages had to be consistent. This was coupled with the desire to produce different levels of debug messages but to avoid excessive overhead if debugging was not enabled.

ACKNOWLEDGMENTS

The author wishes to thank Stephen Berczuk for his helpful comments, particularly for pointing out the benefits of nested Diagnostic Contexts.

REFERENCES

[Adams+96] Adams, Michael, et al. "Fault-Tolerant Telecommunication System Patterns." In *Pattern Languages of Program Design* 2. Reading, MA: Addison-Wesley, 1996, pp. 549–573, and this volume, Chapter 4.

[Buschmann+96] Buschmann, Frank, et al. *Pattern-Oriented Software Architecture: A System of Patterns.* Chichester, England: John Wiley and Sons, 1996, pp. 263–276.

[Cunn95] Cunningham, Ward. "The CHECKS Pattern Language of Information Integrity." In *Pattern Languages of Program Design.* Reading, MA: Addison-Wesley, 1995, pp. 145–155.

[Gamma+95] Gamma, Erich, et al. *Design Patterns: Elements of Reusable Object-Oriented Software.* Reading, MA: Addison-Wesley, 1995.

[Somm96] Sommerlad, Peter. "Command Processor." In *Pattern Languages of Program Design* 2. Reading, MA: Addison-Wesley, 1996, pp. 65–74.

8

PATTERN: HALF-OBJECT + PROTOCOL (HOPP)

Gerard Meszaros

Applicability. Once you decide upon your objects and their associations, it is time to determine how your objects will be mapped into the address spaces in which they will execute. This pattern helps determine where the objects are placed and their positions relative to the address space boundaries.

Problem. Sometimes objects must appear in more than one computing context (that is, address space). How can we make the difference between one and multiple address spaces (for example, single versus distributed processing) transparent?

Forces. The forces affecting the placement of objects into address spaces include complexity, distribution, information availability, cost, and performance.

Many computer systems are forced to be implemented across multiple address spaces for reasons of cost, size, physical distribution, disparity of programming environments, regulatory reasons, and so on. Sometimes these systems can be easily decomposed into objects that each live in exactly one address space. Some objects are constrained to exist in certain address spaces by coupling to hardware (such as sensors, disk drives, and so on), and others can easily be placed based on such couplings. Sometimes, however, a con-

©1995 Nortel Networks. Originally published in *Pattern Languages of Program Design*, vol 1., J.O. Coplien and D.C. Schmidt, eds. (Reading, MA: Addison-Wesley, 1995), pp. 129–132. Used with permission from the author.

cept exists in both spaces, so you can't easily decompose it; or an object may have to interact with other objects in more than one address space, because it requires information from more than one address space to carry out its behavior. Similarly, unsolicited requests arriving from objects in either address space may need to be handled. See Figure 8.1.

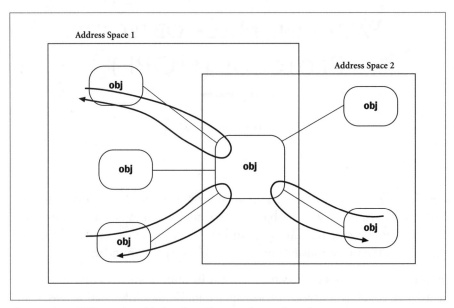

Figure 8.1. Where should the distribution boundary be?

In the figure, the single-headed arrows represent particular "use-cases" that require the participation of the object needing to be represented in both address spaces. In this case, neither address space can carry out the task in isolation. Therefore, at least one object may have to exist in more than one address space. The object or objects in question may have to be split into one or more objects per address space. Splitting an object across the address spaces introduces additional complexity, since a single object is simpler than two half-objects with a protocol between them. (We use the term "half-object" to refer to each distinct part of the object even though each part may implement significantly more than 50 percent of the object's functionality.) One half-object can implement all the behavior, interacting with the other object whenever it needs information retrieved or actions carried out.

If these interactions are frequent, the cost (in terms of execution time, or delay) of building message objects and sending them to an object in another address space may be unacceptable.

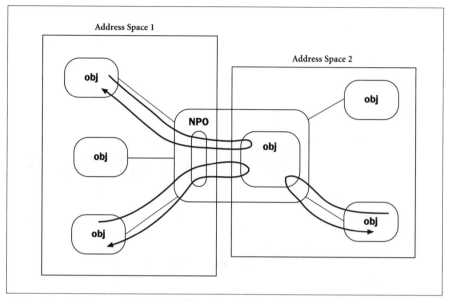

Figure 8.2. The network proxy object (NPO) passes all requests back to the real object.

Splitting an object into two equal parts allows each part to respond to many local requests without consulting the other space, but it may result in duplicated functionality and a need to keep the two objects synchronized. It does isolate the object's interface from the protocol used between the half-objects. See Figure 8.2.

Solution. Divide the object into two interdependent half-objects, one in each address space, with a protocol between them. In each address space, implement whatever functionality is required to interact efficiently with the other objects in that address space. (This may result in duplicated functionality – that is, functions implemented in both address spaces.) Define the protocol between the two half-objects such that it coordinates the activities of the two half-objects and carries the essential information that needs to be passed between the address spaces. See Figure 8.3.

Related Patterns. Once the functions of each half-object are determined, the protocol between them may be defined. This leads to the use of patterns in designing the protocol (Message as Object, Message Parameter as Object) and the mechanisms to handle the creation (information collection, formatting) and reception (parsing, handling) of the message.

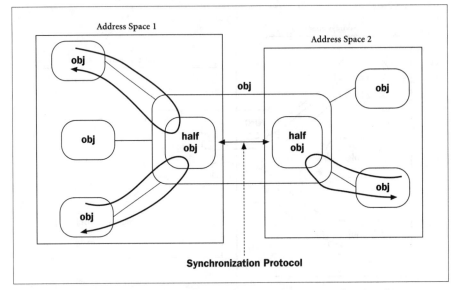

Figure 8.3. Synchronization Protocol. Half-objects respond to local requests; they synchronize their activities through the Synchronization Protocol.

Examples. *Physical distribution:* Non-native debuggers, telephone services distributed across the national telephone network, systems accessing hardware devices (such as sensors), user interfaces remote from information (such as central databases), distributed (replicated) databases.

Size: Systems where functions must be carried out in slave microprocessors due to real-time costs of the function.

Disparity of Programming Environments: A user interface for a C++ debugger implemented in Smalltalk.

Regulatory Reasons: Service control points (SCPs) in the telephone network contain software created by the telephone company to modify calls carried through switches in the telephone network. This software may not be allowed to run in a switch. (This is also an example of disparate programming environments, since switches have proprietary environments while SCPs typically have UNIX-based environments.)

9

ABSTRACT SESSION:
AN OBJECT STRUCTURAL PATTERN

Nat Pryce

OBJECT-ORIENTED FRAMEWORKS are structured in terms of client/server relationships between objects; an object's services are invoked by client objects through the operations of its interface. A common design requirement is for a server object to maintain state for each client that it is serving. Typically this is implemented by returning handles or untyped pointers to the client that are used to identify the per-client data structure holding its state. The lack of strong typing can lead to obscure errors that complicate debugging and maintenance. The Abstract Session pattern allows objects to maintain per-client state with full type safety and no loss of efficiency.

INTENT

The intent of this pattern is to allow a server object with many client objects to maintain per-client state and maintain type-safety.

ALSO KNOWN AS

Service Access Point (SAP), Context, Service Handler

MOTIVATION

Object-oriented frameworks are structured in terms of client/server[1] relationships between objects; an object's services are invoked by client objects through the operations of its interface. Typically, object interactions are defined in terms of abstract interfaces, which increase the reusability and extensibility of the framework because the set of client and server types that can be used together is not bounded and can easily be extended by framework users.

A common design requirement is for a server object to maintain state for each client that it is serving. When the interactions between the server and client objects are defined in terms of abstract interfaces, per-client state cannot be stored in the client objects themselves because different server implementations will have to store different information. This problem is usually solved by using the Session pattern [Lea1995], which imposes a three-phase protocol on the interactions between the client and the server:

1. Clients make an initial "request" call to the server when they begin to use its services. The server responds by allocating a per-client data structure for the new client and returns an identifier of that data structure to the client.

2. The client passes the identifier it received as an argument to subsequent operations on the server. The server uses that identifier to find the per-client information it holds about the caller.

3. When the client has finished using the server, it makes a final "release" call to the server, passing in the identifier that the server uses to find and deallocate the appropriate per-client data structure.

Implementing the Session pattern involves resolving the following forces:

- Per-client state. The server object must be able to store state about each client that is using its services.

- Efficiency. Invocation of service operations should involve minimum run-time overhead.

- Safety. The implementation should catch the use of incorrect session identifiers. Ideally, such errors should be caught at compile-time.

---

[1]In the context of this pattern, the term *server* is used to denote an object that provides a service to "client" objects within the framework and in no way implies any notion of distribution between clients and servers.

Implementations of the Session pattern typically use one of two methods to map from identifiers to the data structures used internally to store per-client state:

- Untyped pointers. Identifiers are defined to be untyped pointers that the server object initializes to point to an implementation-specific data structure and casts to the appropriate type on each invocation. For example, the 16-bit Windows API [Petzold1990] uses untyped pointers to identify windows and other system resources allocated for an application.

- Handles. Identifiers are defined to be values of simple types, such as integers, or opaque values. The server uses a private associative container to map between identifiers and implementation-specific data structures and must perform a lookup each time a client makes a request. For example, the UNIX file API [Lewine1991] uses integer handles to identify open files.

The choice of whether to use untyped pointers or handles is one of safety versus run-time efficiency. Untyped pointers are efficient, but passing an incorrect pointer to a server could cause the program to corrupt memory or crash. Using handles as indices to an associative container allows incorrect identifiers to be detected at run-time but at the expense of performing a lookup on each invocation, which can be costly if many invocations are made during a time-critical part of a program. Both approaches are unsafe; a client can pass an incorrect identifier to the server without the errors being caught at compile-time.

EXAMPLE: NETWORK COMMUNICATION

Consider a communication protocol service that provides reliable transmission of data streams, such as the TCP/IP or Novell SPX protocols provide. The protocol manager itself is implemented as an object that provides services to connect to remote endpoints and accept incoming connections. Client objects wanting to connect to a remote endpoint must request a connection from the protocol object before being able to transmit and receive data. The protocol object must maintain state information, such as unacknowledged packets and flow-control information, for each connection, and thus clients must have some way to identify the connection that they are using to transmit or receive data. When the client has finished transmitting data, it must close the session to release any resources held for the session by the protocol manager.

The following code demonstrates a possible error when using untyped handles. The code uses the UNIX Sockets API [Stevens1990] to open a TCP/IP network connection to a remote endpoint and receive or transmit integer values. The code is incorrect; the first argument to the write function in line 14 should be the socket identifier sock, but the loop counter is erroneously used instead. Because UNIX uses integer handles to identify sockets, the bug cannot be caught by the compiler and only manifests itself as errors at run-time.

```
1    // Select a protocol and get a socket - i.e.
2    // request a session from the selected protocol
3
4    int sock = socket( SelectProtocol(),
         SOCK_STREAM, 0 );
5
6    // Connect to a remote endpoint
7
8    connect( sock, . . . );
9
10   // Send 10 integers to the remote endpoint
11
12   for( int i = 0; i < 10; i++ ) {
13   int number = GetANumberFromSomewhere(i);
14   write( i, &number, sizeof(number) );
15   }
16   cerr << "Transmitted 10 numbers" << endl;
17
18   // Release the protocol session
19
20   close(sock);
```

SOLUTION

The Abstract Session pattern provides a way for an object to store per-client state without sacrificing type safety or efficiency. A protocol service object, rather than providing a client with a handle to be passed as an argument to the operations of its abstract interface, instead creates an intermediate session object and returns a pointer to the session object to the client. The session object encapsulates the state information for the client that owns the session and is only exposed to the client as an abstract interface through which the client can access the protocol's functionality with full type safety. When the client invokes operations of the session, the session cooperates with the service object to complete the operation. When the client has finished using the protocol, it releases the session, after which any pointers to the session object are invalid.

The class diagram in Figure 9.1 shows how the Abstract Session pattern can be used in an implementation of the TCP protocol. The TCP class represents the TCP protocol service and provides an operation, connect, with which client objects can request a connection to a remote endpoint. The TCP service then creates a new TCPSession object, initiates the handshaking protocol with the remote endpoint, and returns a pointer to the session's ChannelSession interface to the caller. The client object can call operations of the ChannelSession interface to transmit data over the connection.

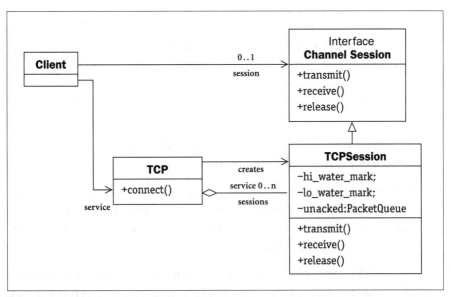

Figure 9.1. Service and Session classes for the TCP protocol and an example Client class.

As shown in Figure 9.2, the TCP object keeps track of the sessions it has created. It demultiplexes each packet received from the IP layer by passing it to the session identified in the packet's header. The session performs protocol processing and then queues the data for reading by the client object that owns it.

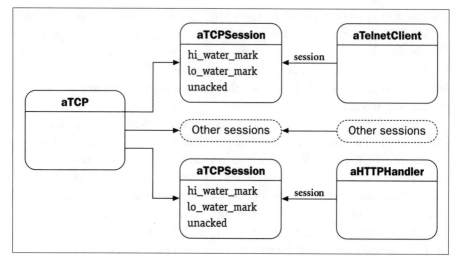

Figure 9.2. Dynamic structure of objects implementing the TCP protocol.

When the client object wants to close the connection, it calls the `release` operation of its session, after which all pointers to the session are invalid.

The Abstract Session pattern successfully resolves the forces outlined above:

- Per-client state. The server object stores state about each client in the session object associated with that client.

- Efficiency. Calling operations of a session object imposes no performance penalty compared to passing untyped pointers to operations of the service object and is more efficient than mapping handles to data structures using some hidden table.

- Safety. The client object invokes operations on the abstract interface of the session object and so never needs to manipulate untyped handles. The session object knows the full type of the service object that created it, and vice versa, so the interactions between them are completely type-safe. When the client invokes an operation on the session, the session can call private operations of the service object, passing the manager a fully typed pointer to itself. The manager does not have to perform unsafe casts to access the state it stores within the session objects.

APPLICABILITY

Use the Abstract Session pattern (Figure 9.3) when

- Interactions between server objects and client objects are defined in terms of abstract interfaces.

- Server objects must maintain state for each client object that makes use of their services.

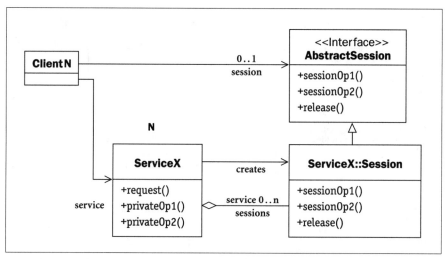

Figure 9.3. Class structure of the Abstract Session pattern.

STRUCTURE AND PARTICIPANTS

- ServiceX (Service). Classes of server objects that create session objects (of type ServiceX::Session) for clients that are bound to them.

- Abstract Session (ChannelSession). The interface through which clients bound to a server object make use of the service provided by that object.

- ServiceX::Session (TCPSession). The session classes used by the ServiceX classes to store information about clients that are bound to them. Clients invoke the AbstractSession interfaces of these objects to interact with the server objects to which they are bound.

- ClientN (HttpHandler, TelnetClient). Objects that are making use of ServiceX through the AbstractSession interface.

COLLABORATIONS

Figure 9.4 illustrates the collaborations between objects in the Abstract Session pattern.

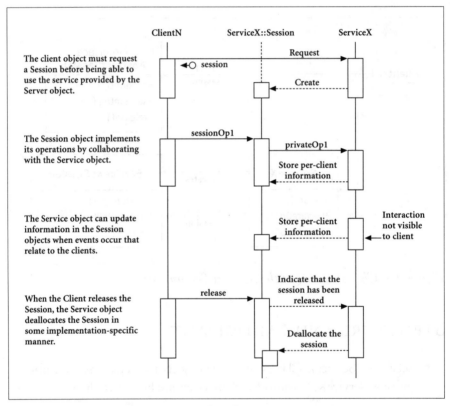

Figure 9.4. Object interactions in the Abstract Session pattern.

- A client object that wants to use a server object requests a session from the server. The server object creates a session object (which conforms to the AbstractSession interface), initializes the session with information about the client, and returns a pointer to the session back to the client.

- The client uses the service provided by the server object by invoking the operations of its session object's AbstractSession interface. The session object cooperates with the server object to complete the invocation.

- The server object uses information stored in the session object to process requests from its clients and can update the per-client information when events occur behind the scenes that relate to the client.

- When a client object has finished using the service provided by the server object, it calls the `release` operation of its session. Forcing clients to release sessions by calling `release` allows a service to hide the way it allocates session objects from its clients. A service could allocate sessions on the heap, in which case the `release` operation would free the session object, or a service could have a fixed number of sessions in an array, in which case `release` would update a record in the service object of the sessions that were unused and could be handed out to new clients.

CONSEQUENCES

The Abstract Session pattern has the following advantages:

- Type safety. Interactions between clients and sessions and between sessions and servers are completely type-safe. This reduces the likelihood of obscure errors, making the code easier to debug and maintain.

- Performance. The interactions between clients and sessions are as fast as or faster than those using unsafe methods such as untyped pointers or handles.

- Flexibility. The use of abstract interfaces and encapsulation of per-client state within each server class reduces coupling between client and server classes. A client can use any server that creates sessions that implement the AbstractSession interface.

- Extensibility. The pattern makes it easy to add server classes to the system; such extensions do not require existing client and server classes to change.

The Abstract Session pattern has the following disadvantages:

- Dangling pointers. It is possible that a session might be referenced and used after it has been released.

- Distribution. It is difficult to pass a session object from the server to the client if the client and server exist in different address spaces. When creating a session, the server must send information to the client to allow the client to create a Proxy [Gamma+1995] session in its local address space. Distributed object brokers, such as CORBA [OMG1995] or DCOM [Rogerson1977], can implement this functionality.

- Multiple languages. It is difficult to call Abstract Sessions from another language, especially from languages that are not object-oriented. This can be solved by writing an Adapter [Gamma+1995] layer that hides session objects behind a set of procedures callable from the other languages and that uses one of the unsafe implementations of the Session pattern to identify session objects.

IMPLEMENTATION

The following implementation issues are worth noting:

1. Use of the heap. Allocating and deallocating memory from the heap is an expensive operation. Forcing clients to discard sessions via the `release` method in the AbstractSession interface, rather than an explicit deallocation of the session object, gives server objects more flexibility in the allocation of session objects. For instance, if the server allocated the session from the heap, the `release` operation would delete the session object. However, a server might preallocate sessions in a cache; when a client invokes the `release` operation of a session, it need only mark that the session is unused rather than perform a heap deallocation. If a server object does not need to store any information about its clients, it can implement the AbstractSession interface itself, perhaps using private inheritance; in this case, the `release` operation would do nothing.

2. C++ smart pointers. A C++ implementation of this pattern can automate the management of session lifetimes by using smart pointer

classes. A smart pointer object would store a pointer to a session interface and release the interface in its destructor. A smart pointer on the stack would automatically release the session when it goes out of scope. A smart pointer held as a member of an object would automatically release the session when the object gets destroyed.

3. Object finalization. In a language with automatic garbage collection and object finalization, the act of releasing a session can be made synonymous with releasing the last reference to the Session object. The functionality of releasing a session can be performed by the finalization method of the Session object and so will be called automatically by the garbage collector.

4. Java outer/inner classes. A Java implementation of this pattern can be simplified using inner classes. The concrete Service class would be implemented as an outer class, and the concrete Session classes would be defined as inner classes. An inner class is associated with an instance of the outer class in which it is defined and can refer directly to the fields and methods of that instance. Thus, inner classes remove the need for explicit delegation from session to service and reduce the possibility of programming errors.

5. Defining server interfaces. If clients are always bound to servers by some third party that knows the complete type of all servers it is using, then server objects do not need to conform to an abstract interface. However, in some systems clients will bind themselves to servers by finding a suitable server object in something like a trader or namespace and then request a session from it; in this case servers will need to conform to some abstract interface that can be used polymorphically.

SAMPLE CODE: COMMUNICATION PROTOCOLS

The following source code expands on the networking example described above in which the program opens a network connection to a remote endpoint and transmits ten integers. The example is taken from an existing object-oriented protocol framework that allows programmers to construct communication protocol software by composing simple components to form protocols with rich functionality tightly tailored to the needs of the application.

The framework defines a number of abstract interfaces and base classes, which are used by protocol implementers, as well as useful abstract data types. The sessions of a protocol layer are accessed through the `Chan-nelSession` interface, by which client objects transmit data. Clients of a protocol layer implement the `ReceiveCallback` interface, to which their session calls back when data is received. Messages are held in `Buffer` objects that perform memory management and segmentation and reassembly of blocks of raw data. Addressing information is encapsulated as `Reference` objects.

Unlike the example code above, an individual protocol can provide multiple service interfaces. For example, our TCP implementation provides an interface named "connect" of type `ConnectService` through which objects can connect to remote endpoints, and an interface named "listen" of type `ListenService` through which objects can request endpoints that listen for incoming connection requests. Service interfaces are abstract, allowing objects to dynamically select the communication protocol to be used at runtime and to acquire the appropriate interface from a factory. For this example, we will consider only the `ConnectService` interface:

```
class ChannelSession {
public:
    virtual bool transmit( Buffer &buf ) = 0;
    virtual void release() = 0;
};

class ReceiveCallback {
public:
    virtual void receive( Buffer &buf ) = 0;
};

class ConnectService {
public:
    virtual ChannelSession *request(
    ReceiveCallback&, const Reference& ) = 0;

};
```

Application-layer communication abstracts (such as distributed object invocation, queued message ports, or event dissemination) communicate by marshaling typed data into and out of `Buffer` objects that are transmitted by these protocol interfaces. It is useful to encapsulate the code to manage the ownership of a protocol session within a reusable base class. For instance, the `ClientEndpoint` class below is the base class for objects that can be connected to a remote endpoint and communicate with that endpoint over a channel through a `ChannelSession` interface. The `bind` method is used to hand ownership of a session that has been acquired by some third party over to the endpoint object. The interaction abstraction derived from `ClientEndpoint` uses the session to transmit and receive data and releases the session when it is destroyed.

```
class ClientEndpoint : public ReceiveCallback {
public:
    /* Receive callback interface: implement in
     * derived classes
     */
    virtual void receive( Buffer & ) = 0;
    /* Binding interface: attach the session object
     * of the channel used by this endpoint
     *
     */
    bool bound() const { return _transport != 0; }
    void bind( ChannelSession *transport ) {
    _transport = transport; }

protected:
    ClientEndpoint() : _transport(0) {}
    /* Allow derived classes access to the private
     *_transport session
     */
    bool transmit( Buffer& ) {
    return _transport -> transmit(); }
    void releaseTransport() { if(_transport)
    _transport- release(); }

    ~ClientEndpoint() { releaseTransport(); }

    private:
    ChannelSession *_transport;
};
```

The programmer can define appropriate interaction abstractions by deriving from the `ClientEndpoint` class. Here we assume that they have already implemented the classes `Port<T>`, encapsulating queued message ports, and `PortClient<T>`, by which a client can transmit values to a remote message port over a transport channel. We will not describe the implementation in any detail since it involves marshaling and the use of thread synchronization libraries that are not germane to the issue.

```
template <class T>
class PortClient : public ClientEndpoint {
public:
    bool out( T &message ) {
        Buffer buf;
        ... marshal message into the buffer...
        return transmit(buf);
    }
};
```

The main application code then looks as follows:

```
1   PortClient<int> send;
2   Reference remote_server =
    GetReferenceFromSomewhere();
3
4   // Select a protocol and get the interface of
5   // its connect service
6
7   ConnectService &connect = SelectProtocol ();
8
9   // Acquire a ChannelSession connecting the Port
10  // Client to a remote Port and pass ownership of
11  // it to the PortClient.
12  ChannelSession *session =
13      connect.request( sender, remote_server );
14  send.bind(session);
15
16  // Send 10 integers
17
18  for( int i = 0; i < 10; i++ ) {
19      int number = GetANumberFromSomewhere(i);
20      send.out(number);
21  }
22
23  // Ending the program will cause the PortClient
24  // object to be destroyed, which will
25  // automatically release the protocol session.
26
27  cerr << "Transmitted 10 integers" << endl;
```

Lines 12 to 14 show the use of the Abstract Session pattern. The program selects a protocol service and requests that the service connect the `PortClient` object to a remote `Port`. The connect service returns a `ChannelSession` that manages the state of the connection, and the program hands ownership of the session to the `PortClient`. When the program calls the `send` operation of the `PortClient` from line 20, the `PortClient` object marshals the integer into a buffer and transmits it over the `ChannelSession`. When the `PortClient` goes out of scope at the end of the program, its destructor releases the session, closing the connection.

KNOWN USES

The Abstract Session pattern is widely used in the implementation of object-oriented communication protocol software. The x-kernel framework [Hutchinson+1991] and the ACE communications toolkit [Schmidt1994] both use this pattern.

Microsoft's Object Linking and Embedding (OLE) framework [Microsoft1993] uses the Abstract Session pattern for managing the size and location of embedded objects. An object such as a word-processing document that can contain embedded objects is known as a "container" and stores pointers to the `IOleObject` interfaces of its embedded objects. Through this interface the container can, among other things, query the required size of the embedded object and set the size and position of the object. When a new `IOleObject` is embedded in the container, the container creates a Session object, known as a client-site, in which it stores information about the actual position and size of the embedded object. The client-site object implements the `IOle-ClientSite` interface that the container passes to the embedded object and through which the embedded object can request to be resized. When an embedded object makes a resize request through its `IOle-ClientSite` interface, the container updates the size and position of all its embedded objects based on the information stored in the client-site session objects.

The Java Abstract Windowing Toolkit (AWT) [Gosling+1996] uses the Abstract Session pattern in several places. An example is the `Graphics` interface, which provides a common interface for drawing graphics on a variety of devices, such as windows, bitmaps, and printers. An object that wants to draw onto a device asks the device to create a graphics context object and receives a reference to the object's `Graphics` interface. The graphics context stores the current drawing state, such as the current font, background and foreground colors, and other states required to render drawing operations onto the associated device.

RELATED PATTERNS

The Abstract Session pattern is one way of implementing the Session pattern [Lea1995].

It is also related to the Facade, Factory Method, and Mediator patterns from the GoF book [Gamma+1995]:

- The Facade pattern uses a single intermediate object to hide the complexities of a framework of cooperating objects from the users of that framework. In contrast, the Session pattern uses multiple intermediate objects to decouple objects that provide a service from the objects that use that service and to provide type-safe interaction between objects that interact only through abstract interfaces.

- The Server object uses the Factory Method to create sessions for a client. This ensures that sessions can be initialized correctly by the server object.

- A Mediator object controls the interaction of multiple cooperating objects. The Server object of the Abstract Session pattern can be viewed as a form of Mediator controlling the interaction of all of its clients. The session objects can be viewed as simple Mediators controlling the interaction of the server and a single client.

The Acceptor and Connector patterns [Schmidt1995] are both examples of higher-level patterns that make use of the Abstract Session pattern.

The Abstract Session pattern can be used to implement an Adapter [Gamma+1995] around objects or nonobject-oriented libraries that use an unsafe implementation of the Session pattern.

ACKNOWLEDGMENTS

The author acknowledges many stimulating discussions with members of the Department of Computing, Imperial College, during the crystallization of this pattern and the writing of this chapter, in particular Steve Crane, Naranker Dulay, and Hal Fosså. The author also would like to thank Doug Schmidt, who shepherded this pattern through its submission to EuroPLoP '97 and suggested many improvements. Last but not least, many thanks to those who gave comments on the paper at EuroPLoP '97 and all who made the workshop such an enjoyable and rewarding experience.

We acknowledge the financial support of British Telecommunications plc through the Management of Multiservice Networks project.

REFERENCES

[Gamma+1995] E. Gamma, R. Helm, R. Johnson, and J. Vlissides. *Design Patterns: Elements of Reusable Object-Oriented Software.* Reading, MA: Addison-Wesley, 1995.

[Gosling+1996] J. Gosling, F. Yellin, and The Java Team. *The Java Application Programming Interface.* Volume 2: *Window Toolkit and Applets.* Reading, MA: Addison-Wesley, 1996.

[Hutchinson+1991] N.C. Hutchinson and L.L. Peterson. "The x-kernel: An Architecture for Implementing Network Protocols." *IEEE Transactions on Software Engineering,* 17(1): 64–76, 1991.

[Lea1995] D. Lea. *Sessions.* Paper presented at ECOOP '95, Aarhus, Denmark, 1995.

[Lewine1991] D. Lewine. *POSIX Programmer's Guide: Writing Portable Unix Applications.* Sebastopol, CA: O'Reilly & Associates, 1991.

[Microsoft1993] Microsoft Corporation (ed.). *Object Linking and Embedding Version 2 (OLE2) Programmer's Reference,* volumes 1 and 2. Redmond, WA: Microsoft Press, 1993.

[OMG1995] The Object Management Group. *The Common Object Request Broker: Architecture and Specifications, Version 2.0.* The Object Management Group, OMG Headquarters, 492 Old Connecticut Path, Framingham, MA 01701, 1995.

[Petzold1990] C. Petzold. *Programming Windows.* Redmond, WA: Microsoft Press, 1990.

[Rogerson1997] D. Rogerson. *Inside COM – Microsoft's Component Object Model.* Redmond, WA: Microsoft Press, 1997.

[Schmidt1994] D.C. Schmidt. "ACE: An Object-Oriented Framework for Developing Distributed Applications." In *Proceedings of the 6th USENIX C++ Technical Conference*. Cambridge, MA: USENIX Association, April 1994.

[Schmidt1995] D.C. Schmidt. "Acceptor and Connector: Design Patterns for Actively and Passively Initializing Network Services." In J.O. Coplien and D.C. Schmidt (eds.), *Pattern Languages of Program Design*. Reading, MA: Addison-Wesley, 1995.

[Stevens1990] W.R. Stevens. *Unix Network Programming*. Englewood Cliffs, NJ: Prentice-Hall, 1990.

10

BODYGUARD

Fernando Das Neves and Alejandra Garrido

INTENT

THE INTENT OF THE BODYGUARD PATTERN is to allow objects to be shared and to control access to them in a distributed environment without system-level support for distributed objects. *Bodyguard* is an object behavioral pattern that simplifies the management of object sharing over a network. It provides message dispatching validation and assignment of access rights to objects in nonlocal environments to prevent incorrect access to an object in collaborative applications.

MOTIVATION

To illustrate the Bodyguard pattern, consider a distributed environment for building and browsing the common knowledge of a team about World Wide Web pages, like the one depicted in Figure 10.1. Pages are collected by WWW browsers as team members visit WWW nodes. Those browsers capture pages, create WWW Page objects, and pass these objects to a repository running on a different host, which tentatively classifies the pages.

The repository is simultaneously accessed by many tools. Let us focus on object sharing among the repository and the tools. The repository can be

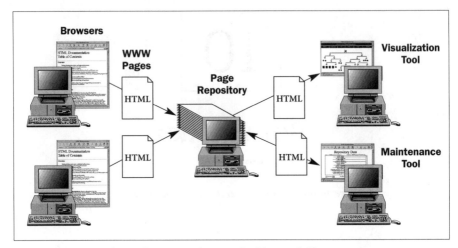

Figure 10.1. Tools working together, probably on different computers, over a common repository of WWW pages. Some of the tools can add pages to the repository (like browsers), others can inspect them (Visualization tool), and others can perform both activities (Maintenance tool).

consulted by two kinds of tools: those that are used to analyze and query the repository content and those that are in charge of cleaning and organizing the repository (by deleting irrelevant pages and reclassifying some others that were mistakenly classified).

The forces that need to be considered in this problem are:

- The need to share objects among a server and many accessing and updating tools, marshaling messages to support the communication.

- The need to control access rights to prevent improper access to any object that is distributed, depending on the context usage. In this example, querying and visualization tools should not be allowed to delete entries in the repository.

- The need to provide support for distributed objects. Sometimes an operating system does not support distributed objects (as CORBA does), or you do not want to pay the price for the flexibility and wide range of service those systems provide when you do not need all of them. Also there are applications with limited needs for object distribution running on platforms (for example, low-end UNIX boxes) where the supposition of CORBA availability conspires against the portability of the application.

A preliminary solution could be achieved by exchanging data with standard operating system mechanisms like RPC and message-passing, but there is an impedance mismatch between applications that benefit from objects throughout their design and the sharing of these objects using these low-level mechanisms.

What we need is to decouple the object sharing from communication and from access control. In the example, the repository would only be in charge of maintaining pages and replying to queries for the pages it contains. An object that we call `Transporter` would be in charge of message marshaling and communication between different servers. We can use proxies to maintain surrogate objects in remote sites. A special object, called `Bodyguard`, would be in charge of maintaining and controlling access rights to the objects for different message categories. These objects and their relationships comprise the Bodyguard pattern.

The *Bodyguard* pattern is an alternative to being impeded by platform-dependent data-transport system calls and the unclear separation of access control from data transport. It allows decoupling of access control from transport mechanisms and dynamic change of access rights and method dispatching.

The following two figures show how the WWW page-sharing scheme looks when it is designed following the Bodyguard pattern. Figure 10.2 shows the scheme from the point of view of the Maintenance Tool asking to delete a page. Figure 10.3 shows how, using the same scheme, the Visualization tool is prohibited from deleting the page.

The essential components of the Bodyguard pattern are (1) the object to be shared, (2) the object that controls the access to that object (`Bodyguard`, and (3) the object that is in charge of the communication among hosts (`Transporter`). There is one `Transporter` in every host. Each `Transporter` may know all the objects that can be shared, and so the objects can assure the `Transporter` exclusive access to them. Proxies redirect messages to their `Bodyguards` and optionally pack the messages as objects. If the messages are allowed, according to the `Bodyguard`'s access rights, then the local `Transporter` sends the request to the remote `Transporter`, which in turn unpacks the request and sends the message to the real object the proxy stands for.

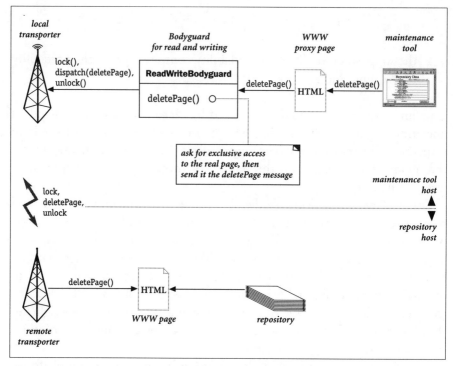

Figure 10.2. The page-sharing scheme for the Maintenance tool. The tool sends messages to the proxy page, which in turn delegates the message to the Bodyguard *to check. Since this* Bodyguard *allows writing operations, the message* deletePage() *is sent to the real page. In this example, the repository is not notified of the operations.*

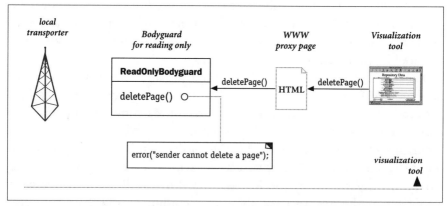

Figure 10.3. The page-sharing scheme instantiated for the Visualization tool, showing how ReadOnlyBodyguard *(a kind of* Bodyguard *that does not allow modification messages) denies the request to delete a page. Note that since the* Bodyguard *denies the request, there is no communication with its transporter or between transporters.*

212

APPLICABILITY

Use the Bodyguard pattern when you

- Have control over the construction of applications that access shared objects.

- Need to share objects in a distributed environment with a common object implementation, but the platform lacks system-level support for distributed objects (CORBA or the like), and authentication control is not mandatory.

- Need to synchronize and pool messages passed to shared objects.

- Need fine-grained control of access restrictions, depending on who requests to share the object.

- Need dynamic change in access rights.

- Need identity checking and assignment of access rights to objects in order to prevent incorrect behavior from objects of an application, but not to guard against security violations from those objects.

Do not use the Bodyguard pattern when

- Your application demands strict authentication of object identity in order to grant access rights and to prevent unauthorized access to restricted information.

- You need support for complex distributed object services, like licensing, externalization, and querying (as with CORBAServices).

- You have a very heterogenous environment, with various object models (like different inheritance and exception propagation models) and different network protocols.

STRUCTURE

The structure of the Bodyguard pattern is illustrated in the OMT diagram shown in Figure 10.4. In the examples and Figures 10.2, 10.3, and 10.4, WWWPages correspond to RealSubjects, WWWProxyPages are Proxy instances, and ReadWriteBodyguard and ReadOnlyBodyguard are `SpecializedBodyguards`. When a tool needs a page, it asks the Repository for the page. If the Repository has the desired page, it answers affirmatively, and a `WWWProxyPage` is created by the `Transporter` at the tool location. Depending on the access rights assigned to the new proxy page by the Repository, an instance of `ReadWriteBodyguard` or `ReadOnlyBodyguard` is created and designated as the bodyguard of the new Proxy Page. A `ProxyPage` class would provide a template for message dispatching. Instances of a `Transporter` class work as an external interface for communication I/O, marshal messages and their parameters, and register objects that can be shared or their remote images (proxies plus `Bodyguards`). Classes `ReadOnlyBodyguard` and `ReadWrite-Bodyguard` provide conformance checking for message dispatching, for example, `ReadOnlyBodyguard` will refuse to delete a page.

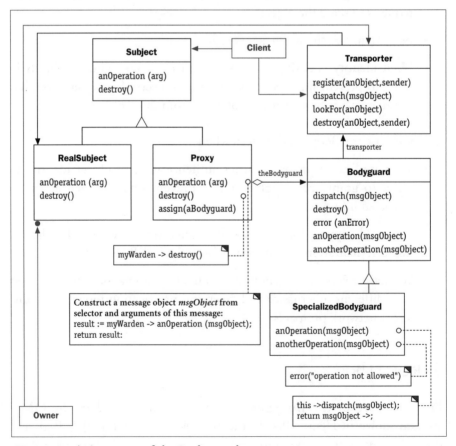

Figure 10.4. Structure of the Bodyguard pattern.

PARTICIPANTS

The following delineations define the participants and their roles in the pattern.

- Real Subject:
  - defines the object meant to be shared.

- Transporter:
  - controls the communication I/O, performing the marshaling that is necessary in order to encode objects and messages to be sent over the communication channel. In fact, we will have a `Transporter` in each remote machine so that marshaling will be encapsulated among the different instances, making it transparent to the rest of the application.
  - registers the associations of shared objects and remote proxies.
  - communicates with other `Transporters` to optionally implement atomic operations over shared objects, such as locking and total reference count of objects.
  - creates proxies of shared objects upon requests to access them.

- Bodyguard:
  - works as a mediator between `Proxy` and `Transporter` instances by sending method-dispatching requests, notifying objects of destruction, and optionally handling error notifications. `Bodyguard` is an abstract class; `SpecializedBodyguard` is the one that implements concrete `Bodyguards`.
  - controls client's access to the real subject, asking the `Transporter` to carry messages to the `RealSubject`, when permitted.
  - specifies the protocol that will be implemented by `SpecializedBodyguards`.

- SpecializedBodyguard:
  - implements methods to provide conformance checking for message dispatching, both in access rights restrictions and low-level synchronization and exclusion. There will be a subclass of `SpecializedBodyguard` for each kind or group of operations that needs a particular access right.

- Proxy
  - acts as a surrogate to the real subject.

- provides an interface identical to `RealSubject`.
- maintains a reference to a `Bodyguard` for the `RealSubject` and delegates every request to it.

COLLABORATIONS

- An object that is intended to be shared will be passed as a parameter of the register message sent to the `Transporter` in order to become broadly known (see Figure 10.5). The `Transporter` then records the object. The sender of the register message is designated as the owner of the object and is allowed to destroy the object.

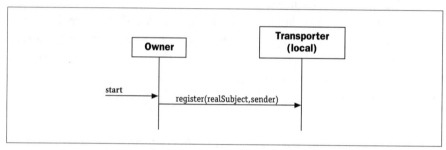

Figure 10.5. Interaction diagram for Object Registration.

- The first access to a remote object is performed by asking the local `Transporter` for it. The `Transporter` will search for the object in the network. If it finds the object, then it will create a local `Bodyguard` and `Proxy` to control access to the remote object (see Figure 10.6).

- In subsequent transactions, when a client needs to send a request to the remote object, the client will interact with the `Proxy` that, in turn, delegates the request to the `Bodyguard`. The `Bodyguard` will check the validity of the request and, when appropriate, communicate with its local `Transporter`, which is in charge of sending the requests to the `Transporter` in the remote host. The remote `Transporter` will then send the request to the remote object and send back the proper response (see Figure 10.7).

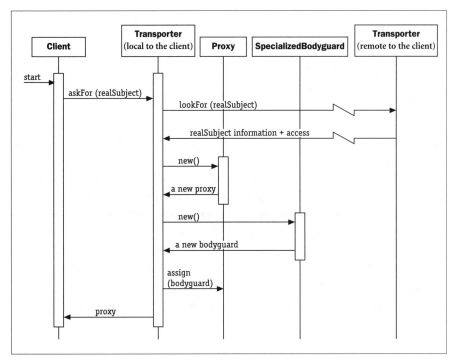

Figure 10.6. Interaction diagram for Remote Object Access.

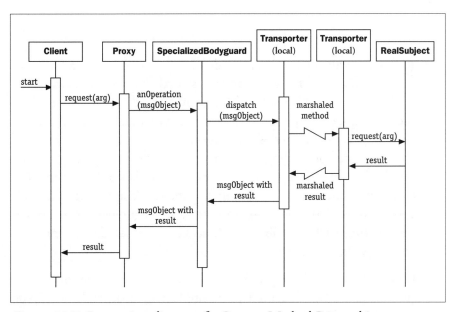

Figure 10.7. Interaction diagram for Remote Method Dispatching.

CONSEQUENCES

The Bodyguard pattern decouples access control from transport mechanisms, allowing the dynamic change of access rights. This decoupling allows the separation of data transport from the definition of different types of access rights over the objects meant to be shared, and from synchronization control. It also isolates the access restriction mechanism, because `Bodyguards` are only visible for proxies and not for external objects.

It trades generality for simplicity. In situations with restricted requisites and limited resources, the Bodyguard pattern offers an object-sharing scheme that is easier to understand and implement than a full, system-level object-sharing system. Bodyguards may also be used to record debugging or tracing information as complete messages, queued messages, and so forth.

As a drawback, the pattern implies augmenting the levels of indirection to reach an object. If communication speed is more important than access validation, then a scheme in which objects talk directly to each other should be implemented.

VARIANTS

Variations on the Bodyguard pattern as described include the following:

- Rights Assignment by Class vs. Identity. At the moment a `Transporter` receives a request to access a shared object and the availability of the object is confirmed, the `Transporter` has to decide which access rights to assign and create the corresponding `Bodyguard`. Access rights can be divided into general categories and one of the categories assigned depending upon the class of the client belongs to and the kind of object it is requesting (or upon the class of the object to be shared plus the object identity of the client). Assignment by class is best performed by the `Transporters`; assignment by identity is best performed by collaboration between `Transporter` and the object owner.

- General Bodyguards vs. Protocol Bodyguards. The number of `Bodyguard` subclasses that need to be implemented depends heavily on how specific the control should be and the different access rights combinations. Bodyguards implement access control by the definition of a set of operations that express the general categories in which methods can be classified. Every operation stands for a kind of access, like reading, writing, and deleting. Proxy instances send requests for method dispatching by calling the proper type of operation in their Bodyguards for the category the method belongs to.

Granularity of the set of operations varies depending on the security enforcement needed by the classes whose instances will be shared. It ranges from checking only reading and writing permissions to extreme cases in which every operation in a Proxy has the same operation in a Bodyguard. In that case, operations in the Bodyguard are implemented knowing the semantics of the operations they will control in a particular Proxy, at the cost of having to code a particular Bodyguard for every protocol to be checked. It should be noted that it is not always necessary to implement a Bodyguard subclass for every class whose objects are going to be shared. Instead, a single Bodyguard can be used for a whole hierarchy. For example, in Smalltalk a single CollectionBodyguard class can be used to control the Collection hierarchy for a single access right, as the protocol is completely defined in the abstract class Collection.

IMPLEMENTATION

Message marshaling, or the way proxies redirect a message invocation to their Bodyguards for checking and dispatching, and the way the Transporter expresses that remote invocation, depends heavily on the language.

Languages that keep meta-information about classes make it easier to know what method we are trying to remotely dispatch and to send that knowledge to the remote site. For instance, messages in Smalltalk are objects in themselves. For any message it is possible to obtain a symbol describing the message selector (message header). Conversely, having a selector and a class, it is possible to find the method that matches the selector. This means that an easy path exists from a message to a symbol and back, a path the Transporter can use to marshal the message.

On the other hand, there are languages that discard class and object meta-information at compile time. For those languages, a message object needs to be explicitly created by a `Bodyguard` every time one of its methods is called. The `Bodyguard` then checks access rights, the `Transporter` at the origin marshals the parameter, and the `Transporter` at the destination decodes the message invocation and calls the real object.

Sometimes a back-end operation is implemented to provide the meta-information the language discards and to add accessory information for garbage collection and atomic operations. A language-independent implementation of a back-end facility for supporting distributed objects on languages with no metaclass protocol can be found in *Amadeus* [McHugh93+].

PARTICIPANT IMPLEMENTATION

- Proxies. A detailed explanation of implementations of proxies for remote access can be found in [Rohnert96] as *Remote Proxies*.

- Transporter. They manage the shared objects residing on every host. A Transporter is composed of two concurrent units. One is in charge of marshaling the arguments of a message for a remote message invocation and deciding for each argument whether to pass-by-proxy or pass-by-copy [McCullough87]. Some values cannot be passed by proxy, such as numbers in hybrid languages like C++. The second unit manages the communication in the opposite direction, from a remote host to a local object.

  Transporter implementation can vary from a concurrent process to an independent daemon, depending on the complexity and flexibility of the services provided. Nevertheless, the context of the problem that Bodyguard addresses and all of the implementations to date suggest using one process or many collaborative processes. Either can be implemented using the Reactor pattern [Schmidt95]. Reactor manages three different handlers. `RequestAcceptor` is created in every host to receive incoming requests for sharing an object that resides on that host. It checks that the object resides there and sends a message "OK to share" (the object ID on the host and an access right). At that time, a Message Handler is created by the `RequestAcceptor` for receiving marshaled messages from a given host, if no such acceptor already exists.

  At the host where the request for a remote object began, an `OK_to_shareAcceptor` waits for acknowledgment to create the remote proxy and the associated `Bodyguard`, depending on the rights the originating `Bodyguard` has determined. After the acknowledgment is received, the `OK_to_shareAcceptor` is eliminated from its `Receptor`.

- Object Creation. `Transporters` must create `Proxy` instances upon requests to access shared objects. The strategy to create a `Proxy` depends on the implementation. If the `Transporter` can access all instance variables of the object, and if the object has a copy operator, then it can clone a new object from a prototype object. If the `Transporter` is able to know all classes and it can keep metaclass information, as in Distributed Smalltalk [Bennett87], then it can directly create the instances from the class information. In the most general case, it can use a separate hierarchy of Abstract Factories [Gamma+95].

- Access rights. If access rights are going to change dynamically, it could be the case that some object that references a shared object needs to know whether that object is local or remote, shared or private, and the remote object's current access rights before performing an operation. This behavior could be achieved even before the object is shared, by implementing a default protocol in the `Subject` class and redefining it in its `Proxy` subclass. Methods like `isShared()` or `isRemote()` can be implemented in the `Subject` class to give a default answer when the queried action has not yet been performed (that is, answering false for `isShared()` and `isRemote()`). At the local site, messages are answered automatically by the object by being inherited; at the remote site, messages are answered by the `Proxy`, which asks the `Bodyguard` when necessary.

- Object destruction and garbage collection. `Transporters` have to be notified of object creation and destruction in order to keep the list of shared objects up to date. This is not a problem in languages with explicit object destruction; the moment the object destructor is called, it is trapped by the `Proxy`. In those languages with garbage collection, either a hook can be triggered at the moment of object destruction (like the *finalize* method in Smalltalk-80 [ParcPlace94]) or the garbage collector must be modified to check for local and remote references, as is the case in Distributed Smalltalk [Bennett87]. Object destruction is one of the access rights the `Bodyguard` grants or prohibits.

RELATED PATTERNS

Gamma and Rohnert discuss some issues and housekeeping tasks related to remote proxies [Gamma+95, Rohnert96]. It is evident that we need proxies to provide a local representative for an object in a different address space and to count references to the real object. Gamma and Rohnert also discuss "protection proxies," those which also provide access control. Nevertheless, the Proxy pattern is not enough for a distributed environment, because there is no explicit description of how to achieve low-level synchronization mechanisms. The Bodyguard pattern uses the Proxy pattern but enriches the structure with additional control (`Bodyguard`) and transport-related (`Transporter`) objects.

The Reactor and Acceptor patterns [Schmidt95] are also related to the Bodyguard pattern in the way in which the `Transporter` works. Reactor and Acceptor interact in order to receive login requests and create handlers for them. `Transporters` perform similar functions each time a remote shared request is made, creating proxies and `Bodyguards` in order to control access. `Transporter` and Reactor both pull incoming messages and maintain the association between objects and their proxies, or handlers and their callbacks and clients, respectively. Nevertheless, many differences may be found in the intents of these patterns, because although both operate in distributed environments, Reactor is intended for a client/server architecture, whereas Bodyguard pattern is designed for a peer-to-peer environment.

The Bodyguard pattern is also strongly related to the Broker pattern [Buschmann+96]. In one sense, Bodyguard is a specialized Broker structure (a kind of "Indirect Broker System" in the Broker taxonomy). `Transporters` take the place of Brokers and handle the task of message unmarshaling of server-side proxies. The `Proxy` class in the Bodyguard pattern stands for client-side proxies in the Broker. The main difference between the Bodyguard and Broker Patterns is that Broker is a high-level pattern; it describes interactions among subsystems like the transport subsystem (client proxy, broker, bridge) and language-mapping (server-side broker, object interfaces). As such, the typical application of the Broker pattern involves large-scale and possibly heterogeneous networks that have total independence from system-specific details as a mandatory requirement. There is also a great distance between the Broker pattern and a concrete implementation like CORBA; a large amount of detail must be filled in before being able to produce an implementation.

Bodyguard is a mid-level pattern, in that it expresses a design closer to actual implementation than does the Broker. As is apparent in the following section, the environment of a Bodyguard instantiation is more restricted than that of a Broker. It involves cooperative applications, usually developed as a set, that use access control to ensure global stability in shared objects, rather than ensuring their security. In the example related under Motivation, `Bodyguards` check that read/write protocols are not violated by any tool.

When `Transporters` need to create `Proxies` and `Bodyguards`, Abstract Factories [Gamma+95] is one of the more general schemes to manage this, although as previously described, it is often the case that simpler schemes, although less general, are used for the sake of performance.

KNOWN USES

Dollimore shows an implementation of shared objects with access restriction in Eiffel [Dollimore+93]. Objects are represented remotely by proxies, which are associated with a Bodyguard known as a "filter." Proxies and filters together build a Private Access Channel, which guards against unauthorized methods. Access rights can be changed by replacing the filter. Proxies manage remote invocation of methods by RPC and do not approach the remote object directly, but through the filter associated with the object.

Another forwarding mechanism for object sharing is implemented in Smalltalk-80, which is composed of proxies on the remote side and transporters (known as `TransporterRooms`) on both sides [McCullough87]. An associated `PolicyMaker` is used to decide whether to pass message parameters by proxy or by value. Object creation is directly managed by `TransporterRooms` that work together with a distributed garbage collector to manage the list of available share objects. No access control is provided. `TransporterRooms` are implemented as concurrent processes.

Distributed Smalltalk (DS) [Bennett87] melds the `Bodyguard` role with the Transporter role (collectively known in DS as `RemoteObject-Table`). In DS it is possible to allow or inhibit access to an object, and also to designate an object as an "agent" of another object. Agents can process messages or redirect them to another object in a manner similar to the way `Bodyguards` filter messages and redirect them. DS has no way of giving different access rights to proxies; access control is allowed only at the host where the original object resides. Local objects are created by the `Remote-ObjectTable` and are directly managed by the `messageProcess`, which works in coordination with a distributed garbage collector. `RemoteObjectTable` is implemented by three concurrent processes.

ACKNOWLEDGMENTS

The authors would like to thank the PLoP '96 shepherd and all the people in the winters' workshops at PLoP '96 and OOPSLA '95 for their useful comments for improvement.

REFERENCES

[Bennett87] J. Bennett. "The Design and Implementation of Distributed Smalltalk." In the *Proceedings of OOPSLA '87: A Conference on Object-Oriented Programming Systems, Languages and Applications*. Orlando, FL: ACM Press, 1987.

[Buschmann+96] F. Buschmann, R. Meunier, H. Rohnert, P. Sommerlad, and M. Stal. *Pattern-Oriented Software Architecture: A System of Patterns*. New York: John Wiley & Sons, 1996, pp. 99–122.

[Dollimore+93] J. Dollimore and X. Wang. "The Private Access Channel: A Security Mechanism for Shared Distributed Objects." In *Proceedings of TOOLS 10: Technology of Object-Oriented Languages and Systems*. Englewood Cliffs, NJ: Prentice Hall, 1993.

[Gamma+95] E. Gamma, R. Helm, R. Johnson, and J. Vlissides. *Design Patterns: Elements of Reusable Object-Oriented Software*. Reading, MA: Addison-Wesley, 1995.

[McCullough87] P. McCullough. "Transparent Forwarding: First Steps." In *Proceedings of OOPSLA '87: A Conference on Object-Oriented Programming Systems, Languages and Applications*. Orlando, FL: ACM Press, 1987.

[McHugh+93] C. McHugh, and V. Cahill. "Eiffel**: An Implementation of Eiffel on Amadeus, a Persistent, Distributed Applications Support Environment." In *Proceedings of TOOLS 10: Technology of Object-Oriented Languages and Systems*. Englewood Cliffs, NJ: Prentice Hall, 1993.

[ParcPlace94] *Visual Works Object Reference*. Santa Clara, CA: ParcPlace Systems, Inc., 1994.

[Rohnert96] H. Rohnert. "The Proxy Pattern Revisited." In J.M. Vlissides, J.O. Coplien, and N.L. Keith (eds.), *Pattern Languages of Program Design* 2. Reading, MA: Addison-Wesley, 1996, pp. 105–118.

[Schmidt95] D. Schmidt. "Reactor: An Object Behavioral Pattern for Concurrent Event Demultiplexing and Dispatching." *In Pattern Languages of Program Design*. J.O. Coplien, D.C. Schmidt, eds. Addison-Wesley, 1995, 529–545.

[Stal95] M. Stal. "The Broker Architectural Framework." A workshop on Concurrent, Parallel and Distributed Patterns of Object-Oriented Programming held at OOPSLA '95.

11

WORTH A THOUSAND WORDS

James O. Coplien

IN MY MARCH COLUMN, I underscored the geometric nature of patterns, and pointed out that *Nature of Order* [1] – Alexander's forthcoming work – underscores this aspect of patterns that has been there all along. Alexander has always emphasized the importance of a sketch as the essence of a pattern, a point I've emphasized in many past columns.

Many contemporary patterns lack pictures or, if they do have sketches, they are cast in standard design notations. These design notations can't communicate what Alexander wants to communicate in a sketch – that's one of the points we'll address in this column.

Pictures portray structure. Some early software patterns are about little more than data structure. But patterns are more than that: they are also a process that tells us how to make the thing in the picture, that tells us what problem it solves.

So every pattern sketch comes with a process – a text that tells us when we must build the thing depicted in the sketch, and how to build it. There are some principles behind these processes, deeper, more general processes of piecemeal growth. Those, too, were described in the March column.

It's process that distinguishes useful patterns from patterns that we simply observe in the world around us. The process part of these pictures is the first step to generativity, and generativity is a first step to solving difficult problems. The sketches of a pattern language combine to build emergent structures we can't foresee in individual patterns. The sketches, and the processes that combine them, are tied closely together. So it was in Alexander's early work; we'll look at that below, too.

© 1998 Lucent Technologies. Originally published in *C++ Report* 10(5), May/June 1998, pp. 51–54, 71, 101 Communications. Used with permission from the author.

But first, we need to look at sketches and geometry, identified as important system elements in the March column. Let's start here.

THE SKETCH

Alexander emphasizes again and again the importance of the sketch for a pattern, a point I've emphasized in this column many times. Alexander's concern for geometry helps bring this emphasis into focus. The sketch shows not only the major relationships between parts – which is the facet of patterns that perhaps most interested the object-oriented software community – but it relates directly to our sense of aesthetics. People share the cognitive processes by which they appreciate beauty, and the sketch appeals to that universal sense of aesthetics.

The software designer is no stranger to design diagrams using standard notations. How are Alexander's sketches different from OMT, UML, or Booch notation? My colleague Joe Davison has an interesting theory: He notes that OMT diagrams don't easily compose, whereas sketches do. (Try composing OMT diagrams for two patterns you use together.) Such composition is fundamental to piecemeal growth, and I think our current notations are antithetical to such an approach to software. I recently evaluated an OO analysis and design course from a prominent vendor: Software maintenance was conspicuous in its absence.

Alexander's early work [2] portrayed system structure in a simple set of composable diagrams. Each element not only captured a geometric structure, but encoded requirements addressed by the element. For example, in his work on Indian villages, the element:

is a demonstration farm that embodies requirements such as getting the best cotton and cash crop, food grain crop, and vegetable crop; reflects the fact that crops must be brought home from the fields; improves the quality of fodder available; demonstrates projects that spread by example; gives more power and respect to the Panchayat, etc.

This element:

is a water distribution system for the fields; it captures requirements such as the need to divide land among sons of successive generations, the desire of people to own land personally, cooperative farming, maintenance of irrigation facilities, and abolition of Zamindari and uneven land distribution. And the element:

is a water collection unit built in the highest corner of the village at right angles to the terrain. It's designed to reclaim uncultivated land, develop horticulture, accommodate full collection of underground water for irrigation and monsoon water for use, drain the land to prevent waterlogging, support a healthy plant ecology, address road and dwelling erosion, etc. The small filled circles are springs or wells.

These elements can be combined into a village:

Each drawing isn't just a sketch, but has behind it a set of requirements that come together in the structure representing it. The structure of a village brings together these elements to minimize conflict between requirements. Alexander guides this integration by making a graph of the dependencies between requirements; the village structure emerges from the graph. That is, there is a process for assembling these elements in meaningful ways, a process that is germane to the elements themselves.

Note that at a fundamental level this is analogous to principles deep beneath the object paradigm. Parnas' original work on modularity emphasized that modules hid "design secrets," which strikes me as similar to the way Alexander's pictures embody design constraints [3].

This formative work of Alexander led to patterns and later to his theory of centers; the same themes recur in each of these manifestations. For example, we see a foreshadowing of forces in the encapsulation of requirement dependencies in each of these elements, and we see the geometric groundwork that would play out to a degree in patterns and more strongly in *Nature of Order*. And we see a strong process presence in each stage of development. One factor common to the above notation and to patterns is the cultural sensitivity of the design elements. The theory of centers is more universal in scope.

I thought a long time about what it would mean to carry these recurring themes into software, particularly with the emphases brought forth in the theory of centers. Alexander postulated criteria to judge whether such a theory for software would capture what he wanted to capture in architecture:

> In effect, the core software issue is this, I think: I have been wondering what kind of entity there is – if one had to choose a type of entity of which it could be said that it is the only component, the essential and single component of all computer programs, what is it?
>
> Is it a function?
>
> Is it a list?
>
> Is it (probably) something else?
>
> Could one say that every successful program is a function of functions?
>
> Could one say that every successful program is a list of lists (lambda calculus)?
>
> In architecture, anyway, there is such a thing because one can say, accurately and truthfully, that every building is a center made of centers. That is one of the key insights in *Nature of Order*. Indeed in 3D space, every living structure is a center made of centers. But software structures do not live in 3D space.
>
> So for software structures one must ask: What kind of x is there that makes it true to say that every successful program is an x of x's?

That is the only question which will let us find out what the equivalents of centers in software really are. It is only when we begin to identify such an x, that the whole domain of possible programs would become visible, in a meaningful way [4].

Might it be reflection? Instantiation (including recursion)? Recursion itself? I thought about this for a while, focusing on Alexander's earlier suggestion to me that a theory of beauty in software would parallel the theory of centers only if the "space" on which it were based comprised dimensions with homogeneous units. It couldn't be time in one dimension, space in another, features in a third, and so forth. I conceded that geometry itself – the space of the code on the page – was a good starting point. A great program is a center of centers, and the centers are geometric.

And then I took things a step further to deal with the predominate computer science models that are preoccupied with time and space. Data structures are spatial, but functions are temporal (following the bouncing program counter through time). Program visualization techniques have long portrayed the temporal dimension of programs in spatial renditions. I theorized that functional languages might provide a good formalism to fold the time dimension back into space.

That's where I was when I wrote the March column. Alexander responded:

> I found your article, and your idea about the spatial structure of a computer program rather amazing. At first I thought, this cannot be, it seemed trivial – and then it began to dawn on me that it might be true, there was more structure than I had expected, visible in that form – and it might indeed give real clues as to the goodness of the program. Your report on Dick Gabriel's work is also very enlightening in this regard and I am delighted he is getting such good results. . . .[5]

And that brings us up to this column, where we scrutinize geometry a bit more and consider the relationship between sketches, patterns, and the theory of centers.

BEYOND HOPP

After I wrote my last column, I went back and revisited the sketches in Gerard Meszaros' HOPP [6]. You'll remember that I portrayed HOPP like this:

What's missing in this diagram? If you look at the picture, the place where the two `HalfCalls` interact is itself a latent center. This makes sense from an application perspective: The coordination of the activities of two half calls is an activity – a center – in its own right. In the text of HOPP, Gerard chose to use the word "between" (instead of, for example, "connecting") to describe the Protocol that is the final "P" in HOPP. And the original picture begs to make the center explicit.

My colleague Warren Montgomery took a look at this and noted: "Half objects are 1 – 1 and almost always asymmetric in responsibilities and initiative. `Call` models can have grouped relationships and be symmetric."

Let's rework the picture to emphasize these geometric properties of the pattern. We apply a structure-preserving transformation that increases the wholeness of the system; in this case, we do so by making the latent center explicit. We might better depict HOPP like this:

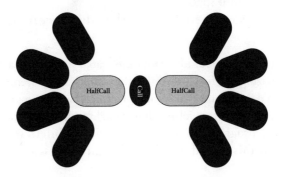

I've also added the objects (the black blobs) that interact with the `Half-Calls` as Gerard depicted it in the original version of HOPP. And the model is now more symmetric about "call." This is important; in his mail, Warren went on to point out:

> Making the model symmetric, if you can, leads to great simplifications. [A system I worked on] started out symmetric, no notion of originating and terminating terminal processes, just terminal processes. The `call` protocols were all symmetric. This made it very easy to take the next step of going to multi-party calls. . . .

The hardware . . . defined something called a tiepoint and everyone connected to a tiepoint was magically conferenced together. . . . No worrying about adding bridges and re-doing connections, just add people to tiepoints and the call goes from 2-way to 3-way to n-way automagically. . . .

Communication among the half calls on the same terminal started out being implemented through variables in terminal data structures, which was ad-hoc, and asymmetric with respect to the communication with half calls on the same call. The limitations quickly became apparent as we started to do more features that caused three or more calls to appear on a terminal at one time. The terminal multicast also formed a symmetry with respect to the tiepoint multicast that satisfied some sense of a need for closure. . . .

I . . . drew the conclusion that

- State machines are best handled by double dispatch from one reception point;

- State machines need ways to wildcard on both state and input . . .

- The utility of enter/leave actions that take place always on entering or leaving a state no matter how you get there became obvious as well.

The result again has symmetry, wildcarding in both dimensions, actions on enter and leave, state and input equally. . . .[7]

As a practical consideration, you need a `Call` center between the `Half-Call` centers. Why? For the same reason that airlines have hub cities: It makes call routing more straightforward while reducing the need for complete network connectivity. This is called three-part call processing or global call processing, a common pattern of telecommunications software architecture. Each `HalfCall` handles the "half" of a call for a particular subscriber, and `Call` itself provides the communication between them. In feature-rich systems, `Call` may be more than a connection between two `HalfCalls`, functioning much like the human operator in antique telephone systems.

When one brings these considerations of symmetry down to the nuts and bolts of telecom software, patterns emerge. Patterns are just culturally sensitive centers. Bob Hanmer of Lucent Technologies has written up the following pattern:

Name: 3 Part Call Processing

Alias: Add A Switch

Problem: Efficient interfacing between many signaling types.

Context: Toll switching where each switching center must communicate with many various signaling types.

Forces: Want flexibility to interwork between any signaling types.

More signaling types are being developed constantly.

There are some common functions that are signaling type-independent.

It is expensive to make changes to every existing signaling type to add new functions.

Want centralization and standardization, for ease of maintenance and to facilitate understanding.

Solution: Distribute call processing into something that can be processed by three separate pieces: incoming trunk handling, outgoing trunk handling, and non-trunk-specific (common) pieces.

Resulting Context: The parts of the software that know about signaling types only need to know about the ones that they process. They have been isolated from all other signaling types.

Non-signaling-specific types of functions are concentrated into separate modules for each of maintenance.

Sketch:

Rationale: Easily extensible. To add new signaling types, add the trunk handlers and make minor changes to some common functions.

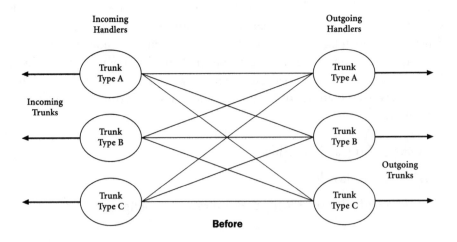

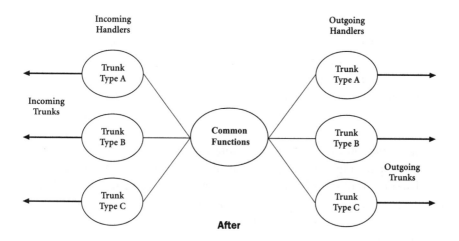

This pattern applies for the same reason that we have telephone switches – the complexity of direct connections between each node in a network.

Author: Robert Hanmer, 5/9/1995 [8]

With an explicit Call center, we can easily add more HalfCalls onto the call. Each HalfCall still handles the interactions with its own subscriber, while the Call center again functions like the operator. For a three-way call, we might have a picture like this:

Here, I've reshaped `Call` to more explicitly show how it connects the `HalfCalls` together. (Who says objects have to be round?) The call as a whole emerges as a center.

The parts are composable. Some of them, like `Call`, carry important design meaning. The figure emerges as a result of several processes – the process of design, and the process of three phone subscribers setting up a three-way call.

Should we call this some kind of notation? Maybe. I'm proposing we hold a "centers painting workshop" at EuroPLoP this year with the guidance of our Lateral Thinking Coordinator, George Platts. It seems a useful way to put down on paper the way we think about programs. Maybe it's an avenue to give dignity to the chalkboard diagrams we all do, whose folk semantics are discarded in the translation to most formal notations.

Can we see this structure in the source code? Unfortunately not, or at least not easily, for most programming languages and environments. But perhaps there is a programming paradigm, or language, where this structure is visible in the source. It's crucial to make the symmetries visible. Such an environment might provide a radical departure from the common patterns of contemporary software development. Such an environment might also fold aspects of process into the geometry of the program as well, as Alexander intended that his Indian village diagrams should communicate requirements and intent. I believe that one research challenge for the pattern community today is to explore what such an environment would look like. I'll talk more about that in the July/August *C++ Report*.

SIGNPOSTS

Well, that's it for this month. In the next article, I'll further explore the concepts of recursion, iteration, instantiation, and other ideas important to software geometry.

REFERENCES

1. Alexander, C. *The Nature of Order,* draft.
2. Alexander, C. "The Determination of Components for an Indian Village." In *Developments in Design Methodology,* N. Cross, ed. Chichester, England: John Wiley and Sons, 1984, 33–56.

3. Parnas, D.L. "Designing Software for Ease of Extension and Construction." In *Proceedings of the Third International Conference on Software Engineering,* May 1978.

4. Alexander, C. Personal correspondence, December 11, 1997.

5. Alexander, C. Personal correspondence, December 28, 1997.

6. Meszaros, G. "Pattern: Half-Object + Protocol (HOPP)." In *Pattern Languages of Program Design* 2. Vlissides, J., N. Kerth and J. Coplien, eds. Reading, MA: Addison-Wesley, 1996.

7. Montgomery, W.A. Personal correspondence, January 9, 1998.

8. Carestia, P.D., and F.S. Hudson. "No. 4 ESS: Evolution of the Software Structure." *Bell System Technical Journal,* 60(6):1167–1201, Jul./Aug. 1981.

12

A Pocket-Sized Broker

Don S. Olson

S OMETIMES YOU DON'T NEED the Victorinox Champion. Sure, every blade and screwdriver, the awl, punch, can opener, reamer, corkscrew, magnifying glass, pen, scissors, pliers, fish scaler, ruler, toothpick, tweezers, hook disgorger, saw, and nail file has its use, and does indeed get used once in a while. But it's an awfully huge knife to lug around when one blade and the toothpick are all you ever use. It's good to be prepared for all possibilities – don't get me wrong – but sometimes you not only can do with less, you can get away with it, too. You might even be better off for it.

What follows are four patterns: Transceiver-Parcel; Broker as Intermediary; Broker as Divorce Attorney; Broker as Matchmaker. However whimsical the titles, these are some real parts of an overall architecture that we have found to be very useful, lightweight, and easy to build. Moreover, it was a lot of fun.

Our object in building our particular broker was to remove everything we didn't need, and probably wouldn't need, so that we could immediately do something useful with it. Amazingly, it worked very well. We not only built a product using these pieces, we sold it for real money, and it worked fantastically well once deployed. Even more amazingly, before we were finished with the framework on its first project outing, another team decided it looked useful to them, too. All of a sudden, it was being passed around like the only canteen on a desert hike. Everybody wanted a taste.

Broker-based architectures certainly aren't novel; in fact, that's an under-

Originally published in *The Patterns Handbook*, Linda Rising, ed. (New York: Cambridge University Press, 1998), pp. 171–181. Used with permission from the author.

statement. One could almost say that we've a plague of them, or something to that effect. They're mostly pretty powerful and very grand, suitable for all occasions. They are the Victorinox Champions. If we'd had the time and money, we might have latched on to any one of them and learned how to use it. Necessity being the mother of invention, however, our poverty of time and money turned into a benefit, and although we won't claim our little pocket-sized broker to be the global solution, it's a pretty good enough solution for a large class of problems.

As an old Russian once said, "Better is the enemy of good enough."

TRANSCEIVER~PARCEL

Problem. You desire to decouple components of an application using one of the Broker patterns. Components will be developed by many people, and they need to spend their time designing the guts of the components, not worrying about their integration. Additionally, it is completely a peer-to-peer system, rather than a client-server model.

Context. You don't care about efficiency, but you want an elastic architecture which you can extend by adding components or reduce by removing them, because every customer, market, or situation has different needs which you want to be able to meet without taking a meat-axe to some monolithic application. All your components should use the same method of communication, but you don't want them to have to know what the actual method of communication is for the environment; hence the commitment to the Broker idea.

Forces

- Each component must be able to both send and receive messages.
- Components may be distributed or exist in the same process.
- You want the dumbest broker imaginable; that is, all it knows are parcels.
- As far as communication goes, you want the dumbest components possible.

Solution. Each transceiver can send and receive parcels, which contain a `visit` method [see Visitor Pattern, GoF95]. The broker, when routing a parcel, invokes an `execute` method on the receiving transceiver, passing the address of the parcel as an argument. The transceiver in turn invokes the visit method on this parcel, which contains whatever method calls the parcel needs to make to cause the transceiver to do the bidding of its originator (another transceiver).

In the most generic version, the visit method of all parcels would invoke the same method in any transceiver, which in turn could encapsulate whatever mysterious machinations occur to perform the service. In our implementation, however, many of the method calls from parcel visit methods were negotiated between developers of the transceivers. This could have added unwanted coupling, but was managed and controlled sufficiently such that anyone on the team, desiring to use any transceiver, could simply examine the .h file for that transceiver's public interface. Additionally, one of our development rules was that the developer responsible for a given transceiver was also responsible for developing the parcels which would visit it. So, the developer of the requesting transceiver only had to create the parcel(s) for which the receiving transceiver subscribes. The parcel to be sent, having been developed specifically for communicating with that transceiver, contained the correct type for which the transceiver subscribed to induce the broker to route it, and voila! communication between components. The transceivers could vary with absolutely no effect on either the parcels or the transceivers sending them.

Resulting Context. New services (i.e., transceivers) can be added to the existing system with no changes to the broker or the other transceivers. Transceivers can add additional services which respond to an existing parcels visit method, or new parcels can be created to extend existing transceivers, or provide communication for new transceivers.

Rationale. This approach allows the creation of the simplest broker that still could support extensions to it such as a secondary registrar (for managing failed transceivers), broadcasting, and other capabilities. The broker and all types of transceivers are derived from the transceiver base class and all types of parcels are derived from the parcel base class so that the communication interfaces among all pieces are easily understood by developers working on them. Integration issues were reduced considerably; in fact, system integration became the least of our concerns. Another benefit was found in training new members to the team, particularly if they had received the same Design Patterns training [see Train Hard, Fight Easy, Olson95]. With the understanding of Visitor [GoF95], Proxy [GoF95], Builder [GoF95], Bridge [GoF95], and State [GoF95], the newcomer could easily grasp the architecture as well as the fundamental building blocks for any existing or future piece of it. *Broker* [POSA196] was not yet published and so we were proceeding with our own peculiar version of that concept adapted to our specific needs and understanding; however, the design was robust, efficient, and general enough to permit immediate reuse in the Local Number Portability, along with nearly all the other components.

Author. Don S. Olson 8/31/96

Originator. The designers and developers of the #800 product team at AG Communication Systems.

GOING POSTAL, OR BROKER AS INTERMEDIARY

Problem. You desire to decouple components of an application.

Context. You don't care about efficiency, but you want an elastic architecture which you can extend by adding components or reduce by removing them, because every customer, market, or situation has different needs which you want to be able to meet without taking a meat-axe to some monolithic application or client-server model. Besides, since your team consists of more than one developer, you don't want to practice the "Big Bang" type of integration at the end of development but would rather be able to dry-run the inevitable at the beginning. You need an architecture that specifies the interfaces in sufficient detail to enable this, but leaves enough wiggle room to add capabilities without perturbations throughout the system.

Forces

- Efficiency is no big thing, but it couldn't hurt. (If it is, see Broker as Matchmaker [Olson95]).

- Decoupling, flexibility, and extensibility are essential, since you're never quite sure what components will be needed.

- Components may be distributed or exist in the same process. (If distributed across processes, or processors, see Broker as Divorce Attorney [Olson95]).

- Components shouldn't care where they are; they should be distributable with absolutely no changes.

- You want the dumbest broker imaginable.

Solution. Create a broker component which understands how to do only two things: register a component called a transceiver, for the messages or parcel it is willing to receive; and route parcels to the transceivers based on the types of parcels for which they have registered. Thus, the broker contains a registrar object, which maintains the list of transceivers and what parcel they desire to receive, and a special transceiver object, which knows how to effectively route the incoming parcel to their destinations based as directed by the registrar.

Resulting Context. Here's the interesting thing: the transceiver from which the broker inherits happens to also be the base class for all components for which the broker routes parcels. (See Transceiver Parcel, [Olson95].) This means that all the pieces of the application, including the broker, communicate through the same mechanism. A transceiver registers with the broker by sending it the only parcel for which the broker itself really subscribes, which the broker handles exactly the same way as any transceiver. The broker, too, invokes the `visit` method on the parcel, which in turn invokes the `register` method on the broker, which hands the sending transceiver's subscription to the registrar. All nonregistration parcels are handed to the registrar which tells the broker where to route them. The broker invokes the `execute` method on the transceiver(s) which subscribe(s) for each parcel type, which in turn invoke(s) the `visit` method on the parcel, which in turn invokes whatever methods it cares to on the visited transceiver.

As in many human bureaucracies, the broker, though the most visible to the transceivers in the system, is hardly the brains of the operation. The registrar is like the secretary who maintains the files and writes the executive's speeches and controls the itinerary; the broker does as told by its registrar.

Rationale. One of the joys of this model was in explaining it to other people. First it was necessary to describe the Visitor pattern [GoF95], then our own use of it in the Transceiver-Parcel patterns. After that, all that remained was to show how the broker was a special kind of transceiver, pass on a few sample transceiver-parcel pairs, and turn them loose building new components. It really was that simple, and that was one of the primary objectives. The remaining objectives of easy distribution, redistribution, and improved efficiency are covered through the variations described in the accompanying patterns Broker as Divorce Attorney (in a really ugly divorce) and Broker as Matchmaker.

Real-life Analog. This is familiar to anyone who invests in the stock market, and, I assume, is the model referred to most generally when the term "broker" is used in computing. You, the investor, want to do something smart with your money, and since stocks are touted for their superior long-range return on investment, you decide to put some of your money into the market. Of course, most of us have no idea how the stock market really works. In order for the market to work effectively, it has to be made easy for us to move our money in and out and around. If, in order to invest, we had to fly to New York, take a cab to the New York Stock Exchange, master the arcane hand signals, learn who's who, etc., etc., I can't imagine that the flood of money that has flowed into the market recently from small investors would have amounted to more than a few drips (no reflection on small investors, really). In reality, we deal with brokers. We give our money cheerfully to the broker with instructions as to where we want it to go. The broker then does whatever it is he or she does to execute our instructions, making the telephone calls, sending faxes, e-mail, messengers, whatever it takes to buy our selected stocks. We, as clients, don't care or need to know precisely how this all happens so long as we receive acknowledgment that it has been accomplished. The broker insulates us from the arcane protocols of the stock market, geographic and time differences, even cultural and linguistic shifts. When we want information on our investments, we can contact the broker who will send us a nice report (and, analogously, the Visitor, will invoke our "read" method on the report). The broker may even arrange for periodic reporting of the progress of our investments (a version of direct brokering – see below) so we don't have to continually interrupt his or her busy day. Unless we're particularly compulsive about daily fluctuations, we can work entirely through our broker, from initial investment to ultimate redemption, after we've made our mountain of money. Or, as one friend describes the client-broker relationship, "turn your money and my experience into my money and your experience."

We indirectly communicate with the market through the broker. Everything is done through the broker, and he/she serves as our only interface to the complexities that comprise the market. It's easy for us, as clients, and makes greater efficiency possible. The drawbacks arise when we are unable to contact our broker. If the broker is out, whether for lunch or embezzlement, we are utterly and completely without recourse, at least for the near future. So for simplifying our lives we accept dependency on the broker. Oh, and we also must accept the *mordida* ("little bite") that the broker places on us in the form of commissions. In the computing world, we might equate this to the time penalty of routing all communications through the broker. You don't get something for nothing, after all.

See Also. Broker [POSA196], Visitor [GoF95]

Author. Don S. Olson 8/31/96

Originator. The designers and developers of the #800 product team at AG Communication Systems.

Going to Court, or Broker as Divorce Attorney (in a really ugly divorce)

Problem. Your broker-based application will be distributed across processes and/or processors, but how it might be distributed may vary.

Context. Perhaps an entire family of products is to be based on this architecture, to be delivered on a variety of platforms, scaled to all sizes of systems, from small, single processor, to multi-processor, distributed installations. As use of these products increases, such as traffic demands in the telecommunications business, redistribution may be necessary. In other words, how the components will be grouped or scattered will be different from delivery to delivery and product to product.

Forces

- All components might exist in the same process.

- Components might as easily be distributed.

- The day may come when components need to be redistributed.

- New components may be added.

- Components may be removed.

- All of this change, addition, and removal may have to be dynamic (i.e., while the existing system is running).

Solution. Use one broker per process (or more, if you are so inclined). Each broker should have a proxy for each type of transceiver it appears to have in its own address space. The proxy fields the parcels routed to it by stripping out their essential information, packing this data into the necessary messaging package for that implementation, and sends it off to some gateway, which each broker also possesses. The gateway performs the inverse process of the proxy, by extracting the information, repackaging it into the parcel it was originally, and routing this to the local broker for delivery. The gateways in our implementation were parcel factories [GoF95], and all shared a single input queue per process.

Resulting Context. No transceiver really knows where another transceiver exists, nor does the broker, to whom proxies look just like the transceivers they represent. The broker remains as dumb as ever, and the transceivers can live in blissful ignorance of how their parcels actually get to their destinations.

Rationale. This is another case all too common in real life, and unfortunately, despite its benefits in computing, it can be quite unpleasant for humans experiencing it. Consider an ugly divorce case. Let's not dwell on details or circumstances, but suppose that one or both parties are so angry that they care only to deal through their attorneys or have been instructed to do so by their attorneys. (Soon-to-be-ex) wife speaks to her attorney, who in turn speaks to the attorney of (soon-to-be-ex) husband, who then relays the message to his client. Buried in this transaction are the filters and protocols the two attorneys must apply to effectively stay within their legal and ethical bounds. The benefits of this model are that the estranged spouses deal with someone familiar to them and in whom they believe they can confide, and their respective attorneys worry about how to effect the desired communication, although it typically occurs over an expensive lunch put on account and added to the $400 per hour fee for acting as brokers of bile and bad news. But to return from that digression, the individual litigants don't have to know the law, or how what they're communicating gets to where it's going, or even where their (soon-to-be-ex) spouse actually is. I'd prefer not to go too deeply into the negative aspects of this means of communication, since rarely in computing do we see an analog of acrimonious divorce proceedings (or the avarice of divorce attorneys), but one penalty is the compounding of the aforementioned *mordida.* When the two clients are fighting over the contents of a single household pot, it seems not at all unusual for the brokering parties to be the true beneficiaries of the convenience of this setup. This might serve as a subtle warning about watching the complexity of your broker-to-broker protocols, or the extent of the network through which they communicate.

In computing, this model allows clients (parties of the first part) of a process to behave as though everything they need (parties of the second part) is in their own address space, or at least within the immediate grasp of the broker with which they are registered. The broker handles tracking down the other client(s) with which the party of the first part wishes to deal, whether that party of the second part resides locally in another process or across the network in some obscure corner of cyberspace. Implicit in this is the possibility that more than two brokers could be involved, a situation which, thankfully, is not typically reflected in divorce proceedings, and which, again thankfully, for which future divorcees mustn't pay. In computing, of course, there may be performance penalties if the number of broker-to-broker connections becomes great, but this is less a consideration when stacked up against the perceived benefits of hiding from clients the protocols necessary for communicating across the network.

Author. Don S. Olson 9/2/96

Originator. The designers and developers of the #800 product team at AG Communication Systems.

Going to the Chapel, or Broker as Matchmaker

Problem. The basic broker architecture is too inefficient for the application.

Context. In many applications, real-time considerations are paramount, as customers may have contractually specified performance. This is not uncommon in the telecommunications area, and for all the simplicity that the basic indirect broker provides, it can get expensive to pass every parcel through it.

Forces

- The basic broker is so nice and clean.

- The basic broker costs too much in processing overhead.

Solution. Allow the broker to perform the first parcel routing as an introduction between the sending and receiving transceivers, supplying the address of the latter to the former (and vice versa, if necessary). After that, the two transceivers can correspond directly with one another. At completion of their communication, the broker will be notified.

Resulting Context. The communication between the two transceivers is much more efficient, having removed the broker from the loop. Of course, if the two transceivers are in different processes, then they must handle the interprocess communication themselves, which requires the equivalent of a proxy for the other transceiver and thus increases coupling. Typically, however, this direct mode of brokering is used when coupling is a minor concern, and efficiency the highest priority, so the tradeoffs usually favor its adoption.

Rationale. Although marriage brokers are not as common as they once were, we still have dating services. In fact, due to the increased working hours needed to earn the cash to fund investments through our stock brokers (the "indirect" model, remember?), some of our number are unable to find the time to seek companionship on our own and have resorted to elite dating services which claim to find us our perfect match, saving us valuable time in weeding through potential candidates, and also insulating us from a great deal of uncertainty, and hence, fun. In any case, the model in real life is copied in our computing model.

In the hope of meeting that special someone, you register with a marriage broker or dating service. The broker in turn checks your profile and sees if a suitable match exists in her network of clients. If there is someone who is "subscribing" for your particular type, the broker arranges for an introduction. This is the point at which your connection becomes direct in that you and the entity with which you want to ultimately interact are directly connected to one another. At this point the broker steps out of the picture. It's between you and your paramour to establish the protocols. In both the real-world model and the computing model, as long as interactions between you and your paramour continue, the broker remains out of the loop. In the event of a break-off in communications, digital or romantic, the broker will want to know so that she/he can serve the client's interest yet again when a suitable match reveals itself.

Author. Don S. Olson 9/2/96

Originator. The designers and developers of the #800 product team at AG Communication Systems.

REFERENCES

[GoF95] Gamma, E., Helm, R., Johnson, R., Vlissides, J. *Design Patterns: Elements of Reusable Architecture.* Reading, MA: Addison-Wesley, 1995.

[Olson95] http://c2.com/cgi-binwili?RegularContributors

[POSA196] Buschmann, F., Meunier, R., Rohnert, H., Sommerlad, P., Stal, M. *Pattern-Oriented Software Architecture: A System of Patterns.* New York: John Wiley & Sons, 1996.

PART 3
EXPERIENCE REPORTS

13

MANAGING CHANGE
WITH PATTERNS

Michael Duell

ABSTRACT

C OSTS ASSOCIATED WITH MODIFYING SOFTWARE are a large part of
an organization's software development budget. Since change is to
be expected, the costs associated with change can be reduced by
preparing for it. Software design patterns associate a problem and context
with a solution to document good design practices. Patterns allow software
designers to evaluate solutions in terms of the aspects of the system most
likely to vary. This chapter uses the INgage™ Intelligent Peripheral Prototype to demonstrate how the use of two patterns, *Layers* and *Mediator*, facili-
tated a major change to the protocol stacks, and isolated object interactions
to make them more maintainable.

INTRODUCTION

One constant in software development is change. Surveys indicated that
during the 1970s, 50% of the average Electronic Data Processing (EDP)
organization's budget was spent on maintenance (ongoing debugging and
modification) [1]. In the 1980s maintenance accounted for 60% of an EDP

organization's budget, and is estimated to account for 80% of the budget for the 1990s [2]. Not only does software change but the rate of change is increasing with time. To make matters worse, early studies indicate that the number of software modifications that are successful the first time decreases with the number of statements modified [3]. As software becomes increasingly more difficult to design, maintain, and modify, organizations cannot afford to ignore the impact of change on software. Change will happen, and good software developers will prepare for it. This chapter discusses how change was anticipated on the INgage™ Intelligent Peripheral Prototype, and how software design patterns were used to manage change.

THE IP PROTOTYPE

An Intelligent Peripheral (IP) is a network element that allows flexible information interactions between a user and the network. Trigger detection points (TDPs) are established in the Service Switching Point (SSP) software which, when encountered, cause the SSP to query the Service Control Point (SCP) for call handling instructions. Once the SCP has provided call handling instructions, the SSP communicates with the IP via Integrated Services Digital Network (ISDN) Primary Rate Interface (PRI) to access resources such as voice response units, announcement units, or Dual Tone Multi Frequency (DTMF) receivers [4]. The specific resources used depend on the services deployed on the IP. AG Communication Systems developed an IP prototype consisting of a control computer, one or more resource computers, and a Time Slot Interchange (TSI) switching matrix communicating with each other over an Ethernet. The basic hardware architecture of this prototype is shown in Figure 13.1. In addition to communication via Ethernet, the control computer supports Signaling System #7 (SS7) communication, and a Man Machine Language (MML) terminal interface. The TSI is connected to the Public Switched Telephone Network (PSTN) via an ISDN PRI. Given a call from a subscriber and instructions received from the SCP in the SS7 network, the IP prototype can connect a subscriber to a resource in the resource computer.

SOFTWARE DESIGN PATTERNS

A software design pattern documents a recurring problem in a given context and a proven solution to that problem [5]. Patterns offer successful solutions

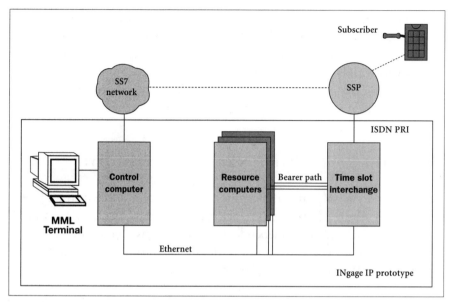

Figure 13.1. The IP prototype hardware architecture.

to recurring problems. Design patterns, properly applied, can make a system more robust to change by allowing some aspect of the system to vary independently of other aspects [6]; thus, the software developer can better prepare for change. The proper use of design patterns helps developers manage change by favoring additive change (adding code using existing interfaces) over invasive change (change which propagates through existing code) [7]. In other words, the software is open for extension but closed for modification [8].

LAYERS

The *Layers* pattern [5] is used to decompose applications into groups of subtasks, such that each group is at an appropriate level of abstraction. Even readers who have not been exposed to patterns will recognize *Layers* in TCP/IP protocol stacks [9], or the OSI model. The use of layers is not a new idea. On the contrary, layered architectures have been around since the 1970s [9], and have become quite common. Layered architectures are commonly used because they offer a successful solution for breaking the dependencies between levels of abstraction. Layers can be used to isolate functions and minimize the amount of information that must be processed at each layer. The result is that layered software is easy to understand and easy to modify [9]. The ease of modification is demonstrated by the use of the TCP/IP protocols on a variety of host hardware and operating systems. The past success with layered architectures supports documenting *Layers* as a pattern. For large systems requiring decomposition into groups of subtasks at different levels of abstraction, layering can offer a proven solution.

USE OF THE LAYERS PATTERN ON THE IP PROTOTYPE

The IP Prototype software architecture was divided into five distinct layers, as shown in Figure 13.2. The original reason for the layering was to make the higher layers platform independent. This goal was accomplished and the prototype software was run on four different platforms: HP Telepace, Tandem, Pentium 90, and Sun Sparc20 workstations.

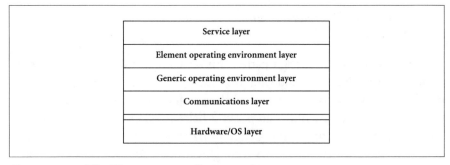

Figure 13.2. The IP prototype software architecture.

While machine independence is clearly a benefit of using the layered architecture, it does not prove that the software is easily modifiable. That test came later when the third-party protocol stacks at the communications layer proved to be a bottleneck. After analyzing the problem, replacing the third-party protocol stacks with a socket interface was determined to be the best course of action. Due to layering, changes required as a result of replacing the communications layer did not propagate beyond the generic operating environment layer (Figure 13.3). Compilation of both the socket interface (at the communications layer) and the Application Programming Interfaces (APIs) at the generic operating environment layer was controlled via a compile-time flag. Based on this flag either the old communications layer or the new one was compiled. As the new code was developed to support the socket interface and APIs, development of code at the Element Operating Environment Layer and Service Layer continued in parallel. After the new communications layer and interfaces to it had been fully tested, the compile-time flag was set and the system incorporated the new communications layer. The transition was smooth. In time, the code for the old communications layer was removed.

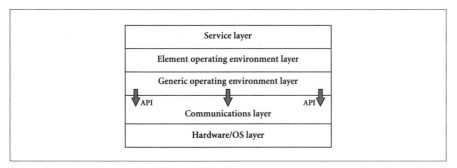

Figure 13.3. Required changes as a result of replacing the communications layer.

The smoothness of this transition stems from the separation of concerns accomplished by the *Layers* pattern. Objects in the higher layers require a means of sending messages, but should not care about how the messages are sent. By defining a fixed message-sending interface, and allowing objects in higher layers to send messages, the details of how the messages are sent can vary.

THE MEDIATOR PATTERN

The intent of *Mediator* [6] is to promote loose coupling by encapsulating object interactions. Once the interactions are encapsulated in the Mediator object, colleague objects can refer to the Mediator object rather than explicitly referring to each other. The interactions are actually constraints, with the Mediator responsible for managing the constraints. The role of the Mediator object is demonstrated by an Air Traffic Control tower, which manages takeoff and landing constraints on aircraft in a terminal area. Since constraints on multiple objects are centralized in a Mediator rather than distributed over the colleague objects, changes in the constraints can be accomplished by

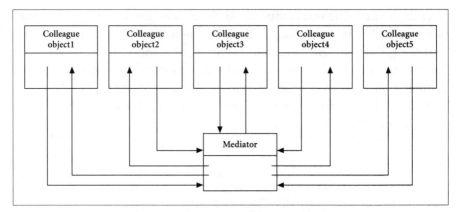

Figure 13.4. Object diagram for the Mediator *pattern.*

changing the Mediator without modifying the colleague objects. An object diagram of the *Mediator* pattern is shown in Figure 13.4.

USE OF THE MEDIATOR PATTERN ON THE IP PROTOTYPE

Two types of constraints were required within the INgage™ IP Prototype. Before establishing a socket connection, certain APIs in the Generic Operating Environment Layer (Figure 13.3) were required to wait until other connections had first been established [10]. Also, before beginning a session (flow of information), certain device objects had to wait until other device objects had initiated sessions. The rationale behind the constraints was to guarantee that resources would be available and that call control could be provided via the SS7 network prior to terminating a call to the INgage™ IP Prototype.

Conceivably, new services on the IP Prototype could require different constraints on the order of device connections. Since the process of establishing a connection or session is independent of an imposed order, the change should be possible without modifying the connection or session establishment code.

BENEFITS OF USING MEDIATOR

Mediator was chosen to make anticipated changes easier to manage. Since different designers were responsible for each colleague class, it was simpler to provide a common set of **Mediator** methods, rather than designing a complex interface to be shared by all five classes. By isolating the classes from their interactions, it became obvious that the interactions were not properties of the colleague classes. Since the classes maintained their essential properties once their interactions were encapsulated in the Mediator, each resulting class model was a truer representation of its interface, and could be understood without knowledge of the other classes. For example, TSI device objects in the Element Operating Layer could communicate with the TSI without knowledge of the connection state of resource computers.

Testing the objects in isolation was also greatly simplified. The Mediator was unit tested without any of the colleague objects by invoking its methods from a driver. The colleague objects were tested without the need to write stubs for all of the other colleague objects. On the target hardware, connections were simulated by reporting them to the Mediator object. These simulated connections made it possible to test a colleague object independently of other colleague objects.

At one point, the synchronous blocking connect method of the API for the TSI had to be changed to an asynchronous, non-blocking connect. This change was accomplished without impacting the connection logic of any other API colleague classes. When changes to an interaction (constraint) are made, they are isolated to the one class where the interactions are encapsulated. When a change in the Mediator is made, rigorous re-test of the colleague objects is not required, since none of their behaviors will change. Since the interaction between the colleague objects is separated from the objects themselves, rigorous unit testing of the Mediator is sufficient to ensure confidence in the change.

CONCLUSION

Change is inevitable in software. Since change is inevitable, good software designers will prepare for it. Software design patterns offer a method of documenting proven designs and evaluating aspects that can vary [6]. By designing for change on the INgage™ IP Prototype, required changes were localized to a few key objects, rather than being propagated throughout the system. Testing those localized changes proved to be easier, since the interfaces between objects remained constant. Evaluating anticipated change, and choosing the appropriate design patterns to accommodate that change, promises to reduce the escalating cost of modifying software and increase the percentage of changes that are successful on the first attempt.

ACKNOWLEDGMENTS

The author would like to thank Pat McDaid of Dovetail Computing, Bill Opdyke of Lucent Technologies, Linda Rising and Roger Tomas of AG Communication Systems, and Greg Utas of Nortel for reviewing this chapter and offering constructive suggestions for improvement.

REFERENCES

1. Yourdon E., and L. Constantine, *Structured Design.* Englewood Cliffs, NJ: Prentice Hall, 1979.

2. Pressman, R., *Software Engineering: A Practitioner's Approach.* New York: McGraw-Hill, 1992.

3. Boehm, B.W., "Software and Its Impact: A Quantitative Assessment." *Datamation,* Vol. 19, No. 5, May 1973, pp. 48–59.

4. Russell, T., *Signaling System #7.* New York: McGraw Hill, 1995.

5. Buschman, F., R. Meunier, H. Rohnert, P. Sommerlad, and M. Stal, *Pattern-Oriented Software Architecture: A System of Patterns.* Chichester, England: John Wiley & Sons, 1996.

6. Gamma, E., R. Helm, R. Johnson, and J. Vlissides, *Design Patterns: Elements of Reusable Object-Oriented Software.* Reading, MA: Addison-Wesley, 1995.

7. Vlissides, J. "Subject-Oriented Design." *C++ Report,* Vol. 10, No. 2, February 1998, pp. 41–45.

8. Martin, R.C., *Designing Object-Oriented C++ Applications Using the Booch Method.* Englewood Cliffs, NJ, Prentice Hall, 1995.

9. Feit, S. *TCP/IP Architecture, Protocols, and Implementation.* New York: McGraw-Hill, 1993.

10. Duell, M. "Experience Using Design Patterns to Decouple Object Interactions on the INgage™ IP Prototype." In *The Patterns Handbook: Techniques, Strategies, and Applications,* ed. L. Rising. Cambridge, UK: Cambridge University Press, 1997.

14

Using Design Patterns to
Build a Framework for
Multimedia Networking

Just A. van den Broecke and James O. Coplien

Introduction

ADVANCES IN BROADBAND NETWORKING and multimedia computing are expected to open a wealth of new applications, such as teleshopping, video on demand, and teleconferencing. Although many exciting new services will enter our workplaces and living rooms, providers and manufacturers face unknown challenges in the areas of:

- Application/end-user services,

- Network and multimedia standards, and

- Hardware platforms and operating systems/environments

The future, however, is unpredictable, so definitive requirements are not available. How can we design our products to allow each area to evolve gratefully and independently?

Distributed system services are applying standard programming interfaces

Originally published in *Bell Labs Technical Journal,* Winter 1997, pp. 166–187. © 1997 Lucent Technologies. Used with permission from the authors.

Panel 1. Abbreviations, Acronyms, and Terms

API: Application programming interface. Programming-level functions providing the services of a software component.

ATM: Asynchronous transfer mode. High-speed packet switching technique with fixed-size packets.

B-ISDM: Broadband integrated services digital network.

CM: Conference management.

CORBA: Common Object Request Broker Architecture. Standard for distributed object technology defined by the Object Management Group.

DLL: Dynamic link library.

FSM: Finite state machine.

GloveView®-2000: ATM switch marketed by Lucent Technologies.

GUI: Graphical user interface.

ISDN: Integrated services digital network.

ITU: International Telecommunications Union.

middleware: Distributed system services provided through standard application programming interfaces.

MM: Multimedia. The meaningful integration of multiple media types with at least one time-dependent media type.

N-ISDN: Narrowband integrated services digital network.

OMG: Object Management Group. Industrial consortium that defines standards for object technology.

OS: Operating systems.

POSA: Reference to the book *Pattern-Oriented Software Architecture* [10].

QoS: Quality of Service. Quality of a network path expressed by parameters such as cost, delay, probability of loss, probability of undetected errors, and throughput.

RPC: Remote procedure call. Calling a function on a remote system as if it were a local function call.

TCP/IP: Transmission control protocol/Internet protocol.

TINA-C: Telecommunications Information Networking Architecture Consortium. International consortium that defines an open architecture (TINA) for telecommunications systems for the broadband, multimedia, and information era.

UML: Unified Modeling Language.

Winsock2: An application programming interface for transparent network programming using Microsoft Windows.

and protocols to help facilitate heterogeneity in operating systems, networks, and hardware devices. Standard programming interfaces make it easier to develop applications for a variety of platforms, and standard protocols enable programs to operate together. These distributed system services are called *middleware* [1], because they sit "in the middle," layering above the operating system and networking software and below specific applications. Middleware can offer a set of general-purpose services, such as remote procedure call (RPC) and messaging, and may be specific to a particular domain, such as distributed databases or network management. Middleware for applications that combine networking and multimedia (audio, video, and data) is a topic of active research [2,3] and standardization. [4,5]

MediaBuilder is a middleware framework that targets the domain of networked multimedia applications. It supports areas such as session management, application protocols, and multimedia devices. Applications can be created by extending the framework and/or by reusing components developed with the framework. MediaBuilder was developed by the PLATINUM project (see Panel 2). Within this project, MediaBuilder was used to build a teleconferencing application that runs over an asynchronous transfer mode (ATM) network infrastructure.

The MediaBuilder software architecture is shaped by a collection of cooperating software patterns. *Patterns* – reusable microarchitectures that contribute to an overall architecture [6] – are an emerging discipline that helps designers understand and apply proven solutions to recurring design prob-

Panel 2. The PLATINUM Project

The PLATform providing Integrated services to New Users of Multimedia (PLATINUM) project had two main goals: (1) to build a high-speed network based on switched ATM, and (2) to develop distributed multimedia applications that use this network.

ATM technology is already deployed in the backbone of existing networks. The goal of the PLATINUM project was to make native ATM available to desktop computers via signaling. This would enable applications to request and use connections of bandwidths as high as 155 Mb/s. End users could experience multimedia services such as teleconferencing with high-quality audio and video.

Figure 14.1 shows a simplified picture of the PLATINUM platform. The cloud in the middle currently contains a single GlobeView®-2000 ATM switch developed and manufactured by Lucent Technologies. The two terminals shown in the figure are standard PCs running Microsoft Windows NT. The three functional layers shown are the network layer, the MediaBuilder middleware layer, and applications.

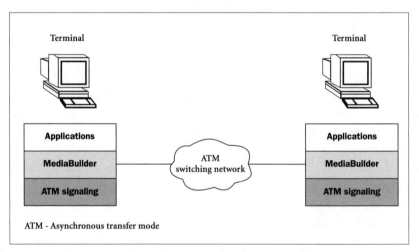

Figure 14.1. Network configuration for the PLATINUM project

The network layer allows users to establish ATM connections by providing ATM signaling protocols (terminals and the switch) and call processing (the switch). The PLATINUM project makes it possible to negotiate connection characteristics such as bandwidth and connection topology (for example, multipoint for conferencing) through the switch.

The MediaBuilder middleware layer makes applications oblivious to underlying networks and provides components for application creation. It offers applications a generic session management service that adapts to a variety of networks, such as ATM (used in the project) or the Internet. Reusable components are provided for a variety of user protocols and for the local mapping of media streams to multimedia devices such as sound cards and cameras. The applications also allow end users to share media such as audio, video, whiteboard, and documents.

The project was conducted between January 1995 and July 1996. Contributors from industry, research institutes, and universities included Lucent Technologies (The Netherlands and the U.S.), AT&T Global Information Solutions (GIS) Germany (now NCR), Deutsche Telekom Germany, Telematics Research Center (TRC, The Netherlands), and the Center for Telematics and Information Technology (CTIT, The Netherlands). PLATINUM was built on earlier work done in the European RACE program [15] and AT&T Fast-Track. See also Klapwijk et al. [19] and Ouibrahim and van den Broecke [20].

lems. The body of literature for the patterns of object-oriented programming [7], telecommunications architecture [8,9], and many other software areas is growing.

In this chapter we focus on the main patterns that contribute to the MediaBuilder architecture. We show how patterns can be used to address design issues within the domain of networked multimedia applications and how they can be woven together to shape an architecture. The description of the MediaBuilder architecture, therefore, is illustrative rather than exhaustive.

The remaining sections are divided as follows: "Patterns" defines what patterns are, presents an example, and describes how to use patterns to build a framework. "MediaBuilder Architecture" shows how existing and new design patterns are woven together to address the issues affecting multimedia networking. "Application Example" presents a conferencing application built with MediaBuilder. "Conclusions" summarizes this chapter's findings, and "Future Directions" projects how MediaBuilder will evolve.

Patterns

In this section we define patterns, their form, and the relationship between patterns and frameworks. We show how a pattern can generate a microarchitecture from a general-purpose design pattern that meets an important application need. The notation used throughout this chapter is also presented.

What Are Patterns?

Patterns support a problem-solving discipline with rapidly growing acceptance in the software architecture and design community. A *pattern* is a structured document that describes a solution to a problem in a context. It captures the key design constructs, practices, and mechanisms of core competencies such as object-oriented development or fault-tolerant system deign. Not necessarily object oriented, patterns supplement general-purpose design by capturing expert solutions in a form that helps developers solve difficult, recurring problems. Patterns are being widely used for teaching, for documentation, and as design aids.

A pattern describes the core structure of a solution at a level high enough to generalize to many specific situations. Just as a dress pattern can be used to cut out many dresses of slightly different style, size, and trim, so a software pattern is a general solution that can be tailored to fit. For example, the *Observer* pattern, presented in the next section, describes a *dependency registration* structure, in which one piece of software is affected by changes that take place in another piece of software. Many aspects of the solution in this widely recurring software problem are subtle and difficult for programmers to solve. The *Observer* pattern describes the core elements of a working solution, but still leaves many implementation details to the discretion of the developer. Patterns tell the developer what to do without specifying how to do it; they are abstract, yet not vague.

A pattern has several sections beyond the solution. It describes the problem being addressed and the context in which it arises. It also describes the design tradeoffs – called *forces* – that it strives to balance. A pattern provides a *rationale,* which explains how the forces are balanced, and a *resulting context,* which describes new problems that arise because of the pattern or special situations that call for attention to other patterns. Together, these sections define a *pattern form*. Several popular pattern forms exist, all of which have these basic elements, but each of which adds other elements, such as applicability and intent, to emphasize specific design concerns. This form helps developers understand the problem, the solution, and the relationship between them, which enables developers to tailor an appropriate solution. A pattern is much more than a simple pairing of problem to solution.

The term *design pattern* usually refers to a collection of 23 patterns described in a book by Gamma, Helm, Johnson, and Vlissides [7], also called the "Gang of Four" patterns, referring to the four authors. These patterns follow the GoF form, which is widely emulated in the industry. They describe design solutions to problems that arise in object-oriented design. The patterns are largely independent of programming language, tools, and design methods, yet are specific enough for a novice programmer to implement. Familiarity with GoF patterns is, in many respects, a measure of competence in object-oriented programming.

The patterns described in this chapter are related to object-oriented design. Some are GoF patterns that we have applied to the domain of multimedia networking. A recent book by Buschmann et al., of Siemens [10], provided a valuable source for several other patterns that we have used. It has been dubbed the "POSA" book, an acronym of its title, *Pattern-Oriented Software Architecture*. The pattern form we use is described in "Pattern Form and Notation," later in this section.

THE OBSERVER PATTERN

The *Observer* pattern, from the GoF collection, serves to "define a one-to-many dependency between objects so that when one object changes state, all its dependents are notified and updated automatically." [7] The pattern is popularly used in human/machine interface designs to keep the user interface current with values of variables in a program. But that is just one specific use of *Observer*; the pattern can be generalized to fit many dependency registration problems.

Most good patterns have strong visual analogies. Figure 14.2 shows the structure of a typical *Observer* implementation (see "Pattern Form and Notation," later in this section, for the notation used). The intent of the pattern

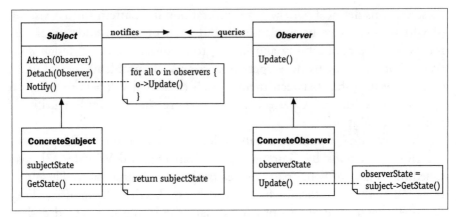

Figure 14.2. The Observer pattern.

is to keep the state of ConcreteObserver consistent with that of ConcreteSubject. The structure uses general-purpose abstract base classes Observer and Subject to decouple the dependency registration logic of the two classes. When ConcreteSubject goes to a new state, it notifies its observers (Notify()) so they can make their states consistent with the change. The notification takes place through the Notify() interface of the abstract Subject base class. The ConcreteObserver may then use GetState() to query the ConcreteSubject for state change details.

If we captured *Observer* in a higher-level design abstraction – for example, as a set of C++ abstract base classes – we would obscure important design components and design relationships. The purpose of a pattern is not to hide design secrets, but to clarify the relationships between the parts. Furthermore, a given software artifact such as a function or class may participate in several patterns at once; the partitioning is not strictly hierarchical. A pattern is sufficiently general that no single implementation may generalize to meet developer needs, so it is counterproductive to make it fit a single context.

Observer might be reused a million times without being implemented exactly the same way twice. If we use one invocation to propagate the notification event, followed by a reciprocal request for detailed state change information, the two actions can be combined by providing state information as an argument to the Notify() operation of the Observer class. This is not a new pattern, but rather a variant of the same pattern.

BUILDING FRAMEWORKS WITH PATTERNS

We can think of some patterns as abstract descriptions of small software frameworks. A *framework* is a partial program for a problem domain. A developer can extend a framework at its external interfaces to build a complete, running application. Most object-oriented programming languages are rich in constructs to extend existing abstractions. For example, *inheritance* allows the designer to incrementally define a new type (for example, class) in terms of an existing one. Templates (sometimes called parameterized types) allow even more general-purpose parameterization of algorithms, user-defined types, and data structures.

Patterns are more abstract; they describe the major components and the relationships among them without the detail of coding mechanisms. As we described earlier for the *Observer* pattern, one pattern may generate many viable implementations. A good pattern factors common changes from the recurring, stable structure. A developer should be able to conveniently capture specific application needs in new code, and then to just as conveniently hook this code into the framework using mechanisms supported by the programming language. One thing that keeps patterns abstract is their ability to remain flexible in application-specific variations.

A single pattern can generate a microarchitecture that can serve as a reusable framework. For example, a developer might use the *Observer* pattern as the architectural foundation for network conferencing. A state change in one terminal usually implies state changes or actions at other terminals. If one terminal goes mute (temporarily turns off its audio channel), other terminals may want to display an icon identifying the terminal that is muted. If one terminal goes on hook (hangs up), other terminals must be told that they should no longer try to communicate with that terminal. We can think of this use of *Observer* as a conference management framework that can easily accommodate many classes of change, such as the addition of new terminals or terminal types, the way call states are computed or represented, and many others. This architecture separates the addition of new features (such as private subconferences) from the underlying framework common to all features.

Most useful frameworks, such as the ET++ framework [11], are rich in patterns, combining many microarchitectures into a larger structure. The resulting framework can be documented by new patterns that describe how to extend it for specific desired behaviors.

PATTERN FORM AND NOTATION

Class diagrams drawn in this document use the Unified Modeling Language (UML) notation [12] (see Panel 3). We also introduce an extension of the UML notation to show patterns together with classes (see Panel 4). Pattern names are set in italics, and class names are set in the Courier type font.

Panel 3. Unified Modeling Language

Jointly, Grady Booch [21], James Rumbaugh et al. [22], and Ivar Jacobson [23], have recently started to define the Unified Modeling Language (UML) [12], which is expected to become a main industry standard. We use a subset of the UML notation, whose notation elements are summarized below.

Figure 14.3 shows a class diagram. Classes are depicted as rectangles, each of which includes three compartments – the class name, attributes, and operations, respectively (see SessionComponent). Class names are shown in bold, abstract class names in bold italics. The compartments for attributes and operations are optional. Inheritance is indicated by a solid arrow from the subclass to the superclass (for example, Party inherits from SessionComponent). General associations between classes are drawn as solid lines, optionally labeled with the direction and nature of the association (SessionComponent notifies SessionObserver). An aggregation, or "whole-part," relationship is shown as an association with a diamond at the class that is the container (Session contains Party). Comments are depicted by a rectangle with a flipped corner and a dashed line connecting it to the commented element.

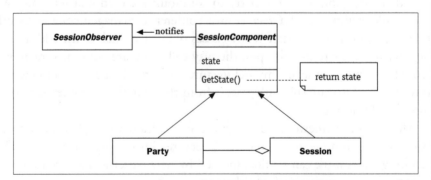

Figure 14.3. An example of a class diagram in UML notation.

Booch describes a potential extension to the UML to include patterns [24]. A pattern can be regarded as a template or a recipe to generate an instance of the classes that a designer uses in his or her design. These classes will conform to the roles of the pattern's classes. Patterns are drawn as ellipses. A designer's class that plays a role in a pattern is depicted by a dashed arrow pointing from the class to the pattern, labeled with the role being played.

We have also used this notation to show relationships between patterns. First, a role within a pattern may be played by another pattern, shown by the same notation, that is, a labeled dashed arrow from the pattern that conforms to a role. Second, a pattern can be a variant of a more abstract or better known pattern in a different domain, shown by a dashed arrow from the variant pattern to the base pattern. No label is used because the entire variant pattern conforms to the base pattern.

Figure 14.4, excerpted from the MediaBuilder architecture, illustrates the notation. The pattern *Session Control & Observation* conforms to the *Model View Controller* pattern. The *Session Control & Observation* pattern has three participants: `SessionControl`, `Session-Model`, and `SessionObserver`. The class `SessionControl-Command` plays the `SessionControl` role and the `Command` role within the *Command* pattern. The pattern *Parties & Media as First Class Citizens* plays the `SessionModel` role. The class `Medium-Builder` plays a `SessionObserver` role. As used here, conformance is not the same as inheritance, but rather compliance with the behavior of the pattern or one of its participant's roles.

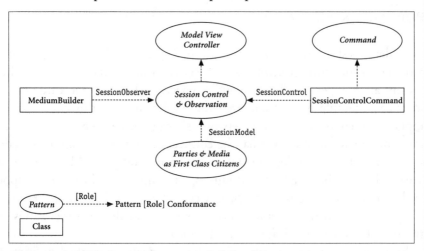

Figure 14.4. UML notation extended for design patterns.

The pattern form we use in this chapter contains the following sections:

- **Name.** The name of the pattern.

- **Context.** The situations in which the pattern may apply.

- **Problem.** The problem that the pattern addresses.

- **Forces.** Constraints related to the problem and/or tradeoffs shaping the solution.

- **Solution.** The principles of the solution.

- **Resulting context.** The benefits and liabilities of applying the pattern.

- **Examples.** Where and how the pattern has been applied within Media-Builder.

- **See Also.** References to related patterns.

MEDIABUILDER ARCHITECTURE

This section shows how existing and new design patterns address issues within the domain of multimedia networking and how these patterns are woven together to shape the MediaBuilder architecture.

PURPOSE AND SERVICES

Consider a desktop telephony application. Typically, this type of application provides connection control and transport of audio data streams. These streams are mapped locally to an audio device, such as a sound card. A more advanced example is a teleconferencing application. In this case, multiple applications cooperate over the network, sharing media such as video, audio, and whiteboard. In these media, the connection procedures and connection topologies (for example, multicast) are more complex. Multiple media streams have to be locally mixed (audio) or composed (video) and mapped to their corresponding multimedia devices. The sophistication of the under-lying network protocols and services, such as bridging, determines the amount of work an application must perform.

MediaBuilder allows software designers to create networked multimedia applications rapidly. It offers both a framework and a set of reusable components developed with that framework, as shown in Figure 14.5. Applications can be created by extending the framework and/or by selecting from components.

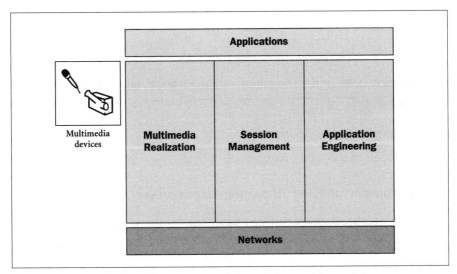

Figure 14.5. A functional overview of the MediaBuilder architecture.

Functionally, MediaBuilder is located between end-user applications, networks, and multimedia devices. Its applications can be used on different types of networks and their associated protocols. For example, the current MediaBuilder implementation runs on both ATM signaling networks and the Internet.

The services that MediaBuilder provides fall into three functional areas. Session management provides services that enable applications to control communication sessions. Multimedia realization deals with user protocols/multimedia streams and their mapping to local multimedia devices. Application engineering provides services to configure and instantiate framework components. The sections that follow discuss each functional area in more detail.

Session Management. Session management allows applications to establish a shared context. Applications modify and negotiate this context through the session management application programming interface (API). This API provides a high-level service that is independent of the underlying network. API services are used to:

- Set up/release a session,

- Add/delete parties and/or media,

- Join/leave a session,

- Reinstate a session,

- Modify characteristics of media and/or parties,

- Support roles and permissions of parties with respect to session management,

- Contact directory services, and

- Respond to incoming requests.

The two main functions of session management are:

- Mapping between user quality of service (QoS), such as sharing a video medium, and a network QoS, such as bandwidth and multicast; and

- Negotiating the session context with peer session management entities.

Multimedia Realization. Multimedia realization carries out the context negotiated by session management. This involves establishing transport connections for the end-to-end exchange of multimedia data, application protocols, and local mapping on multimedia devices. Initially, session management establishes an agreement between two users to share – for example, audio and video facilities – and then multimedia realization makes the connections that allow them to see and hear each other.

A set of base classes for application protocols, object communication, and finite state machines (FSMs) help develop new protocols and handle real-time sensitive streams. Extensible adapter classes provide a variety of standard transport services, such as native ATM or transmission control protocol/Internet protocol (TCP/IP). Services for buffering, splitting/combining, and multithreading support real-time streams, such as audio and video.

Multimedia devices – video cameras, speakers, microphones, audio files, and windows to display a shared whiteboard, and others – are producers and/or consumers of multimedia information. Base class abstractions are used to develop multimedia devices that support specific hardware or operating systems (OS)/multimedia interfaces.

Application Engineering. Components developed in each area described above can be reused. Reusable components may be individual classes or more extensive "building blocks" that, when selected and combined, can create (engineer) applications. Application engineering is supported by:

- A repository of available components,

- Configuration services to select and combine components, and

- Run-time mechanisms that allow components to be dynamically linked, created, and attached to the framework.

Components available for reuse include audio, video, shared whiteboard, reliable multicast, shared object protocol, ATM signaling control, and conference management.

ARCHITECTURAL OVERVIEW

This section summarizes the seven main patterns of the MediaBuilder framework, which are described in detail in subsequent sections.

Figure 14.6 shows the main design patterns, their relationships, and their external interfaces (small gray ellipses). Each pattern belongs to one of the functional areas introduced above – session management, multimedia realization, or application engineering. Although many more patterns contribute to the architecture, these seven patterns form the backbone of the MediaBuilder framework and determine its basic behavior.

The *Facade* pattern [7] is applied within MediaBuilder to give applications a common, high-level interface, the session management API, while shielding clients from the details of how a session is controlled.

The *Command* pattern [7] encapsulates a request as a class. It is applied within MediaBuilder to execute network-specific control procedures through which a session context is negotiated.

The *Session Control & Observation* pattern controls and maintains the state of a session and notifies those interested in that state. The pattern's three participants are realized using additional patterns, as shown in Figure 14.3. The session state (SessionModel) is modeled using the pattern *Parties & Media as First Class Citizens*. SessionControl, which controls the session state, is realized using the *Command* pattern [7]. SessionObservers have an interest in the session state.

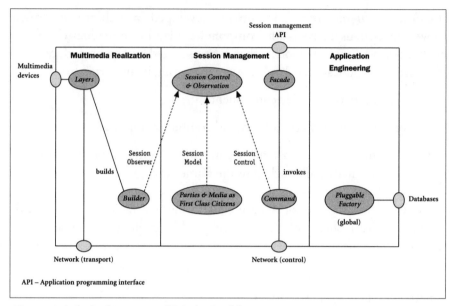

Figure 14.6. Architecture of MediaBuilder patterns.

The *Builder* pattern [7] is a specialized `SessionObserver` applied to build a realization of a session context (the `SessionModel`) that is local to the application. This involves creating and linking transport connections, application protocols, and local multimedia devices. These elements are structured according to the *Layers* pattern

The *Pluggable Factory* pattern provides a global service for configuring and instantiating framework components. A database holds a repository of components that can be reused in different applications.

SESSION MANAGEMENT PATTERNS

The four patterns that contribute to session management are *Session Control & Observation, Parties & Media as First Class Citizens, Facade,* and *Command.*

Session Control & Observation. MediaBuilder separates session control (session management) from session usage (multimedia realization). This concept is similar to the separation between control and user planes in the integrated services digital network (ISDN). Using the *Session Control & Observation* pattern, MediaBuilder links session management and multimedia realization.

Name – Session Control & Observation.

Context – Advanced signaling protocols, such as in narrowband ISDN (N-ISDN) and broadband ISDN (B-ISDN), separate control protocols (in the C plane) from user protocols (in the U plane). C plane protocols negotiate characteristics of U plane protocols. Clients such as terminal applications and switch call processing will have to integrate actions in these two planes. In addition, clients often need to maintain complex state information related to entities such as calls, parties, and connections. This information may be used for billing, connection modification, and status display.

Problem – How should responsibilities between classes that implement control and usage functions be decoupled?

Forces

- Usage functions should be triggered from control functions.

- A direct coupling between control and use inhibits these functions from evolving independently.

Solution – Divide these responsibilities among three classes: `Session-Model`, `SessionObserver`, and `SessionControl`. `Session-Model` maintains the state and notifies `SessionObservers` of state changes. `SessionControl` executes network-specific control procedures using `NetworkControl` on behalf of a `Client`. `SessionControl` reflects the (intermediate) results in the `SessionModel`. `SessionObserver` acts on state changes from the `SessionModel`. Specialized `SessionObservers` can handle the (instantiation of) protocols in the U plane or other usage functions such as billing or status display. Figure 14.7 a shows an example of the pattern's class structure.

This solution is a specialization of the *Model-View-Controller* pattern [13].

Examples – The message trace diagram (Figure 14.7b) shows a sample of how the pattern is used in an N-ISDN application. The `SessionModel` consists of a single `Call` object. `SessionControl` is represented by the object `OutgoingSetup` and interacts with `Call` and a `Q.931API` object (a `NetworkControl`). Two `SessionObservers` are shown: a `SpeechApplet`, which is responsible for handling audio functions (transport and presentation), and a `StatusDisplay`, which graphically monitors the call state.

Resulting Context – The pattern integrates control and usage aspects for sessions, while allowing these functions to evolve separately. For example,

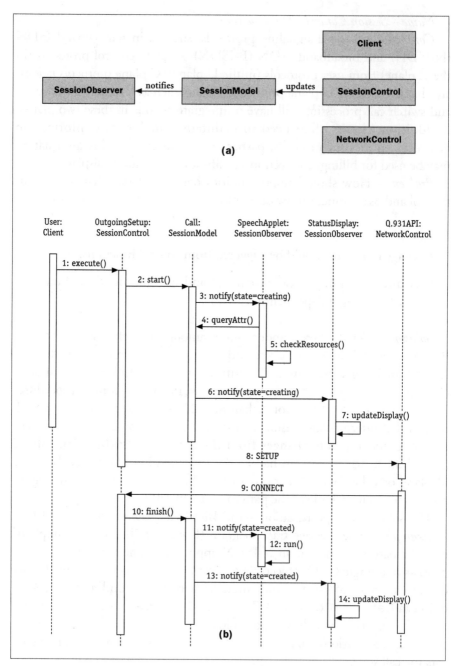

Figure 14.7. (a) A class structure example of the Session Control &
Observation pattern. (b) An application example of the Session Control
& Observation pattern.

new `SessionObserver` types may be developed and attached to the `SessionModel` without a need to change `SessionModel` or `SessionControl`. Similarly, `SessionControl` may be updated by additional control procedures or architectures.

The pattern does not enforce a particular distribution of its participating classes. For example, `SessionControl` and `SessionModel` may reside on a central server, while clients may maintain `SessionObservers`. Notifications from `SessionModel` will be carried from the server to clients. Smart caching of `SessionModel` within clients may reduce overhead for `SessionModel` queries over the network.

See Also – Buschmann et al. [10] described several variants of the *Model View Controller* pattern.

Parties & media as first class citizens. The pattern *Parties & Media as First Class Citizens* was applied to shape the main structure of the `SessionModel` role within the *Session Control & Observation* pattern.

Name – *Parties & Media as First Class Citizens.*

Context – Clients conducting a session involving multiple parties and connections must maintain complex state information. As the session proceeds, this state is modified in various ways, such as adding new connections and removing parties. For example, clients of broadband ATM protocols, such as International Telecommunications Union (ITU) Q.2931 [14], have to track parties and connections involved in a call.

The relationship between parties and connections (who is connected to whom) is often modeled from different viewpoints (that is, local view versus global view).

Problem – Different viewpoints often require complex conversions between models. How can we define and relate session entities that enable a single model to represent both a local and a global view?

Forces

- At times, parties in a session need to maintain connections.

- At times, connections need to maintain parties.

- A session release should clear all parties and connections.

- Services such as third-party call setup require a global view at the initiator.

Solution – Have each session (`Session`) maintain parties (`Party`) and media (`Medium`) involved in the session. Use a third object (`Party-`

MediumEdge) to maintain the state for each Party associated with Medium. Parties and media are thus first class citizens within a session. Figure 14.8 shows this structure.

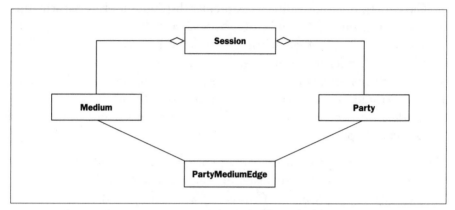

Figure 14.8. A class structure example of the Parties & Media as First Class Citizens pattern.

Medium embodies attributes common to all Party objects sharing it, such as agreed video coding. PartyMediumEdge represents aspects that are local to each Party with respect to that Medium, such as permissions and send/receive directivity. Another way of viewing the model is as a matrix of Medium and Party objects, where cells represent PartyMedium-Edge objects.

Resulting Context – Any topology of parties and media can be represented. The session context can be modified by adding/deleting any combination of Medium, Party, and PartyMediumEdge. For example, a new Party can be added to an existing Medium by adding a Party and a Party-MediumEdge.

The pattern does not imply any particular distribution. Objects comprising a model may be distributed or centralized.

Examples – Figure 14.9 shows the session model developed for Media-Builder. It applies the pattern twice, integrating a user-level context (Session, Party, Medium, PartyMediumEdge), as well as a communication context (Association, Connection, PartyAssociation-tionEdge). The communication context can represent various (logical) connection topologies, such as point-to-point or multipoint.

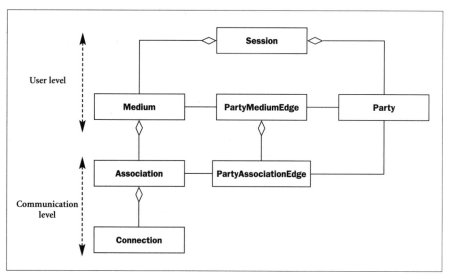

Figure 14.9. A MediaBuilder session model.

The session management API presents the user/QoS portion of the model. See the *Facade* pattern, discussed below.

Known Uses – A similar modeling approach has been applied in related projects for broadband (ATM) signaling. [15,16]

Facade. The *Facade* pattern, summarized here, is described in Gamma et al. [7]

Name – Facade.

Context – A system is structured into subsystems to reduce complexity.

Problem – How can coupling between subsystems be minimized?

Forces – High-level interfaces shield clients from the complexities of a subsystem, but they also hide lower-level functionality that clients with specialized needs may require.

Solution – Provide a high-level interface through a class (Facade) that shields clients from the lower-level functions of subsystem classes. Facade maps a high-level interface to low-level interfaces within a subsystem (see Figure 14.10a). Specialized clients may still access subsystem classes directly.

Resulting Context

- The pattern reduces the number of objects that clients have to deal with, making the subsystem easier to use.

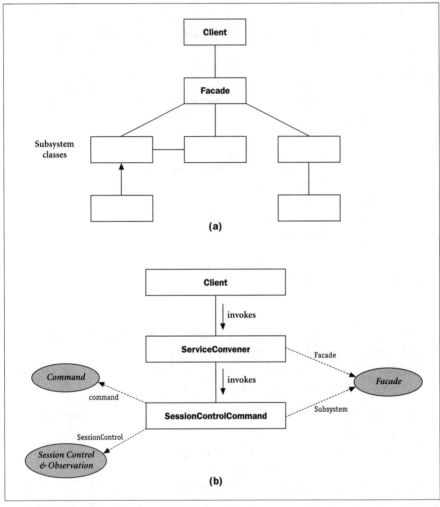

Figure 14.10. (a) The Facade pattern (see Gamma et al., [7] pp. 185–193). (b) Using the Facade pattern in MediaBuilder.

- The pattern promotes weak coupling between subsystems and their clients, making the evolution of subsystems less likely to affect clients.

- A client can still access subsystem classes as needed.

Examples – Facade is applied in MediaBuilder to realize the session management API (see Figure 14.10b). The `ServiceConvener` class plays the `Facade` role, and `SessionControlCommand` is a subsystem class. `ServiceConvener`, which application clients invoke to modify the session, instantiates and invokes one or more `SessionControlCommands` to carry out the request.

See Also – *Command Processor,* described in Buschmann et al. [10], combines elements of *Facade* and *Command.*

Command. The *Command* pattern is applied to modify the session state in cooperation with peer session management entities. *Command* is described in Gamma et al. [7], and summarized below.

Name – *Command.*

Content – A system to which clients can add new operations. These operations are invoked by the system and operate in a client-specific context. For example, we describe how to add a new type of signaling to MediaBuilder for performing session management.

Problem – How can the system invoke client-specific operations without knowing what they are or the context in which they will operate?

Forces

- The operation may be asynchronous – that is, the response to a request is not automatically returned.

- The client should be able to undo the operation before it is completed.

Solution – Encapsulate an operation as a class that declares an interface for its execution (`Command`). The actual execution is implemented in a derived class (`ConcreteCommand`). For example, `Command` may declare a pure virtual member function – `execute()` – that is overloaded in `ConcreteCommand`. Similarly, the operation can be canceled by overloading a pure virtual `undo()` member function.

Resulting Context – *Command* decouples the system invoking the operation from the object that knows how to perform or undo it, in this case, `ConcreteCommand`.

Examples – MediaBuilder applies *Command* to realize session management procedures (see Figure 14.10b). `SessionControlCommand` plays a role in two other patterns, `Session Control & Observation` (the `SessionControl` role) and *Facade* (the `Subsystem` role). `SessionControlCommand` can be specialized for different types of underlying networks and control architectures, such as central server or distributed.

ServiceConvener, the invoker of the SessionControlCommand, does not need specific knowledge of these technologies. ServiceConvener uses the *Pluggable Factory* pattern (see "Application Engineering Patterns" later in this chapter) to create the appropriate SessionControlCommand and calls on its specialized execute() or undo() function. For example, within the PLATINUM project (see Panel 2), SessionControlCommand is specialized for ATM signaling procedures.

See Also – *Command Processor,* described in Buschmann et al. [10], combines elements of the *Facade* and *Command* patterns.

MULTIMEDIA REALIZATION PATTERNS

Multimedia realization patterns address two issues:

- Modeling application protocols/streams and their relationships with multimedia devices and network transport media, using the *Layers* pattern; and

- Controlling the life cycle of application protocols/streams according to state changes in the session context, using the *Builder* pattern.

Layers. The *Layers* pattern is described in Buschmann et al. [10] Although the pattern's applicability is much wider, our summary is adapted to the domain of networking protocols.

Name – *Layers.*

Context – A system of networking protocols requires decomposition.

Problem – How should protocol components be modeled?

Forces

- Higher-level protocol components depend on lower-level ones.

- Components should be interchangeable.

- The highest and lowest protocol levels interact with system boundaries, such as applications and drivers.

Solution – Structure the system into an appropriate number of protocol layers, with the highest protocol layer on top and the lowest on the bottom. An actual design can have many variations (see "Examples," below).

Examples – Within MediaBuilder, an application protocol stack has to interact at both ends with external boundaries. Multimedia devices are at the top, and network transport connections, such as native ATM or TCP/IP, are at the bottom. The stack itself may consist of several layers of protocols, but it may also be empty if a transport connection is directly coupled to a multimedia device (such as a native ATM stream coupled to a video window). We also need to cater to stack topologies, in which multimedia devices and transport media have a many-to-many relationship. For example, multiple incoming audio streams are sometimes mixed (called combining) and sent to both a speaker device and an audio file (known as splitting).

Figure 14.11 shows the basic class structure. A protocol stack consists of layered components (`StackElements`). Each component can be a "true" layer (`Layer`), such as a protocol, or can provide adaptation (`Adapter`) to the user level (`PresenterAdapter`) or the network level (`TransportAdapter`). Layers may be specialized to split (`Splitter`) or combine (`Combiner`) media streams. Other layers can implement protocols (`ProtocolLayer`, not shown).

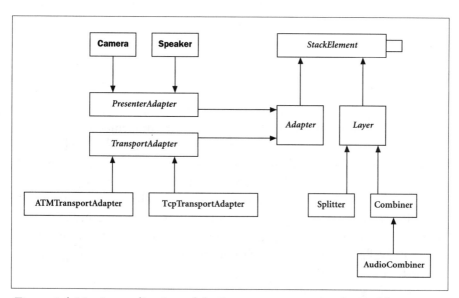

Figure 14.11. An application of the Layers pattern in MediaBuilder.

See Also – Hüni et al. [17] describe how GoF patterns such as *Strategy, Visitor,* and *Command* are applied in a framework for network protocols.

Builder. The *Builder* pattern, described in Gamma et al., [7] is summarized here.

Name – Builder.

Context – Construction of a composition of objects.

Problem – How can we make the construction process and the composition transparent to the client?

Forces – The number of possible compositions is open ended.

Solution – Separate the construction of the composition from its representation to allow the same construction process to create different compositions. The construction process is provided by an abstract class, the `Builder`. The client instructs `Builder` to build a composition. By overloading `Builder`, the client can force it to create different compositions.

Examples – Within MediaBuilder, *Builder* is applied to create a concrete representation of the session context that is local to the application. This consists of a protocol stack with attached multimedia devices and transport connections (see the *Layers* pattern). The class `MediumBuilder` conforms to both *Builder* and the role of *SessionObserver* within the *Session Control & Observation*. It controls the life cycle of the protocol stack according to session state changes.

APPLICATION ENGINEERING PATTERNS

The design patterns discussed in the sections "Session Management Patterns" and "Multimedia Realization Patterns" are implemented as a set of base classes that together determine the basic behavior of the MediaBuilder framework. Extensions of these classes are specialized for technologies such as multimedia types or ATM signaling control. These extended classes, which form a layer of components on top of the abstract framework, are available for reuse. New applications can be created by selecting and combining components at a level higher than a programming language. This is sometimes called "programming without programming." The *Pluggable Factory* pattern addresses these issues.

Name – Pluggable Factory.

Context – Provide reusable extensions of a (C++) framework. An object-oriented framework contains cooperating base classes that framework users can customize for their applications. The dilemma here is that the framework must instantiate these classes, even though it only knows about its base classes, which it cannot instantiate. The patterns *Factory Method* and *Abstract Factory* [7] provide a solution based on abstract interfaces with signatures returning a base class object. Users can customize the implementation of these interfaces through inheritance such that an instance of their concrete class is returned. This type of mechanism can be regarded as an object-oriented form of application callback. Many frameworks use *Factory*-type patterns. However, framework users still have to explicitly overload factory interfaces. Deriving new classes requires updating the factory and recompiling the application.

Problem – How can we make a factory whose product line can be configured by plugging in derived classes created by the framework? For example, if we introduce a fax medium into a MediaBuilder application, we need classes for a fax protocol and a fax multimedia device (see the *Layers* pattern). How can we add these to the application without recompiling or even stopping the application?

Solution – Extend the GoF factory patterns by symbolically creating objects from a repository (see Figure 14.12). Engineers (`Engineer`) configure component classes in a repository (`Repository`), each class of which has a symbolic name. When a client (`Client`) requests it, a reseller (`Reseller`) is able to instantiate a class from the repository through its symbolic name. Clients can also query the repository to get a list of class names. Implementing `Repository` works best with libraries that can be dynamically loaded, such as dynamic link libraries (DLLs) under Microsoft Windows. Initialization files can store the class names and the specific library name that creates and implements them.

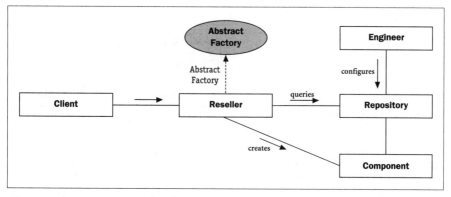

Figure 14.12. An example of the Pluggable Factory pattern in MediaBuilder.

Resulting Context – Adding components to the repository can extend an application. The repository can also store symbolic relationships between components, enabling engineers to create applications by combining components.

Examples Within MediaBuilder, *Pluggable Factory* provides a simple form of application engineering. By configuring class relationships in a file, it uses a repository of specialized classes to build larger components. At certain points, MediaBuilder will request *Pluggable Factory* for the creation of objects. For example, it may request that a voice connection be created by the base class `AudioSpeakerAdapter`. A user may have developed `MySpeakerAdapter` from `AudioSpeakerAdapter` to specify off-line that this class should be instantiated at run-time.

EXPANDED ARCHITECTURE

Figure 14.13 expands Figure 14.3 by showing key classes of the Media-Builder architecture.

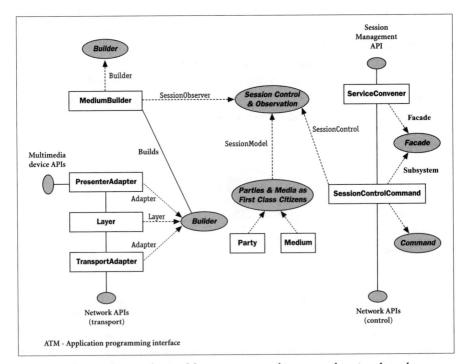

Figure 14.13. The MediaBuilder patterns architecture showing key classes.

`ServiceConvener`, which provides the Session Management API, enables a user program to modify a session context by adding, deleting, and modifying session objects such as `Party` and `Medium`. `ServiceConvener` invokes specialized `SessionControlCommands` that handle the control procedures.

`SessionControlCommand` conforms to the *Command* pattern and the `SessionControl` role within the *Session Control & Observation* pattern. It is responsible for modifying the session state. `SessionControlCommand` objects are customized to use specific control architectures and network control APIs to carry out functions such as ATM signaling.

The state of the session is realized with the pattern *Parties & Media as First Class Citizens*. This context is shared by all MediaBuilder instances participating in that context. It constitutes a global view consisting of a graph of objects such as all `Parties`, `Media`, their associations (`PartyMediumEdges`), and the connection topology used to provide end-to-end transport flows. Only `SessionControlCommand` objects make changes to the session state. `SessionObserver` objects are "views" of the session context. They are notified when the session changes state and can act on these changes according to their roles (see the paragraph below).

The `MediumBuilder` is a `SessionObserver` that builds a concrete local representation of the session context using the structure of the *Layers* pattern. This representation comprises stacks of streams and protocols, as well as multimedia devices attached to them.

Layers integrates protocol layering (using `Layer` classes) and adaptation to boundaries (using `Adapter` classes) at the ends of a protocol stack. `TransportAdapters` map a specific transport interface, such as ATM or TCP/IP, to a common transport interface. `PresenterAdapters` work like multimedia devices. For example, a `CameraPresenterAdapter` maps video input streams from a camera device (driver) to the next lower element in the stack, which can be either a `Layer` or `TransporterAdapter` object.

The `Reseller/Repository` classes (not shown in Figure 14.13) provide global services for configuring and instantiating components. The classes discussed above determine basic behavior, but the objects that carry out these responsibilities are created through the `Reseller`. The framework calls on the `Reseller` to create objects to carry out specific tasks. Using the *Pluggable Factory* pattern, the `Reseller` creates specific objects that are configured from overloaded classes in a repository. For example, the `ServiceConvener` asks the `Reseller` to create an `Outgoing-AddSessionControlCommand` when a user adds objects (such as a `Party`) to a session. Depending on how the repository was configured, the `Reseller` will return a specialized `OutgoingAddSessionControlCommand` (for example, for a specific type of ATM signaling). The repository also holds relationships between classes, such as the specific `SessionObservers` that are to be created for objects within the session model.

APPLICATION EXAMPLE

The conference management (CM) application is a desktop tool for teleconferencing. It allows a user to share multiple media with one or more users. Several meetings can be held concurrently by a CM application. To manage these sessions, CM provides an easy-to-use control interface that visually reflects the session state (see "Parties & Media as First Class Citizens," earlier in this chapter). Vertically, it shows the participants in a group meeting, horizontally the media. Intersections show the participation status of each participant in a medium. Double arrows indicate that the participant both sends and receives on each medium.

Each participant can configure his or her own participation and media and that of other participants by using the "Add Participant" and "Add Medium" buttons. By clicking on the buttons of the participant/medium intersections, the participant can alter his or her own status and that of other participants. A user can also save an active meeting in a file and later return to the same meeting by loading that file. Participants can be given roles and permissions with respect to session management. These permissions are checked by the framework and reflected in the user interface, for example, by disabling particular buttons.

Only the graphical user interface (GUI) is specific to the CM application. All other functions are provided by reusing MediaBuilder components. Networking functions are configured to use ATM signaling and native ATM streams (for optimal performance). The Medium Realization part reuses components like audio, video, and shared whiteboard. New multimedia components can be added (plugged in) without recompiling the application. The "Add Medium" button lets the user choose from a list of media available in the repository. When a medium is added to a session, its related protocols and multimedia devices are also automatically instantiated.

CONCLUSIONS

Patterns are a valuable tool to structure, communicate, and document the complex design issues that arise when combining networking and multimedia. Our experience with MediaBuilder showed us that designing with patterns was not a matter of "finding all the patterns and proceeding with the implementation." We started the MediaBuilder design with a single pattern *(Session Control & Observation)*. During the course of the design, and even in the implementation, we discovered and applied additional patterns. Through iteration, the basic framework took shape. As the development team grew comfortable with patterns, they assimilated its language into their vocabulary. For example, one could hear phrases like: "Okay, let's apply *Command* here." The ability to communicate in abstract structures rather than detailed objects was another benefit of using patterns.

The patterns described in the GoF [7] and POSA [10] books are, in our opinion, a valuable starting point for projects and organizations that would like to apply design patterns.

FUTURE DIRECTIONS

We are continuing to develop MediaBuilder, particularly in these areas:

- A pilot project with users of teleteaching and remote medical consultation,

- Server applications,

- Additional desktop (client) applications,

- Support for Internet-related networking standards,

- Networking through Winsock2 provider modules, and

- Longer-term evolution to a CORBA/TINA-C architecture. [4, 18]

ACKNOWLEDGMENTS

We thank all the reviewers of this paper – especially Doug McIlroy, Mark Bradac, Ferry van Geffen, and Hamza Ouibrahim, all from Lucent Technologies – for their comments and helpful suggestions.

REFERENCES

1. P.A. Bernstein, *Middleware – An Architecture for Distributed Systems.* White Paper CRL 93/6, Digital Equipment Corporation, Mar. 2, 1993.

2. A.A. Lazar, *Control, Management and Telemedia (COMET) Research Group – Activity Report.* Center for Telecommunications Research, Columbia University, New York City, Aug. 1996.

3. A.A. Lazar and K.S. Lim, "Programmability and Service Creation for Multimedia Networks." *Fifth IEEE International Symposium on High-Performance Distributed Computing.* Syracuse, NY, Aug. 1996, pp. 217–223.

4. Telecommunications Information Networking Architecture Consortium (TINA-C), *Overall Concepts and Principles of TINA.* TINA-C Deliverable version 1.0, 1995. http://www.tinac.com

5. *Multimedia Communications Forum.* http://www.mmcf.org/

6. K. Beck and R.E. Johnson, "Patterns Generate Architectures." *Proceedings of ECOOP94,* Bologna, Italy, July 1994, pp. 139–149. http://st-www.cs.uiuc.edu/users/patterns/papers

7. E. Gamma, R. Helm, R.E. Johnson, and J. Vlissides, *Design Patterns – Elements of Reusable Object-Oriented Software.* Reading, MA: Addison-Wesley, 1995.

8. G. Meszaros, "A Pattern Language for Improving Capacity of Reactive Systems." *Pattern Languages of Program Design* 2, ed. J. Vlissides et al. Reading, MA: Addison-Wesley, 1996, pp. 575–592.

9. M. Adams et al., "Fault-Tolerant Telecommunication System Patterns." *Pattern Languages of Program Design* 2, ed. J. Vlissides et al. Reading, MA: Addison-Wesley, 1996, pp. 549–562, and this volume, Chapter 4.

10. F. Buschmann, R. Meunier, H. Rohnert, P. Sommerlad, and M. Stal, *Pattern-Oriented Software Architecture – A System of Patterns.* New York: John Wiley, 1996.

11. E. Gamma, *Object-Oriented Software Development Based on ET++, Design Patterns, Class Library, Tools* (in German). Berlin: Springer-Verlag, 1992.

12. G. Booch, J. Rumbaugh, and I. Jacobson, *Unified Method for Object-Oriented Development.* Documentation Set 0.91, Rational Software Corporation, Sept. 1995. http://www.rational.com/ot/uml

13. G.E. Krasner and S.T. Pope, "A Cookbook for Using the Model-View-Controller User Interface Paradigm in SmallTalk-80." *Journal of Object-Oriented Programming,* Vol. 1, No. 3, Aug. 1988, pp. 26–49.

14. ITU Q.2931, *Broadband Integrated Services Digital Network (B-ISDN) – Digital Subscriber Signaling No. 2 (DSS 2). User Network Interface Layer 3 Specification for Basic Call/Connection Control.* International Telecommunications Union, 1995.

15. *Service Description Framework and B-ISDN Service Descriptions.* RACE II/MAGIC Deliverable 3, June 1993. http://www.analysys.com/race

16. S. Minzer, "A Signaling Protocol for Complex Multimedia Services." *IEEE Journal of Selected Areas in Communications,* Vol. 9, NO. 9, Dec. 1991, pp. 97–114.

17. H. Hüni, R.E. Johnson, and R. Engel, "A Framework for Network Protocol Software." *OOPSLA '95 Proceedings, ACM SIGPLAN Notices,* Austin, TX, Oct. 1995, pp. 358–369.

18. *Object Management Group.* http://www.omg.org/ http://st-www.cs.uiuc.edu/users/patterns/papers

19. A. Klapwijk, H. Ouibrahim, and U. Behnke, "PLATINUM: A Platform for New Users of Multimedia." *European Conference on Networks & Optical Communications (NOC '96).* Heidelberg, Germany, June 1996, pp. 115–122.

20. H. Ouibrahim and J.A. van den Broecke, "Multiparty/Multimedia Services to Native ATM Desktops." *Fifth IEEE International Symposium on High-Performance Distributed Computing.* Syracuse, NY, Aug. 1996, pp. 203–208.

21. G. Booch, *Object-Oriented Analysis and Design with Applications,* 2nd ed. Redwood City, CA: Benjamin/Cummings, 1994.

22. J. Rumbaugh et al., *Object-Oriented Modeling and Design.* Englewood Cliffs, NJ: Prentice-Hall, 1991.

23. I. Jacobson, *Object-Oriented Software Engineering – A Use Case Driven Approach.* Workingham, U.K.: Addison-Wesley, 1992.

24. G. Booch, "Patterns and Protocols." *Report on Object-Oriented Analysis and Design (ROAD),* Vol. 2, No. 3, May–June 1996, pp. 2–8.

FURTHER READING

J.O. Coplien and D.C. Schmidt, eds. *Pattern Languages of Program Design*. Addison-Wesley, 1995.

J.O. Coplien, *Software Patterns*. New York: SIGS Publications, June 1996.

R.P. Gabriel, *Patterns of Software: Tales from the Software Community*. Oxford, U.K.: Addison-Wesley, Aug. 1996.

15

OPENWEBSERVER:
AN ADAPTIVE WEB SERVER
USING SOFTWARE PATTERNS

Junichi Suzuki and Yoshikazu Yamamoto

ABSTRACT

THE EXPLOSIVE GROWTH of the Web requires servers to be extensible and configurable. This chapter describes our adaptive web server, OpenWebServer, which uses the *Reflection* architectural pattern. The server supports the dynamic adoption of functionality, such as introducing additional protocols, modifying execution policies, and tuning system performance. This is achieved by specifying and coordinating metaobjects that represent various aspects within the web server. We present a Java version of OpenWebServer, and describe its design using *Reflection* and other design patterns: *Singleton, Bridge, Mediator, Observer,* and *Decorator*. These patterns provide a better-factored design and allow the web server to evolve continually beyond static and monolithic servers.

INTRODUCTION

As the Internet is becoming more ubiquitous, the Web is increasingly used for many purposes. The explosive growth of the Web places larger and more challenging demands on servers. An effective design for Internet-based servers is required. This chapter describes our experience in designing a web server that addresses many of the current challenges facing web servers.

CHALLENGES FACING WEB SERVERS

Current web servers must:

- Connect with various systems such as groupware, database management systems, mobile agent engines, and transaction processing monitors.

- Integrate generic communication environments including CORBA (Common Object Request Broker Architecture) and DCOM (Distributed Component Object Model).

- Extend server functionality by introducing additional network protocols or content data types.

- Change server execution policies – e.g., optimize concurrency, connection management, request handling, and cache management.

- Adapt to the execution environment – e.g., ATM networks and electronic devices such as network routers, printers, or copiers.

Every user may not require the same functionality in a web server. Therefore, a web server should be flexible enough to meet a wide range of requirements on demand. Most web servers, unfortunately, are monolithic. They provide a fixed and limited set of capabilities. When additional functionality is required, the usual solution involves shutting down the system, modifying one or more components, integrating them with existing components, and restarting the system. This solution is often difficult or expensive to maintain, and does not allow the server to be used during the upgrade. Therefore, it is typical to take the "scrap-and-build" approach for a given requirement, where the software is rewritten from scratch because it may be more economically feasible. A dynamically adaptable web server architecture based on reusable components is an attractive alternative for extensive and intrusive changes.

ADAPTABILITY OF WEB SERVERS

Most web servers lack the adaptability to enable the system's evolution. Designers cannot know or predict all possible uses of the system. A service or configuration that is appropriate at one point may not be useful later, and the system may not evolve transparently.

The *Reflection* architectural pattern enables the system to maintain information about itself and use this information to remain changeable and extensible [1]. This chapter addresses the problem of adaptability and describes our use of patterns to build an adaptive web server. We consider the use of *Reflection* for specifying various aspects (e.g., structure and/or behavior) of an open-ended system that can be dynamically adapted. OpenWebServer is developed on top of AISF (Adaptive Internet Server Framework) [2], an adaptive framework for Internet servers. This chapter presents a Java version of OpenWebServer.

The remainder of this chapter is organized as follows: The first section introduces the concept and benefits of *Reflection*. The next section presents the advantage of developing a web server based on design patterns. The following section presents some applications of the adaptability of OpenWebServer. The next section describes design patterns used in the implementation phase. In the last two sections, we conclude with a note on the current status of the project and present future work.

THE REFLECTION ARCHITECTURAL PATTERN

In general, the meta-architecture that *Reflection* embodies introduces the notion of "object/metaobject separation." A metaobject or metalevel object contains information about the internal structure and/or behavior of one or more baselevel objects or baseobjects, which includes the application logic. In other words, metaobjects can track and control certain aspects (e.g., structure and/or behavior) of baseobjects. A set of metaobjects is called a metaspace or metalevel. A set of baseobjects is called a baselevel.

Reflection is the ability of a program to manipulate as data something that represents the state of the program to adjust to changing requirements. The goal of reflection is to allow a baseobject to reflect on its own execution state and eventually alter it to change its meaning during execution. In contrast to reflection, reification is the process of making something accessible that is normally unavailable in the baselevel (e.g., programming environment) or is hidden from the programmer. For the execution of a baseobject to be supervised, it must first be reified into the corresponding metalevel. The interfaces a baseobject uses to access its metalevel are called Metaobject Protocols, or MOPs. The relationships are illustrated in Figure 15.1.

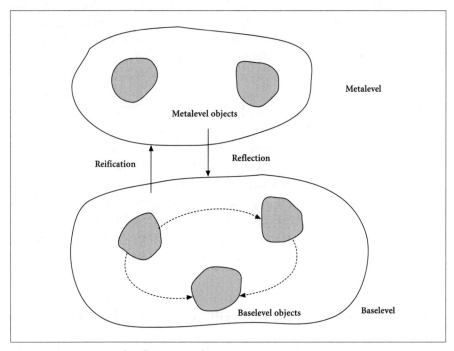

Figure 15.1. Typical reflective architecture.

CONCEPTUAL FRAMEWORK AND ADVANTAGES OF OPENWEBSERVER

OpenWebServer contains a metalevel that supports a wide range of aspects of web servers. It provides a set of fine-grained metaobjects and supplemental utility objects to support the writing of both the baselevel and metalevel. OpenWebServer is implemented within the programmable metalevel and can dynamically adjust itself so that it is executed in the best-tuned condition for a given requirement.

Although modern web servers provide some extension mechanisms like CGI (Common Gateway Interface), server-side APIs, and server-side scripting capability, their extensibility is restricted within the application level. In contrast, OpenWebServer provides a uniform platform where a variety of requirements can be specified from low-level services, such as connection management, request handling, and cache management, into application-level services without breaking the single framework. In other words, the metalevel in OpenWebServer plays the role of a generic "change absorber" for the web server.

The *Reflection* pattern provides the following advantages:

- Separation of concerns. In conventional web servers, the system's basic mechanisms are complicated by policy specifications. This makes it difficult to understand and maintain the system. The separation of the reflective facilities from the underlying mechanisms allows the reuse of feasible policies.

- Improved adaptability and configurability. The metalevel keeps the baselevel open-ended for extension. New requirements can be implemented with relatively minor modifications to baseobjects within the original system. This eliminates the "scrap-and-build" solution in system development.

- Transparency. Metaobject protocols decouple the metalevel and baselevel. This indirection reduces the constraints on both, so the levels can be developed independently. This transparency allows the metalevel to evolve while maintaining backward compatibility with the baselevel.

OpenWebServer is named after the Open-Closed Principle (OCP), which was originally proposed by Bertrand Meyer, and states that software entities should be open for extension but closed for internal modification. This means we should design systems so that objects can be extensible by adding new objects via inheritance or composition, not by modifying the object's internal working code. OpenWebServer is intended to apply the Open-Closed Principle so that the system can evolve by adding new metaobjects or reorganizing them.

METALEVEL DESIGN OF OPENWEBSERVER

This section presents the architectural overview of OpenWebServer and describes the design patterns used to construct the metalevel.

ARCHITECTURAL OVERVIEW

OpenWebServer consists of three packages. The `jp.ac.keio.ows.kernel` package contains the foundation objects to construct and maintain the metalevel. The `jp.ac.keio.ows.meta` package contains series of metaobjects and is controlled by the `kernel` package. The `jp.ac.keio.ows.utility` package contains utility objects to support the writing of both the baselevel and metalevel. It is used by `kernel` and `meta` packages.

The `jp.ac.keio.ows.kernel` package is organized as shown in Figure 15.2, and contains the following objects:

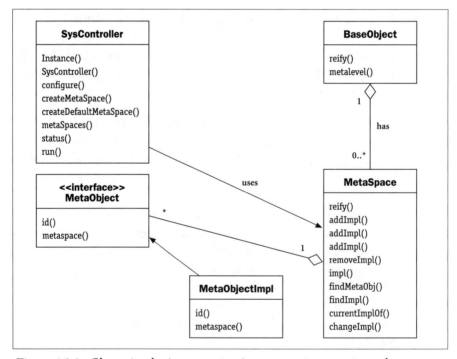

Figure 15.2. Classes in the `jp.ac.keio.ows.kernel` *package.*

- `SysController`. Starts the system by creating appropriate meta-spaces and metaobjects with a configuration file. It also keeps track of system status and system configuration. This object is also responsible for stopping and resuming the system. It is an active object executed on a root thread in the thread hierarchy.

- `MetaSpace`. Represents a metalevel, or metaspace. Multiple metalevels can exist within the system though it usually has a single metalevel. It references every metaobject and coordinates the interaction between them to meet a given requirement. This object is discussed later.

- `MetaObject`. Specifies the interfaces for all metaobjects. This is a base interface class for them. `MetaObjectImpl` and its subclasses provide the implementations of this object. The relationship between `MetaObject` and `MetaObjectImpl` is discussed next.

- `MetaObjectImpl`. Provides an implementation for a `MetaObject`. Multiple implementations can be defined for a single `MetaObject`.

- `BaseObject`. Specifies the interfaces needed to all baseobjects. This is a base class for them.

`SysController` is a *Singleton,* since it has exactly one instance in the system. The *Singleton* pattern ensures a class has just one instance and provides controlled access to it [3]. The following shows its selected interfaces:

```
public class SysController implements Runnable {
  static protected SysController Instance = null;
  protected Thread thread;
  public static SysController Instance(String param)
    {
   if(Instance == null){
    Instance = new SysController(param);
   }
    return Instance;
 }
 private SysController(String param) {
 // ...
   thread = new Thread(this);
   thread.start();
 }
}
```

The static `Instance()` method is used to instantiate or return the unique instance. The constructor is protected and called by `Instance()`. `SysController` creates one or more instances of `MetaSpace` and holds a set of references to them.

`MetaSpace` is an entry point from the baselevel to metalevel. Baseobjects can access `MetaSpace` when communicating with their metalevels. Each baseobject can have zero or more instances of `MetaSpace`. In turn, each `MetaSpace` aggregates zero or more metaobjects (see Figure 15.2).

Baseobjects do not have to be attached to a metalevel, but can be dynamically attached on demand. Attachment on demand is known as lazy reification. Each baseobject can be reified with its method `reify()`, and access its metalevel with the method `metalevel()` (see Figure 15.2). Once a baseobject is reified, it becomes aware of its metalevel, and the corresponding metaobjects are then instantiated by the class `MetaSpace`. The number and type of created metaobjects depend on what the users wish to do.

The `jp.ac.keio.ows.meta` package consists of a collection of metaobjects (see Figure 15.3). To specify metaobjects, we identified services and entities by looking for typical events or constructs found during the execution of web servers. Abstracting these events and constructs, OpenWeb-Server provides the following metaobjects by default:

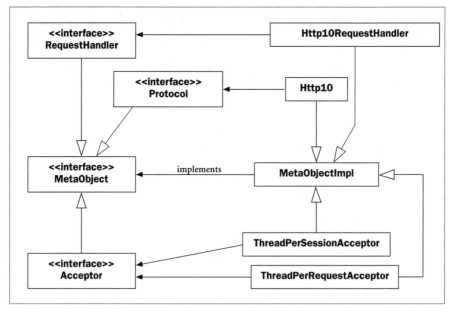

Figure 15.3. Classes in the `jp.ac.keio.ows.meta` *package.*

- `Initializer`. Initializes the network facility along with the current configuration. A typical task is to create one or more sockets according to the current communication protocol and concurrency policy and then instantiate an `Acceptor`.

- `Acceptor`. Waits for and accepts incoming requests. It encapsulates the different concurrency policies for simultaneous access. Once it obtains a request, it asks a `RequestHandler` to process the request given the current configuration (i.e., protocol and concurrency policy).

- `RequestHandler`. Deals with requests from an `Acceptor`. It encapsulates the different policies for interpreting a request, based on the kind of request and target content. It is created on a per-request basis when an `Acceptor` accepts a request. It is executed on a separated thread or the same thread that an `Acceptor` runs on.

- `Protocol`. Defines protocol specific information on a per-protocol basis. It is referenced by a `RequestHandler`.

- `ContentFinder`. Finds a target resource (e.g., HTML/XML files or data within a back-end repository) passed by a `RequestHandler`.

- `Logger`. Records accesses to the web server. `RequestHandler` typically calls it.

- `ExecManager`. Executes external entities like CGI scripts.

These metaobjects represent typical aspects of web servers. They are objects that affect the behavior of other objects, and have the following basic responsibilities [1]:

- Encapsulate system internals that may change.

- Provide an interface to facilitate modifications to the metalevel.

- Control baselevel behavior.

As shown in Figure 15.3, all metaobjects are interface classes derived from `MetaObject` in the `kernel` package. We can add a new metaobject depending on the requirements by deriving from `MetaObject`. Implementations of a metaobject are provided by implementation classes derived from `MetaObjectImpl`. Figure 15.3 shows two implementations attached to `Acceptor`. `ThreadPerRequestAcceptor` and

`ThreadPerSessionAcceptor` implement different concurrency policies of thread per request and thread per session, respectively. Implementation classes are also contained in the `meta` package.

OpenWebServer eliminates the explicit level shifting from baselevel to metalevel, and the explicit reflective function calls found in the traditional reflective programming languages. This is similar to the approach introduced by CodA, a Smalltalk-based meta-architecture [4]. Metaobjects are just like other objects in the system. Reflective computation is executed by direct interaction with the desired metaobjects. Methods of every metaobject within the `kernel` and `meta` packages are considered Metaobject Protocols (MOPs).

DESIGN PATTERNS FOR MODELING METAOBJECTS

Bridge: Decoupling in the previous section a Metaobject and Its Implementations. The metaobjects just described in the previous section are abstractions of typical aspects of web servers, and define their interface and semantics. Their concrete implementations are prepared as classes that implement them and derive from `MetaObjectImpl` (Figures 15.3 and 15.4). The relationship between metaobject and its implementations is based on *Bridge* [3]. The pattern explicitly decouples an interface and its implementation. Permanent binding between them should be avoided in OpenWebServer. The implementation must be dynamically chosen or changed for system adaptability. Also, both the interface and the implementations should be independently extensible; changes in an implementation should have no impact on clients of the interface.

Bridge separates an interface and its implementation using object composition, instead of inheritance, which is typically used for incremental modifications. Object composition should be favored over inheritance, since object composition decouples the early and permanent binding between an object and the semantics of its behavior, and provides more run-time flexibility [2, 3].

OpenWebServer uses a variant of *Bridge*, which includes the interface-implementation relationship, provided by Java, between interface and its implementation. Figure 15.4 depicts a class diagram where this pattern is applied to `Acceptor`. `ThreadPerRequestAcceptor` and `ThreadPerSessionAcceptor` are implementation classes of `Acceptor`. These classes implement `accept()` differently, which contains an infinite loop to wait for incoming requests and dispatches them to a `RequestHandler` along with the current concurrency policy.

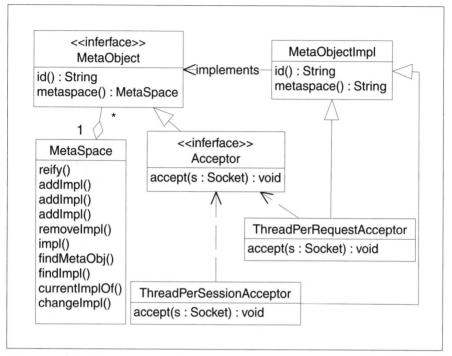

Figure 15.4. Class structure of a metaobject and its implementations.

In our variant of *Bridge*, MetaSpace aggregates implementation objects so that it can change the metaobject's implementation dynamically. It can inspect the current implementation with its currentImpl(), and change it using changeImpl(). The following section describes how Meta-Space maintains a set of metaobjects and their implementations internally.

Bridge allows changing the metaobject's implementation at run-time, depending on the desired execution policy in the web server. It allows dynamic adaptation without system shutdown. *Bridge* has the following benefits for OpenWebServer:

- Decoupling abstraction and implementations.

- Layered architecture that separates the core mechanism and its policy explicitly. This leads to a system that is better factored and easier to maintain.

- Improved adaptability.

DESIGN PATTERNS FOR COORDINATING METAOBJECTS

OpenWebServer encourages metaobjects to specify aspects in web servers and interact with each other to meet design demands. This often causes multiple associations among metaobjects. In the worst case, every metaobject should know all others. Though partitioning a system into well-defined objects generally enhances reusability, lots of interconnections make it less likely that a metaobject can work without the support of others. As a result, the system behaves as if it were monolithic. Moreover, it would be difficult to change a system's behavior transparently due to the spaghetti associations.

Mediator: Isolating the Associations Between Metaobjects. To avoid this situation, we use *Mediator* [3], which encapsulates the interaction of a set of objects and facilitates loose coupling among them by keeping the reference to every object within a mediator object. In OpenWebServer, `MetaSpace` is a mediator object. It controls and coordinates interactions among a set of metaobjects. It acts as an intermediary among the metaobjects in the meta-level. Each metaobject knows only `MetaSpace`, not any other metaobject, thereby reducing the number of interconnections.

Figure 15.5 shows how *Mediator* is applied to the metalevel of OpenWeb-Server. In this figure, `MetaSpace` is an intermediary among `Acceptor` and `Logger`. Each metaobject has an attribute `metaspace` to refer to the metaspace it belongs to, and can call `currentImplOf()` of `Meta-Space` to get the current implementation of a desired metaobject. Figure 15.6 depicts a run-time object structure where three metaobjects indirectly interconnect with `MetaSpace`. `MetaSpace` contains every metaobject and its implementations in the instance variable `components`, typed `Hashtable`. This variable has the mapping of a string entry (key) and `Vector` type value. The former is used to assign the string name of metaobject, and the latter is for the sequence of implementation objects. The current implementation is assigned to the first element of the vector. The method `currentImplOf()` returns the first element, and `changeImpl()` changes the order of elements in the vector. To add an implementation object, the method `addImpl()` is used, which is prepared for every type of metaobject.

Mediator provides the following benefits for OpenWebServer:

- Encapsulation of the interactions between metaobjects.

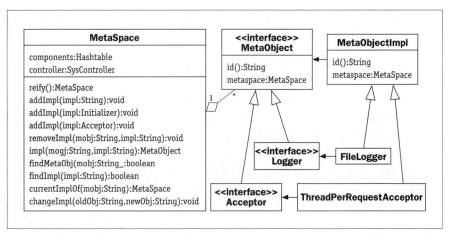

Figure 15.5. A class structure of MetaSpace, *metaobjects, and their implementations based on Mediator.* MetaSpace *is an intermediary among metaobjects and encapsulates their interactions; instead, metaobjects are connected each other directly.*

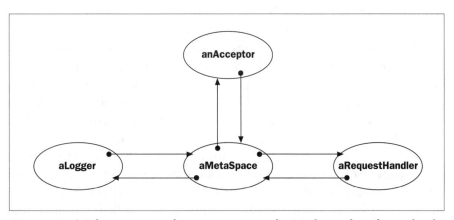

Figure 15.6. The run-time object structure in the Mediator-based metalevel. Here, three metaobjects interconnect indirectly via MetaSpace.

- Loose connections between metaobjects and simplified protocols between them.

- Centralized control for metaobjects.

Mediator+Observer: Propagating the Change of Metaobjects. Decoupling a metaobject and its implementations causes the changes in each metaobject to be localized when the metaobject dynamically alters its implementations. Such changes, however, will occasionally affect other metaobjects and require the event to be transferred to them. For example, a change in the implementation of the `Protocol` metaobject requires a reconfiguration of `RequestHandler`. Therefore, `MetaSpace` must propagate change events to the metaobjects that are interested in the change. Every metaobject should not know the metaobjects that depend on its change.

In this situation, *Observer* [3] can be used for metaobject-mediator communication. This pattern encapsulates the interactions between objects by using a subject to store the state information for observer objects. Figure 15.7 shows that metaobjects (and their implementations virtually) are observers of `MetaSpace`. `Observable` is a subject class and `Observer` is an observer interface class. Whenever the configuration of a metaobject changes, `MetaSpace` propagates the event to other metaobjects using its method `notifyObservers()`. Metaobjects respond to the event with `update()`. `Mediator` is also an observer for `SysController`, because `SysController` sends the system status to `MetaSpace`.

`SysController`, `MetaSpace`, and some metaobjects are usually executed in different threads. Therefore, it is possible to cause deadlock, if an `Observable` issues a change notification in a thread while an `Observer` is trying to check the `Observable`'s instance variable. To avoid the potential deadlock, `MTObservable` is introduced (Figure 15.7). It uses `Notifier` to issue the event notification in a new thread. A `Notifier` is created for a single notification to an observer. This concurrent variant of *Observer* is borrowed from [5]. Note that `Observable` and `Observer` are not those in the `java.util` package, because the instance variable `observers` of `Observable` in JDK is private instead of protected; thus it cannot be used from `MTObservable`.

Observer provides the following benefits for OpenWebServer:

- Loose coupling between metaobjects and the mediator.

- Centralized control to propagate the change events.

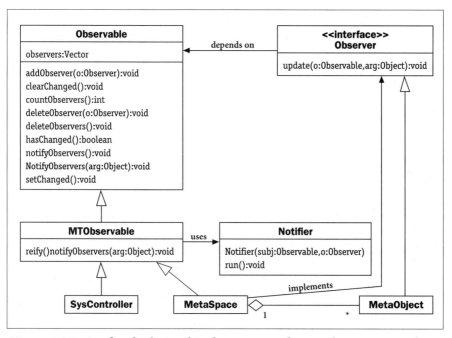

Figure 15.7. A refined relationship for event notification between metaobjects and `MetaSpace` *with Observer.*

- Simplified and more abstract protocol between the mediator and metaobjects.

DESIGN PATTERNS USED FOR UTILITY OBJECTS

OpenWebServer provides supplemental utility objects that allow the asynchronous I/O capability used by a concurrency policy called single-threaded with I/O multiplexing (see also next section). These objects are plugged into a Java package handling I/O streams named `java.io`. This package uses *Decorator* [3]. Figure 15.8 shows `AsyncInputStream` and `NonBlockingStream` are derived from `java.io.FilterInputStream`. The difference in these classes is whether the method `available()` of `java.io.InputStream` is used or not. This method returns the number of bytes that can be read from the stream without blocking. `NonBlockingStream` precedes all `read*()` methods with a call to `available()` to ensure there are data available. The method `available()`, however, does not work well with certain mechanisms like the network socket, and `read()` may not block if `available()` returns 0 [6]. `AsyncInputStream` reports the correct number of bytes that can actually be read asynchronously without using the derived `available()`. It can get available data in a nonblocking manner by spawning a thread that calls blocking `read()` exclusively.

APPLICATIONS

Our first application is to support dynamic reconfiguration of concurrency policy. OpenWebServer provides a series of implementations for `Acceptor`, and can tune the policy at runtime. It supports the following policies:

- Process per request. A simple model to implement, but resource intensive and requires too much overhead.

- Process pool. Alleviates the overhead in the above forking model. It requires mutual exclusion.

- Thread-per-request. Much faster than the forking policy. However, it is not portable for different platforms.

- Thread-per-session. Less resource-intensive than the thread-per-request policy. However, it requires that endpoints use HTTP 1.1 or that the server detect the location of clients for every incoming request.

- Thread pool. Alleviates the overhead of the threading policy. It requires mutual exclusion.

- Single-threaded I/O multiplexing. Conservative of resources and highly portable. It also has less overhead. However, it is fault-sensitive, and the number of simultaneous connections is limited.

For example, OpenWebServer can start as a single-threaded server with I/O multiplexing, and then change itself into a threaded server when the workload (i.e., the access rate) of the server exceeds the predefined threshold.

The second application is the dynamic adaptation of communication protocols. OpenWebServer provides configurations for HTTP 0.9, 1.0, and 1.1 as implementation classes of `Protocol`.

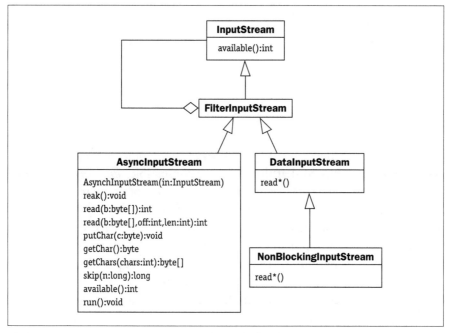

Figure 15.8. AsyncInputStream *and* NonBlockingStream *are used for asynchronous I/O. They are plugged into the Decorator class structure.*

OpenWebServer also has application-level components. We have created a CGI (Common Gateway Interface) capability as an implementation class for ExecManager. Also, it has been integrated with a CSCW (ComputerSupported Collaborative Work) environment where the software design information is shared within the distributed development team [7]. OpenWebServer prepares an implementation for ContentFinder, which finds a requested XML (eXtensible Markup Language) document. It also provides utility objects that parse HTML/XML documents, create their syntax trees, and retrieve elements and attributes in the parsed tree.

The personalization service of HTML/XML documents is implemented with OpenWebServer [8]. The dynamic generation of document presentation is performed based on the context of client-side environment, users, and users' behaviors. The implementations for RequestHandler, ContentFinder, and CacheManager are provided for this purpose.

Our last application is to integrate OpenWebServer with the DOM (Document Object Model) interface and CORBA [7]. DOM is a standard of the World Wide Web Consortium, which provides a series of interfaces for accessing and manipulating XML documents.

DISCUSSION AND RELATED WORK

To evolve the metalevel of OpenWebServer, metaobjects should be fine-grained and black box so that they are plug-compatible. *Evolving Framework* [9] is a pattern language, a set of patterns that describes how to start building a reusable framework, refactor it, and support the development process with appropriate tools. It includes a pattern, *Three examples,* which should be applied to the development of a framework at first. This pattern enables a developer to find hidden abstractions and rebuild proper abstractions by developing at least three applications. We have developed six applications as described in the previous section and have tried to be sure the metalevel contains proper abstractions (i.e, metaobjects). We plan to develop other applications that are even more different from previous ones (see next section). *Evolving Framework* also includes *Hot spots,* a pattern to identify hot spots and encapsulate them with design patterns. Hot spots are the aspects of a problem domain that must be kept flexible. In OpenWebServer, a series of metaobjects represent hot spots and encapsulate some types of changes. Developing its subsequent applications would allow us to find hidden hot spots and refine the metalevel. Currently, we are applying *Fine-grained objects* and *Black-box framework.*

Despite its flexibility, *Reflection* has some liabilities [1]:

- Modifications at the metalevel may cause damage. The robustness of a metalevel is quite important, because incorrect modifications of the metalevel may cause serious damage to the system. The current Open-WebServer cannot detect potential errors that might be caused by the change specifications. Metalevels that allow the safe deletion of metaobjects are of particular interest.

- Increased number of components. The greater the number of aspects that are defined at the metalevel, the greater the number of metaobjects. This may add unnecessary complexity for a simple web server and increase the difficulty in maintaining the metalevel. We are investigating a mechanism that keeps the metalevel lightweight by allowing the safe deletion of metaobjects.

- Lower efficiency. Reflective systems are slower than nonreflective systems, because a single task requires the interaction between baselevel and metalevel. Thus, OpenWebServer is slower than static and monolithic servers. However, we can adjust the trade-off between dynamic adaptability and performance, with the mechanism of lazy reification.

CURRENT PROJECT STATUS AND FUTURE WORK

The current OpenWebServer includes eight metaobjects, twenty-nine implementation objects, and thirty utility objects. It was initially implemented with the Python programming language and, later, with Java. We are investigating other languages to illustrate that the architectural design of Open-WebServer does not depend on a specific language.

As for the metalevel in OpenWebServer, we are aggressively making metaobjects fine-grained. At present, we are dividing `Acceptor` into different metaobjects that deal with concurrency and I/O, as described in [10], because the current `Acceptor` is somewhat coarse. Also, we are experimenting with an alternative mechanism to coordinate metaobjects. As described earlier, OpenWebServer incorporates some design patterns to achieve system evolution. However, composing and coordinating metaobjects to introduce new system behavior requires precise knowledge of the interfaces and implementations of all the metaobjects. Few methodologies have been proposed for metaobject composition. We are developing a framework that enables the relationships between baselevel and metalevel as well as among metaobjects to be more configurable, and to hide the details of the coordination process. We are particularly interested in the deletion of metaobjects from the metalevel. The deletion of metaobjects often brings unexpected fatal errors, while the addition of metaobjects can be handled seamlessly. Our goal is to provide a highly scalable metalevel.

We are also developing applications for OpenWebServer to demonstrate the power of its metalevel and improve it. We plan to introduce additional communication protocols such as LDAP (Lightweight Directory Access Protocol) and SNMP (Simple Network Management Protocol). We also plan to provide real-time streaming functionality for continuous media using RTP

(Realtime Transport Protocol) or RTSP (RealTime Streaming Protocol). New underlying environments of OpenWebServer are also planned including CORBA, embedded environments, and real-time operating systems.

CONCLUSION

This chapter addresses how web servers can meet diverse requirements and describes the advantage of using software patterns that make them adaptable and configurable. We used *Reflection, Singleton, Bridge, Mediator, Observer,* and *Decorator* to achieve it. With these patterns, OpenWebServer makes its aspects open-ended for extension, and allows itself to continually evolve beyond the static and monolithic servers of today. The information on our project is maintained at www.yy.cs.keio.ac.jp/~suzuki/project/aisf/. The original version of this chapter can be also found at this URL, which does not remove some sentences, figures, and references due to the editorial limits.

ACKNOWLEDGEMENTS

We would like to thank Linda Rising, Haruo Akimaru, and Shigeki Yamada for their invitation to this special issue. We are also grateful to Mike Duell, Jeff Garland, and John Goodsen for their helpful comments and suggestions for earlier drafts.

REFERENCES

1. F. Buschmann, R. Meunier, H. Rohnert, P. Sommerlad, and M. Stal, "A System of Patterns: Pattern-Oriented Software Architecture", New York: Wiley, 1996.

2. J. Suzuki and Y. Yamamoto, "Building an Adaptive Web Server with a Meta-Architecture: AISF Approach." In *Proceedings of SPA '98,* March 1998.

3. E. Gamma, R. Helm, R. Johnson, and J. Vlissides, "Design Patterns: Elements of Reusable Object-Oriented Software." Reading, MA: Addison-Wesley, 1995.

4. J. McAffer, "Engineering the Meta Level." In *Proceedings of Reflection '96,* 1996.

5. D. Lea, "Concurrent Programming in Java: Design Principle and Patterns." Reading, MA: Addison-Wesley, 1997.

6. S. Oaks and H. Wong, "Java Threads." O'Reilly & Associates, 1997.

7. J. Suzuki and Y. Yamamoto, "Toward the Interoperable Software Design Models: Quartet of UML, XML, DOM and CORBA." Submitted to IEEE ISESS '99, 1999.

8. J. Suzuki and Y. Yamamoto, "Document Brokering with Agents: Persona Approach." In *Proceedings of WISS'98,* December 1998.

9. D. Roberts and R. Johnson, "Patterns for Evolving Frameworks." In *Pattern Languages of Program Design 3.* R. Martin, D. Riehle, and F. Buschmann, eds. Reading, MA: Addison-Wesley, 1998.

10. J.C. Hu and D.C. Schmidt, "Developing Flexible and High-Performance Web Servers with Frameworks and Patterns." In *ACM Computing Surveys,* May 1998.

16

Applying a Pattern Language
to Develop Application-Level
Gateways

Douglas C. Schmidt

Abstract

Developers of communication applications must address recurring design challenges related to efficiency, extensibility, and robustness. These challenges are often independent of application-specific requirements. Successful developers resolve these challenges by applying appropriate pattern and pattern languages. Traditionally, however, these patterns have been locked in the heads of expert developers or buried deep within complex system source code. The primary contribution of this chapter is to describe a pattern language that underlies object-oriented communication software. In addition to describing each pattern in this language, the chapter illustrates how knowledge of the relationships and trade-offs among the patterns help guide the construction of reusable communication frameworks and applications.

1 Introduction

Communication software is the set of services and protocols that makes possible modern distributed systems and applications, such as web services,

Based on "A Family of Design Patterns for Application-Level Gateways," by Douglas C. Schmidt, which appeared in *Theory and Practice of Object Systems* 2(1), pp. 15–30, 1996. ©1996 John Wiley & Sons, Inc. Used with permission from the author.

distributed objects, collaborative applications, and e-commerce systems [1]. Building, maintaining, and enhancing high-quality communication software is hard, however. Developers must have a deep understanding of many complex issues, such as service initialization and distribution, concurrency control, flow control, error handling, event loop integration, and fault tolerance. Successful communication applications created by experienced software developers must embody effective solutions to these issues.

It is non-trivial to separate the essence of successful communication software solutions from the details of particular implementations. Even when software is written using well-structured object-oriented (OO) frameworks and components, it can be hard to identify key roles and relationships. Moreover, operating system (OS) platform *features*, such as the absence or presence of multi-threading, or application *requirements*, such as best-effort versus fault tolerant error handling, are often different. These differences can mask the underlying architectural commonality among software solutions for different applications in the same domain.

Capturing the core commonality of successful communication software is important for the following reasons:

1. *It preserves important design information for programmers who enhance and maintain existing software.* Often, this information only resides in the heads of the original developers. If this design information is not documented explicitly, therefore, it can be lost over time, which increases software entropy and decreases software maintainability and quality.
2. *It helps guide the design choices of developers who are building new communication systems.* By documenting common traps and pitfalls in their domain, patterns can help developers select suitable architectures, protocols, and platform features without wasting time and effort (re)implementing inefficient or error-prone solutions.

The goal of this chapter is to demonstrate by example an effective way to capture and convey the essence of successful communication software by describing a *pattern language* used to build application-level *gateways*, which route messages between *peers* distributed throughout a communication system. Patterns represent successful solutions to problems that arise when building software [2]. When related patterns are woven together, they form a language that helps to

• Define a vocabulary for talking about software development problems; and

• Provide a process for the orderly resolution of these problems.

Studying and applying patterns and pattern languages helps developers enhance the quality of their solutions by addressing fundamental challenges in communication software development. These challenges include communication of architectural knowledge among developers; accommodating new design paradigms or architectural styles; resolving nonfunctional forces, such as reusability, portability, and extensibility; and avoiding development traps and pitfalls that are usually learned only by costly trial and error [3].

This chapter presents the OO architecture and design of an application-level gateway in terms of the pattern language used to guide the construction of reusable and gateway-specific frameworks and components. Application-level gateways have stringent requirements for reliability, performance, and extensibility. They are excellent exemplars, therefore, to present the structure, participants, and consequences of key patterns that appear in most communication software.

The pattern language described in this chapter was discovered while building a wide range of communication systems, including on-line transaction processing systems, telecommunication switch management systems [4], electronic medical imaging systems [5], parallel communication subsystems [6], avionics mission computers [7], and real-time CORBA object request brokers (ORBs) [8]. Although the specific application requirements in these systems were different, the communication software design challenges were similar. This pattern language therefore embodies design expertise that can be reused broadly in the domain of communication software, well beyond the gateway example described in this chapter.

The remainder of this chapter is organized as follows: Section 2 outlines an OO software architecture for application-level gateways; Section 3 examines the patterns in the pattern language that forms the basis for reusable communication software, using application-level gateways as an example; Section 4 compares these patterns with other patterns in the literature; and Section 5 presents concluding remarks.

2 AN OO SOFTWARE ARCHITECTURE FOR APPLICATION-LEVEL GATEWAYS

A gateway is a mediator [2] that decouples cooperating peers throughout a network and allows them to interact without having direct dependencies on

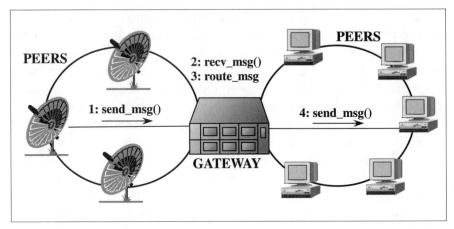

Figure 16.1. The structure and dynamics of peers and an application-level gateway.

each other. As shown in Figure 16.1, messages routed through the gateway contain payloads encapsulated in routing messages. Figure 16.2 illustrates the structure, associations, and internal and external dynamics among objects within a software architecture for application-level gateways. This architecture is based on extensive experience developing gateways for various research and production communication systems. After building many gateway applications it became clear that their software architectures were largely independent of the protocols used to route messages to peers. This realization enabled the reuse of components depicted in Figure 16.2 for thousands of other communication software projects [1]. The ability to reuse these components so systematically stems from two factors:

1. *Understanding the actions and interactions of key patterns within the domain of communication software.* Patterns capture the structure and dynamics of participants in a software architecture at a higher level than source code and OO design models that focus on individual objects and classes. Some of the communication software patterns described in this chapter have been documented individually [1]. Although individual pattern descriptions capture valuable design expertise, complex communication software systems embody scores of patterns. Understanding the relationships among these patterns is essential to document, motivate, and resolve difficult challenges that arise when building communication software. Therefore, Section 3

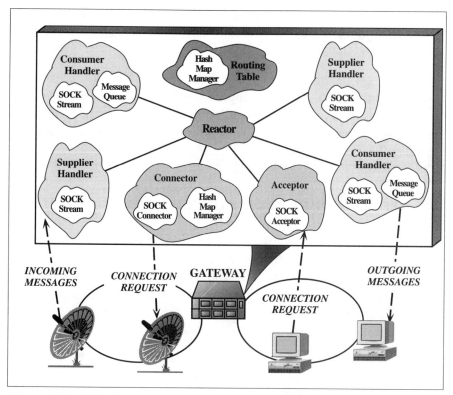

Figure 16.2. The OO gateway software architecture.

describes the interactions and relationships among these patterns in terms of a *pattern language* for communication software. The patterns in this language work together to solve complex problems within the domain of communication software.

2. *Developing an OO framework that implements these patterns.* Recognizing the patterns that commonly occur in many communication software systems helped shape the development of reusable framework components. the gateway systems this chapter is based upon were implemented using the ADAPTIVE Communication Environment (ACE) framework and components that integrated reusable C++ wrapper facades and tasks. These tasks include event demultiplexing, event handler dispatching, connection establishment, routing, dynamic configuration of application services, and concurrency control. In addition, the ACE framework contains implementations of the patterns

319

described in Section 3. The patterns are much richer than their implementation in ACE, however, and have been applied by many other communication systems, as well.

This section describes how various ACE components have been reused and extended to implement the application-independent and application-specific components in the communication gateway shown in Figure 16.2. Following this overview, Section 3 examines the pattern language that underlies the ACE components.

2.1 APPLICATION-INDEPENDENT COMPONENTS

Most components in Figure 16.2 are based on ACE components that can be reused in other communication systems. The only components that are not widely reusable are the `Supplier` and `Consumer Handlers`, which implement the application-specific details related to message formats and the gateway's routing protocol. The behavior of the application-independent components in the gateway is outlined below.

Interprocess Communication (IPC) Components. The `SOCK Stream`, `SOCK Connector`, and `SOCK Acceptor` components encapsulate the socket network programming interface [9]. These components are implemented using the *Wrapper Facade* pattern [1], which simplifies the development of portable communication software by shielding developers from low-level, tedious, and error-prone socket-level programming. In addition, they form the foundation for higher-level patterns and ACE components described below.

Event Demultiplexing Components. The `Reactor` is an OO event demultiplexing mechanism based on the *Reactor* pattern [1] described in Section 3.3. It channels all external stimuli in an event-driven application through a single demultiplexing point. This design permits single-threaded applications to wait on event handles, demultiplex events, and dispatch event handlers efficiently. Events indicate that something significant has occurred, e.g., the arrival of a new connection or work request. The main source of events in the gateway are (1) connection events that indicate requests to establish connections and (2) data events that indicate routing messages encapsulating various payloads, such as commands, status messages, and bulk data transmissions.

Initialization and Event Handling Components. Establishing connections between endpoints involves two roles: (1) the *passive role,* which initializes an endpoint of communication at a particular address and waits passively for the other endpoint to connect with it, and (2) the *active role,* which actively initiates a connection to one or more endpoints that are playing the passive role. The `Connector` and `Acceptor` are factories [2] that implement active and passive roles for initializing network services, respectively. These components implement the *Acceptor-Connector* pattern, which is described in Section 3.5. The gateway uses these components to establish connections with peers and produce initialized `Supplier` and `Consumer Handlers`.

To increase system flexibility, connections can be established in the following two ways:

1. *From the gateway to the peers,* which is often done to establish the initial system configuration of peers when the gateway first starts up.
2. *From a peer to the gateway,* which is often done after the system is running whenever a new peer wants to send or receive routing messages.

In a large system, dozens or hundreds of peers may be connected to a single gateway. To expedite initialization, therefore, the gateway's `Connector` can initiate all connections asynchronously rather than synchronously. Asynchrony helps decrease connection latency over long delay paths, such as wide-area networks (WANs) built over satellites or long-haul terrestrial links. The underlying `SOCK Connector` [9] contained within a `Connector` provides the low-level asynchronous connection mechanism. When a `SOCK Connector` connects two socket endpoints via TCP it produces a `SOCK Stream` object, which is then used to exchange data between that peer and the gateway.

Message Demultiplexing Components. The `Map Manager` efficiently maps external ids, such as peer routing addresses, onto internal ids, such as `Consumer Handlers`. The gateway uses a `Map Manager` to implement a `Routing Table` that handles the demultiplexing and routing of messages internally to a gateway. The `Routing Table` maps addressing information contained in routing messages sent by peers to the appropriate set of `Consumer Handlers`.

Message Queueing Components. The `Message Queue` [9] provides a generic queueing mechanism used by the gateway to buffer messages in

Consumer Handlers while they are waiting to be routed to peers. A Message Queue can be configured to run efficiently and robustly in single-threaded or multi-threaded environments. When a queue is instantiated, developers can select the desired concurrency strategy. In multi-threaded environments, Message Queues are implemented using the *Monitor Object* pattern [1].

2.2 APPLICATION-SPECIFIC COMPONENTS

In Figure 16.2 only two of the components – Supplier and Consumer Handlers – are specific to the gateway application. These components implement the Non-blocking Buffered I/O pattern described in Section 3.6. Supplier and Consumer Handlers reside in the gateway, where they serve as proxies for the original source and the intended destination(s) of routing messages sent to hosts across the network. The behavior of these two gateway-specific components is outlined below.

Supplier Handlers. Supplier Handlers are responsible for routing incoming messages to their destination(s). The Reactor notifies the Supplier Handler when it detects an event on that connection's communication endpoint. After the Supplier Handler has received a complete routing message from that endpoint it consults the Routing Table to determine the set of Consumer Handler destinations for the message. It then requests the selected Consumer Handler(s) to forward the message to the appropriate peer destinations.

Consumer Handlers. A Consumer Handler is responsible for delivering routing messages to their destinations reliably. It implements a flow control mechanism to buffer bursts of routing messages that cannot be sent immediately due to transient network congestion or lack of buffer space at a receiver. Flow control is a transport layer mechanism that ensures a source peer does not send data faster than a destination peer can buffer and process the data. For instance, if a destination peer runs out of buffer space, the underlying TCP protocol instructs the associated gateway's Consumer Handler to stop sending messages until the destination peer consumes its existing data.

A gateway integrates the application-specific and application-independent components by customizing, instantiating, and composing the ACE components described above. As shown in Figure 16.3 `Supplier` and `Consumer Handlers` inherit from a common ancestor: the ACE `Svc Handler` class, which is produced by `Connectors` and `Acceptors`. Each `Svc Handler` is a local Proxy [2] for a remotely connected peer. It contains a `SOCK Stream`, which enables peers to exchange messages via connected socket handles.

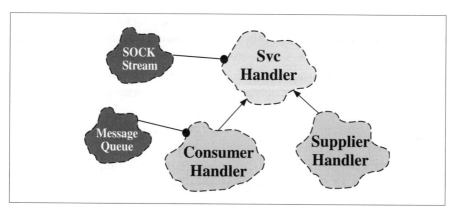

Figure 16.3. Supplier and consumer handler inheritance hierarchy.

A `Consumer Handler` is implemented in accordance with the Non-blocking Buffered I/O pattern. Thus, it uses an `ACE Message Queue` to chain unsent messages in the order they must be delivered when flow control mechanisms permit. After a flow controlled connection opens up, the ACE framework notifies its `Consumer Handler`, which starts draining the `Message Queue` by sending messages to the peer. If flow control occurs again this sequence of steps is repeated until all messages are delivered.

To improve reliability and performance, the gateways described in this chapter utilize the Transmission Control Protocol (TCP). TCP provides a reliable, in-order, non-duplicated bytestream service for application-level gateways. Although TCP connections are inherently bi-directional, data sent from peer to the gateway use a different connection than data sent from the gateway to the peer. There are several advantages to separating input connections from output connections in this manner:

- It simplifies the construction of gateway `Routing Tables`;

- It allows more flexible connection configuration and concurrency strategies;

- It enhances reliability since `Supplier` and `Consumer Handlers` can be reconnected independently if errors occur on a connection.

3 A Pattern Language for Application-Level Gateways

The previous sections described the structure and functionality of an application-level gateway. Although this architectural overview helps to clarify the behavior of key components in a gateway, it does not reveal the deeper relationships and roles that underly these software components. In particular, the architecture descriptions do not motivate *why* a gateway is designed in this particular manner or why certain components act and interact in certain ways. Understanding these relationships and roles is crucial to develop, maintain, and enhance communication software.

An effective way to capture and articulate these relationships and roles is to describe the *pattern language* that generates them. Studying the pattern language that underlies the gateway software provides the following two benefits:

1. *It identifies successful solutions to common design challenges.* The pattern language underlying the gateway architecture transcends the particular details of the application and resolves common challenges faced by communication software developers. A thorough understanding of this pattern language enables widespread reuse of gateway software architecture in other systems, even when reuse of its algorithm, implementations, interfaces, or detailed designs is not feasible [10].

2. *It reduces the effort of maintaining and enhancing gateway software.* A pattern language helps to capture and motivate the collaboration between multiple classes and objects. This is important for developers who must maintain and enhance a gateway. Although the roles and relationships in a gateway design are embodied in the source code, extracting them from the surrounding implementation details can be costly and error-prone.

3.1 Strategic Patterns

Figure 16.4 illustrates the following five *strategic* patterns that form a portion of the language that generates connection-oriented, application-level gateways:

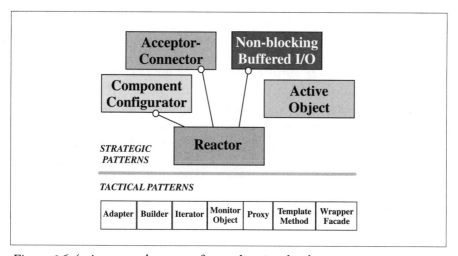

Figure 16.4. A pattern language for application-level gateways.

- *Reactor* [1]. This pattern structures event-driven applications, particularly servers, that receive requests from multiple clients concurrently but process them iteratively.

- *Active object* [1]. This pattern decouples method execution from method invocation to enhance concurrency and simplify synchronized access to objects that reside in their own threads of control.

- *Component configurator* [1]. This pattern allows an application to link and unlink its component implementations at run-time without having to modify, recompile, or statically relink the application. It also supports the reconfiguration of components into different processes without having to shut down and re-start running processes.

- *Acceptor-connector* [1]. This pattern decouples connection establishment and service initialization from service processing in a networked system.

- *The non-blocking buffered I/O pattern.* This pattern decouples input mechanisms and output mechanisms so that data can be routed correctly and reliably without blocking application processing unduly.

The five patterns in this language are strategic because they significantly influence the software architecture for applications in a particular domain, which in this case is the domain of communication software and gateways.

For example, the Non-blocking Buffered I/O pattern described in Section 3.6 ensures that message processing is not disrupted or postponed indefinitely when a gateway experiences congestion or failure. This pattern helps to sustain a consistent quality-of-service (QoS) for gateways that use reliable connection-oriented transport protocols, such as TCP/IP or IPX/SPX. A thorough understanding of the strategic communication patterns described in this chapter is essential to develop robust, efficient, and extensible communication software, such as application-level gateways.

3.2 TACTICAL PATTERNS

The application-level gateway implementation also uses many *tactical* patterns, such as the following:

- *Adapter* [2]. This pattern transforms a non-conforming interface into one that can be used by a client. The gateway uses this pattern to treat different types of routing messages, such as commands, status information, and bulk data, uniformly.

- *Builder* [2]. This pattern provides a factory for building complex objects incrementally. The gateway uses this pattern to create its Routing Table from a configuration file.

- *Iterator* [2]. This pattern decouples sequential access to a container from the representation of the container. The gateway uses this pattern to connect and initialize multiple Supplier and Consumer Handlers with their peers.

- *Monitor object* [1]. This pattern synchronizes concurrent method execution to ensure that only one method at a time runs within an object. It also allows an object's methods to schedule their execution sequences co-operatively. The gateway uses this pattern to synchronize the multi-threaded configuration of its Message Queues.

- *Proxy* [2]. This pattern provides a local surrogate object that acts in place of a remote object. The gateway uses this pattern to shield the main gateway routing code from delays or errors caused by the fact that peers are located on other host machines in the network.

- *Template method* [2]. This pattern specifies an algorithm where some steps are supplied by a derived class. The gateway uses this pattern to selectively override certain steps in its `Connector` and `Acceptor` components so that failed connections can be restarted automatically.

- *Wrapper facade* [1]. This pattern encapsulates the functions and data provided by existing non-OO APIs within more concise, robust, portable, maintainable, and cohesive OO class interfaces. The ACE framework uses this pattern to provide an OS-independent set of component network programming components used by the gateway.

Compared to the five strategic patterns outlined above, which are domain-specific and have broad design implications, these tactical patterns are domain-independent and have a relatively localized impact on a software design. For instance, Iterator is a tactical pattern used in the gateway to process entries in the `Routing Table` sequentially without violating data encapsulation. Although this pattern is domain-independent and thus widely applicable, the problem it addresses does not impact the application-level gateway software design as pervasively as strategic patterns, such as Non-blocking Buffered I/O or Reactor. A thorough understanding of tactical patterns is essential, however, to implement highly flexible software that is resilient to changes in application requirements and platform environments.

The remainder of this section describes each of the strategic patterns in detail and explains how they are used in the gateway.

3.3 THE REACTOR PATTERN

Intent. The Reactor pattern structures event-driven applications, particularly events, that receive requests from multiple clients concurrently but process them iteratively.

Motivation and Forces. Single-threaded applications must handle events from multiple sources without blocking indefinitely on any particular source. The following forces impact the design of single-threaded, event-driven communication software:

1. *The need to demultiplex multiple types of events from multiple sources of events efficiently within a single thread of control.* Often, events from multiple sources within an application process must be handled at the event demultiplexing level. By handling events at this level, there may be no need for more complicated threading, synchronization, or locking within an application.

2. *The need to extend application behavior without requiring changes to the event dispatching framework.* Demultiplexing and dispatching mechanisms are often application-independent and can therefore be reused. In contrast, the event handler policies are more application-specific. By separating these concerns, application policies can change without affecting lower-level framework mechanism.

Solution. Apply the Reactor pattern to wait synchronously for the arrival of indication events on one or more event sources such as connected socket handles. Integrate the mechanisms that demultiplex and dispatch the events to services that process them. Decouple these event demultiplexing and dispatching mechanisms from the application-specific processing of indication events within the services.

Structure, Participants, and Implementation. Figure 16.5 illustrates the structure and participants in the Reactor pattern. The `Reactor` defines an interface for registering, removing, and dispatching concrete event handler objects, such as `Supplier` or `Consumer Handlers` in the gateway. An implementation of this interface provides a set of application-independent mechanisms. These mechanisms perform event demultiplexing and dispatching of application-specific event handlers in response to various types of input, output, and timer events.

An `Event Handler` specifies an abstract interface used by a `Reactor` to dispatch callback methods defined by objects that register to events of interest. A concrete event handler is a class that inherits from `Event Handler` and selectively overrides callback method(s) to process events in an application-specific manner.

Dynamics.Figure 16.6 illustrates the dynamics among participants in the Reactor pattern. These dynamics can be divided into the following two modes:

1. *Initialization mode,* where `Concrete Event Handler` objects are registered with the `Reactor`.

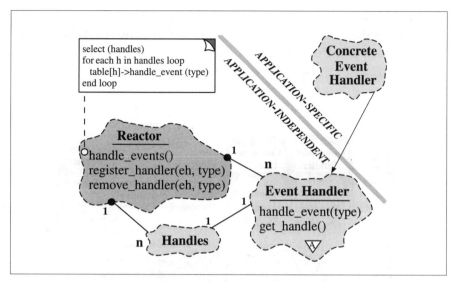

Figure 16.5. Structure and participants in the Reactor pattern.

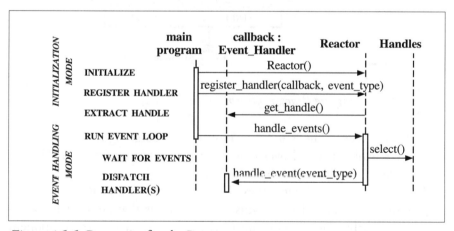

Figure 16.6. Dynamics for the Reactor pattern.

2. *Event handling mode,* where the Reactor invokes upcalls on registered objects, which then handle events in an application-specific way.

Usage. The Reactor is used for the following types of event dispatching
operations in the gateway:

1. *Input events.* The `Reactor` dispatches each incoming routing message to the `Supplier Handler` associated with its socket handle, at which point the message is routed to the appropriate `Consumer Handler(s)`. This use-case is shown in Figure 16.7.

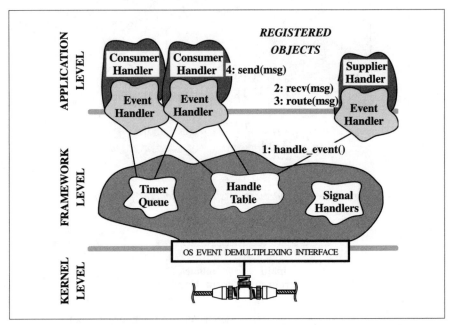

Figure 16.7. Using the Reactor pattern in the gateway.

2. *Output events.* The `Reactor` ensures that outgoing routing messages are reliably delivered over flow controlled `Consumer Handlers`, as described in Sections 3.6 and 3.7.
3. *Connection completion events.* The `Reactor` dispatches events that indicate the completion status of connections that are initiated asynchronously. These events are used by the `Connector` component described in Section 3.5.
4. *Connection request events.* The `Reactor` also dispatches events that indicate the arrival of passively initiated connections. These events are used by the `Acceptor` component described later.

The Reactor pattern has been used in many single-threaded event-driven frameworks, such as the Motif, Interviews [11], System V STREAMS [12], the ACE OO communication framework [9], and implementations of

COBRA [8]. In addition, it provides the event demultiplexing infrastructure for all of the other strategic patterns presented below.

3.4 THE COMPONENT CONFIGURATOR PATTERN

Intent. The Component Configurator pattern allows an application to link and unlink its component implementations at run-time without having to modify, recompile, or statically relink the application. It also supports the reconfiguration of components into different processes without having to shut down and re-start running processes.

Motivation and Forces. The following forces impact the design of highly flexible and extensible communication software.

1. *The need to defer the selection of a particular implementation of a component until very late in the design cycle.* Deferring these configuration decisions until installation-time or run-time significantly increases the design choices available to developers. For example, run-time context information can be used to guide implementation decisions and components can be (re)configured into applications dynamically.

2. *The need to build complete applications by composing or scripting multiple independently developed components.* Much of the recurring component configuration and initialization behavior of applications should be factored out into reusable methods. This separation of concerns allows new versions of components to be linked into an application at run-time without disrupting concurrently executing components.

Solution. Apply the Component Configurator pattern to decouple component interfaces from their implementations and make applications independent of the point(s) in time at which component implementations are configured into application processes.

Structure, Participants, and Implementation. Figure 16.8 illustrates the structure and participants of the Component Configurator pattern. This pattern reuses the Reactor pattern's `Reactor` and `Event Handler` for its event demultiplexing and dispatching needs. The `Component` is a subclass of `Event Handler` that adds interfaces for initializing and terminating C++ objects when they are linked and unlinked dynamically. Application-specific components inherit from `Component` and selectively override

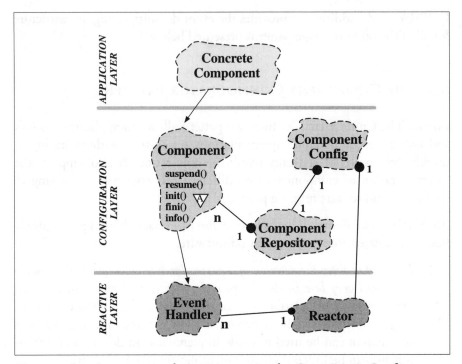

Figure 16.8. Structure and participants in the Component Configurator pattern.

in `init` and `fini` methods to implement custom initialization and termination behavior, respectively.

The `Component Repository` records which `Components` are currently linked and active. The `Component Config` is a facade [2] that orchestrates the behavior of the other components. It also provides a single access point for linking, activating, suspending, resuming, and unlinking `Components` into and out of an application at run-time.

Dynamics. Figure 16.9 illustrates the dynamics between participants in the Component Configurator pattern. These dynamics can be divided into the following two modes:

1. *Configuration mode,* which dynamically links or unlinks `Components` to and from an application.
2. *Event handling mode,* which process incoming events using patterns such as Reactor or Active Object [1].

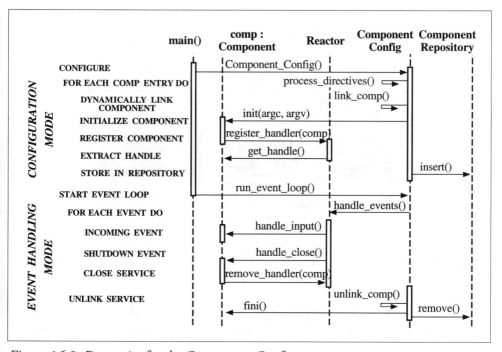

Figure 16.9. Dynamics for the Component Configurator pattern.

Usage. The Component Configurator pattern is used in the gateway as shown in Figure 16.10. The `Reactive Gateway` component is a single-threaded implementation of the gateway that can be dynamically linked via commands in a configuration script. To dynamically replace this component with a multi-threaded implementation, the `Component Config` need only reconsult its `comp.conf` file, unlike the `Reactive Gateway`, dynamically link the `Thread-per Connection Gateway` or `Thread Pool Gateway`, and initialize the new implementation. The `Component Config` facade uses dynamic linking to implement the Component Configurator pattern efficiently.

The Component Configurator pattern is used in the Windows NT Service Control Manager (SCM), which allows a master SCM process to initiate and control administrator-installed service components automatically. In general, modern operating systems, such as Solaris, Linux, and Windows NT, provide support for dynamically configured kernel-level device drivers that implement the Component Configurator pattern. Another use of the

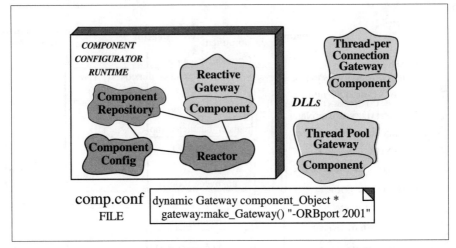

Figure 16.10. Using the Component Configurator pattern in the gateway.

Component Configurator pattern is the applet mechanism in Java, which supports dynamic downloading, initializing, starting, stopping, and terminating of Java applets.

3.5 THE ACCEPTOR-CONNECTOR PATTERN

Intent. The Acceptor-Connector pattern decouples connection establishment and service initialization from service processing in a networked system.

Motivation and Forces. Connection-oriented applications, such as our application-level gateway, and middleware, such as CORBA, are often written using lower-level network programming interfaces, like sockets [13]. The following forces impact the initialization of services when using these lower-level interfaces:

1. *The need to reuse connection establishment code for each new service.* Key characteristics of services, such as the communication protocol or the data format, should be able to evolve independently and transparently from the mechanisms used to establish the connections. Since service characteristics change more frequently than connection establishment mechanisms, separating these concerns helps to reduce software coupling and increase code reuse.

2. *The need to make the connection establishment code portable across platforms that contain different network programming interfaces.* Parameterizing the Acceptor-Connector's mechanisms for accepting connections and performing services helps to improve portability by allowing the wholesale replacement of these mechanisms. This makes the connection establishment code portable across platforms that contain different network programming interfaces, such as sockets but not TLI, or vice versa.

3. *The need to enable flexible service concurrency policies.* After a connection is established, peer applications use the connection to exchange data to perform some type of service, such as remote login or HTML document transfer. A service can run in a single thread, in multiple threads, or multiple processes, regardless of how the connection was established or how the services were initialized.

4. *The need to ensure that a passive-mode I/O handle is not accidentally used to read or write data.* By strongly decoupling the connection establishment logic from the service processing logic, passive-mode socket endpoints cannot be used incorrectly, e.g., by trying to read or write data on a passive-mode listener socket used to accept connections. This eliminates an important class of network programming errors.

5. *The need to actively establish connections with a large number of peers efficiently.* When an application must establish connections with a large number of peers efficiently over long-delay WANs it may be necessary to use asynchrony and initiate and complete multiple connections in non-blocking mode.

Solution. Apply the Acceptor-Connector pattern to decouple the connection and initialization of peer services in a networked application from the processing these peer services perform after they are connected and initialized.

Structure, Participants, and Implementation. Figure 16.11 illustrates the layering structure of participants in the Acceptor-Connector pattern. The `Acceptor` and `Connector` components are factories that assemble the resources necessary to connect and activate `Svc Handlers`. `Svc Handlers` are components that exchange messages with connected peers.

The participants in the Connection Layer of the Acceptor-Connector pattern leverage the Reactor pattern. For instance, the `Connector`'s asynchronous initialization strategy establishes a connection after the `Reactor` notifies it that a previously initiated connection request to a peer has com-

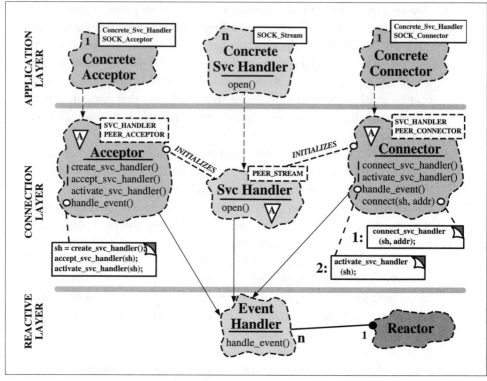

Figure 16.11. Structure and participants in the Acceptor-Connector pattern.

pleted. Using the Reactor pattern enables multiple Svc Handlers to be initialized asynchronously within a single thread of control.

To increase flexibility, Acceptor and Connector components can be parameterized by a particular type of IPC mechanism and SVC HANDLER. The IPC mechanism supplies the underlying transport mechanism, such as C++ wrapper facades for sockets or TLI, used to establish a connection. The SVC HANDLER specifies an abstract interface for defining a service that communicates with a connected peer. A Svc Handler can be parameterized by a PEER STREAM endpoint. The Acceptor and Connector components associate this endpoint with its peer when a connection is established.

By inheriting from Event Handler, a SVC handler can register with a Reactor and use the Reactor pattern to handle its I/O events within the same thread of control as the Acceptor or Connector.

Conversely, a SVC Handler can use the Active Object pattern and handle its I/O events in a separate thread. Section 3.7 evaluates the tradeoffs between these two patterns.

Parameterized types are used to decouple the Acceptor-Connector pattern's connection establishment strategy from the type of service and the type of connection mechanism. Developers supply template arguments for these types to produce Application Layer Acceptor or Connectors such as the Connector used by the gateway to initialize its Supplier and Consumer Handlers. This design enables the wholesale replacement of the SVC HANDLER and IPC mechanism, without affecting the Acceptor-Connector pattern's service initialization strategy.

Note that a similar degree of decoupling could be achieved via inheritance and dynamic binding by using the Abstract Factory or Factory Method patterns described in [2]. Parameterized types were used to implement this pattern since they improve run-time efficiency. In general, templates trade compile- and link-time overhead and space overload for improved run-time performance.

Dynamics. Figure 16.12 illustrates the dynamics among participants for the Acceptor component of the pattern. These dynamics are divided into the following three phases:

1. *Endpoint initialization phase,* which creates a passive-mode endpoint encapsulated by PEER ACCEPTOR that is bound to a network address, such as an IP address and port number. The passive-mode endpoint listens for connection requests from peers. This endpoint is registered with the Reactor, which drives the event loop that waits on the endpoint for connection requests to arrive from peers.

2. *Service activation phase.* Since an Acceptor inherits from an Event Handler the Reactor can dispatch the Acceptor's handle_event method when connection request events arrive. This method performs the Acceptor's Svc handler initialization strategy, which (1) assembles the resources necessary to create a new Concrete Svc Handler object, (2) accepts the connection into this object, and (3) activates the Svc Handler by calling its open hook method.

3. *Service processing phase.* After the Svc Handler is activated, it processes incoming event messages arriving on the PEER STREAM. A Svc Handler can process incoming event messages using patterns such as Reactor or the Active Object [1].

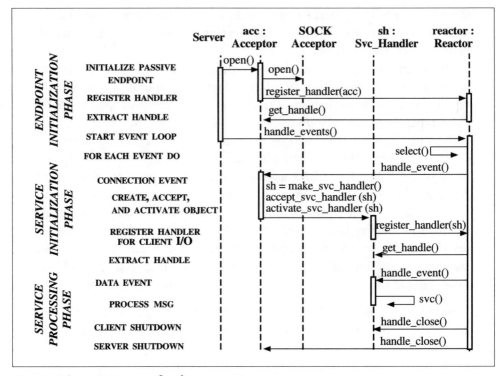

Figure 16.12. Dynamics for the Acceptor *component.*

The dynamics among participants in the Connector component of the pattern can be divided into the following three phases:

1. *Connection initiation phase,* which actively connects one or more Svc Handlers with their peers. Connections can be initiated synchronously or asynchronously. The Connector's connect method implements the strategy for establishing connections actively.
2. *Service initialization phase,* which activates a Svc Handler by calling its open method when its connection completes successfully. The open method of the Svc Handler then performs service-specific initialization.
3. *Service processing phase,* which performs the application-specific service processing using the data exchanged between the Svc Handler and its connected peer.

Figure 16.13 illustrates these three phases of dynamics using *asynchronous* connection establishment. Note how the Connector's connection initiation phase is separated *temporally* from the service initialization phase. This design enables multiple connection initiations to proceed in parallel within a single thread of control. The dynamics for synchronous connection establishment is similar. In this case, the Connector combines the connection initiation and service initialization phases into a single blocking operation.

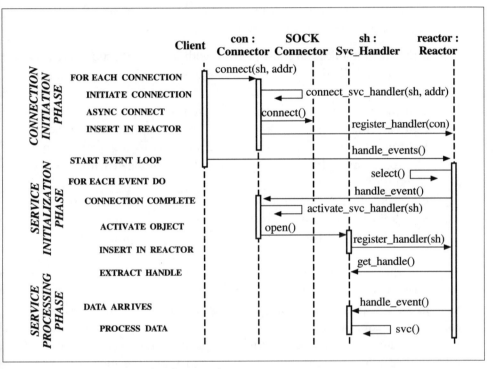

Figure 16.13. Dynamics for the asynchronous Connector *component.*

In general, synchronous connection establishment is useful for the following situations:

- If the latency for establishing a connection is very low, such as establishing a connection with a server on the same host via the loopback device.

- If multiple threads of control are available and it is feasible to use a different thread to connect each Svc Handler synchronously.

- If a client application cannot perform useful work until a connection is established.

In contrast, asynchronous connection establishment is useful for the following situations:

- If the connection latency is high and there are many peers to connect with, e.g., establishing a large number of connections over a high-latency WAN.

- If only a single thread of control is available, e.g., if the OS platform does not provide application-level threads.

- If the client application must perform additional work, such as refreshing a GUI, while the connection is in the process of being established.

It is often the case that network services, such as our application-level gateway, must be developed without knowing if they will connect synchronously or asynchronously. Therefore, components provided by a general-purpose network programming framework must support multiple synchronous and asynchronous use-cases.

The Acceptor-Connector pattern increases the flexibility and reuse of networking framework components by separating the connection establishment logic from the service processing logic. The only coupling between (1) `Acceptor` and `Connector` components and (2) a `Svc Handler` occurs in the service initialization phase, when the `open` method of the `Svc Handler` is invoked. At this point, the `Svc Handler` can perform its service-specific processing using any suitable application-level protocol or concurrency policy.

For instance, when messages arrive at a gateway, the `Reactor` can be used to dispatch `Supplier Handlers` to frame the messages, determine outgoing routes, and deliver the messages to their `Consumer Handlers`. However, `Consumer Handlers` can send the data to the remote destinations using a different type of concurrency mechanism, such as Active Objects described in Section 3.7.

Usage. Figure 16.14 illustrates how the `Acceptor` component of the Acceptor-Connector pattern is used by the gateway when it plays the passive connection role. In this case, peers connect to gateway, which uses the `Acceptor` to decouple the passive initialization of `Supplier` and `Consumer Handlers` from the routing tasks performed after a handler is initialized.

Figure 16.15 illustrates how the `Connector` component of the Acceptor-Connector pattern is used by the gateway to simplify the task of connecting to a large number of peers. In this case, peer addresses are read from

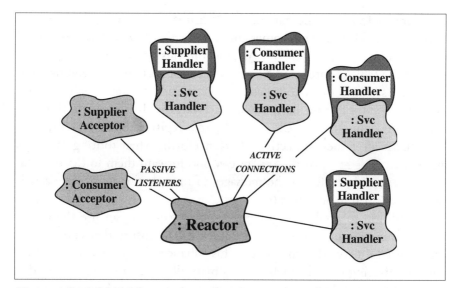

Figure 16.14. Using the Acceptor *component in the gateway.*

a configuration file during gateway initialization. The gateway uses the Builder pattern [2] to bind these addresses to dynamically allocated Consumer Handlers or Supplier Handlers. Since these handlers inherit from Svc Handler, all connections can be initiated asynchronously using the Iterator pattern [2]. The connections are then completed in parallel using the Connector.

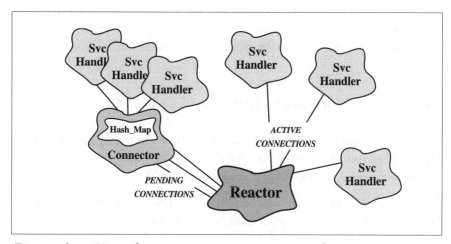

Figure 16.15. Using the Connector *component in the gateway.*

Figure 16.15 shows the state of the `Connector` after four connections have been established. Three other connections that have not yet completed are owned by the `Connector`. As shown in this figure, the `Connector` maintains a table of three `Handlers` whose connections are pending completion. As connections complete, the `Connector` removes each connected `Channel` from its table and activates it. In the single-threaded implementation `Supplier Handlers` register themselves with the `Reactor` after they are activated. Henceforth, when routing messages arrive, `Supplier Handlers` receive and forward them to `Consumer Handlers`, which deliver the messages to their destinations (these activities are described in Section 3.6).

In addition to establishing connections, a gateway can use the `Connector` in conjunction with the `Reactor` to ensure that connections are restarted if network errors occur. This enhances the gateway's fault tolerance by ensuring that channels are automatically reinitiated when they disconnect unexpectedly, e.g., if a peer crashes or an excessive amount of data is queued at a `Consumer Handler` due to network congestion. If a connection fails unexpectedly, an exponential-backoff algorithm can restart the connection efficiently by using the timer dispatching capabilities of the `Reactor`.

The intent and general architecture of the Acceptor-Connector pattern is found in network server management tools like `inetd` [13] and `listen` [14]. These tools utilize a master Acceptor process that listens for connections on a set of communication ports. Each port is associated with a communication-related service (such as the standard Internet services `ftp`, `telnet`, `daytime`, and `echo`). When a service request arrives on a monitored port, the Acceptor process accepts the request and dispatches an appropriate preregistered handler that performs the service.

3.6 The Non-blocking Buffered I/O Pattern

Intent. The Non-blocking Buffered I/O pattern decouples input mechanisms and output mechanisms so that data can be routed correctly and reliably without blocking application processing unduly.

Motivation and Forces. Message routing in a gateway must not be disrupted or postponed indefinitely when congestion or failure occurs on incoming and outgoing network connections. Thus, the following forces must be resolved when building robust connection-oriented gateways:

1. *The need to prevent misbehaving connections from disrupting the QoS of well-behaved connections.* Input connections can fail because peers disconnect. Likewise, output connections can flow control as a result of network congestion. In these types of cases, the gateway must not perform blocking `send` or `recv` operations on any single connection since (1) the entire gateway can hang indefinitely or (2) messages on other connections cannot be sent or received and the QoS provided to peers will degrade.

2. *The need to allow different concurrency strategies for processing input and output.* Several concurrency strategies can be used to process input and output, including (1) single-threaded processing using the Reactor pattern (Section 3.3) and (2) multi-threaded processing using the Active Object pattern (Section 3.7). Each strategy is appropriate under different situations, depending on factors such as the number of CPUs, context switching overhead, and number of peers.

Solution. Apply the Non-blocking Buffered I/O pattern to decoupling input processing from output processing to prevent blocking and allow customized concurrency strategies to be configured flexibly into an application.

Structure, Participants, and Implementation. Figure 16.16 illustrates the layer structuring of participants in the Non-blocking Buffered I/O pattern. The I/O Layer provides an event source for `Supplier Handlers` and an event sink for `Consumer Handlers`. A `Supplier Handler` uses a `Routing Table` to map routing messages onto one or more `Consumer Handlers`. If messages cannot be delivered to their destination peers immediately they are buffered in a `Message Queue` for subsequent transmission.

Since `Supplier Handlers` are decoupled from `Consumer Handlers` their implementations can vary independently. This separation of concerns is important since it allows the use of different concurrency strategies for input and output. The consequences of this decoupling are discussed further in Section 3.7.

Dynamics. Figure 16.7 illustrates the dynamics among participants in the Non-blocking Buffered I/O pattern. These dynamics can be divided into three phases:

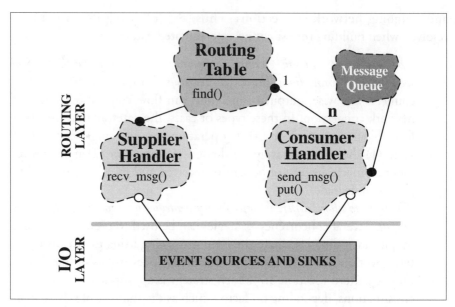

Figure 16.16. Structure and Participants in the Non-blocking Buffered I/O pattern.

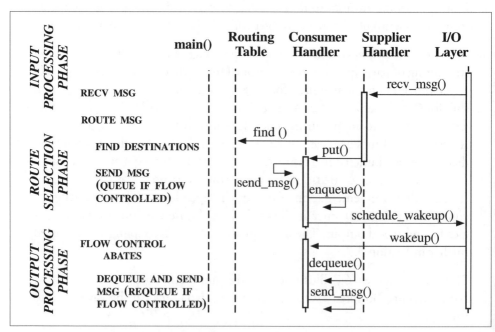

Figure 16.17. Dynamics for the Non-blocking Buffered I/O pattern.

1. *Input processing phase,* where `Supplier Handlers` reassemble incoming TCP segments into complete routing messages *without* blocking the application process.
2. *Route selection phase.* After a complete message has been reassembled, the `Supplier Handler` consults a `Routing Table` to select the `Consumer Handler(s)` responsible for sending the routing messages to their peer destinations.
3. *Output processing phase,* where the selected `Consumer Handlers` transmit the routing messages to their destination(s) *without* blocking the application process.

Usage. The other strategic patterns in this chapter – i.e., Reactor, Connector, Acceptor, and Active Object – can be applied to many types of communication software. In contrast, the Non-blocking Buffered I/O pattern is more coupled with gateway-style applications that route messages between peers. A primary challenge of building a reliable connection-oriented gateway centers on avoiding blocking I/O. This challenge centers primarily on reliably managing *flow control* that occurs on the connections used by `Consumer Handlers` to forward messages to peers. If the gateway blocked indefinitely when sending on a congested connection then incoming messages could not be routed, even if those messages were destined for non-flow controlled `Consumer Handlers`.

The remainder of this section describes how the Non-blocking Buffered I/O pattern can be implemented in a single-threaded, reactive version of the gateway (Section 3.7 examines the multi-threaded, Active Object version of the Non-blocking Buffered I/O pattern). In this implementation, the Non-blocking Buffered I/O pattern uses a `Reactor` as a cooperative multi-tasking scheduler for gateway I/O operations on different connections within a single thread. Single-threading eliminates the following overhead:

- *Synchronization* – e.g., access to shared objects like the `Routing Table` need not be serialized; and

- *Context switching* – e.g., all messages routing can occur within a single thread.

In the reactive implementation of the Non-blocking Buffered I/O pattern, the `Supplier Handlers` and `Consumer Handlers` are descendants of `Event Handler`. This layered inheritance design enables the gateway to route messages by having the `Reactor` dispatch the han-

`dle_event` methods of `Supplier` and `Consumer Handlers` when messages arrive and flow control conditions subside, respectively.

Using the Reactor pattern to implement the Non-blocking Buffered I/O pattern involves the following steps:

1. *Initialize non-blocking endpoints.* The `Supplier` and `Consumer Handler` handles are set into non-blocking mode after they are activated by an `Acceptor` or `Connector`. The use of non-blocking I/O is essential to avoid blocking that can otherwise occur on congested network links.

2. *Input message reassembly and routing.* Routing messages are received in fragments by `Supplier Handlers`. If an entire message is not immediately available, the `Supplier Handler` must buffer the fragment and return control to the event loop. This is essential to prevent "head of line" blocking on `Supplier channels`. When a `Supplier Channel` successfully receives and frames an entire message it uses the `Routing Table` to determine the appropriate set of `Consumer Handlers` that will deliver the message.

3. *Message delivery.* The selected `Consumer Handlers` try to send the message to the destination peer. Messages must be delivered reliably in "first-in, first-out" (FIFO) order. To avoid blocking, all `send` operations in `Consumer Handlers` must check to make sure that the network link is not flow controlled. If it is *not,* the message can be sent successfully. This path is depicted by the `Consumer Handler` in the upper right-hand corner of Figure 16.18. If the link *is* flow controlled, however, the Non-blocking Buffered I/O pattern implementation must use a different strategy. This path is depicted by the `Consumer Handler` in the lower right-hand corner of Figure 16.18.

To handle flow controlled connections, the `Consumer Handler` inserts the message it is trying to send into its `Message Queue`. It then instructs the `Reactor` to call back to the `Consumer Handler` when the flow control conditions abate, and returns to the main event loop. When it is possible to try to `send` again, the `Reactor` dispatches the `handle_event` method on the `Consumer Handler`, which then retries the operation. This sequence of steps may be repeated multiple times until the entire message is transmitted successfully.

Note that the gateway always returns control to its main event loop immediately after every I/O operation, regardless of whether it sent or

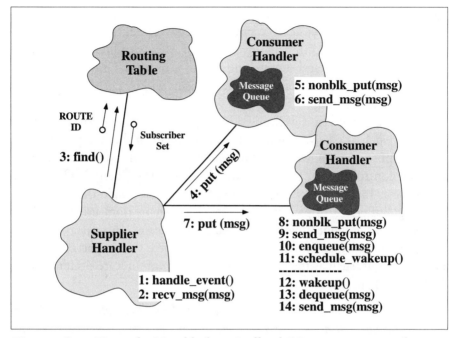

Figure 16.18. Using the Non-blocking Buffered I/O pattern in a single-threaded reactive gateway.

received an entire message. This is the essence of the Non-blocking Buffered I/O pattern – it correctly routes the messages to peers without blocking on any single I/O channel.

3.7 THE ACTIVE OBJECT PATTERN

Intent. The Active Object pattern decouples method execution from method invocation to enhance concurrency and simplify synchronized access to objects that reside in their own threads of control.

Motivation and Forces. All the strategic patterns used by the single-threaded gateway in Section 3.6 are layered upon the Reactor pattern. The Acceptor-Connector and Non-blocking Buffered I/O patterns both use the Reactor as a scheduler/dispatcher to initialize and route messages within a single thread of control. In general, the Reactor pattern forms the central event loop in single-threaded reactive systems. For example, in the single-threaded gateway implementation, the `Reactor` provides a coarse-grained form of concurrency control that serializes the invocation of event handlers at the level of event demultiplexing and dispatching within a process. This eliminates the need for additional synchronization mechanisms within a gateway and minimizes context switching.

The Reactor pattern is well suited for applications that use short-duration callbacks, such as passive connection establishment in the Acceptor pattern. It is less appropriate, however, for long-duration operations, such as blocking on flow controlled `Consumer Handlers` during periods of network congestion. In fact, much of the complexity in the single-threaded Non-blocking Buffered I/O pattern implementation stems from using the Reactor pattern as a cooperative multi-tasking mechanism. In general, this pattern does not adequately resolve the following force that impacts the design of applications, such as the gateway, that must communicate simultaneously with multiple peers.

1. *The need to ensure that blocking read and write operations on one endpoint does not detract from the QoS of other endpoints.* Network services are often easier to program if blocking I/O is used rather than reactive non-blocking I/O [1]. The simplicity occurs because execution state can be localized in the activation records of a thread, rather than decentralized in a set of control blocks maintained explicitly by application developers.

Solution. Apply the Active Object pattern to decouple method invocation on an object from method execution. Method invocation should occur in the client's thread of control, whereas method execution should occur in a separate thread. Moreover, design the decoupling so the client thread appears to invoke an ordinary method.

Structure, Participants, and Implementation. Figure 16.19 illustrates the structure and participants in the Active Object pattern. The `Proxy` exports the active object's public methods to clients. The `Scheduler` determines the next method to execute based on synchronization and scheduling constraints. The `Activation List` maintains a queue of pending `Method Requests`. The `Scheduler` determines the order in which these `Method Requests` are executed (a FIFO scheduler is used in the gateway to maintain the order of message delivery). The `Servant` maintains object state shared by the implementation methods.

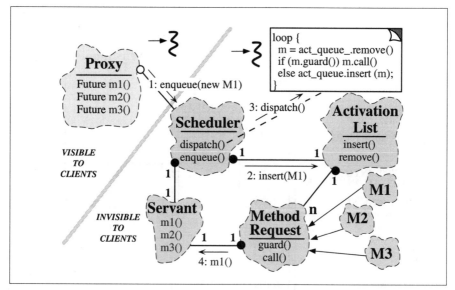

Figure 16.19. Structure and participants in the Active Object pattern.

Dynamics. Figure 16.20 illustrates the dynamics among participants in the Active Object pattern. These dynamics are divided into the following three phases:

1. *Method Request construction.* In this phase, the client application invokes a method defined by the Proxy. This triggers the creation of a Method Request, which maintains the argument bindings to the method, as well as any other bindings required to execute the method and return a result. A binding to a Future object is returned to the caller of the method.

2. *Scheduling/execution.* In this phase the Scheduler acquires a mutual exclusion lock, consults the Activation Queue to determine which Method Request(s) meet the synchronization constraints. The Method Request is then bound to the current Servant and the method is allowed to access/update the Servant's state.

3. *Return result.* The final phase binds the result of the Method Request to a Future [15], which passes return values back to the caller when the method finishes executing. A Future is a synchronization object that enforces "write-once, read-many" synchronization.

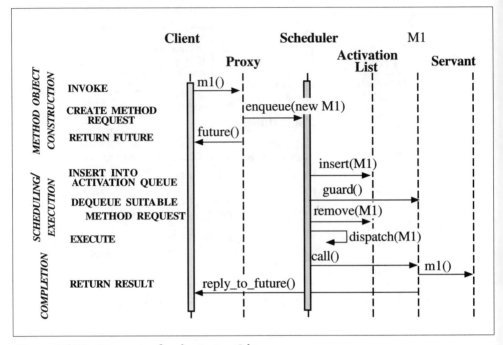

Figure 16.20. Dynamics for the Active Object pattern.

Subsequently, any readers that rendezvous with the Future will evaluate the future and obtain the result value. The Future and the Method Request can be garbage collected when they are no longer needed.

Usage. The gateway implementation described in Section 3.6 is single-threaded. It uses the Reactor pattern implementation of the Non-blocking Buffered I/O pattern as a cooperative multi-tasking scheduler that dispatches events of interest to a gateway. After implementing a number of single-threaded gateways it became clear that using the Reactor pattern as the basis for all gateway routing I/O operations was error-prone and hard to maintain. For example, it was hard to remember why control must be returned promptly to the Reactor's event loop when I/O operations cannot proceed. This misunderstanding became a common source of errors in single-threaded gateways.

To avoid these problems, a number of multi-threaded gateways were built using variations of the Active Object pattern. This pattern allows Consumer Handlers to block independently when sending messages to peers. The remainder of this section describes how Consumer Handlers can be multi-threading using the Active Object pattern.[1] This modification simplified the implementation of the Non-blocking Buffered I/O pattern substantially since Consumer Handlers can block in their own active object thread without affecting other Handlers. Implementing the Consumer Handlers as active objects also eliminated the subtle and error-prone cooperative multi-tasking programming techniques required when using the Reactor to schedule Consumer Handlers.

Figure 16.21 illustrates the Active Object version of the Non-blocking Buffered I/O pattern. Note how much simpler it is compared with the Reactor solution in Figure 16.18. This simplification occurs since the complex output scheduling logic is moved into the Active Objects, rather than being the responsibility of application developers.

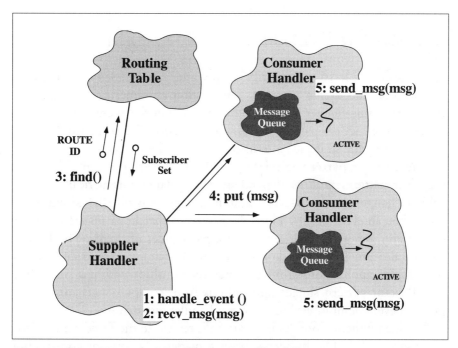

Figure 16.21. Using the Non-blocking Buffered I/O pattern in a multi-threaded Active Object gateway.

---

[1]While it is possible to apply the Active Object pattern to the Supplier Handlers this has less impact on the gateway design because the Reactor already supports non-blocking input.

It is also possible to observe the difference in complexity between the single-threaded and multi-threaded gateways by examining the source code that implements the Non-blocking Buffered I/O pattern in production gateway systems. It is hard to identify the reasons for this complexity simply by inspecting the source code, due to all the error handling and protocol-specific details surrounding the implementation. These details tend to disguise the key insight: *the main difference between the complexity of the single-threaded and multi-threaded solutions arise from the choice of the Reactor pattern rather than the Active Object pattern.*

This chapter has explicitly focused on the interactions and tradeoffs between the Reactor and Active Object patterns to clarify the consequences of different design choices. In general, documenting the interactions and relationships between closely related patterns is a challenging and unresolved topic that is being addressed by the patterns community.

4 RELATED PATTERNS

Other sources [2, 16, 1] identify, name, and catalog many fundamental architectural and design patterns. This section examines how the patterns described in this chapter relate to other patterns in this literature. Note that many of the tactical patterns outlined in Section 3.2 form the basis for implementing the strategic patterns presented in this chapter.

The Reactor pattern is related to the Observer pattern [2]. In the Observer pattern, *multiple* dependents are updated automatically when a subject changes. In the Reactor pattern, a handler is dispatched automatically when an event occurs. Thus, the Reactor dispatches a *single* handler for each event, although there can be multiple sources of events. The Reactor pattern also provides a Facade [2]. The Facade pattern presents an interface that shields applications from complex relationships within a subsystem. The Reactor pattern shields applications from complex mechanisms that perform event demultiplexing and event handler dispatching.

The Component Configurator pattern is related to the Builder and Mediator patterns [2]. The Builder pattern provides a factory for constructing complex objects incrementally. The Mediator coordinates interactions between its associates. The Component Configuration pattern provides a factory for configuring and initializing components into an application at run-time. At run-time, the Component Configurator pattern allows the components offered by an application to be incrementally modified without disturbing executing components. In addition, the Component Configurator pattern coordinates the interaction between components configured into an application and external administrators that want to update, suspend, resume, or remove components at run-time.

The Acceptor-Connector pattern is related to the Template Method, Strategy, and Factory Method patterns [2]. In the Template Method pattern, an algorithm is written such that some steps are supplied by a derived class. In the Factory Method pattern, a method in a subclass creates an associate that performs a particular task, but the task is decoupled from the protocol used to create the task. The `Acceptor` and `Connector` components in the Acceptor-Connector pattern are factories that use template methods or strategies to create, connect, and activate handlers for communication channels. The intent of the Acceptor-Connector pattern is similar to the Client/Dispatcher/Server pattern described in [16]. They both are concerned with separating active connection establishment from the subsequent service. The primary difference is that the Acceptor-Connector pattern addresses both passive/active and synchronous/asynchronous connection establishment.

The Non-blocking Buffered I/O pattern is related to the Mediator pattern [2], which decouples cooperating components of a software system and allows them to interact without having direct dependencies among each other. The Non-blocking Buffered I/O pattern is specialized to resolve the forces associated with network communication. It decouples the mechanisms used to process input messages from the mechanisms used to process output mechanisms to prevent blocking. In addition, the Non-blocking Buffered I/O pattern allows the use of different concurrency strategies for input and output channels.

5 CONCLUDING REMARKS

This chapter illustrates the application of a pattern language that enables widespread reuse of design expertise and software components in production communication gateways. The patterns in this language illustrate the structure of, and collaboration between, objects that perform core communication software tasks. The tasks addressed by these patterns include event demultiplexing and event handler dispatching, connection establishment and initialization of application services, concurrency control, and routing.

The pattern language and ACE framework components described in this chapter have been reused by the author and his colleagues in many production communication software systems ranging from telecommunication, electronic medical imaging, and avionics projects [10, 5, 7] to academic research projects [9,8]. In general, this pattern language has aided the development of components and frameworks in these systems by capturing the structure and dynamics of participants in a software architecture at a level higher than (1) source code and (2) OO design models that focus on individual objects and classes.

An in-depth discussion of our experiences and lessons learned using patterns appeared in [4]. An ACE-based example of single-threaded and multi-threaded gateways that illustrates all the patterns in this paper is freely available at www.cs.wustl.edu/~schmidt/ACE.html.

REFERENCES

1 D.C. Schmidt, M. Stal, H. Rohnert, and F. Buschmann, *Pattern-Oriented Software Architecture: Patterns for Concurrency and Distributed Objects,* Volume 2. New York: Wiley & Sons, 2000.

2 E. Gamma, R. Helm, R. Johnson, and J. Vlissides, *Design Patterns: Elements of Reusable Object-Oriented Software.* Reading, MA: Addison-Wesley, 1995.

3 J.O. Coplien and D.C. Schmidt, eds., *Pattern Languages of Program Design.* Reading, MA: Addison-Wesley, 1995.

4 D.C. Schmidt, "Experience Using Design Patterns to Develop Reusable Object-Oriented Communication Software," *Communications of the ACM (Special Issue on Object-Oriented Experiences),* vol. 38, October 1995.

5 I. Pyarali, T.H. Harrison, and D.C. Schmidt, "Design and Performance of an Object-Oriented Framework for High-Performance Electronic Medical Imaging," in *Proceedings of the 2nd Conference on Object-Oriented Technologies and Systems* (Toronto, Canada), USENIX, June 1996.

6 D.C. Schmidt and T. Suda, "Measuring the Performance of Parallel Message-based Process Architectures," in *Proceedings of the Conference on Computer Communications (INFOCOM)* (Boston, MA), pp. 624–633, IEEE, April 1995.

7 T.H. Harrison, D.L. Levine, and D.C. Schmidt, "The Design and Performance of a Real-time CORBA Event Service," in *Proceedings of OOPSLA '97* (Atlanta, GA), ACM, October 1997.

8 D.C. Schmidt and C. Cleeland, "Applying a Pattern Language to Develop Extensible ORB Middleware." See this volume, Chapter 18.

9 D.C. Schmidt, "Applying Design Patterns and Frameworks to Develop Object-Oriented Communication Software," in *Handbook of Programming Languages* (P. Salus, ed.), Macmillan Computer Publishing, 1997.

10 D.C. Schmidt and P. Stephenson, "Experiences Using Design Patterns to Evolve System Software Across Diverse OS Platforms," in *Proceedings of the 9th European Conference on Object-Oriented Programming* (Aarhus, Denmark), ACM, August 1995.

11 M.A. Linton, J. Vlissides, and P. Calder, "Composing User Interfaces with Inter-Views," *IEEE Computer,* vol. 22, pp. 8–22, February 1989.

12 D. Ritchie, "A Stream Input-Output System," *AT&T BelL Labs Technical Journal,* vol. 63, pp. 311–324, October 1984.

13 W.R. Stevens, *UNIX Network Programming,* First Edition. Englewood Cliffs, NJ: Prentice Hall, 1990.

14 S. Rago, *UNIX System V Network Programming.* Reading, MA: Addison-Wesley, 1993.

15 R.H. Halstead, Jr., "Multilisp: A Language for Concurrent Symbolic Computation," *ACM Trans. Programming Languages and Systems,* vol. 7, pp. 501–538, October 1985.

16 F. Buschmann, R. Meunier, H. Rohnert, P. Sommerlad, and M. Stal, *Pattern-Oriented Software Architecture – A System of Patterns.* Wiley and Sons, 1996.

17

APPLYING DESIGN PATTERNS TO FLEXIBLY CONFIGURE NETWORK SERVICES IN DISTRIBUTED SYSTEMS*

Douglas C. Schmidt

ABSTRACT

THIS CHAPTER DESCRIBES how design patterns help to enhance the flexibility and extensibility of communication software by permitting network services to evolve independently of the strategies used to passively initialize the services. The chapter makes three contributions to the study and development of configurable distributed applications. First, it identifies five orthogonal dimensions of passive service initialization: service advertisement, endpoint listening, service handler creation, passive connection establishment, and service handler activation. Second, the chapter illustrates how design patterns have been used to build a communication software framework that supports flexible configuration of different strategies for each of these five dimensions. Third, the chapter demonstrates how design patterns and frameworks are being used successfully to develop highly configurable production distributed systems.

Based on "A Family of Design Patterns for Flexibly Configuring Network Services in Distributed Systems" by Douglas C. Schmidt, which appeared in *Proceedings of the International Conference on Configurable Distributed Systems, Annapolis, MD, May 6–8, 1996.* © 1996 IEEE. Used with permission from the author.

*This research is supported in part by a grant from SiemensMED.

1 INTRODUCTION

Despite dramatic increases in network and host performance, developing extensible communication software for distributed systems remains hard. *Design patterns* [1] are a promising technique for capturing and articulating proven techniques for developing extensible distributed software. A design pattern captures the static and dynamic structures and collaborations of components in a software architecture. It also aids the development of extensible components and frameworks by expressing the structure and collaboration of participants in a software architecture at a level higher than (1) source code or (2) object-oriented design models that focus on individual objects and classes.

This chapter examines design patterns that form the basis for flexibly configuring network services in applications built by the author and his colleagues for a number of production distributed systems. Due to stringent requirements for reliability and performance, these projects provided an excellent testbed for capturing and articulating the key structure, participants, and consequences of design patterns for building extensible distributed systems.

The primary focus of this chapter is the `Acceptor` component in the *Acceptor-Connector* pattern [2]. This design pattern decouples connection establishment and service initialization from service processing in a networked system. The `Acceptor` component is a role in this pattern that enables the tasks performed by network services to evolve independently of the strategies used to initialize the services *passively.*

When instantiated and used in conjunction with other patterns, such as Reactor [2] and Strategy [1], the Acceptor-Connector pattern provides a reusable component in the ACE framework [3]. ACE provides a rich set of reusable object-oriented components that perform common communication software tasks. These tasks include event demultiplexing, event handler dispatching, connection establishment, routing, dynamic configuration of application services, and concurrency control.

This chapter is organized as follows: Section 2 motivates the Acceptor-Connector pattern by illustrating how it has been applied in production application-level `Gateways`; Section 3 outlines the `Acceptor` component of the Acceptor-Connector pattern; Section 4 illustrates how to implement `Acceptors` flexibly and efficiently by applying the Wrapper Facade [2], Strategy, Bridge, Factory Method, and Abstract Factory design patterns [1]; Section 5 outlines how `Acceptors` have been used to implement application-level `Gateways`; Section 6 discusses related patterns; and Section 7 presents concluding remarks.

2 BACKGROUND AND MOTIVATION

2.1 SEPARATING CONNECTION ESTABLISHMENT AND SERVICE INITIALIZATION

Many network services, such as remote login, file transfer, and WWW HTML document transfer, use connection-oriented protocols, such as TCP, to deliver data reliably between two or more communication endpoints. Establishing connections between endpoints involves the following two roles:

1. The *passive role,* which initializes an endpoint of communication at a particular address and waits passively for the other endpoint(s) to connect with it.
2. The *active* role, which actively initiates a connection to one or more endpoints that are playing the passive role.

The intent of the Acceptor-Connector pattern described in this chapter is to decouple passive initialization of a service from the tasks performed after the service is initialized. This pattern was discovered by generalizing from extensive experience building reusable communication frameworks for a range of distributed systems [3]. In all these systems, the tasks performed by a service are independent of the following:

- *Which endpoint initiated the connection.* Connection establishment is inherently asymmetrical since the passive endpoint *waits* whereas the active endpoint *initiates* the connection. After the connection is established, however, data may be transferred between endpoints in a manner that obeys a service's communication protocol, which can be structured as peer-to-peer, request-response, oneway streaming, etc.

- *The network programming interfaces and underlying protocols used to establish the connection.* Different network programming interfaces, such as sockets or TLI, provide different routines to establish connections using various underlying transport protocols. After a connection is established, however, data may be transferred between endpoints using standard read/write system calls that communicate between separate endpoints in a distributed application.

- *The strategies used to initialize the service.* The processing tasks performed by a service are typically independent of the initialization strategies used to (1) advertise the service, (2) listen for connection requests from peers, (3) create a service handler to process those requests, (4) establish the connection with the peers, and (5) execute the service handler in one or more threads or processes. Explicitly decoupling these initialization strategies from the service behavior itself enhances the extensibility, reusability, and portability of the service.

2.2 MOTIVATING EXAMPLE

Figure 17.1 illustrates how the Acceptor-Connector pattern has been used to implement multi-service, application-level Gateways, which is described further in [4]. A Gateway is a mediator [1] that routes the data between services running on Peers located throughout a wide area and local area network. From the Gateway's perspective, Peer services differ solely in their message framing formats and payload types. Several types of data, such as status information, bulk data, and commands, are exchanged by services running on the Gateway and the Peers. Peers are located throughout local area networks (LANs) and wide-area networks (WANs) and are used to monitor and control network resources, such as satellites, call centers, or remote branch offices.

The Gateway uses a connection-oriented interprocess communication (IPC) mechanism, such as TCP, to transmit data between its connected Peers. Connection-oriented protocols simplify application error handling and can enhance performance over long-delay WANs. Each commu-

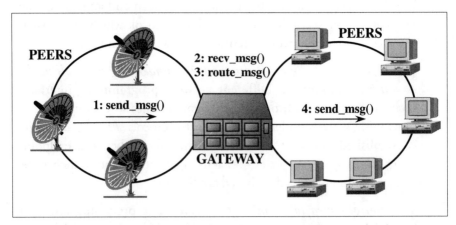

Figure 17.1. A connection-oriented, multi-service application-level Gateway.

nication service in the `Peers` sends and receives status information, bulk data, and commands to and from the `Gateway` using separate TCP connections. Each connection is bound to a unique address, e.g., an IP address and port number. For instance, bulk data sent from a ground station `Peer` through the `Gateway` is connected to a different port than status information sent by a tracking station peer through the `Gateway` to a ground station `Peer`. Separating connections in this manner allows more flexible routing strategies and more robust error handling if connections fail or become flow controlled.

One way to design the `Peers` and `Gateway` is to tightly couple the connection roles with the network services. For instance, the `Gateway` could be hard-coded to play the active connection role and initiate connections for all its services. To accomplish this, it could iterate through a list of `Peers` and synchronously connect with each of them. Likewise, `Peers` could be hard-coded to play the passive role and accept the connections and initialize their services. Moreover, the active and passive connection code for the `Gateway` and `Peers`, respectively, could be implemented with conventional network programming interfaces like sockets or TLI. In this case, a `Peer` could call `socket`, `bind`, `listen`, and `accept` to initialize a passive-mode listener socket and the `Gateway` could call `socket` and `connect` to actively initiate a data-mode connection socket. After the connections were established, the `Gateway` could route data for each type of service it provided.

However, the tightly coupled design outlined above has the following drawbacks:

- *Limited extensibility and reuse of the Gateway and Peer software.* For example, the mechanisms used to establish connections and initialize services are independent of the type of routing service, e.g., status information, bulk data, or commands, performed by the `Gateway`. In general, these services tend to change more frequently than the connection and initialization mechanisms.

- Inflexible connection roles. There are circumstances where the Gateway must play the passive connection role and the Peers play the active role. Therefore, tightly coupling the software that implements connection establishment with the software that implements the service makes it hard to (1) reuse existing services, (2) extend the `Gateway` by adding new routing services and enhancing existing services, and (3) reconfigure the connection roles played by `Peers` and the `Gateway`.

- *Non-portable and error-prone interfaces.* Using low-level network programming, such as sockets or TLI, is non-portable and error-prone. These low-level interfaces do not provide adequate type-checking since they utilize low-level I/O handles. It is easy to accidentally misuse these interfaces in ways that cannot be detected until runtime.

Therefore, a more flexible and efficient way to design the `Peers` and `Gateway` is to use the *Acceptor* pattern.

3 THE ACCEPTOR-CONNECTOR PATTERN

This section presents a brief overview of the Acceptor-Connector pattern. A comprehensive discussion is available in [2].

Intent. The intent of the Acceptor-Connector pattern is to decouple connection establishment and service initialization from service processing in a networked system.

Forces. The Acceptor-Connector pattern resolves the following forces for distributed applications that use connection-oriented communication protocols:

1. *The need to reuse connection establishment code for each new service.* Key characteristics of services, such as the communication protocol or the data format, should be able to evolve independently and transparently from the mechanisms used to establish the connections. Since service characteristics change more frequently than connection establishment mechanisms, separating these concerns helps to reduce software coupling and increase code reuse.
2. *The need to make the connection establishment code portable across platforms that contain different network programming interfaces.* Parameterizing the Acceptor-Connector's mechanisms for accepting connections and performing services helps to improve portability by allowing the wholesale replacement of these mechanisms. This makes the connection establishment code portable across platforms that contain different network programming interfaces, such as sockets but not TLI, or vice versa.

3. *The need to enable flexible service concurrency policies.* After a connection is established, peer applications use the connection to exchange data to perform some type of service, such as remote login or HTML document transfer. A service can run in a single thread, in multiple threads, or multiple processes, regardless of how the connection was established or how the services were initialized.

4. *The need to ensure that a passive-mode I/O handle is not accidentally used to read or write data.* By strongly decoupling the connection establishment logic from the service processing logic, passive-mode socket endpoints cannot be used incorrectly, e.g., by trying to read or write data on a passive-mode listener socket used to accept connections. This eliminates an important class of network programming errors.

5. *The need to actively establish connections with large numbers of peers efficiently.* When an application must establish connections with a large number of peers efficiently over long-delay WANs it may be necessary to use asynchrony and initiate and complete multiple connections in non-blocking mode.

Structure and Participants. The structure of the key participants in the Acceptor-Connector pattern is illustrated in Figure 17.2. The Acceptor and Connector components are factories that assemble the resources necessary to connect and activate Svc_Handlers. Svc_Handlers are components that exchange messages with connected Peers.

The participants in the Connection Layer of the Acceptor-Connector pattern can leverage off the Reactor pattern. For instance, the Connector's asynchronous initialization strategy establishes a connection after a reactor notifies it that a previously initiated connection request to a Peer has completed. Using the Reactor pattern enables multiple Svc_Handlers to be initialized asynchronously within a single thread of control.

To increase flexibility, Acceptor and Connector components can be parameterized by a particular type of IPC mechanism and SVC_HANDLER. The IPC mechanism supplies the underlying transport mechanism, such as C++ wrapper facades [2] for sockets or TLI, used to establish a connection. The SVC_HANDLER specifies an abstract interface for defining a service that communicates with a connected Peer. A Svc_Handler can be parameterized by a PEER_STREAM endpoint. The Acceptor and Connector components associate this endpoint to its Peer when a connection is established.

By inheriting from Event_Handler, a Svc_Handler can register

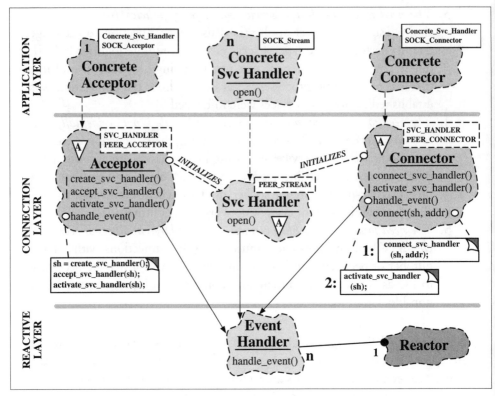

Figure 17.2. Structure of participants in the Acceptor-Connector pattern.

with a `Reactor` and use the Reactor pattern to handle its I/O events within the same thread of control as the `Acceptor` or `Connector`. Conversely, a `Svc_Handler` can use the Active Object pattern and handle its I/O events in a separate thread. The tradeoffs between these two patterns is described in [4].

Figure 17.2 illustrates how parameterized types can be used to decouple the Acceptor-Connector pattern's connection establishment strategy from the type of service and the type of connection mechanism. Application developers supply template arguments for these types to produce Application Layer `Acceptor` or `Connectors`. This design enables the whole-sale replacement of the `SVC_HANDLER` and IPC mechanism, without affecting the Acceptor-Connector pattern's service initialization strategy.

Note that a similar degree of decoupling could be achieved via inheritance and dynamic binding by using the Abstract Factory or Factory Method patterns

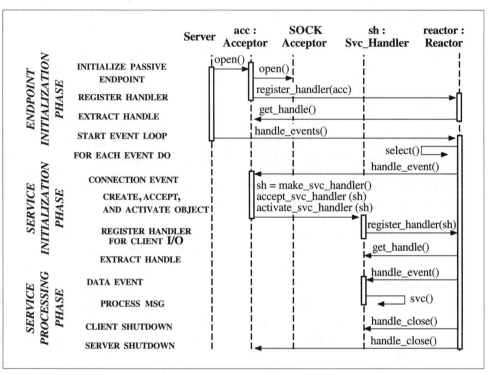

Figure 17.3. Dynamics for the `Acceptor` *component.*

described in [1]. Parameterized types were used to implement this pattern since they improve run-time efficiency. In general, templates trade compile- and link-time overhead and space overhead for improved run-time performance.

Dynamics. Figure 17.3 illustrates the dynamics among participants for the `Acceptor` component of the pattern. These dynamics are divided into the following three phases:

1. *Endpoint initialization phase,* which creates a passive-mode endpoint encapsulated by `PEER_ACCEPTOR` that is bound to a network address, such as an IP address and port number. The passive-mode endpoint listens for connection requests from `Peers`. This endpoint is registered with the `Reactor`, which drives the event loop that waits on the endpoint for connection requests to arrive from `Peers`.

2. *Service activation phase.* Since an `Acceptor` inherits from an `Event Handler` the `Reactor` can dispatch the `Acceptor`'s `handle_event` method when connection request events arrive.

This method performs the `Acceptor`'s `Svc_Handler` initialization strategy, which (1) assembles the resources necessary to create a new `Concrete_Svc_Handler` object, (2) accepts the connection into this object, and (3) activates the `Svc_Handler` by calling its `open` hook method.

3. *Service processing phase.* After the `Svc_Handler` is activated, it processes incoming event messages arriving on the `PEER_STREAM`. A `Svc_Handler` can process incoming event messages in accordance with patterns, such as the Reactor or the Active Object [2].

The dynamics among participants in `Connector` component of the pattern can be divided into the following three phases:

1. *Connection initiation phase,* which actively connects one or more `Svc_Handlers` with their peers. Connections can be initiated synchronously or asynchronously. The `Connector`'s `connect` method implements the strategy for establishing connections actively.

2. *Service initialization phase,* which activates a `Svc_Handler` by calling its `open` method when its connection completes successfully. The `open` method of the `Svc_Handler` then performs service-specific initialization.

3. *Service processing phase,* which performs the application-specific service processing using the data exchanged between the `Svc_Handler` and its connected `Peer`.

4 APPLYING DESIGN PATTERNS TO DEVELOP EXTENSIBLE ACCEPTORS

This section describes how to implement a highly configurable instance of the `Acceptor` component from the Acceptor-Connector pattern by applying other design patterns, in particular Wrapper Facade [2], Strategy, Bridge, Factory Method, and Abstract Factory [1]. These patterns enable an `Acceptor` to flexibly configure alternative strategies for *service advertisement, endpoint listening, service handler creation, service connection acceptance,* and *service activation.* In this section, we focus on the `Svc_Handler` and the `Acceptor` components shown in Figure 17.2. The `Connector` component can be implemented similarly.

4.1 THE SVC_HANDLER CLASS

This abstract C++ class provides a generic interface for processing services. Applications customize this class to perform a particular type of service. The C++ interface for the `Svc_Handler` is shown below:

```
template <class PEER_STREAM>
        // Type of IPC mechanism.
class Svc_Handler {
public:
  // Pure virtual method (defined by subclass).
  virtual int open (void) = 0;

protected:
  // Instance of IPC mechanism.
  PEER_STREAM stream_;
};
```

Each `Svc_Handler` contains a communication endpoint, called `peer_stream`, of parameterized type PEER_STREAM. This endpoint is used to exchange data between the `Svc_Handler` and its connected peer. After a connection is successfully accepted, an `Acceptor` activates a `Svc_Handler` by calling its `open` method. This pure virtual method must be overridden by a concrete `Svc_Handler` subclass and performs service-specific initializations.

4.2 THE ACCEPTOR CLASS

This abstract C++ class implements the generic strategy for passively initializing network services, which are implemented as concrete `Svc_Handlers`. An `Acceptor` instance coordinates the following five orthogonal dimensions of passive service initialization:

1. *Service advertisements,* which initializes the `peer_acceptor_` endpoint and announces the availability of the service to interested peers.
2. *Endpoint listening,* which waits passively for peers to actively initiate connections on the `peer_acceptor_` endpoint.
3. *Service handler creation,* which creates and initializes a concrete `Svc_Handler` that can communicate with the new peer.

4. *Passive connection establishment,* which uses the `peer_acceptor_` endpoint to accept a connection initiated actively by a peer.
5. *Service handler concurrency activation,* which determines the type of concurrency mechanism used to process data exchanged with peers.

The `Acceptor`'s `open` method is responsible for handling the first two dimensions. The `Acceptor`'s `accept` method is responsible for handling the remaining three dimensions.

The following interface illustrates the methods and data members in the `Acceptor` class:

```
template <class SVC_HANDLER,
  // Type of service handler.
  class PEER_ACCEPTOR>
  // Type of passive connection mechanism.
class Acceptor {
public:
  // Defines the initialization strategies.
  typedef Strategy_Factory<SVC_HANDLER,
                            PEER_ACCEPTOR>
        STRATEGY_FACTORY;

  // Initialize listener endpoint at <addr>
  // according to specified <init_strategies>.
  virtual void open
    (const PEER_ACCEPTOR::PEER_ADDR &addr,
    STRATEGY_FACTORY *init_strategies);

  // Embodies the strategies for creating,
  // connecting, and activating <SVC_HANDLER>'s.
  virtual void accept (void);

protected:
  // Defines strategy to advertise endpoint.
  virtual void advertise_svc
    (const PEER_ACCEPTOR::PEER_ADDR &);

  // Defines the strategy to listen for active
  // connections from peers.
  virtual void make_listener (PEER_ACCEPTOR *);

  // Defines <SVC_HANDLER> creation strategy.
  virtual SVC_HANDLER *make_svc_handler (void);
```

```
        // Defines <SVC_HANDLER> connection strategy.
        virtual void accept_svc_handler (SVC_HANDLER *);

        // Defines <SVC_HANDLER> concurrency strategy.
        virtual int activate_svc_handler (SVC_HANDLER *);

    private:
        // Pointers to objects that implement the
        // <Acceptor>'s initialization Strategies.
        Advertise_Strategy<PEER_ACCEPTOR::PEER_ADDR>
          *listen_strategy_;
        Listener_Strategy<PEER_ACCEPTOR>
          *listen_strategy_;
        Creation_Strategy<SVC_HANDLER
          *create_strategy_;
        Accept_Strategy<SVC_HANDLER, PEER_ACCEPTOR>
          *accept_strategy_;
        Concurrency_Strategy<SVC_HANDLER>
          *concurrency_strategy_;
    };
```

The Acceptor is a C++ template that is parameterized by a particular
type of PEER_ACCEPTOR and SVC_HANDLER. The PEER_ACCEPTOR
is the type of transport mechanism used by the Acceptor to passively
establish the connection. The SVC_HANDLER is the type of service that
processes the data exchanged with its connected peer. Parameterized types
are used to efficiently decouple the service initialization strategies from the
type of Svc_Handler, network programming interface, and transport
layer connection protocol. This design improves the extensibility of the
Acceptor and Svc_Handler components by allowing the wholesale
replacement of various strategies.

Figure 17.4 visually depicts the relationship between the classes that comprise the Acceptor implementation. The five strategies supported by the
Acceptor to passively initialize Svc_Handlers are illustrated and
described below.

1. *Service advertisement strategies.* The Acceptor uses its service advertisement strategy to initialize the PEER_ACCEPTOR endpoint and to
   announce the availability of the service to interested peers. Figure 17.5
   illustrates the common strategies configured into the Acceptor to
   advertise services:

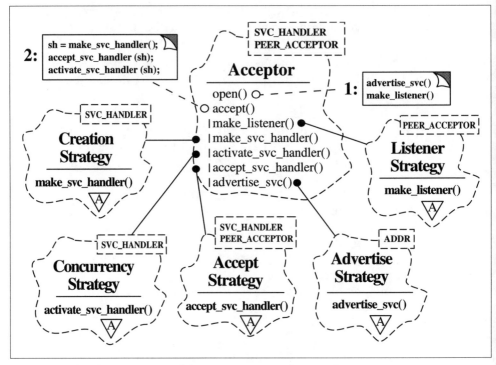

Figure 17.4. Class structure of the `Acceptor` *class implementation.*

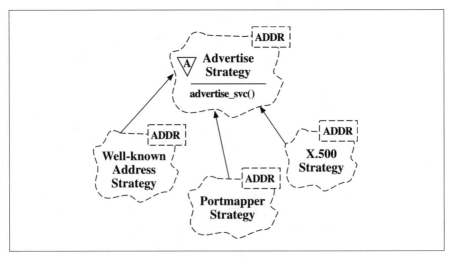

Figure 17.5. Alternative service advertising strategies.

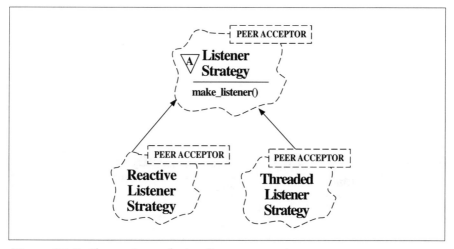

Figure 17.6. Alternative endpoint listener strategies.

Well-known addresses, such as Internet port numbers and host names:

Endpoint portmappers, such as those used by Sun RPC and DCE;

X.500 directory service, which is an ISO OSI standard for mapping names to values in a distributed system.

2. *Endpoint listener strategies.* The Acceptor uses its endpoint listening strategy to wait passively for peers to actively initiate a connection to the PEER_ACCEPTOR endpoint. Figure 17.6 illustrates the following common strategies configured into the Acceptor to wait for connections:

Reactive listeners, which use an event-demultiplexer, such as a Reactor [2], to listen passively on a set of endpoints in a single thread of control;

Threaded listeners, which use a separate thread of control for each listener.

3. *Service handler creation strategies.* The Acceptor uses its creation strategy to initialize a Svc_Handler that will communicate with the new peer. Figure 17.7 illustrates the following common strategies configured into the Acceptor to create Svc_Handlers:

Demand creation, which allocates a new Svc_Handler for every new connection;

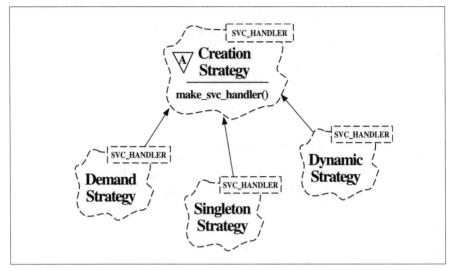

Figure 17.7. Alternative `Svc_Handler` *creation strategies.*

Singleton creation, which only creates a single `Svc_Handler` that is recycled for every connection;

Dynamic creation, which does not store the `Svc_Handler` object in the application process until it is required, at which point the object is dynamically linked into the process from a shared library.

4. *Passive connection establishment strategies.* The `Acceptor` uses its passive connection establishment strategy to accept a new connection initiated actively by a peer. Figure 17.8 illustrates the following common strategies configured into the `Acceptor` to accept connections from peers:

Connection-oriented (CONS) establishment, which uses connection-oriented protocols, such as TCP, SPX, or TP4;

Connectionless (CLNS) establishment, which uses the Adapter pattern [1] to utilize a uniform interface for connectionless protocols.

5. *Service handler concurrency activation strategies.* The `Acceptor` uses its activation strategy to determine the type of concurrency mechanism a `Svc_Handler` will use to process data exchanged with its peer. Figure 17.9 illustrates the following common strategies configured into the `Acceptor` to activate `Svc_Handlers`:

Reactive activation, where all `Svc_Handlers` execute within a single thread of control by using the Reactor pattern [2];

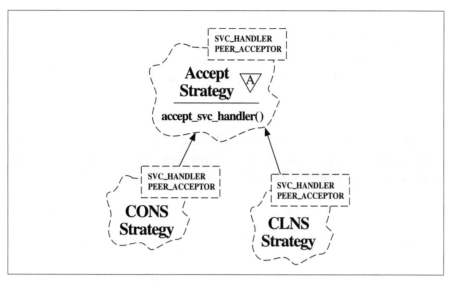

Figure 17.8. Alternative `Svc_Handler` *connection acceptance strategies.*

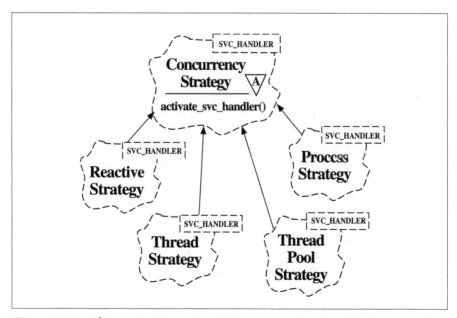

Figure 17.9. Alternative `Svc_Handler` *concurrency activation strategies.*

Thread activation, where each `Svc_Handler` executes within its own separate thread;

Thread pool activation, where each `Svc_Handler` executes within a pool of threads to increase performance on multi-processors;

Process activation, where each `Svc_Handler` executes within a separate process.

The next section illustrates how different `Acceptors` can be configured flexibly to support alternative strategies without requiring changes to its external interface design or internal implementation.

4.3 USING DESIGN PATTERNS TO IMPLEMENT AN EXTENSIBLE ACCEPTOR

The ACE implementation of the Acceptor-Connector pattern applies the Wrapper Facade [2], Factory Method, Strategy, Bridge, and Abstract Factory patterns described in [1]. These patterns facilitate the flexible and extensible configuration and use of the initialization strategies discussed above. Below, each pattern used in the ACE `Acceptor` is described, the design forces it resolves are outlined, and an example of how the pattern is used to implement the `Acceptor` is presented.

Using the Wrapper Facade Pattern. The Wrapper Facade [2] pattern encapsulates the functions and data provided by existing non-OO APIs within more concise, robust, portable, maintainable, and cohesive OO class interfaces. The ACE `Acceptor` uses the Wrapper Facade pattern to provide a uniform interface that encapsulates differences between non-uniform network programming mechanisms, such as sockets, TLI, named pipes, and STREAM pipes.

Figure 17.10 illustrates how the ACE `Acceptor` uses the Wrapper Facade pattern to enhance its portability across platforms that contain different network programming interfaces, such as sockets but not TLI, or vice versa. In this example, the `PEER_STREAM` template argument of the `Svc_Handler` class can be instantiated with either a `SOCK_Stream` or a `TLI_Stream`, depending on whether the platform supports sockets or TLI. The Wrapper Facade pattern ensures that these two classes can be used identically by different instantiations of the `Svc_Handler` class.

Using the Strategy Pattern. The Strategy pattern [1] defines a family of

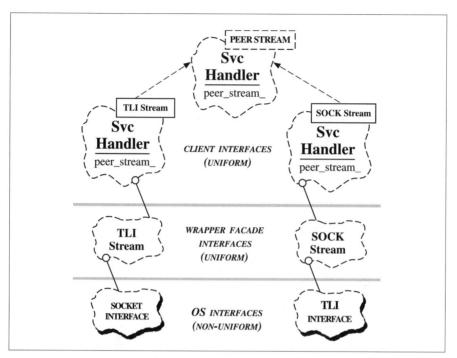

Figure 17.10. Using the Wrapper Facade pattern.

algorithms, encapsulates each one as an object, and makes them interchangeable. The ACE `Acceptor` uses this pattern to determine the passive
initialization strategies used to create, accept, and execute a
`Svc_Handler`. By using the Strategy pattern, an application can configure different initialization strategies *without* modifying the following algorithm used by `accept` as follows:

```
template <class SVC_HANDLER, class PEER_ACCEPTOR>
    void
Acceptor<SVC_HANDLER, PEER_ACCEPTOR>::accept (void)
{
  // Create a new <SVC_HANDLER>.
  SVC_HANDLER *svc_handler =
    make_svc_handler ();

  // Accept connection from the peer.
  accept_svc_handler (svc_handler);

  // Activate <SVC_HANDLER>.
  activate_svc_handler (svc_handler);
}
```

Figure 17.11 illustrates how the Strategy pattern is used to implement the `Acceptor`'s concurrency strategy. When the `Acceptor` is initialized, its `Strategy_Factory` configures the designated concurrency strategy. As shown in Figure 17.9, there are a number of alternative strategies. The particular strategy illustrated in Figure 17.11 activates each `Svc_Handler` to run in a separate thread of control. Since all concurrency algorithms are encapsulated in a uniform interface, however, it is easy to replace this strategy with an alternative one, such as running the `Svc_Handler` in a separate process.

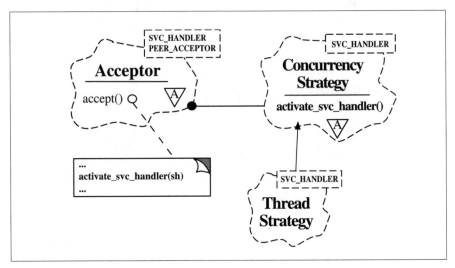

Figure 17.11. Using the Strategy pattern.

Using the Bridge Pattern. The Bridge pattern [1] decouples an abstraction from its implementation so that the two can vary independently. The ACE `Acceptor` uses this pattern to provide a stable, uniform interface that is both open (i.e., extensible) and closed (i.e., does not require direct code changes).

Figure 17.12 illustrates how the Bridge pattern is used to implement the `Acceptor`'s connection acceptance strategy (the Bridge pattern is used for all the other `Acceptor` strategies, as well). When a connection is established with a peer, the `Acceptor`'s `accept` method invokes the `accept_svc_handler` method. Instead of performing the passive connection acceptance strategy directly, however, this method forwards the method to the appropriate subclass of `Accept_Strategy`. In the example shown in Figure 17.12, this subclass establishes the connection using a con-

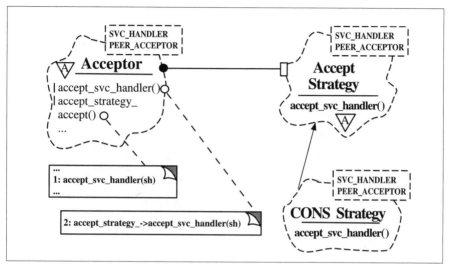

Figure 17.12. Using the Bridge pattern.

nection-oriented protocol. Since the Bridge pattern is used, however, an application can change the `Acceptor`'s connection acceptance strategy to an alternative strategy. For example, it can change to the connectionless version shown in Figure 17.8 without requiring any changes to the code in `accept`.

Another advantage of using the Bridge pattern is that a subclass of the `Acceptor` can override its `make_*` methods to avoid the additional overhead of indirecting through strategy objects on every call. In this case, the `accept` method uses the Template Method pattern [1]. In the Template Method version of `accept` the steps in the `Acceptor`'s passive initialization algorithm are fixed, but can be overridden by derived classes.

Using the Factory Method Pattern. The Factory Method pattern [1] defines a stable interface for initializing a component, but allows subclasses to specify the details of the initialization. The ACE `Acceptor` uses this pattern to allow each initialization strategy used by the `Acceptor` to be extended without modifying the `Acceptor` or `Svc_Handler` implementations.

Figure 17.13 illustrates how the Factory Method pattern is used to transparently extend the `Acceptor`'s creation strategy. The `Creation_Strategy` base class contains a factory method called `make_svc_handler`. This method is invoked by the `make_svc_handler` Bridge method in the `Acceptor` to create the appropriate type of concrete `Svc_Handler`, as follows:

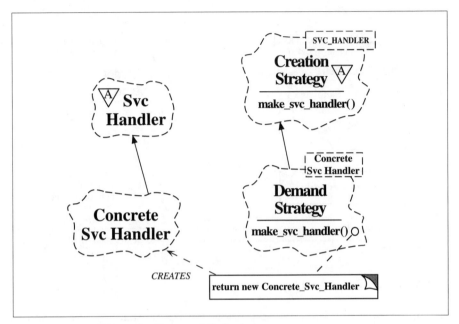

Figure 17.13. Using the Factory Method pattern.

```
template <class SVC_HANDLER, class PEER_ACCEPTOR>
    void
Acceptor<SVC_Handler, PEER_ACCEPTOR>::accept (void)
{
    creation_strategy_->make_svc_handler ();
}
```

An implementation of a creation strategy based on the *demand* strategy could be implemented as follows:

```
template <class SVC_HANDLER> SVC_HANDLER *
Demand_Strategy<SVC_HANDLER>::make_svc_handler
    (void) {
    // Implement the ``demand'' creation
    // strategy allocating a new <SVC_HANDLER>.
    return new SVC_HANDLER;
}
```

Note that it is the responsibility of the `Acceptor`'s `Strategy_Factory` to determine the type of subclass associated with the `creation_strategy_`.

Using the Abstract Factory Pattern. The Abstract Factory pattern [1] provides a single interface that creates families of related objects without requiring the specification of their concrete classes. The `Acceptor` uses this pattern to simplify its interface by localizing all five of its initialization strategies into a single class. The Abstract Factory pattern also ensures that all selected strategies can work together correctly.

Figure 17.14 illustrates how the Abstract Factory pattern is used to implement the `Status_Acceptor` taken from the `Gateway` example described in Section 5. This example instantiates the following `Strategy_Factory` template:

```
template <class SVC_HANDLER,
         // Type of service handler.
         class PEER_ACCEPTOR>
         // Type of passive connection
  class Strategy_Factory {
```

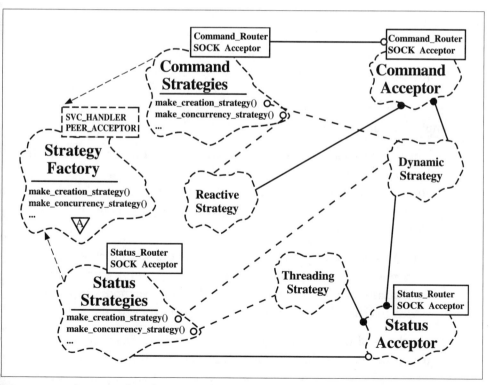

Figure 17.14. Using the Abstract Factory pattern.

```
public:
  Strategy_Factory
    (Advertise_Strategy<PEER_ACCEPTOR::PEER_ADDR> *,
     Listener_Strategy<PEER_ACCEPTOR> *,
     Creation_Strategy<SVC_HANDLER> *,
     Accept_Strategy<SVC_HANDLER, PEER_ACCEPTOR> *,
     Concurrency_Strategy<SVC_HANDLER> *);

  // Factory methods called by Acceptor::open().
  Advertise_Strategy<PEER_ACCEPTOR::PEER_ADDR>
    *make_advertise_strategy (void);
  Listener_Strategy<PEER_ACCEPTOR>
    *make_listener_strategy (void);
  Creation_Strategy<SVC_HANDLER>
    *make_create_strategy (void);
  Accept_Strategy<SVC_HANDLER, PEER_ACCEPTOR>
    *make_accept_strategy (void);
  Concurrency_Strategy<SVC_HANDLER>
    *make_concurrency_strategy (void);

  // ...
```

Figure 17.14 shows the creation and concurrency strategies – the other strategies are handled similarly. The Status_Strategies factory instructs the Status_Acceptor to dynamically create each Status_Router, which will execute in its own thread of control. This example illustrates the following points:

- The Abstract Factory pattern is often used in conjunction with the Factory Method pattern. For example, the Strategy_Factory abstract factory simplifies the interface to the Acceptor by consolidating all five initialization strategy factory methods in a single class.

- The Abstract Factory pattern ensures that the various strategies can work together correctly. For instance, the Strategy_Factory can be subclassed and its various make_* Factory Methods can be overridden to create different types of initialization strategies.

- Subclasses of the Strategy_Factory abstract factory can be used to ensure that conflicting initialization strategies are not configured accidentally. For example, the *singleton* creation strategy may conflict with the *thread* concurrency strategy since multiple threads of control will attempt to access a single communication endpoint. A `Strat-egy_Factory` subclass can be defined to check for these conflicts and report an error at configuration time.

5 EXAMPLE: IMPLEMENTING EXTENSIBLE APPLICATION-LEVEL GATEWAYS USING THE ACCEPTOR

This section illustrates how the application-level `Gateway` described in Section 2 uses the pattern-based `Acceptor` component from Section 4 to simplify the task of passively initializing services whose connections are initiated actively by `Peers`. In this example the `Peers` play the active role in establishing connections with the `Gateway`.

Defining Svc_Handlers for Routing Peer Messages. The three classes shown below, `Status_Router`, `Bulk_Data_Router`, and `Command_Router`, process routing messages received from `Peers`. These classes inherit from `Svc_Handler`, which allows them to be passively initialized by an `Acceptor`, as shown in Figure 17.15. Each class is instantiated with a specific type of C++ IPC wrapper facade that exchanges data with its connected peer. For example, the classes below use a `SOCK_Stream` as the underlying data transport delivery mechanism. `SOCK_Stream` is an ACE C++ wrapper facade that encapsulates the data transfer functions in the socket interface. By virtue of the Strategy pattern, however, it is easy to vary the data transfer mechanism by parameterizing the `Svc_Handler` with a different `PEER_STREAM`, such as a `TLI_Stream`.

The `Status_Router` class routes status data sent to and received from `Peers`:[1]

```
class Status_Router :
  public Svc_Handler<SOCK_Stream>
{
public:
    // Performs router initialization.
```

---

[1]To save space, these examples have been simplified by omitting most of the detailed protocol logic and error handling code.

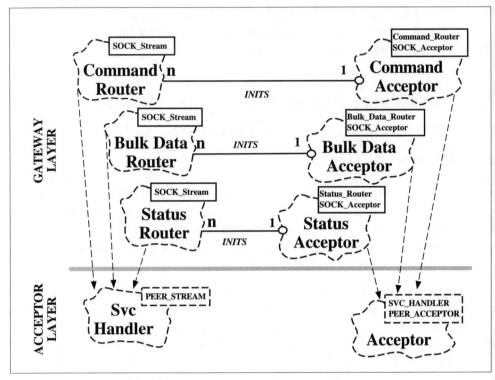

Figure 17.15. Structure of Acceptor *participants in the* Gateway.

```
virtual int open (void);
// Receive and route status data from/to peers.
virtual int handle_event (void);
// ...
```

The Bulk_Data_Router class routes bulk data sent to and received from Peers

```
class Bulk_Data_Router :
  public Svc_Handler<SOCK_Stream>
{
public:
  // Performs router initialization.
  virtual int open (void);
  // Receive and route bulk data from/to peers.
  virtual int handle_event (void);
  // ...
```

The `Command_Router` class routes bulk data sent to and received from Peers:

```
class Command_Router :
  public Svc_Handler<SOCK_Stream>
{
public:
  // Performs router initialization.
  virtual int open (void);
  // Receive and route command data from/to peers.
  virtual int handle_event (void);
  // ...
```

Defining Acceptor Factories to Create Svc_Handlers. The three classes shown below are instantiations of the `Acceptor` template:

```
// Typedefs that instantiate <Acceptor>s for
// different types of routers.
typedef Acceptor<Status_Router, SOCK_Acceptor>
        Status_Acceptor;
typedef Acceptor<Bulk_Data_Router, SOCK_Acceptor>
        Bulk_Data_Acceptor
typedef Acceptor<Command_Router, SOCK_Acceptor>
        Command_Acceptor;
```

These typedefs instantiate the `Acceptor` template with concrete parameterized type arguments for `SVC_HANDLER` and `PEER_ACCEPTOR`. A `SOCK_Acceptor` wrapper facade is used as the underlying `PEER_ACCEPTOR` in order to accept a connection passively. Parameterizing the `Acceptor` with a different `PEER_ACCEPTOR`, such as `TLI_Acceptor`, is easy since the IPC mechanisms are encapsulated in C++ wrapper facade classes. The three objects shown below are instances of these classes that create and activate `Status_Routers`, `Bulk_Data_Routers`, and `Command_Routers`, respectively:

```
// Accept connection requests from
// Gateway and activate Status_Router.
static Status_Acceptor status_acceptor;

// Accept connection requests from
// Gateway and activate Bulk_Data_Router.
static Bulk_Data_Acceptor bulk_data_acceptor;

// Accept connection requests from
```

```
    // Gateway and activate Command_Router.
    static Command_Acceptor command_acceptor;
```

Defining Strategies to Initialize Svc_Handlers. The three classes shown below are instantiations of the `Strategy_Factory` defined in Section 4.2:

```
    // Typedefs that instantiate different types
    // of <Strategy_Factory>.
    typedef Strategy_Factory<Status_Router,
                             SOCK_Acceptor>
            Status_Strategies;
    typedef Strategy_Factory<Bulk_Data_Router,
                             SOCK_Acceptor>
            Bulk_Data_Strategies;
    typedef Strategy_Factory<Command_Router,
                             SOCK_Acceptor>
            Command_Strategies;
```

These typedefs instantiate the `Strategy_Factory` template with concrete parameterized type arguments for SVC_HANDLER and PEER_ACCEPTOR. The three objects shown below instantiate these classes to specify the initialization strategies for `Status_Routers`, `Bulk_Data_Routers`, and `Command_Routers`, respectively:

```
    // Creates a multi-threaded <Status_Router>.
    Status_Strategies threaded
      (new Well-Known_Addr,
       new Reactive_Listener (Reactor::instance ()),
       new Demand,
       new CONS,
       new Multi_Thread);

    // Creates a multi-processed <Bulk_Data_Router>.
    Bulk_Data_Strategies process
      (new Well_Known_Addr,
       new Reactive_Listener (Reactor::instance ()),
       new Demand,
       new CONS,
       new Multi_Process);

    // Creates a single-thread reactive <Command_Router>.
    Command_Strategies reactive
      (new Well_Known_Addr,
```

```
new Reactive_Listener (Reactor::instance ()),
new Demand,
new CONS,
new Reactive (Reactor::instance ());
```

Each `Strategy_Factory` configuration shown above uses the *well known address* service advertisement strategy, the *reactive* listener strategy, the *demand* `Svc_Handler` creation strategy, and the *connection-oriented* acceptance strategy. To illustrate the flexibility of the Acceptor-Connector pattern, however, each `Strategy_Factory` implements a different concurrency strategy, as follows:

- When the `Status_Router` is activated by `Status_Acceptor` it runs in a separate thread.

- When activated by `Bulk_Data_Acceptor`, the `Bulk_Data_Router` runs as a separate process.

- When activated by `Command_Acceptor`, the `Command_Router` runs in the same thread as with the `Reactor` singleton [1], which is used to demultiplex connection requests for the three `Acceptor` factories.

Note how changing the concurrency strategy does not affect the `Acceptor` class. Thus, the `Acceptor`'s generic strategy for passively initializing services can be reused, while permitting specific details, such as the `PEER_ACCEPTOR`, `SVC_HANDLER`, and selected initialization strategies, to change flexibly.

The Main Gateway Function. The main gateway initializes the `Acceptors` with their well-known ports and initialization strategies, as follows:

```
// Main program for the Gateway.

int main (void) {
  // Initialize Acceptors with their well-known
  // ports and their initialization strategies.
  status_acceptor.open
    (INET_Addr (STATUS_PORT), &threaded);
  bulk_data_acceptor.open
    (INET_ADDr (BULK_DATA_PORT), &process);
```

```
command_acceptor.open
  (INET_Addr (COMMAND_PORT), &reactive);

// Loop forever handling connection request
// events and processing data from peers.
for (;;)
  Reactor::instance ()->handle_events ();
}
```

The listener strategy configured for each `Acceptor` is reactive. Therefore, the program enters an event loop that uses the `Reactor` singleton to detect all connection requests from `Peers` within a single thread of control. When connections arrive, the `Reactor` singleton dispatches the associated `Acceptor`, which (1) creates an appropriate type of `Svc_Handler` on demand to perform the service, (2) accepts the connection into the handler, and (3) activates the handler. The concurrency strategy configured into each `Acceptor` dictates how every `Svc_Handler` it creates will process events.

Figure 17.16 illustrates the relationship between Acceptor-Connector pattern components in the `Gateway` after four connections have been established. The various `*Routers` exchange data with their connected `Peers` using the type of concurrency strategy designated by their

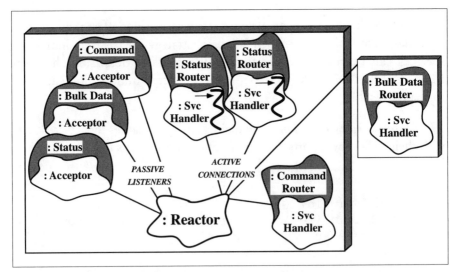

Figure 17.16. Object diagram for the `Gateway` *Acceptor-Connector pattern.*

`Strategy_Factories`. Meanwhile, the `*Acceptor`s continue to listen for new connections.

5.1 Known Uses

UNIX Network Superservers. Superserver implementations such as Inetd [5], Listen [6], and the Service Configurator [7] from the ACE framework use a master acceptor process that listens for connections on a set of communication ports. In Inetd, for example, each port is associated with a service, such as the standard Internet services `FTP`, `TELNET`, `DAYTIME`, and `ECHO`. The acceptor process decouples the functionality of the Inetd superserver into two separate parts: one for establishing connections and another for receiving and processing requests from peers. When a service request arrives on a port monitored by Inetd, it accepts the request and dispatches an appropriate pre-registered handler to perform the service.

CORBA Object Request Brokers (ORBs). The ORB Core layer in many implementations of CORBA [8] uses the Acceptor-Connector pattern to passively and actively initialize connection handlers when clients request ORB services. For example, [9] describes how the Acceptor-Connector pattern is used to implement the ORB Core portion in The ACE ORB (TAO), which is a high-performance and real-time implementation of CORBA.

Web Browsers. The HTML parsing components in Web browsers such as Netscape and Internet Explorer use the asynchronous version of the connector component to establish connections with servers associated with images embedded in HTML pages. This pattern allows multiple HTTP connections to be initiated asynchronously. This avoids the possibility of the browser's main event loop blocking.

Ericcson EOS Call Center Management System. This system uses the Acceptor-Connector pattern to allow application-level Call Center Manager event servers [10] to establish connections actively with passive supervisors in a networked center management system.

Project Spectrum. The high-speed medical image transfer subsystem of project Spectrum [11] uses the Acceptor-Connector pattern to establish connections passively and initialize application services for storing large medical images. Once connections are established, applications send and receive multi-megabyte medical images to and from the image stores.

ACE. Implementations of the generic `Svc_Handler`, `Connector`, and `Acceptor` components described in the Implementation section are provided as reusable C++ classes in the ACE framework [3]. Java ACE [12] is a version of ACE implemented in Java that provides components corresponding to the participants in the Acceptor-Connector pattern.

6 RELATED PATTERNS

[1, 13, 2] identify and catalog many architectural and design patterns. This section examines how the patterns described in this chapter relate to other patterns in the literature.

The intent of the Acceptor-Connector pattern is similar to the Configuration pattern [14]. The Configuration pattern decouples structural issues related to configuring services in distributed applications from the execution of the services themselves. This pattern has been used in frameworks for configuring distributed systems, such as Regis [15], to support the construction of a distributed system from a set of components. In a similar way, the Acceptor-Connector pattern decouples service initialization from service processing. The primary difference is that the Configuration pattern focuses more on the active composition of a chain of related services, whereas the Acceptor-Connector pattern focuses on the passive initialization of a service handler at a particular endpoint. In addition, the Acceptor-Connector pattern also focuses on decoupling service behavior from the service's concurrency strategies.

The intent of the Acceptor-Connector pattern is similar to that of the Client-Dispatcher-Server pattern [13] in that both are concerned with the separation of active connection establishment from subsequent service processing. The primary difference is that the Acceptor-Connector pattern addresses passive and active connection establishment and initialization of both synchronous and asynchronous connections. In contrast, the Client-Dispatcher-Server pattern focuses on synchronous connection establishment.

The service handlers that are created by acceptors and connectors can be coordinated using the Abstract Session pattern [16], which allows a server object to maintain state for many clients. Likewise, the Half Object plus Protocol pattern [17] can help decompose the responsibilities of an end-to-end service into service handler interfaces and the protocol used to collaborate between them.

The Acceptor-Connector pattern may be viewed as an object creational pattern [1]. A creational pattern assembles the resources necessary to create an object and decouples the creation and initialization of the object from subsequent use of the object. The Acceptor-Connector pattern is a factory that creates, passively connects, and initializes service handlers. Its `accept` method implements the algorithm that listens passively for connection requests, then creates, accepts, and activates a handler when the connection is established. The handler performs a service using data exchanged on the connection. Thus, the subsequent behavior of the service is decoupled from its initialization strategies.

7 CONCLUDING REMARKS

This chapter describes the Acceptor-Connector pattern and illustrates how its `Acceptor` component has been implemented using other patterns to develop highly flexible communication software. In general, the Acceptor-Connector pattern is applicable whenever connection-oriented applications have the following characteristics:

- The behavior of a distributed service does not depend on the steps required to passively or actively connect and initialize a service.

- Connection requests from different peers may arrive concurrently, but blocking or continuous polling for incoming connections on any individual peer is inefficient.

The Acceptor-Connector pattern provides the following benefits for network applications and services:

It enhances the reusability, portability, and extensibility of connection-oriented software. The Acceptor-Connector pattern decouples mechanisms for connection establishment and service initialization, which are application-independent and thus reusable, from the services themselves, which are application-specific. For example, the application-independent mechanisms in the `Acceptor` are reusable components that know how to establish a connection passively and to create and activate its associated

`Svc_Handler`. In contrast, the `Svc_Handler` knows how to per-form application-specific service processing.

This separation of concerns decouples connection establishment from service handling, thereby allowing each part to evolve indepen-dently. The strategy for establishing connections actively was written once, placed into the ACE framework, and reused via inheritance, object composition, and template instantiation. Thus, the same passive connec-tion establishment code need not be written for each application. In con-trast, services may vary according to different application requirements. By parameterizing the `Acceptor` with a `Svc_Handler`, the impact of this variation is localized to a single point in the software.

Improves application robustness. By strongly decoupling the `Acceptor` from the `Svc_Handler` the passive-mode `PEER_ACCEPTOR` cannot accidentally be used to read or write data. This eliminates a class of subtle errors that can arise when programming with weakly typed network pro-gramming interfaces such as sockets or TLI.

However, the Acceptor-Connector pattern can also exhibit the following drawbacks:

Additional indirection. The Acceptor-Connector pattern can incur addi-tional indirection compared to using the underlying network program-ming interfaces directly. However, languages that support parameterized types, such as C++, Ada, or Eiffel, can implement these patterns with no significant overhead when compilers inline the method calls used to implement the patterns.

Additional complexity. The Acceptor-Connector pattern may add unneces-sary complexity for simple client applications that connect with only one server and perform one service using a single network programming interface. However, the use of generic acceptor and connector wrapper facades may simplify even these use cases by shielding developers from tedious, error-prone and non-portable low-level network programming mechanisms.

Open-source implementations of the Acceptor-Connector and Reactor patterns are available at `www.cs.wustl.edu/~schmidt/ ACE.html`. This URL contains complete source code, documentation, and example test drivers for the C++ components developed as part of the ACE framework [3] developed at the University of California, Irvine and at Washington University, St. Louis.

REFERENCES

1. E. Gamma, R. Helm, R. Johnson, and J. Vlissides, *Design Patterns: Elements of Reusable Object-Oriented Software.* Reading, MA: Addison-Wesley, 1995.

2. D.C. Schmidt, M. Stal, H. Rohnert, and F. Buschmann, *Pattern-Oriented Software Architecture: Patterns for Concurrency and Distributed Objects,* Volume 2. New York, NY: Wiley & Sons, 2000.

3. D.C. Schmidt, "Applying Design Patterns and Frameworks to Develop Object-Oriented Communication Software," in *Handbook of Programming Languages* (P. Salus, ed.), Macmillan Computer Publishing, 1997.

4. D.C. Schmidt, "Applying a Pattern Language to Develop Application-Level Gateways." See this volume, Chapter 16.

5. W.R. Stevens, *UNIX Network Programming,* First Edition. Englewood Cliffs, NJ: Prentice Hall, 1990.

6. S. Rago, *UNIX System V Network Programming.* Reading, MA: Addison-Wesley, 1993.

7. P. Jain and D.C. Schmidt, "Service Configurator: A Pattern for Dynamic Configuration of Services," in *Proceedings of the 3rd Conference on Object-Oriented Technologies and Systems,* USENIX, June 1997.

8. Object Management Group, *The Common Object Request Broker: Architecture and Specification,* 2.3 ed., June 1999.

9. D.C. Schmidt and C. Cleeland, "Applying a Pattern Language to Develop Extensible ORB Middleware." See this volume, Chapter 8.

10. D.C. Schmidt and T. Suda, "An Object-Oriented Framework for Dynamically Configuring Extensible Distributed Communication Systems," *IEE/BCS Distributed Systems Engineering Journal (Special Issue on Configurable Distributed Systems),* vol. 2, pp. 280–293, December 1994.

11. G. Blaine, M. Boyd, and S. Crider, "Project Spectrum: Scalable Bandwidth for the BJC Health System," *HIMSS, Health Care Communications,* pp. 71–81, 1994.

12. P. Jain and D. Schmidt, "Experiences Converting a C++ Communication Software Framework to Java," *C++ Report,* vol. 9, January 1997.

13. F. Buschmann, R. Meunier, H. Rohnert, P. Sommerlad, and M. Stal, *Pattern-Oriented Software Architecture – A System of Patterns.* Wiley and Sons, 1996.

14. S. Crane, J. Magee, and N. Pryce, "Design Patterns for Binding in Distributed Systems," in *The OOPSLA '95 Workshop on Design Patterns for Concurrent, Parallel, and Distributed Object-Oriented Systems* (Austin, TX), ACM, October 1995.

15. J. Magee, N. Dulay, and J. Kramer, "A Constructive Development Environment for Parallel and Distributed Programs," in *Proceedings of the 2nd International Workshop on Configurable Distributed Systems* (Pittsburgh, PA), pp. 1–14, IEEE, March 1994.

16. N. Pryce, "Abstract Session," in *Pattern Languages of Program Design* (B. Foote, N. Harrison, and H. Rohnert, eds.). Reading, MA: Addison-Wesley, 1999, and this volume, Chapter 9.

17. G. Meszaros, "Half-object plus Protocol," in *Pattern Languages of Program Design* (J.O. Coplien and D.C. Schmidt, eds.). Reading, MA: Addison-Wesley, 1995, and this volume, Chapter 8.

18

APPLYING A PATTERN LANGUAGE TO DEVELOP EXTENSIBLE ORB MIDDLEWARE*

Douglas C. Schmidt and Chris Cleeland

ABSTRACT

DISTRIBUTED OBJECT COMPUTING forms the basis of next-generation communication software. At the heart of distributed object computing are Object Request Brokers (ORBs), which automate many tedious and error-prone distributed programming tasks. Like much communication software, conventional ORBs use statically configured designs, which are hard to port, optimize, and evolve. Likewise, conventional ORBs cannot be extended without modifying their source code, which forces recompilation, relinking, and restarting running ORBs and their associated application objects.

This chapter makes two contributions to the study of extensible ORB middleware. First, it presents a case study illustrating how a pattern language can be used to develop dynamically configurable ORBs that can be customized for

Based on "Applying a Pattern Language to Develop Extensible ORB Middleware," by Douglas C. Schmidt and Chris Cleeland, which appeared in *IEEE Communications* 37(4), April 1999, pp. 54–63. © 1999 IEEE. Used with permission from the author.

*This work was supported in part by ATD, BBN, Boeing, Cisco, DARPA contract 9701516, Motorola Commercial Government and Industrial Solutions Sector, Motorola Laboratories, Siemens, and Sprint.

specific application requirements and system characteristics. Second, we quantify the impact of applying this pattern language to reduce the complexity and improve the maintainability of common ORB tasks, such as connection management, data transfer, demultiplexing, and concurrency control.

1 INTRODUCTION

Four trends are shaping the future of commercial software development. First, the software industry is moving away from *programming* applications from scratch to *integrating* applications using reusable components [1]. Second, there is great demand for *distribution technology* that provides remote method invocation and/or message-oriented middleware to simplify application collaboration. Third, there are increasing efforts to define standard software infrastructure frameworks that permit applications to interwork seamlessly throughout *heterogeneous* environments [2]. Finally, next-generation distributed applications such as video-on-demand, teleconferencing, and avionics require *quality-of-service* (QoS) guarantees for latency, bandwidth, and reliability [3].

A key software technology supporting these trends is *distributed object computing (DOC) middleware.* DOC middleware facilitates the collaboration of local and remote application components in heterogeneous distributed environments. The goal of DOC middleware is to eliminate many tedious, error-prone, and non-portable aspects of developing and evolving distributed applications and services. In particular, DOC middleware automates common network programming tasks, such as object location, implementation startup (i.e., server and object activation), encapsulation of byte-ordering and parameter type size differences across dissimilar architectures (i.e., parameter marshaling), fault recovery, and security. At the heart of DOC middleware are *Object Request Brokers* (ORBs), such as CORBA [4], DCOM [5], and Java RMI [6].

This chapter describes how we have applied a *pattern language* to develop and evolve dynamically configurable ORB middleware that can be extended more readily than statically configured middleware. In general, pattern languages help to alleviate the continual re-discovery and re-invention of software concepts and components by conveying a family of related solutions to standard software development problems [7]. For instance, pattern languages are useful for documenting the roles and relationships among participants in common communication software architectures [8]. The pattern language presented in this chapter is a generalization of the one presented in [9] and has been used successfully to build flexible, efficient, event-driven, and concurrent communication software, including ORB middleware.

To focus our discussion, this chapter presents a case study that illustrates how we have applied this pattern language to develop *The ACE* ORB (TAO) [10]. TAO is a freely available, highly extensible ORB targeted for applications with real-time QoS requirements, including avionics mission computing [11], multimedia applications [12], and distributed interactive simulations [13]. A novel aspect of TAO is its extensible design, which is guided by a pattern language that enables the ORB to be customized dynamically to meet specific application QoS requirements and network/endsystem characteristics.

The remainder of this chapter is organized as follows: Section 2 presents an overview of CORBA and TAO, Section 3 motivates the need for dynamic configuration and describes the pattern language that resolves key design challenges faced when developing extensible ORBs; Section 3.5 evaluates and quantifies the contribution of the pattern language to ORB middleware; and Section 4 presents concluding remarks.

2 Overview of CORBA and TAO

This section outlines the CORBA reference model and describes the enhancements that TAO provides for high-performance and real-time applications.

2.1 Overview of the CORBA Reference Model

CORBA Object Request Brokers (ORBs) [14] allow clients to invoke operations on distributed objects without concern for the following issues:

Object Location. A CORBA object can be either collocated with the client or distributed on a remote server, without affecting its implementation or use.

Programming Language. The languages supported by CORBA include C, C++, Java, Ada95, COBOL, and Smalltalk, among others.

OS Platform. CORBA runs on many OS platforms, including Win32,

UNIX, MVS, and real-time embedded systems, such as VxWorks, Chorus, and LynxOS.

Communication Protocols and Interconnects. The communication protocols and interconnects that CORBA runs on include TCP/IP, IPX/SPX, FDDI, ATM, Ethernet, Fast Ethernet, embedded system backplanes, and shared memory.

Hardware. CORBA shields applications from side effects stemming from hardware diversity, such as different storage layouts and data type sizes/ranges.

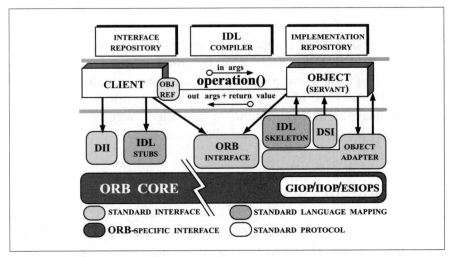

Figure 18.1. Components in the CORBA reference model.

Figure 18.1 illustrates the components in the CORBA reference model, all of which collaborate to provide the portability, interoperability, and transparency outlined above.

Each component in the CORBA reference model is outlined below:

Client. A client is a *role* that obtains references to objects and invokes operations on them to perform application tasks. Objects can be remote or collocated relative to the client. Clients can access remote objects just like a local object, i.e., object→operation(args). Figure 18.1 shows how the underlying ORB components described below transmit remote operation requests transparently from client to object.

Object. In CORBA, an object is an instance of an OMG Interface Definition Language (IDL) interface. Each object is identified by an *object reference,* which associates one or more paths through which a client can access an object on a server. An *object ID* associates an object with its implementation, called a servant, and is unique within the scope of an Object Adapter. Over its lifetime, an object has one or more servants associated with it to implement its interface.

Servant. This component implements the operations defined by an OMG IDL interface. In object-oriented (OO) languages, such as C++ and Java, servants are implemented using one or more class instances. In non-OO languages, such as C, servants are typically implemented using functions and `structs`. A client never interacts with servants directly, but always through objects identified by object references. Together, an object and its servant form an implementation of the Bridge pattern [15], with *object* as the *RefinedAbstraction* and *servant* as the *ConcreteImplementor.*

ORB Core. When a client invokes an operation on an object, the ORB Core is responsible for delivering the request to the object and returning a response, if any, to the client. An ORB Core is implemented as a run-time library linked into client and server applications. For objects executing remotely, a CORBA-compliant ORB Core communicates via a version of the General Inter-ORB Protocol (GIOP), such as the Internet Inter-ORB Protocol (IIOP) that runs atop the TCP transport protocol. In addition, custom Environment-Specific Inter-ORB protocols (ESIOPs) can also be defined [16].

ORB Interface. An ORB is an abstraction that can be implemented various ways (e.g., one or more processes or a set of libraries). To decouple applications from implementation details, the CORBA specification defines an interface to an ORB. This ORB interface provides standard operations to initialize and shut down the ORB, convert object references to strings and back, and create argument lists for requests made through the *dynamic invocation interface* (DII).

OMG IDL Stubs and Skeletons. IDL stubs and skeletons serve as a "glue" between the client and servants, respectively, and the ORB. Stubs implement the *Proxy* pattern [15] and provide a strongly typed, *static invocation interface* (SII) that marshals application parameters into a common message-level representation. Conversely, skeletons implement the *Adapter* pattern

[15] and demarshal the message-level representation back into typed parameters that are meaningful to an application.

IDL Compiler. An IDL compiler transforms OMG IDL definitions into stubs and skeletons that are generated automatically in an application programming language, such as C++ or Java. In addition to providing programming language transparency, IDL compilers eliminate common sources of network programming errors and provide opportunities for automated compiler optimizations [17].

Dynamic Invocation Interface (DII). The DII allows clients to generate requests at run-time, which is useful when an application has no compile-time knowledge of the interface it accesses. The DII also allows clients to make *deferred synchronous* calls, which decouple the request and response portions of two-way operations to avoid blocking the client until the servant responds. CORBA SII stubs support both synchronous and asynchronous *two-way*, i.e., request/response, and *one-way*, i.e., request-only operations.

Dynamic Skeleton Interface (DSI). The DSI is the server's analogue to the client's DII. The DSI allows an ORB to deliver requests to servants that have no compile-time knowledge of the IDL interface they implement. Clients making requests need not know whether the server ORB uses static skeletons or dynamic skeletons. Likewise, servers need not know if clients use the DII or SII to invoke requests.

Object Adapter. An Object Adapter is a composite component that associates servants with objects, creates object references, demultiplexes incoming requests to servants, and collaborates with the IDL skeleton to dispatch the appropriate operation upcall on a servant. Object Adapters enable ORBs to support various types of servants that possess similar requirements. This design results in a smaller and simpler ORB that can support a wide range of object granularities, lifetimes, policies, implementation styles, and other properties.

Interface Repository. The Interface Repository provides run-time information about IDL interfaces. Using this information, it is possible for a program to encounter an object whose interface was not known when the program was compiled, yet be able to determine what operations are valid on the object and make invocations on it using the DII. In addition, the Interface Repository provides a common location to store additional information associated with interfaces to CORBA objects, such as type libraries for stubs and skeletons.

Implementation Repository. The Implementation repository [18] contains information that allows an ORB to activate servers to process servants. Most of the information in the Implementation Repository is specific to an ORB or OS environment. In addition, the Implementation Repository provides a common location to store information associated with servers, such as administrative control, resource allocation, security, and activation modes.

2.2 OVERVIEW OF TAO

TAO is a high-performance, real-time ORB endsystem targeted for applications with deterministic and statistical QoS requirements, as well as best-effort requirements. TAO's ORB endsystem contains the network interface, OS, communication protocol, and CORBA-compliant middleware components and services shown in Figure 18.2. TAO supports the standard OMG CORBA reference model [14] and Real-Time CORBA specification [19], with enhancements designed to ensure efficient, predictable, and scalable QoS behavior for high-performance and real-time applications. In addition, TAO is well-suited for general-purpose distributed applications. Below, we outline the features of TAO's components shown in Figure 18.2.

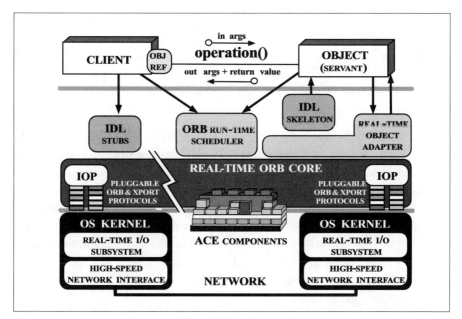

Figure 18.2. Components in the TAO real-time ORB endsystem.

Optimized IDL Stubs and Skeletons. IDL stubs and skeletons perform marshaling and demarshaling of application operation parameters, respectively. TAO's IDL compiler generates stubs/skeletons that can selectively use highly optimized compiled and/or interpretive (de)marshaling [20]. This flexibility allows application developers to selectively trade off time and space, which is crucial for high-performance, real-time, and/or embedded distributed systems.

Real-Time Object Adapter. An Object Adapter associates servants with the ORB and demultiplexes incoming requests to servants. TAO's real-time Object Adapter uses perfect hashing [21] and active demultiplexing [22] optimizations to dispatch servant operations in constant $O(1)$ time, regardless of the number of active connections, servants, and operations defined in IDL interfaces.

Run-Time Scheduler. TAO's run-time scheduler [19] maps application QoS requirements, such as bounding end-to-end latency and meeting periodic scheduling deadlines, or ORB endsystem/network resources, such as CPU, memory, network connections, and storage devices. TAO's run-time scheduler supports both static [10] and dynamic [23] real-time scheduling strategies.

Real-Time ORB Core. An ORB Core delivers client requests to the Object Adapter and returns responses (if any) to clients. TAO's real-time ORB Core [24] uses a multi-threaded, preemptive, priority-based connection and concurrency architecture [20] to provide an efficient and predictable CORBA protocol engine. TAO's ORB Core allows customized protocols to be plugged into the ORB without affecting the standard CORBA application programming model [25].

Real-Time I/O Subsystem. TAO's real-time I/O (RIO) subsystem [26] extends support for CORBA into the OS. RIO assigns priorities to real-time I/O threads so that the schedulability of application components and ORB endsystem resources can be enforced. When integrated with advanced hardware, such as the high-speed network interfaces described below, RIO can (1) perform early demultiplexing of I/O events onto prioritized kernel threads to avoid thread-based priority inversion and (2) maintain distinct priority streams to avoid packet-based priority inversion. TAO also runs efficiently and as predictably as possible on conventional I/O subsystems that lack advanced QoS features.

High-Speed Network Interface. At the core of TAO's I/O subsystem is a "daisy-chained" network interface consisting of one or more ATM Port Interconnect Controller (APIC) chips [27]. The APIC is designed to sustain an aggregate bidirectional data rate of 2.4 Gbps using zero-copy buffering optimization to avoid data copying across endsystem layers. In addition, TAO runs on conventional real-time interconnects, such as VME backplanes and multi-processor shared memory environments, as well as TCP/IP.

TAO Internals. TAO is developed using lower-level middleware called ACE [28], which implements core concurrency and distribution patterns [8] for communication software. ACE provides reusable C++ wrapper facades and framework components that support the QoS requirements of high-performance, real-time applications and higher-level middleware like TAO. ACE and TAO run on a wide range of OS platforms, including Win32, most versions of UNIX, and real-time operating systems, such as Sun/Chorus ClassiX, LynxOS, and VxWorks.

To expedite our project goals, and to avoid re-inventing existing components, we based TAO on SunSoft IIOP, which is a freely available C++ reference implementation of the Internet Inter-ORB Protocol (IIOP) version 1.0. Although SunSoft IIOP provides core features of a CORBA ORB it also has the following limitations.

Lack of Standard ORB Features. Although SunSoft IIOP provides an ORB Core, an IIOP 1.0 protocol engine, and a DII and DSI implementation, it lacks an IDL compiler, an Interface Repository and Implementation Repository, and a Portable Object Adapter (POA). TAO implements all these missing features and provides newer CORBA features, asynchronous method invocations [29], real-time CORBA [19] features [30], and fault tolerance CORBA features [31, 32].

Lack of IIOP Optimizations. Due to the excessive marshaling/demarshaling overhead, data copying, and high levels of function call overhead, SunSoft IIOP performs poorly over high-speed networks. Therefore, we applied a range of optimization principle patterns [22] that improved its performance considerably [33]. The principles that directed our optimizations include: (1) optimizing for the common case, (2) eliminating gratuitous waste, (3) replacing general-purpose methods with efficient special-purpose ones, (4) precomputing values, if possible, (5) storing redundant state to speed up expensive operations, (6) passing information between layers, and (7) optimizing for processor cache affinity.

This chapter does not discuss how TAO solves the limitations with SunSoft IIOP outlined above, which are described in detail in [10, 20]. Instead, we focus on how TAO uses patterns to implement an ORB that overcomes the following SunSoft IIOP limitations while simultaneously preserving its QoS capabilities:

Lack of Portability. Like most communication software, SunSoft IIOP is programmed directly using low-level networking and OS APIs, such as sockets, `select`, and POSIX Pthreads. Not only are these APIs tedious and error-prone, they are also not portable across OS platforms, e.g., many operating systems lack Pthreads support. Section 3.3.1 illustrates how we use the *Wrapper Facade* pattern [15] to improve TAO's portability.

Lack of Configurability. Like many ORBs and other middleware, SunSoft IIOP is configured *statically,* which makes it hard to extend without modifying its source code directly. This violated a key design goal of TAO, namely *dynamic* adaptation to diverse application requirements and system environments. Sections 3.3.7, 3.3.6, and 3.3.8 explain how we used the *Abstract Factory* [15], *Strategy* [15], and *Component Configurator* [8] patterns to simplify the TAO's configurability for different use-cases.

Lack of Software Cohesion. Like many applications, SunSoft IIOP focuses on solving a specific problem, i.e., implementing an ORB Core and an IIOP protocol engine. It accomplishes this using a tightly coupled, ad-hoc implementation that hard-codes key ORB design decisions. How we used *Abstract Factory* and *Strategy* to decrease the unnecessary coupling and increase cohesion when evolving SunSoft IIOP to TAO is explained later in this chapter.

3 APPLYING A PATTERN LANGUAGE TO BUILD EXTENSIBLE ORB MIDDLEWARE

3.1 WHY WE NEED DYNAMICALLY CONFIGURABLE MIDDLEWARE

A key motivation for ORB middleware is to offload complex, lower-level distributed system infrastructure tasks from application developers to ORB developers. ORB developers are responsible for implementing reusable middleware components that handle connection management, interprocess communication, concurrency, transport endpoint demultiplexing, scheduling, dispatching, (de)marshaling, and error handling. These components are typically compiled into a run-time ORB library, linked with application objects that use the ORB components, and executed in one or more OS processes.

Although this separation of concern can simplify application development, it can also yield inflexible and inefficient applications and middleware architectures. The primary reason is that many conventional ORBs are configured *statically* at compile-time and link-time by ORB developers, rather than *dynamically* at installation-time or run-time by application developers. Statically configured ORBs have the following drawbacks [28].

Inflexibility. Statically configured ORBs tightly couple each component's *implementation* with the *configuration* of internal ORB components, i.e., which components work together and how they work together. As a result, extending statically configured ORBs requires modifications to existing source code. In commercial non-open-source ORBs, this code may not be accessible to application developers.

Even if source code is available, extending statically configured ORBs requires recompilation and relinking. Moreover, any currently executing ORBs and their associated objects must be shut down and restarted. This static reconfiguration process is not well suited for application domains, such as telecom call processing, that require 7×24 availability [34].

Inefficiency. Statically configured ORBs can be inefficient, both in terms of space and time. Space inefficiency can occur if unnecessary components are always statically configured into an ORB. This can increase the ORB's memory footprint, forcing applications to pay a space penalty for features they do not require. Overly large memory footprints are particularly problematic for embedded systems, such as cellular phones or telecom switch line cards [35].

Time inefficiency can stem from restricting an ORB to use statically configured algorithms or data structures for key processing tasks, thereby making it hard for application developers to customize an ORB to handle new use-cases. For instance, real-time avionics systems [11] often can instantiate all their servants off-line. These systems can benefit from an ORB that uses perfect hashing or active demultiplexing [36] to demultiplex incoming requests to servants. Thus, ORBs that are configured statically to use a general-purpose, "one-size-fits-all" demultiplex *strategy*, such as dynamic hashing, may perform poorly for mission-critical systems.

In theory, the drawbacks with static configuration described above are *internal* to ORBs and should not affect application developers directly. In practice, however, application developers are inevitably affected since the quality, portability, usability, and performance of the ORB middleware is reduced. Therefore, an effective way to improve ORB extensibility is to develop ORB middleware that can be both statically *and* dynamically configured.

Dynamic configuration enables the selective integration of customized implementations for key ORB strategies, such as connection management, communication, concurrency, demultiplexing, scheduling, and dispatching. This design allows ORB developers to concentrate on the *functionality* of ORB components, without committing themselves prematurely to a specific *configuration* of these components. Moreover, dynamic configuration enables application developers and ORB developers to change design decisions late in the system life-cycle, i.e., at installation-time or run-time.

Figure 18.3 illustrates the following key dimensions of ORB extensibility:

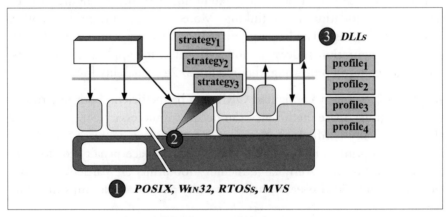

Figure 18.3. Dimensions of ORB extensibility.

1. *Extensibility to retarget the ORB on new platforms,* which requires that the ORB be implemented using modular components that shield it from non-portable system mechanisms, such as those for threading, communication, and event demultiplexing. OS platforms such as

POSIX, Win32, VxWorks, and MVS provide a wide variety of system mechanisms.

2. *Extensibility via custom implementation strategies,* which can be tailored to specific application requirements. For instance, ORB components can be customized to meet periodic deadlines in real-time systems [11]. Likewise, ORB components can be customized to account for particular system characteristics, such as the availability of asynchronous I/O or high-speed ATM networks.

3. *Extensibility via dynamic configuration of custom strategies,* which takes customization to the next level by dynamically linking only those strategies that are necessary for a specific ORB "personality." For example, different application domains, such as medical systems or telecom call processing, may require custom combinations of concurrency, scheduling, or dispatch strategies. Configuring these strategies at run-time from dynamically linked libraries (DLLs) can (1) reduce the memory footprint of an ORB and (2) make it possible for the application developers to extend the ORB without requiring access or changes to the original source code.

Below, we describe the pattern language applied to enhance the extensibility of TAO along each dimension outlined above.

3.2 OVERVIEW OF PATTERN LANGUAGE THAT IMPROVES ORB EXTENSIBILITY

This section uses TAO as a case study to illustrate a pattern language that can help developers of applications and ORBs build, maintain, and extend communication software by reducing the coupling between components. Figure 18.4 shows the patterns in the pattern language that we applied to develop an extensible ORB architecture for TAO. It is beyond the scope of this chapter to describe each pattern in detail or to discuss all the patterns used within TAO. Instead, we focus on how key patterns can improve the extensibility and performance of comprehensive descriptions of these patterns and [8] explain how the patterns can be woven together to form a pattern language.

The intent and usage of the patterns in this language are outlined below.

Wrapper Facade [8]. This pattern encapsulates the functions and data provided by existing non-OO APIs within more concise, robust, portable,

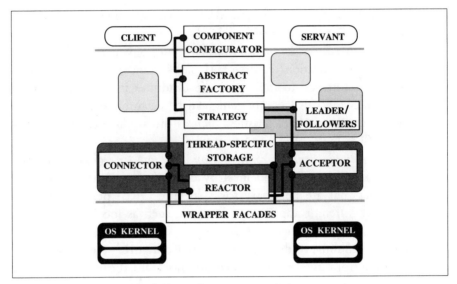

Figure 18.4. Applying a pattern language to TAO.

maintainable, and cohesive OO class interfaces. TAO uses this pattern to avoid tedious, non-portable, and non-typesafe programming of low-level, OS-specific system calls, such as the Socket API or POSIX threads.

Reactor [8]. This pattern structures event-driven applications, particularly servers, that receive requests from multiple clients concurrently but process them iteratively. TAO uses this pattern to notify ORB-specific handlers synchronously when I/O events occur in the OS. The Reactor pattern drives the main loop in TAO's ORB Core, which accepts connections and receives/sends client requests/responses.

Acceptor-Connector [8]. This pattern decouples connection establishment and service initialization from service processing in a networked system. TAO uses this pattern in the ORB Core on servers and clients to passively and actively establish GIOP connections that are independent of the underlying transport mechanisms.

Leader/Followers [8]. This pattern provides an efficient concurrency model in which multiple threads take turns to share a set of event sources to detect, demultiplex, dispatch, and process service requests that occur on the event sources. TAO uses this pattern to facilitate the use of multiple concurrency strategies that can be configured flexibly into its ORB Core at run-time.

Thread-Specific Storage [8]. This pattern allows multiple threads to use a "logically global" access point to retrieve an object that is local to a thread, without incurring locking overhead for each access to the object. TAO uses this pattern to minimize lock contention and priority inversion for real-time applications.

Strategy [15]. This pattern provides an abstraction for selecting one of several candidate algorithms and packaging it into an object. TAO uses this pattern throughout its software architecture to extensibly configure custom ORB strategies for concurrency, communication, scheduling, and demultiplexing.

Abstract Factory [15]. This pattern provides a single component that builds related objects. TAO uses this pattern to consolidate its dozens of *Strategy* objects into a manageable number of abstract factories that can be reconfigured en masse into clients and servers conveniently and consistently. TAO components use these factories to access related strategies without specifying their subclass name explicitly.

Component Configurator [8]. This pattern allows an application to link and unlink its component implementations at run-time without having to modify, recompile, or statically relink the application. It also supports the reconfiguration of components into different processes without having to shut down and re-start running processes. TAO uses this pattern to dynamically interchange *abstract factory* implementations in order to customize ORB personalities at run-time.

The patterns constituting this pattern language are not limited to ORBs or communication middleware. They have been applied in many other communication application domains, including telecom call processing and switching, avionics flight control systems, multimedia teleconferencing, and distributed interactive simulations.

3.3 How to Use a Pattern Language to Resolve ORB Design Challenges

In the following discussion, we outline the forces underlying the key design challenges that arise when developing extensible real-time ORBs. We also describe which pattern(s) in our pattern language are used in TAO. In addition, we show how the absence of these patterns in an ORB leaves these forces unresolved. To illustrate this latter point concretely, we compare TAO with SunSoft IIOP. Since TAO evolved from the SunSoft IIOP release, it provides an ideal baseline to evaluate the impact of patterns on the software qualities of ORB middleware.

3.3.1 Encapsulate Low-Level System Mechanisms with the Wrapper Facade Pattern

Context. One role of an ORB is to shield application-specific clients and servants from the details of low-level systems programming. Thus, ORB developers, rather than application developers, are responsible for tedious, low-level network programming tasks, such as demultiplexing events, sending and receiving GIOP messages across the network, and spawning threads to execute client requests concurrently. Figure 18.5 illustrates a common approach used by SunSoft IIOP, which is programmed internally using system mechanisms, such as sockets, `select`, and POSIX threads.

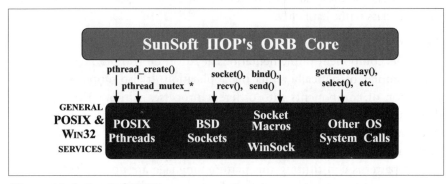

Figure 18.5. SunSoft IIOP operating system interaction.

Problem. Developing an ORB is hard. It is even harder if developers must wrestle with low-level system mechanisms written in languages like C, which often yield the following problems:

- *ORB developers must have intimate knowledge of many OS platforms.* Implementing an ORB using system-level C APIs forces developers to deal with non-portable, tedious, and error-prone OS idiosyncracies, such as using untyped socket handles to identify transport endpoints. Moreover, these APIs are not portable across OS platforms. For example, Win32 lacks POSIX Pthreads and has subtly different semantics for sockets and `select`.

- *Increased maintenance effort.* One way to build an ORB is to handle portability variations via explicit conditional compilation directives in ORB source code. However, using conditional compilation to address platform-specific variations *at all points of use* increases the complexity of the source code, as shown in Section 3.5. Extending such ORBs is hard since platform-specific details are scattered throughout the implementation source code files.

- *Inconsistent programming paradigms.* System mechanisms are accessed through C-style function calls, which cause an "impedance mismatch" with the OO programming style supported by C++, the language we use to implement TAO.

How can we avoid accessing low-level system mechanisms when implementing an ORB?

Solution → the Wrapper Facade pattern. An effective way to avoid accessing system mechanisms directly is to use the *Wrapper Facade* pattern [8], which is a variant of the Facade pattern [15]. The intent of the Facade pattern is to simplify the interface for a subsystem. The intent of the Wrapper Facade pattern is more specific: it provides typesafe, modular, and portable OO interfaces that encapsulate lower-level, stand-alone system mechanisms, such as sockets, `select`, and POSIX threads. In general, the Wrapper Facade pattern should be applied when existing system-level APIs are non-portable and non-typesafe.

Using the Wrapper Facade pattern in TAO. TAO accesses all system mechanisms via the wrapper facades provided by ACE [28]. Figure 18.6 illustrates how the ACE C++ wrapper facades improve TAO's robustness and portability by encapsulating and enhancing native OS concurrency, communication, memory management, event demultiplexing, and dynamic linking mechanisms with typesafe OO interfaces. The OO encapsulation provided by ACE alleviates the need for TAO to access weakly typed system APIs directly. Thus, C++ compilers can detect type system violations at compile-time rather than waiting for the problems to occur at run-time.

The ACE wrapper facades use C++ features to eliminate performance penalties that would otherwise be incurred from its additional type safety and layer of abstraction. For instance, inlining is used to avoid the overhead of calling small methods. Likewise, static methods are used to avoid the overhead of passing a C++ `this` pointer to each invocation.

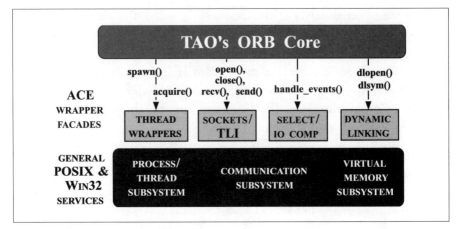

Figure 18.6. Using the Wrapper Facade pattern to encapsulate native OS mechanisms.

Although the ACE wrapper facades resolve several common low-level development problems, they are just the first step towards developing an extensible ORB. The remaining patterns described in this section build on the encapsulation provided by the ACE wrapper facades to address more challenging ORB design issues.

3.3.2 Demultiplexing ORB Core Events Using the Reactor Pattern

Context. An ORB Core is responsible for demultiplexing I/O events from multiple clients and dispatching their associated event handlers. For instance, a server-side ORB Core listens for new client connections and reads/writes GIOP requests/responses from/to connected clients. To ensure responsiveness to multiple clients, an ORB Core uses OS event demultiplexing mechanisms to wait for CONNECTION, READ, and WRITE events to occur on multiple socket handles. Common event demultiplexing mechanisms include select, WaitForMultipleObjects, I/O completion ports, and threads.

Figure 18.7 illustrates a typical event demultiplexing sequence for SunSoft IIOP. In (1), the server enters its event loop by (2) calling get_request on the Object Adapter. The get_request method then (3) calls the static method block_for_connection on the server_endpoint. This method manages all aspects of server-side connection management, ranging from connection establishment to GIOP protocol handling. The

ORB remains blocked (4) on `select` until the occurrence of I/O event, such as a connection event or a request event. When a request event occurs, `block_for_connection` demultiplexes that request to a specific `server_endpoint` and (5) dispatches the event to that endpoint. The GIOP Engine in the ORB Core then (6) retrieves data from the socket and passes it to the Object Adapter, which demultiplexes it, demarshals it, and (7) dispatches the appropriate method upcall to the user-supplied servant.

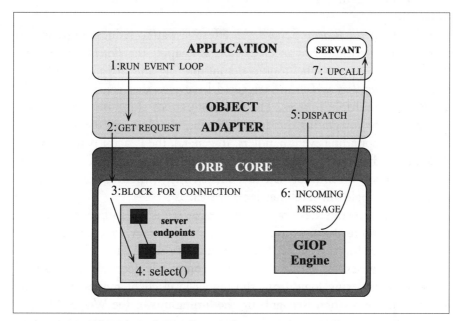

Figure 18.7. The SunSoft IIOP event loop.

Problem. One way to develop an ORB Core is to hard-code it to use one event demultiplexing mechanism, such as `select`. Relying on just one mechanism is undesirable, however, since no single scheme is efficient on all platforms or for all application requirements. For instance, asynchronous I/O completion ports are highly efficient on Windows NT [37], whereas synchronous threads are an efficient demultiplexing mechanism on Solaris [33].

Another way to develop an ORB Core is to tightly couple its event demultiplexing code with the code that performs GIOP protocol processing. For instance, the event demultiplexing logic of SunSoft IIOP is not a self-contained component. Instead, it is closely intertwined with subsequent processing of client request events by the Object Adapter and IDL skeletons. In this case, however, the demultiplexing code cannot be reused as a blackbox component by other communication middleware applications, such as HTTP servers [37] or video-on-demand servers. Moreover, if new ORB strategies for threading or Object Adapter request scheduling algorithms are introduced, substantial portions of the ORB Core must be rewritten.

How then can an ORB implementation decouple itself from a specific event demultiplexing mechanism and decouple its demultiplexing code from its handling code?

Solution → *the Reactor pattern.* An effective way to reduce coupling and increase the extensibility of an ORB Core is to apply the *Reactor* pattern [8]. This pattern supports synchronous demultiplexing and dispatching of multiple *event handlers,* which are triggered by events that can arrive concurrently from multiple sources. The Reactor pattern simplifies event-driven applications by integrating the demultiplexing of events and the dispatching of their corresponding event handlers. In general, the Reactor pattern should be applied when applications or components, such as an ORB Core, must handle events from multiple clients concurrently, without becoming tightly coupled to a single low-level mechanism, such as `select`.

Note that applying the Wrapper Facade pattern is not sufficient to resolve the event demultiplexing problems outlined above. A wrapper facade for `select` may improve ORB Core potentiality somewhat. However, this pattern alone does not resolve the need to completely decouple the low-level event demultiplexing logic from the higher-level client request processing logic in an ORB Core. Recognizing the limitations of the Wrapper Facade pattern, and then applying the Reactor pattern to overcome the limitations, is one of the benefits of applying a pattern language, rather than just isolated patterns.

Using the Reactor pattern in TAO. TAO uses the Reactor pattern to drive the main event loop in its ORB Core, as shown in Figure 18.8. A TAO server (1) initiates an event loop in the ORB Core's `Reactor,` where it (2) remains blocked on `select` until an I/O event occurs. When a GIOP request event occurs, the `Reactor` demultiplexes the request to the appropriate event handler, which is the GIOP `Connection_Handler` that is associated with each connected socket. The `Reactor` (3) then calls `Connection_Handler::handle_input`, which (4) dispatches the request to TAO's Object Adapter. The Object Adapter demultiplexes the request to the appropriate upcall method on the servant and (5) dispatches the upcall.

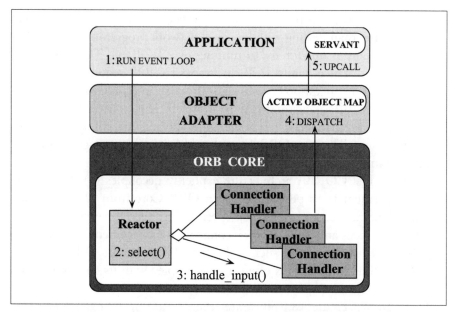

Figure 18.8. Using the Reactor Pattern in TAO's event loop.

The Reactor pattern enhances the extensibility of TAO by decoupling the event handling portions of its ORB Core from the underlying OS event demultiplexing mechanisms. For example, the `WaitForMultipleObjects` event demultiplexing system call can be used on Windows NT, whereas `select` can be used on UNIX platforms. Moreover, the Reactor pattern simplifies the configuration of new event handlers. For instance, adding a new `Secure_Connection_Handler` that performs encryption/decryption of all network traffic will not affect the `Reactor`'s implementation. Finally, unlike the event demultiplexing code in SunSoft IIOP, which is tightly coupled to one use-case, the ACE implementation of the Reactor pattern [8] used by TAO has been applied in many other OO event-driven applications ranging from HTTP servers [37] to real-time avionics infrastructure [11].

3.3.3 Managing Connections in an ORB Using the Acceptor-Connector Pattern

Context. Managing connections is another key responsibility of an ORB Core. For instance, an ORB Core that implements the IIOP protocol must establish TCP connections and initialize the protocol handlers for each IIOP `server_endpoint`. By localizing connection management logic in the

413

ORB Core, application-specific servants can focus solely on processing client requests, rather than dealing with low-level network programming tasks.

An ORB Core is not *limited* to running over IIOP and TCP transports, however. For instance, while TCP can transfer GIOP requests reliably, its flow control and congestion control algorithms can preclude its use as a real-time protocol [10]. Likewise, it may be more efficient to use a shared memory transport mechanism when clients and servants are collocated on the same endsystem. Thus, an ORB Core should be flexible enough to support multiple transport mechanisms [16].

Problem. The CORBA architecture explicitly decouples (1) the connection management tasks performed by an ORB Core from (2) the request processing performed by application-specific servants. However, a common way to implement an ORB's *internal* connection management activities is to use low-level network APIs, such as Sockets. Likewise, the ORB's connection establishment protocol is often tightly coupled with its communication protocol.

For example, Figure 18.9 illustrates the connection management structure of SunSoft IIOP. The client-side of SunSoft IIOP implements a hard-coded connection caching *strategy* that uses a linked list of `client_endpoint` objects. As shown in Figure 18.9, this list is traversed to find an unused endpoint whenever (1) `client_endpoint::lookup` is called. If no unused `client_endpoint` to the server is in the cache, a new connection (2) is initiated; otherwise an existing connection is reused. Likewise, the server-side uses a linked list of `server_endpoint` objects to generate the read/write bitmasks required by the (3) `select` event demultiplexing mechanism. This list maintains passive transport endpoints that (4) accept connections and (5) receive requests from clients connected to the server.

The problem with SunSoft IIOP's design is that it tightly couples (1) the ORB's connection management implementation with the socket network programming API and (2) the TCP/IP connection establishment protocol with the GIOP communication protocol, thereby yielding the following drawbacks:

- *Inflexibility.* If an ORB's connection management data structures and algorithms are too closely intertwined, substantial effort is required to modify the ORB Core. For instance, tightly coupling the ORB to use the Socket API makes it hard to change the underlying transport mechanism, e.g., to use shared memory rather than Sockets. Thus, it

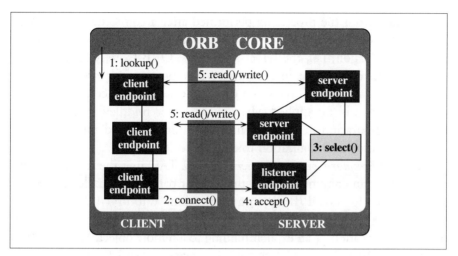

Figure 18.9. Connection management in SunSoft IIOP.

can be hard to port such a tightly coupled ORB Core to new communication mechanisms, such as ATM, Fibrechannel, or shared memory, or different network programming APIs, such as TLI or Win32 Named Pipes.

- *Inefficiency.* Many internal ORB strategies can be optimized by allowing both ORB developers and application developers to select appropriate implementation late in the software development cycle, e.g., after systematic performance profiling. For example, to reduce lock contention and overhead, a multi-threaded, real-time ORB client may need to store transport endpoints in thread-specific storage [8]. Similarly, the concurrency strategy for a CORBA server might require that each connection run in its own thread to eliminate per-request locking overhead. If connection management mechanisms are hard-coded and tightly bound with other internal ORB strategies, however, it is hard to accommodate efficient new strategies.

How then can an ORB Core's connection management components support multiple transports and allow connection-related behaviors to be (re)configured flexibly late in the development cycle?

Solution → the Acceptor-Connector pattern. An effective way to increase the flexibility of ORB Core connection management and initialization is to apply the *Acceptor-Connector* pattern [8]. This pattern decouples connection initialization from the processing performed after a connection endpoint is initialized. The `Acceptor` component in this pattern is responsible for *passive* initialization, i.e., the server-side of the ORB Core. Conversely, the `Connector` component in the pattern is responsible for *active* initialization, i.e., the client-side of the ORB Core. In general, the Acceptor-Connector pattern should be applied when client/server middleware must allow flexible configuration of network programming APIs and must maintain proper separation of initialization roles.

Using the Acceptor-Connector pattern in TAO. TAO uses the Acceptor-Connector pattern in conjunction with the Reactor pattern to handle connection establishment for GIOP/IIOP communication. Within TAO's client-side ORB Core, a `Connector` initiates connections to servers in response to an operation invocation or an explicit binding to a remote object. Within TAO's server-side ORB Core, an `Acceptor` creates a GIOP `Connection Handler` to service each new client connection. `Acceptors` and `Connection_Handlers` both derive from an `Event_Handler`, which enables them to be dispatched automatically by a `Reactor`.

TAO's `Acceptors` and `Connectors` can be configured with any transport mechanisms, such as Sockets or TLI, provided by the ACE wrapper facades. In addition, TAO's `Acceptor` and `Connector` can be imbued with custom strategies to select an appropriate concurrency mechanism, as described in Section 3.3.4.

Figure 18.10 illustrates the use of *Acceptor-Connector* strategies in TAO's ORB Core. When a client (1) invokes a remote operation, it makes a `connect` call through a `Strategy_Connector`. This `Strategy_Connector` (2) consults its *connection strategy* to obtain a connection. In this example, the client uses a "caching connection strategy" that recycles connections to the server and only creates new connections when existing connections are all busy. This caching strategy minimizes connection setup time, thereby reducing end-to-end request latency.

In the server-side ORB Core, the `Reactor` notifies TAO's `Strategy_Acceptor` to (3) accept newly connected clients and create `Connection_Handlers`. The `Strategy_Acceptor` delegates the choice of concurrency mechanism to one of TAO's *concurrency* strategies, e.g., reactive, thread-per-connection, or thread-per-priority, described in Section 3.3.4. After a `Connection_Handler` is activated (4) within the ORB Core, it performs the requisite GIOP protocol processing (5) on a connection and ultimately dispatches (6) the request to the appropriate servant via TAO's Object Adapter.

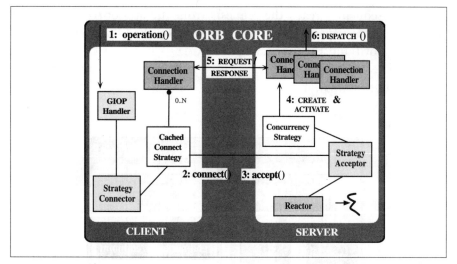

Figure 18.10. Using the Acceptor-Connector pattern in TAO's connection management.

3.3.4 Simplifying ORB Concurrency Using the Leader/Followers Pattern

Context. After the Object Adapter has dispatched a client request to the appropriate servant, the servant executes the request. Execution may occur in the same thread of control as the `Connection_Handler` that received it. Conversely, execution may occur in a different thread, concurrent with other request executions.

The Real-Time CORBA specification [38] defines a thread pool API. In addition, the CORBA specification defines an interface on the POA for an application to specify that all requests be handled by a single thread or be handled using an ORB's internal multi-threading policy. To meet application QoS requirements, it is important to develop ORBs that implement these various concurrency APIs efficiently [24]. Concurrency allows long-running operations to execute simultaneously without impeding the progress of other operations. Likewise, preemptive multi-threading is crucial to minimize the dispatch latency of real-time systems [11].

Concurrency is often implemented via the multi-threading capabilities available on OS platforms. For instance, SunSoft IIOP supports the two concurrency architectures shown in Figure 18.11: a single-threaded Reactive architecture and a thread-per-connection architecture. SunSoft IIOP's reactive concurrency architecture uses `select` within a single thread to dispatch each arriving request to an individual `server_endpoint` object, which subsequently reads the requests from the appropriate OS kernel queue. In (1), a request arrives and is queued by the OS. Then, `select` fires, (2) notifying the associated `server_endpoint` of a waiting request. The `server_endpoint` finally (3) reads the request from the queue and processes it.

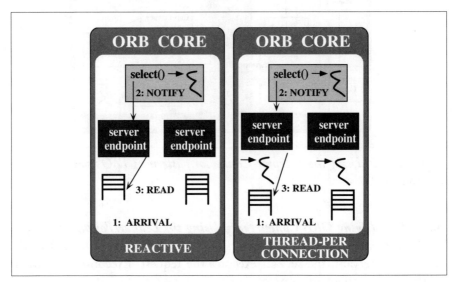

Figure 18.11. SunSoft IIOP concurrency architectures.

In contrast, SunSoft IIOP's thread-per-connection architecture executes each `server_endpoint` in its own thread of control, servicing all requests arriving on that connection within its thread. After a connection is established, `select` waits for events on the connection's descriptor. When (1) requests are received by the OS, the thread performing `select` (2) reads one from the queue and (3) hands it off to a `server_endpoint` for processing.

Problem. In many ORBs, the concurrency architecture is programmed directly using the OS platform's multi-threading API, such as the POSIX threads API [39]. However, there are several drawbacks to this approach:

- *Non-portable.* Threading APIs are highly platform-specific. Even IEEE standards, such as POSIX threads [39], are not available on many widely used OS platforms, including Win32, VxWorks, and pSoS. Not only is there no direct syntactic mapping between APIs, but there is no clear mapping of semantics either. For instance, POSIX threads support deferred thread cancellation, whereas Win32 threads do not. Moreover, although Win32 has a thread termination API, the Win32 documentation strongly recommends *not* using it since it does not release all thread resources after a thread exits. Moreover, even POSIX Pthread implementations are non-portable since many UNIX vendors support different drafts of the Pthreads specification.

- *Hard to program correctly.* Portability aside, programming a multi-threaded ORB is hard since application and ORB developers must ensure that access to shared data is serialized properly in the ORB and its servants. In addition, the techniques required to robustly terminate servants executing concurrently in multiple threads are complicated, non-portable, and non-intuitive.

- *Non-extensible.* The choice of an ORB concurrency strategy depends largely on external factors like application requirements and network/endsystem characteristics. For instance, reactive single-threading [8] is an appropriate strategy for short duration, compute-bound requests or a uni-processor. If these external factors change, however, an ORB's design should be extensible enough to handle alternative concurrency strategies, such as thread pool or thread-per-priority [24].

When ORBs are developed using low-level threading APIs, they are hard to extend with new concurrency strategies *without* affecting other ORB components. For example, adding a thread-per-request architecture to Sun-Soft IIOP would require extensive changes in order to (1) store the request in a *thread-specific storage* (TSS) variable during protocol processing, (2) pass the key to the TSS variable through the scheduling and demarshaling steps in the Object Adapter, and (3) access the request stored in TSS before dispatching the operation on the servant. Thus, there is no easy way to modify SunSoft IIOP's concurrency architecture without drastically changing its internal structure.

How then can an ORB support a simple, extensible, and portable concurrency mechanism?

Solution → *the Leader/Follower pattern.* An effective way to increase the portability, correctness, and extensibility of ORB concurrency strategies is to apply the *Leader/Followers* pattern [8]. This pattern provides an efficient concurrency model in which multiple threads take turns to share a set of event sources to detect, demultiplex, dispatch, and process service requests that occur on the event sources. In general, the Leader/Followers pattern should be used when an application needs to minimize context switching, synchronization, and data copying, while still allowing multiple threads to run concurrently.

While *Wrapper Facades* provide the basis for portability, they are simply a thin syntactic veneer over the low-level native OS APIs. Moreover, a facade's semantic behavior may still vary across platforms. Therefore, the Leader/Followers pattern defines a higher-level concurrency abstraction that shields TAO from the complexity of low-level thread facades. By raising the level of abstraction for ORB developers, the Leader/Followers pattern makes it easier to define more portable, flexible, and conveniently programmed ORB concurrency strategies. For example, if the number of threads in the pool is 1, the Leader/Followers pattern behaves just like the Reactor pattern.

Using the Leader/Followers pattern in TAO. TAO uses the Leader/Followers pattern to demultiplex GIOP events to `Connection_Handlers` handlers within a pool of threads. When using this pattern, an application pre-spawns a *fixed* number of threads. When these threads invoke TAO's standard `ORB::run` method, one thread will become the leader and wait for a GIOP event. After the leader thread detects the event, it promotes an arbitrary thread to become the next leader and then demuliplexes the event to its associated `Connection_Handler`, which processes the event concurrently with respect to other threads in the ORB. This sequence of steps is shown in Figure 18.12.

As shown in Figure 18.12, a pool of threads is allocated and a leader thread is chosen to `select` (1) on connections for all servants in the server process. When a request arrives, this thread reads it (2) into an internal buffer. If this is a valid request for a servant, a follower thread in the pool is released to become the new leader (3) and the leader thread dispatches the upcall (4). After the upcall is dispatched, the original leader thread becomes a follower and returns to the thread pool. New requests are queued in socket endpoints until a thread in the pool is available to execute the requests.

3.3.5 Reducing Lock Contention and Priority Inversions with the Thread-Specific Storage Pattern

Context. The Leader/Followers pattern allows applications and components in the ORB to run concurrently. The primary drawback to concurrency, however, is the need to *serialize* access to shared resources. In an ORB,

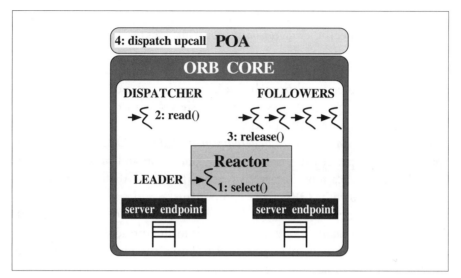

Figure 18.12. Using the Leader/Followers pattern to structure TAO's concurrency strategies.

common shared resources include the dynamic memory heap, an ORB pseudo-object reference created by the `CORBA::ORB_init` initialization factory, the *Active Object* Map in a POA [22], and the `Acceptor`, `Connector`, and `Reactor` components described earlier. A common way to achieve serialization is to use mutual-exclusion locks on each resource shared by multiple threads.

Problem. In theory, multi-threading an ORB can improve performance by executing multiple instruction streams simultaneously. In addition, multithreading can simplify internal ORB design by allowing each thread to execute synchronously, rather than reactively or asynchronously. In practice, however, multi-threaded ORBs often perform no better, or even worse, than single-threaded ORBs due to (1) the cost of acquiring/releasing locks and (2) priority inversions that arise when high- and low-priority threads contend for the same locks [40]. In addition, multi-threaded ORBs are hard to program due to complex concurrency control protocols used to avoid race conditions and deadlocks.

Solution → the Thread-Specific Storage pattern. An effective way to minimize the amount of locking required to serialize access to resources shared within an ORB is to use the *Thread-Specific Storage* pattern [8]. This pattern allows multiple threads in an ORB to use one logically global access point to retrieve thread-specific data *without* incurring locking overhead for each access.

In general, the Thread-Specific Storage pattern should be used when the data shared by objects within each thread must be accessed through a globally visible access point that is "logically" shared with other threads, but "physically" unique for each thread.

Using the Thread-Specific Storage pattern in TAO. TAO uses the Thread-Specific Storage pattern to minimize lock contention and priority inversion for real-time applications. Internally, each thread in TAO uses thread-specific storage to store its ORB Core components, e.g., `Reactor`, `Acceptor`, and `Connector`. When a thread accesses any of these components, they are retrieved using a `key` as an index into the thread's internal thread-specific state, as shown in Figure 18.13. Thus, no additional locking is required to access thread-specific ORB state.

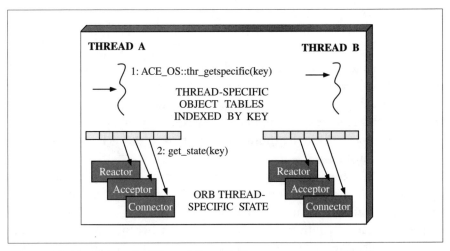

Figure 18.13. Using the Thread-Specific Storage pattern in TAO.

3.3.6 Support Interchangeable ORB Behaviors with the Strategy Pattern

Context. Extensible ORBs must support multiple request demultiplexing and scheduling strategies in their Object Adapters. Likewise, they must support multiple connection establishment, request transfer, and concurrent request processing strategies in their ORB Cores.

Problem. One way to develop an ORB is to provide only static, non-extensible strategies, which are typically configured in the following ways:

- *Preprocessor macros.* Some strategies are determined by the value of preprocessor macros. For example, since threading is not available on all OS platforms, conditional compilation is often used to select a feasible concurrency model.

- *Command-line options.* Other strategies are controlled by the presence or absence of flags on the command-line. For instance, command-line options can be used to selectively enable ORB concurrency strategies for platforms that support multi-threading [24].

While these two configuration approaches are widely used, they are inflexible. For instance, preprocessor macros only support compile-time strategy selection, whereas command-line options convey a limited amount of information to an ORB. Moreover, these hard-coded configuration strategies are divorced completely from any code they might affect. Thus, ORB components that want to use these options must (1) know of their existence, (2) understand their range of values, and (3) provide an appropriate implementation for each value. Such restrictions make it hard to develop highly extensible ORBs that are composed from transparently configurable strategies.

How then does an ORB (1) permit replacement of subsets of component strategies in a manner orthogonal and transparent to other ORB components and (2) encapsulate the state and behavior of each strategy so that changes to one component do not permeate throughout an ORB haphazardly?

Solution → the Strategy pattern. An effective way to support multiple transparently "pluggable" ORB strategies is to apply the *Strategy* pattern [15]. This pattern factors out similarities among algorithmic alternatives and explicitly associates the name of a strategy with its algorithm and state. Moreover, the Strategy pattern removes lexical dependencies on strategy implementations since applications access specialized behaviors only through common base class interfaces. In general, the Strategy pattern should be used when an application's behavior can be configured via multiple interchangeable strategies.

Using the Strategy pattern in TAO. TAO uses a variety of strategies to factor out behaviors that are often hard-coded in conventional ORBs. Several of these strategies are illustrated in Figure 18.14. For instance, TAO supports multiple request demultiplexing strategies (e.g., perfect hashing vs. active demultiplexing [36]) and dispatching strategies (i.e., FIFO vs. rate-based) in its Object Adapter, as well as connection management strategies (e.g., process-wide cached connections vs. thread-specific cached connections) and handler concurrency strategies (e.g., Reactive vs. variations of Leader/Followers) in its ORB Core.

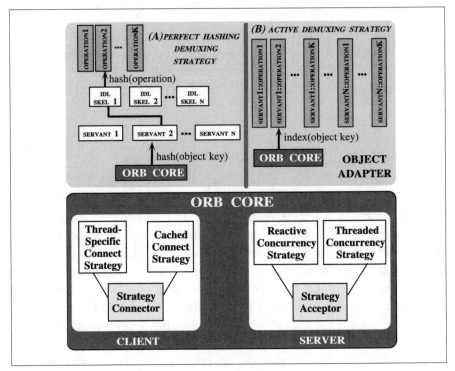

Figure 18.14. ORB Core and POA strategies in TAO.

3.3.7 Consolidate ORB Strategies Using the Abstract Factory Pattern

Context. There are many potential strategy variants supported by TAO. Table 18.1 shows a simple example of the strategies used to create two configurations of TAO. Configuration 1 is an avionics application with deterministic real-time requirements [11]. Configuration 2 is an electronic medical imaging application [41] with high throughput requirements. In general, the forces that must be resolved to compose all ORB strategies correctly are the need to (1) ensure the configuration of semantically compatible strategies and (2) simplify the management of a large number of individual strategies.

Table 18.1. Example Applications and Their ORB Strategy Configurations

Application	Concurrency	Dispatching	Demultiplexing	Protocol
		Strategy Configuration		
Avionics	Thread-per priority	Priority-based	Perfect hashing	VME backplane
Medical Imaging	Thread-per connection	FIFO	Active demulti-plexing	TCP/IP

Problem. An undesirable side-effect of using the Strategy pattern extensively in complex ORB software – as well as other types of software – is that it becomes hard to manage extensibility for the following reasons:

- *Complicated configuration and evolution.* ORB source code can become littered with hard-coded references to strategy types, which complicates configuration and evolution. For example, within a particular application domain, such as real-time avionics or medical imaging, many independent strategies must act harmoniously. Identifying these strategies individually by name, however, requires tedious replacement of selected strategies in one domain with a potentially different set of strategies in another domain.

- *Semantic incompatibilities.* It is not always possible for certain ORB strategy configurations to interact compatibly. For instance, the FIFO strategy for scheduling requests shown in Table 18.1 may not work with the thread-per-priority concurrency architecture. The problem stems from semantic incompatibilities between scheduling requests in their order of arrival (i.e., FIFO queueing) versus dispatching requests based on their relative priorities (i.e., preemptive priority-based thread dispatching). Moreover, some strategies are only useful when certain preconditions are met. For instance, the perfect hashing demultiplexing strategy is generally feasible only for systems that statically configure all servants off-line [22].

How can a highly configurable ORB reduce the complexities required to manage its myriad strategies, as well as enforce semantic consistency when combining discrete strategies?

Solution → the Abstract Factory pattern. An effective way to consolidate multiple ORB strategies into semantically compatible configurations is to apply the *Abstract Factory* pattern [15]. This pattern provides a single access point that integrates all strategies used to configure an ORB. Concrete subclasses then aggregate compatible application-specific or domain-specific strategies, which can be replaced en masse in semantically meaningful ways. In general, the Abstract Factory pattern should be used when an application must consolidate the configuration of many strategies, each having multiple alternatives that must vary together.

Using the Abstract Factory pattern in TAO. All of TAO's ORB strategies are consolidated into two abstract factories that are implemented as Singletons [15]. One factory encapsulates client-specific strategies, the other factory encapsulates server-specific strategies, as shown in Figure 18.15. These abstract factories encapsulate request demultiplexing, scheduling, and dispatch strategies in the server, as well as concurrency strategies in both client and server. By using the Abstract Factory pattern, TAO can configure different ORB personalities conveniently and consistently.

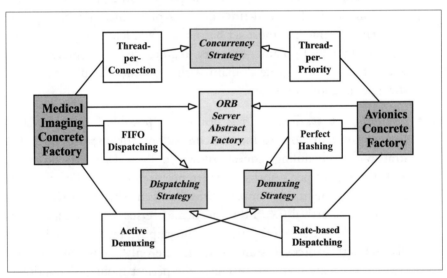

Figure 18.15. Factories used in TAO.

3.3.8 Dynamically Configure ORBs with the Component Configurator Pattern

Context. The cost of many computing resources, such as memory and CPUs, continues to drop. However, ORBs must still avoid excessive consumption of finite system resources. This parsimony is particularly essential for embedded and real-time systems that require small memory footprints and predictable CPU utilization [20]. Many applications can also benefit from the ability to extend ORBs *dynamically*, i.e., by allowing their strategies to be configured at run-time.

Problem. Although the Strategy and Abstract Factory patterns simplify the customization of ORBs for specific application requirements and system characteristics, these patterns can still cause the following problems for extensible ORBs:

- *High resource utilization.* Widespread use of the Strategy pattern can substantially enlarge the number of strategies configured into an ORB, which can increase the system resources required to run an ORB.

- *Unavoidable system downtime.* If strategies are configured statically at compile-time or static link-time using abstract factories, it is hard to enhance existing strategies or add new strategies without (1) changing the existing source code for the consumer of the *strategy* or the *abstract factory*, (2) recompiling and relinking an ORB, and (3) restarting running ORBs and their application servants.

Although it does not use the Strategy pattern explicitly, SunSoft IIOP does permit applications to vary certain ORB strategies at run-time. However, these different strategies must be configured statically into SunSoft IIOP at compile-time. Moreover, as the number of alternatives increases, so does the amount of code required to implement them. For instance, Figure 18.16 illustrates SunSoft IIOP's approach to varying the concurrency *strategy*.

Each area of code that might be affected by the choice of concurrency strategy is trusted to act independently of other areas. This proliferation of decision points adversely increases the complexity of the code, complicating future enhancement and maintenance. Moreover, the selection of the data type specifying the strategy complicates integration of new concurrency architectures because the type (`bool`) would have to change, as well as the programmatic structure `if (do_thread) then ... else ...,` that decodes the strategy specifier into actions.

In general, static configuration is only feasible for a small, fixed number of strategies. However, configuring complex ORB middleware (1) statically complicates evolution, (2) increases system resource utilization, and (3) leads to unavoidable system downtime to modify existing components.

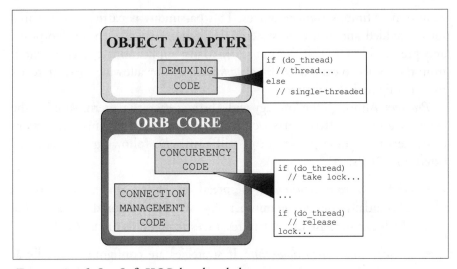

Figure 18.16. SunSoft IIOP hard-coded strategy usage.

How then does an ORB implementation reduce the "overly large, overly static" side-effects stemming from pervasive use of the Strategy and Abstract Factory patterns?

Solution → the Component Configurator pattern. An effective way to enhance the dynamism of an ORB is to apply the *Component Configurator* pattern [8]. This pattern uses explicit dynamic linking [28] mechanisms to obtain, utilize, and/or remove the run-time address bindings of custom strategy and abstract factory objects into an ORB at installation-time and/or run-time. Widely available explicit dynamic linking mechanisms include the dlopen/dlsym/dlclose functions in SRV4 UNIX [42] and the LoadLibrary/GetProcAddress functions in the WIN32 subsystem of windows NT [43]. The ACE wrapper facades used by TAO portably encapsulate these OS APIs.

By using the Component Configurator pattern, the *behaviors* of ORB strategies are decoupled from *when* the strategy implementations are configured into an ORB. For instance, ORB strategies can be linked into an ORB from dynamically linked libraries (DLLs) at compile-time, installation-time, or even during run-time. Moreover, the Component Configurator pattern can reduce the memory footprint of an ORB by allowing application developers and/or system administrators to dynamically link only those strategies that are necessary for a specific ORB personality.

In general, the Component Configurator pattern should be used when

(1) an application wants to configure its constituent components dynamically and (2) conventional techniques, such as command-line options, are insufficient due to the number of possibilities or the inability to anticipate the range of values.

Using the Component Configurator pattern in TAO. TAO uses the Component Configurator pattern in conjunction with the Strategy and Abstract Factory patterns to dynamically install the strategies it requires without (1) recompiling or statically relinking existing code or (2) terminating and restarting an existing ORB and its application servants. This design allows the behavior of TAO to be tailored for specific platforms and application requirements without requiring access to, or modification of, ORB source code.

In addition, the Component Configurator pattern allows applications to customize the personality of TAO at run-time. For instance, during TAO's ORB initialization phase, it uses the dynamic linking mechanisms provided by the OS (and encapsulated by the ACE wrapper facades) to link in the appropriate concrete factory for a particular use-case. Figure 18.17 shows two factories tuned for different application domains supported by TAO: avionics and medical imaging.

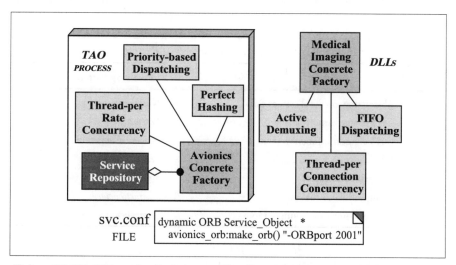

Figure 18.17. Using the Component Configurator pattern in TAO.

In the configuration shown in Figure 18.17, the Component Configurator has consulted the comp.conf script and installed the avionics concrete factory in the process. Applications using this ORB personality will be configured with a particular set of ORB concurrency, demultiplexing, and dispatching strategies. The medical imaging concrete factory resides in a DLL outside of the existing ORB process. To configure a different ORB personality, this factory could be installed dynamically during TAO's ORB server initialization phase.

3.4 SUMMARY OF DESIGN CHALLENGES AND PATTERNS THAT RESOLVE THEM

Table 18.2 summarizes the mapping between ORB design challenges and the patterns in the pattern language that we applied to resolve these challenges in TAO. This table focuses on the forces resolved by individual patterns. However, TAO also benefits from the collaboration among *multiple* patterns in the pattern language. For example, the Acceptor and Connector patterns utilize the Reactor pattern to notify them when connection events occur at the OS level.

Moreover, patterns often must collaborate to alleviate drawbacks that arise from applying them in isolation. For instance, the reason the Abstract Fac-

Table 18.2. Summary of Forces and Their Resolving Patterns

Forces	Resolving Pattern
Abstracting low-level system calls	*Wrapper Facade*
ORB event demultiplexing	*Reactor*
ORB connection management	*Acceptor-Connector*
Efficient concurrency models	*Leader/Followers*
Pluggable strategies	*Strategy*
Group similar initializations	*Abstract Factory*
Dynamic run-time configuration	*Component Configurator*

tory pattern is used in TAO is to avoid the complexity caused by its extensive use of the Strategy pattern. Although the Strategy pattern simplifies the effort required to customize an ORB for specific application requirements and network/endsystem characteristics, it is tedious and error-prone to manage a large number of strategy interactions manually.

3.5 EVALUATING THE CONTRIBUTION OF PATTERNS TO ORB MIDDLEWARE

Section 3.3 described the pattern language used in TAO and qualitatively evaluated how these patterns helped to alleviate limitations with the design of SunSoft IIOP. The discussion below goes one step further and quantitatively evaluates the benefits of applying patterns to ORB middleware.

Where's the Proof? Implementing TAO using a pattern language yielded significant quantifiable improvements in software reusability and maintainability. The results are summarized in Table 18.3. This table compares the following metrics for TAO and SunSoft IIOP:

Table 18.3. Code Statistics: TAO vs. SunSoft IIOP

ORB Task	TAO			SunSoft IIOP		
	# Methods	Total LOC	Avg. v(G)	# Methods	Total LOC	Avg. v(G)
Connection Management (Server)	2	43	7	3	190	14
Connection Management (client)	3	11	1	1	64	16
GIOP Message Send (client/Server)	1	46	12	1	43	12
GIOP Message Read (client/Server)	1	67	19	1	56	18
GIOP Invocation (client)	2	205	26	2	188	27
GIOP Message Processing (client/Server)	3	41	2	1	151	24
Object Adapter Message Dispatch (Server)	2	79	6	1	61	10

1. The number of methods required to implement key ORB tasks (such as connection management, request transfer, socket and request demultiplexing, marshaling, and dispatching).
2. The total non-comment lines of code (LOC) for these methods.
3. The average McCabe Cyclometric Complexity metric $v(G)$ [44] of the methods. The $v(G)$ metric uses graph theory to correlate code complexity with the number of possible basic paths that can be taken through a code module. In C++, a module is defined as a method.

The use of patterns in TAO significantly reduced the amount of ad hoc code and the complexity of certain operations. For instance, the total lines of code in the client-side *Connection Management* operations were reduced by a factor of 5. Moreover, the complexity for this component was substantially reduced by a factor of 16. These reductions in LOC and complexity stem from the following factors:

- These ORB tasks were the focus of our initial work when developing TAO.

- Many of the details of connection management and socket demultiplexing were subsumed by patterns and components in the ACE framework, in particular, Acceptor, Connector, and Reactor.

Other areas did not yield as much improvement. In particular, *GIOP Invocation* tasks actually increased in size and maintained a consistent v(G). There were two reasons for this increase:

1. The primary pattern applied in these cases was Wrapper Facade, which replaced the low-level system calls with ACE wrappers but did not factor out common strategies; and
2. SunSoft IIOP did not trap all the error conditions that TAO addressed much more completely. Therefore, the additional code in TAO is necessary to provide a more robust ORB.

The most compelling evidence that the systematic application of patterns can positively contribute to the maintainability of complex software is shown in Figure 18.18. This figure illustrates the distribution of v(G) over the percentage of affected methods in TAO. As shown in the figure, most of TAO's code is structured in a straightforward manner, with almost 70% of the methods' v(G) falling into the range of 1–5.

In contrast, while SunSoft IIOP has a substantial percentage (55%) of its methods in that range, many of the remaining methods (29%) have v(G) greater than 10. The reason for the difference is that SunSoft IIOP uses a monolithic coding style with long methods. For example, the average length of methods with v(G) over 10 is over 80 LOC. This yields overly complex code that is hard to debug and understand.

In TAO, most of the monolithic SunSoft IIOP methods were decomposed into smaller methods when integrating the patterns. The majority (86%) of TAO's methods have a v(G) under 10. Of that number, nearly 70% have a

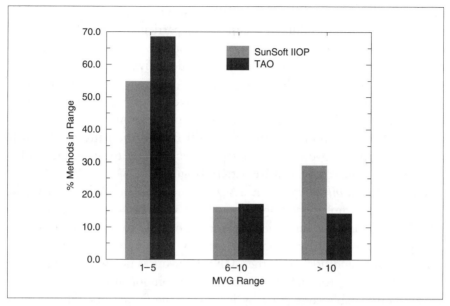

Figure 18.18. Distribution of v(G) over ORB methods.

v(*G*) between 1 and 5. The relatively few (14%) methods in TAO with v(*G*) greater than 10 are largely unchanged from the original SunSoft IIOP Type-Code interpreter. Subsequent releases of TAO have completely removed the TypeCode interpreter and replaced it with stubs and skeletons generated automatically by TAO's IDL compiler. Thus, there is no need for TAO ORB developers to maintain this code any more.

In general, the use of monolithic methods in SunSoft IIOP not only increases its maintenance effort, it also degrades its performance due to reduced processor cache hits [20]. Therefore, we plan to experiment with the application of other patterns, such as *Command* and *Template Method* [15], to simplify and optimize these monolithic methods into smaller, more cohesive methods.

What Are the Benefits? In general, applying a pattern language to TAO yielded the following benefits:

Increased extensibility. Patterns such as Abstract Factory, Strategy, and Component Configurator simplify the configuration of TAO for a particular application domain by allowing extensibility to be "designed into" the ORB. In contrast, DOC middleware lacking these patterns is significantly harder to extend.

Enhanced design clarity. By applying a pattern language to TAO, not only did we develop a more extensible ORB, we also devised a richer vocabulary for expressing ORB middleware designs. In particular, a pattern language captures and articulates the design rationale for complex object-structures in an ORB. Moreover, it helps to demystify and motivate the structure of an ORB by describing its architecture in terms of design forces that recur in many types of software systems. The expressive power of a pattern language enabled us to concisely convey the design of complex software systems, such as TAO. As we continue to learn about ORBs and the patterns of which they are composed, we expect our pattern vocabulary to grow and evolve into an even more comprehensive pattern language.

Increased portability and reuse. TAO is built atop the ACE framework, which provides implementations of many key communication software patterns [28]. Using ACE simplified the porting of TAO to numerous OS platforms since most of the porting effort was absorbed by the ACE framework maintainers. In addition, since the ACE framework is rich with configurable high-performance, real-time network-oriented components, we were able to achieve considerable code reuse by leveraging the framework. This is indicated by the consistent decrease in lines of code (LOC) in Table 18.3.

What Are the Liabilities? The use of a pattern language can also incur some liabilities. We summarize these liabilities below and discuss how we minimize them in TAO.

Abstraction penalty. Many patterns use indirection to increase component decoupling. For instance, the Reactor pattern uses virtual methods to separate the application-specific `Event Handler` logic from the general-purpose event demultiplexing and dispatching logic. The extra indirection introduced by using these pattern implementations can potentially decrease performance. To alleviate these liabilities, we carefully applied C++ programming language features (such as inline functions and templates) and other optimizations (such as eliminating demarshaling overhead [20] and demultiplexing overhead [36]) to minimize performance overhead. As a result, TAO is substantially faster than the original hard-coded SunSoft IIOP [20].

Additional external dependencies. Whereas SunSoft IIOP only depends on system-level interfaces and libraries, TAO depends on wrapper facades in the ACE framework. Since ACE encapsulates a wide range of low-level OS mechanisms, the effort required to port it to a new platform could potentially be higher than porting SunSoft IIOP, which only uses a subset of the OS's APIs. However, since ACE has been ported to many platforms already, the effort to port to new platforms is relatively low. Most sources of platform variation have been isolated to a few modules in ACE.

4 CONCLUDING REMARKS

This chapter presented a case study illustrating how we applied a pattern language to enhance the extensibility of TAO, which is a dynamically configurable ORB that is targeted for distributed applications with high-performance and real-time requirements. We found qualitative and quantitative evidence that the use of this pattern language helped to clarify the structure of, and collaboration between, components that perform key ORB tasks. These tasks include event demultiplexing and event handler dispatching, connection establishment and initialization of application services, concurrency control, and dynamic configuration. In addition, patterns improved TAO's performance and predictability by making it possible to transparently configure lightweight and optimized strategies for processing client requests.

A principal benefit of applying a pattern language to guide TAO's design is that the systematic application of patterns in the language improved the decoupling and object-oriented structure of the ORB significantly. The patterns we used were applied in roughly the same order that they appear in Section 3.3 Each evolution of TAO leveraged the results of prior evolutions. This iterative process revealed new insights on which patterns in the language could be applied and how they might be applied in subsequent stages.

The complete C++ source code, examples, and documentation for ACE and TAO are freely available at URL `www.cs.wustl.edu/~schmidt/TAO.html`.

REFERENCES

1. R. Johnson, "Frameworks = Patterns + Components," *Communications of the ACM,* vol. 40, October 1997.

2. S. Vinoski, "CORBA: Integrating Diverse Applications within Distributed Heterogeneous Environments," *IEEE Communications Magazine,* vol. 14, February 1997.

3. J.A. Zinky, D.E. Bakken, and R. Schantz, "Architectural Support for Quality of Service for CORBA Objects," *Theory and Practice of Object Systems,* vol. 3, no. 1, 1997.

4. Object Management Group, *The Common Object Request Broker: Architecture and Specification,* 2.2 ed., February 1998.

5. D. Box, *Essential COM.* Reading, MA: Addison-Wesley, 1997.

6. A. Wollrath, R. Riggs, and J. Waldo, "A Distributed Object Model for the Java System," *USENIX Computing Systems,* vol. 38, October 1995.

7. D.C. Schmidt, "Experience Using Design Patterns to Develop Reusable Object-Oriented Communication Software," *Communications of the ACM (Special Issue on Object-Oriented Experiences)*, vol. 38, October 1995.

8. D.C. Schmidt, M. Stal, H. Rohnert, and F. Buschmann, *Pattern-Oriented Software Architecture: Patterns for Concurrency and Distributed Objects*, vol. 2. New York, NY: Wiley & Sons, 2000.

9. D.C. Schmidt, "Applying a Pattern Language to Develop Application-Level Gateways." See this volume, Chapter 16.

10. D.C. Schmidt, D.L. Levine, and S. Mungee, "The Design and Performance of Real-Time Object Request Brokers," *Computer Communications*, vol. 21, pp. 294–324, April 1998.

11. T.H. Harrison, D.L. Levine, and D.C. Schmidt, "The Design and Performance of a Real-Time CORBA Event Service," in *Proceedings of OOPSLA '97* (Atlanta, GA), ACM, October 1997.

12. S. Mungee, N. Surendran, and D.C. Schmidt, "The Design and Performance of a CORBA Audio/Video Streaming Service," in *Proceedings of the Hamilton International Conference on System Science*, January 1999.

13. C. O'Ryan, D.C. Schmidt, and D. Levine, "Applying a Scalable CORBA Evens Service to Large-scale Distributed Interactive Simulations," in *Proceedings of the 5th Workshop on Object-Oriented Real-Time Dependable Systems* (Monterey, CA), IEEE, November 1999.

14. Object Management Group, *The Common Object Request Broker: Architecture and Specification*, 2.3 ed., June 1999.

15. E. Gamma, R. Helm, R. Johnson, and J. Vlissides, *Design Patterns: Elements of Reusable Object-Oriented Software*. Reading, MA: Addison-Wesley, 1995.

16. C. O'Ryan, F. Kuhns, D.C. Schmidt, and J. Parsons, "Applying Patterns to Develop a Pluggable Protocols Framework for ORB Middleware," in *Design Patterns in Communications Software* (L. Rising, ed.), Cambridge University Press, 2001.

17. E. Eide, K. Frei, B. Ford, J. Lepreau, and G. Lindstrom, "Flick: A Flexible, Optimizing IDL Compiler," in *Proceedings of ACM SIGPLAN '97 Conference on Programming Language Design and Implementation (PLDI)* (Las Vegas, NV), ACM, June 1997.

18. M. Henning, "Binding, Migration, and Scalability in CORBA," *Communications of the ACM (Special Issue on CORBA)*, vol. 41, October 1998.

19. Object Management Group, *Realtime CORBA Joint Revised Submission*, OMG Document orbos/99-02-12 ed., March 1999.

20. A. Gokhale and D.C. Schmidt, "Optimizing a CORBA IIOP Protocol Engine for

Minimal Footprint Multimedia Systems," *Journal of Selected Areas in Communication (Special Issue on Service Enabling Platforms for Networked Multimedia Systems)*, vol. 17, September 1999.

21. D.C. Schmidt, "GPERF: A Perfect Hash Function Generator," in *Proceedings of the 2nd C++ Conference* (San Francisco, CA), pp. 87–102, USENIX, April 1990.

22. I. Pyarali, C. O'Ryan, D.C. Schmidt, N. Wang, V. Kachroo, and A. Gokhale, "Using Principle Patterns to Optimize Real-Time ORBs," *Concurrent Magazine*, vol. 8, no. 1, 2000.

23. C.D. Gill, D.L. Levine, and D.C. Schmidt, "The Design and Performance of a Real-Time CORBA Scheduling Service," *The International Journal of Time-Critical Computing Systems (Special Issue on Real-Time Middleware)*, vol. 20, no. 2, 2001.

24. D.C. Schmidt, S. Mungee, S. Flores-Gaitan, and A. Gokhale, "Software Architectures for Reducing Priority Inversion and Non-determinism in Real-Time Object Request Brokers," *Journal of Real-Time Systems (Special Issue on Real-Time Computing in the Age of the Web and the Internet)*, to appear 2001.

25. C. O'Ryan, F. Kuhns, D.C. Schmidt, O. Othman, and J. Parsons, "The Design and Performance of a Pluggable Protocols Framework for Real-Time Distributed Object Computing Middleware," in *Proceedings of the Middleware 2000 Conference*, ACM/IFIP, April 2000.

26. F. Kuhns, D.C. Schmidt, C. O'Ryan, and D. Levine, "Supporting High-Performance I/O in QoS-Enabled ORB Middleware," *Cluster Computing: The Journal on Networks, Software, and Applications*, 2000.

27. Z.D. Dittia, G.M. Parulkar, and J.R. Cox, Jr., "The APIC Approach to High Performance Network Interface Design: Protected DMA and Other Techniques," in *Proceedings of INFOCOM '97* (Kobe, Japan), pp. 179–187, IEEE, April 1997.

28. D.C. Schmidt, "Applying Design Patterns and Frameworks to Develop Object-Oriented Communication Software," in *Handbook of Programming Languages* (P. Salus, ed.), Macmillan Computer Publishing, 1997.

29. A.B. Arulanthu, C. O'Ryan, D.C. Schmidt, M. Kircher, and J. Parsons, "The Design and Performance of a Scalable ORB Architecture for CORBA Asynchronous Messaging," in *Proceedings of the Middleware 2000 Conference*, ACM/IFIP, April 2000.

30. C. O'Ryan, D.C. Schmidt, F. Kuhns, M. Spivak, J. Parsons, I. Pyarali, and D. Levine, "Evaluating Policies and Mechanisms for Supporting Embedded, Real-Time Applications with CORBA 3.0," in *Proceedings of the 6th IEEE Real-Time Technology and Applications Symposium* (Washington, DC), IEEE, May 2000.

31. B. Natarajan, A. Gokhale, D.C. Schmidt, and S. Yajnik, "DOORS: Towards High-Performance Fault-Tolerant CORBA," in *Proceedings of the 2nd International Sym-*

posium on Distributed Objects and Applications (DOA 2000) (Antwerp, Belgium), OMB, September 2000.

32. B. Natarajan, A. Gokhale, D.C. Schmidt, and S. Yajnik, "Applying Patterns to Improve the Performance of Fault-Tolerant CORBA," in *Proceedings of the 7th International Conference on High-Performance Computing (HiPC 2000)* (Bangalore, India), ACM/IEEE, December 2000.

33. J. Hu, S. Mungee, and D.C. Schmidt, "Principles for Developing and Measuring High-Performance Web Servers over ATM," in *Proceedings of INFOCOM '98*, March/April 1998.

34. F. Kon, M. Roman, P. Liu, J. Mao, T. Yamane, L. Magalhaes, and R. Campbell, "Monitoring, Security, and Dynamic Configuration with the Dynamic TAO Reflective ORB," in *Proceedings of the Middleware 2000 Conference*, ACM/IFIP, April 2000.

35. M. Roman, M.D. Mickunas, F. Kon, and R. Campbell, "LegORB and Ubiquitous CORBA," in *Reflective Middleware Workshop*, ACM/IFIP, April 2000.

36. A. Gokhale and D.C. Schmidt, Measuring and Optimizing CORBA Latency and Scalability over High-Speed Networks," *Transactions on Computing*, vol. 47, no. 4, 1998.

37. J. Hu and D.C. Schmidt, "JAWS: A Framework for High Performance Web Servers," in *Domain-Specific Application Frameworks: Frameworks Experience by Industry* (M. Fayad and R. Johnson, eds.). Wiley & Sons, 1999.

38. Object Management Group, *OMG Real-Time Request for Proposal*, OMG Document ptc/97-06-20 ed., June 1997.

39. IEEE, *Threads Extension for Portable Operating Systems (Draft 10)*, February 1996.

40. D.C. Schmidt, S. Mungee, S. Flores-Gaitan, and A. Gokhale, "Alleviating Priority Inversion and Non-Determinism in Real-Time CORBA ORB Core Architectures," in *Proceedings of the 4th IEEE Real-Time Technology and Applications Symposium* (Denver, CO), IEEE, June 1998.

41. J. Pyarali, T.H. Harrison, and D.C. Schmidt, "Design and Performance of an Object-Oriented Framework for High-Performance Electronic Medical Imaging," *USENIX Computing Systems*, vol. 9, November/December 1996.

42. R. Gingell, M. Lee, X. Dang, and M. Weeks, "Shared Libraries in SunOS," in *Procedings of the Summer 1987 USENIX Technical Conference* (Phoenix, AZ), 1987.

43. D.A. Solomon, *Inside Windows NT*, 2nd ed. Redmond, WA: Microsoft Press, 1998.

44. T.J. McCabe, "A Complexity Measure," *IEEE Transactions on Software Engineering*, vol. SE-2, December 1976.

19

APPLYING PATTERNS TO DEVELOP A PLUGGABLE PROTOCOLS FRAME-WORK FOR ORB MIDDLEWARE*

Douglas C. Schmidt, Carlos O'Ryan, Ossama Othman,
Fred Kuhns, and Jeff Parsons

ABSTRACT

To be an effective platform for performance-sensitive applications, off-the-shelf CORBA middleware must preserve the communication-layer quality of service (QoS) properties of applications end-to-end. However, the standard CORBA GIOP/IIOP interoperability protocols are not well-suited for applications with stringent message footprint size, latency, and jitter requirements. It is essential, therefore, to develop standard pluggable protocols frameworks that allow custom messaging and transport protocols to be configured flexibly and used transparently by applications.

This chapter provides three contributions to the study of pluggable protocols frameworks for performance-sensitive CORBA middleware. First, we outline the key design challenges faced by pluggable protocols developers.

Based on "The Design and Performance of a Pluggable Protocols Framework for Object Request Broker Middleware," by Carlos O'Ryan, Fred Kuhns, Douglas C. Schmidt, and Jeff Parsons, which appeared in *Middleware 2000: IFIP/ACM International Conference on Distributed Systems Platforms and Open Distributed Processing, New York, NY, April 4–7, 2000,* ©2000 Springer Verlag. Used with permission from the authors.

*This work was supported in part by ATD, BBN, Boeing, Cisco, DARPA contract 9701516, Motorola Commercial Government and Industrial Solutions Sector, Motorola Laboratories, Siemens, and Sprint.

Second, we describe how we resolved these challenges by developing a pluggable protocols framework for TAO, which is our high-performance, real-time CORBA-compliant ORB. Third, we present the results of benchmarks that pinpoint the impact of TAO's pluggable protocols framework on its end-to-end efficiency and predictability.

Our results demonstrate how the application of optimizations and patterns to CORBA middleware can yield both highly flexible/reusable designs and highly efficient/predictable implementations. These results illustrate that (1) CORBA middleware performance is largely an implementation detail and (2) the next generation of optimized, standards-based CORBA middleware can replace many ad hoc and proprietary solutions.

1 INTRODUCTION

Standard CORBA middleware now available off-the-shelf allows clients to invoke operations on distributed components without concern for component location, programming language, OS platform, communication protocols and interconnects, or hardware [1]. However, conventional off-the-shelf CORBA middleware generally lacks (1) support for QoS specification and enforcement, (2) integration with high-speed networking technology, and (3) efficiency, predictability, and scalability optimizations [2]. These omissions have limited the rate at which performance-sensitive applications, such as video-on-demand, teleconferencing, and avionics mission computing, have been developed to leverage advances in CORBA middleware.

To address the shortcomings of CORBA middleware mentioned above, we have developed *The ACE ORB* (TAO) [2], which is an open-source,[1] standards-based, high-performance, real-time ORB endsystem CORBA middleware that supports applications with deterministic and statistical QoS requirements, as well as "best-effort" requirements. This chapter focuses on the design and implementation of a *pluggable protocols framework* that can efficiently and flexibly support high-speed protocols and networks, real-time embedded system interconnects, and standard TCP/IP protocols over the Internet.

At the heart of TAO's pluggable protocols framework is its patterns-oriented OO design [3, 4], which decouples TAO's ORB messaging and transport interfaces from its transport-specific protocol components. This design allows custom ORB messaging and transport protocols to be configured

---

[1]TAO is available at www.cs.wustl.edu/~schmidt/TAO.html.

flexibly and used transparently by CORBA applications. For example, if ORBs communicate over a high-speed networking infrastructure, such as ATM AAL5 or specialized protocols like HPPI, then simpler ORB messaging and transport protocols can be configured to optimize unnecessary features and overhead of the standard CORBA General Inter-ORB Protocol (GIOP) and Internet Inter-ORB Protocol (IIOP). Likewise, TAO's pluggable protocols framework makes it straightforward to support customized embedded system interconnects, such as CompactPCI or VME, under the standard CORBA General Inter-ORB Protocol (GIOP).

For OO researchers and practitioners, the results in this chapter provide two important contributions:

1. We demonstrate empirically that the ability of standards-based CORBA middleware to support high-performance, real-time systems is largely an *implementation detail,* rather than an inherent liability, e.g.:

   TAO's end-to-end one-way latency overhead is only ~100 μsecs using commercial off-the-shelf 200 MHz PowerPCs, a 320 Mbps VMEbus, and VxWorks.

   The overall roundtrip latency of a TAO two-way method invocation using the standard inter-ORB protocol and using a commercial, off-the-shelf Pentium II Xeon 400 MHz workstation running in loopback mode is ~189 μsecs. The ORB middleware accounts for approximately 48% or ~90 μsecs of the total roundtrip latency.

   Using the specialized POSIX local IPC protocol reduces roundtrip latency to ~125 μsecs.

   These results are as fast as, or faster than, many ad hoc, proprietary solutions, thereby motivating the use of well-tuned, standards-based CORBA middleware, even for real-time embedded applications with stringent QoS requirements.

2. We explore how patterns can be applied to resolve key design challenges. TAO's pattern-oriented OO design can be extended to other pluggable protocols frameworks, either in standard middleware or in distributed applications using proprietary middleware.

The remainder of this chapter is organized as follows: Section 2 outlines the CORBA protocol interoperability architecture; Section 3 motivates the requirements for standard CORBA pluggable protocols and outlines TAO's pluggable protocols framework; Section 4 describes the patterns that guide the architecture of TAO's pluggable protocols framework and resolve key design challenges. Section 5 illustrates the performance characteristics of TAO's pluggable protocols framework; Section 6 compares TAO with related work; and Section 7 presents concluding remarks.

2 OVERVIEW OF THE CORBA PROTOCOL INTEROPERABILITY ARCHITECTURE

The CORBA specification [5] defines an architecture for ORB interoperability. Although a complete description of the model is beyond the scope of this chapter, this section outlines the portions of the CORBA specification that are relevant to our present topic, i.e., object addressing and inter-ORB protocols.

CORBA Object Addressing. To identify objects, CORBA defines a generic format called the Interoperable Object Reference (IOR). An object reference identifies one instance of an object and associates one or more paths by which that object can be accessed. The same object may be located by different object references, e.g., if a server is re-started on a new port or migrated to another host. Likewise, multiple server locations can be referenced by one IOR, e.g., if a server has multiple network interfaces connecting it to distinct networks, there may be multiple network addresses.

References to server locations are called *profiles*. A profile provides an opaque, protocol-specific representation of an object location. Profiles can be used to annotate the server location with QoS information, such as the priority of the thread serving each endpoint or redundant addresses to increase fault-tolerance.

CORBA Protocol Model. CORBA Inter-ORB Protocols (IOPs) support the interoperability between ORB endsystems. IOPs define data representation formats and ORB messaging protocol specifications that can be mapped onto standard or customized transport protocols. Regardless of the choice of ORB messaging or transport protocol, however, the same standard CORBA programming model is exposed to the application developers. Figure 19.1 shows the relationships between these various components and layers.

In the CORBA protocol interoperability architecture, the standard *General Inter-ORB Protocol* (GIOP) is defined by the CORBA specification [5]. In addition, CORBA defines a TCP/IP mapping of GIOP, which is called the *Internet Inter-ORB Protocol* (IIOP). ORBs must support IIOP to be "interoperability compliant." Other mappings of GIOP onto different trans-

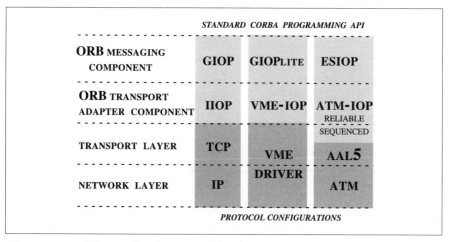

STANDARD CORBA PROGRAMMING API			
ORB MESSAGING COMPONENT	GIOP	GIOPLITE	ESIOP
ORB TRANSPORT ADAPTER COMPONENT	IIOP	VME-IOP	ATM-IOP RELIABLE SEQUENCED
TRANSPORT LAYER	TCP	VME	AAL5
NETWORK LAYER	IP	DRIVER	ATM
PROTOCOL CONFIGURATIONS			

Figure 19.1. Relationship between CORBA Inter-ORB Protocols and transport-specific mappings.

port protocols are allowed by the specification, as are different inter-ORB protocols, which are known as *Environment Specific Inter-ORB Protocols* (ESIOPs).

Regardless of whether GIOP or an ESIOP is used, a CORBA IOP must define a data representation, an ORB message format, an ORB transport protocol or transport protocol adapter, and an object addressing format. For example, the GIOP specification consists of the following:

- *A Common Data Representation (CDR) definition.* CDR is a transfer syntax that maps IDL types from their native host format to a low-level *bi-canonical* representation, which supports both little-endian and big-endian formats. CDR-encoded messages are used to transmit CORBA requests and server responses across a network. All IDL data types are marshaled using the CDR syntax into an *encapsulation,* which is an octet stream that holds marshaled data.

- *GIOP message formats.* The GIOP specification defines seven types of messages that send requests, receive replies, locate objects, and manage communication channels. The following table lists the seven types of messages in GIOP 1.0[2] and the permissible originators of each type:

---

[2]Version 1.1 of GIOP added a Fragment message and version 1.2 relaxes restrictions on message originators.

Message Type	Originator	Value
Request	Client	0
Reply	Server	1
CancelRequest	Client	2
LocateRequest	Client	3
LocateReply	Server	4
CloseConnection	Server	5
MessageError	Both	6

- *GIOP transport adapter.* The GIOP specification describes the features of an ORB transport protocol that can carry GIOP messages. Such protocols must be reliable and connection-oriented. In addition, GIOP defines a connection management protocol and a set of constraints for GIOP message ordering.

- *Object addressing.* An Interoperable Object Reference (IOR) is a sequence of opaque *profiles,* each representing a protocol-specific representation of an object's location. For example, an IIOP profile includes the IP address and port number where the server accepts connections, as well as the object key that identifies an object within a particular server. An IOR may contain multiple profiles because there may be multiple ways to access a server, e.g., through different physical network connections or alternate protocols.

CORBA also defines other attributes that can be associated with a specific profile, group of profiles, or an entire IOR. These attributes are called *tagged components.* Tagged components can contain various types of QoS information dealing with security, server thread priorities, network connections, CORBA policies, or other domain-specific information.

An IIOP version 1.0 profile contains the protocol version, hostname, and port number, as well as an object key that is used to demultiplex an object within a server's Object Adapter. In IIOP version 1.1, a new field was added to the GIOP header that defines a sequence of tagged components, which are name/value pairs that can be used for security, QoS, or other purposes. Tagged components may contain more information than just the object location. For example, IIOP 1.1 defines a flexible mechanism to include QoS parameters, security and authentication tokens, per-object policies for bridging with non-CORBA middleware, character set representations, and alternative addresses for a server.

ESIOP Synopsis. In addition to the standard GIOP and IIOP protocols, the CORBA specification allows ORB implementors to define Environment Specific Inter-ORB Protocols (ESIOP)s. ESIOPs can define unique data representation formats, ORB messaging protocols, ORB transport protocols or transport protocol adapters, and object addressing formats. These protocols can exploit the QoS features and guarantees provided in certain domains, such as telecommunications or avionics, to satisfy performance-sensitive applications that have stringent bandwidth, latency, and jitter requirements.

Only one ESIOP protocol is defined in the CORBA 2.x family of specifications: the DCE Common Inter-ORB Protocol (DCE-CIOP) [5]. The OMG is attempting to standardize other protocols for domains, such as wireless and mobile systems [6], which have unique performance characteristics and optimization points.

3 THE DESIGN OF A CORBA PLUGGABLE PROTOCOLS FRAMEWORK

The CORBA specification provides a standard for general-purpose CORBA middleware. Within the scope of this specification, however, ORB implementors are free to optimize internal data structures and algorithms [7]. Moreover, ORBs may use specialized inter-ORB protocols and ORB services and still comply with the CORBA specification.[3] For example, ORB providers can develop additional ESIOPs for protocols such as ATM or VME, as shown in Figure 19.1.

This section first identifies the limitations of, and requirements for, protocol support in conventional CORBA ORBs. It then describes how TAO's pluggable protocols framework is designed to overcome these limitations.

3.1 PROTOCOL LIMITATIONS OF CONVENTIONAL ORBS

CORBA's standard GIOP/IIOP protocols are well-suited for conventional request/response applications with best-effort QoS requirements [8]. They are not well-suited, however, for high-performance real-time and/or embedded applications that cannot tolerate the message footprint size of GIOP or

---

[3]An ORB *must* implement GIOP/IIOP, however, to be interoperability-compliant.

the latency, overhead, and jitter of the TCP/IP-based IIOP transport protocol. For instance, TCP functionality, such as adaptive retransmissions, deferred transmissions, and delayed acknowledgments, can cause excessive overhead and latency for real-time applications [9]. Likewise, network protocols, such as IPv4, lack packet admission policies and rate control capabilities, which can lead to excessive congestion and missed deadlines in networks and endsystems.

Therefore, applications with more stringent QoS requirements need optimized protocol implementations, QoS-aware interfaces, custom presentation layers, specialized memory management (e.g., shared memory between ORB and I/O subsystem), and alternative transport programming APIs (e.g., sockets vs. VIA [10]). Domains where highly optimized ORB messaging and transport protocols are particularly important include (1) multimedia applications running over high-speed networks, such as Gigabit Ethernet or ATM, and (2) real-time applications running over embedded system interconnects, such as VME or CompactPCI.

Conventional CORBA implementations have the following limitations that make it hard for them to support performance-sensitive applications effectively:

1. *Static protocol configurations.* Conventional ORBs support a limited number of statically configured protocols, often just GIOP/IIOP over TCP/IP.
2. *Lack of protocol control interfaces.* Conventional ORBs do not allow applications to configure key protocol policies and properties, such as peak virtual circuit bandwidth or cell pacing rate.
3. *Single protocol support.* Conventional ORBs do not support simultaneous use of multiple inter-ORB messaging or transport protocols.
4. *Lack of real-time protocol support.* Conventional ORBs have limited or no support for specifying and enforcing real-time protocol requirements across a backplane, network, or Internet end-to-end.

3.2 PLUGGABLE PROTOCOLS FRAMEWORK REQUIREMENTS

The limitations of conventional ORBs described in Section 3.1 make it hard for developers to leverage existing implementations, expertise, and ORB optimizations across projects or application domains. Defining a standard *pluggable protocols framework* for CORBA ORBs is an effective way to address this problem. The requirements for such a pluggable protocols framework for CORBA include the following:

1. *Define standard, unobtrusive protocol configuration interfaces.* To address the limitations of conventional ORBs, a pluggable protocols framework should define a standard set of APIs to install ESIOPs and their transport-dependent components. Most applications need not use this interface directly. Therefore, the pluggable protocols interface should be exposed only to application developers interested in defining new protocols or in configuring existing protocol implementations in novel ways.

2. *Use standard CORBA programming and control interfaces.* To ensure application portability, clients should program to standard application interfaces defined in CORBA IDL, even if pluggable ORB messaging or transport protocols are used. Likewise, object implementators need not be aware of the underlying framework. Developers should be able to set policies, however, that control the ORB's choice of protocols and protocol properties. Moreover, these interfaces should transparently support certain real-time ORB features, such as scatter/gather I/O, optimized memory management, and strategized concurrency models [7].

3. *Simultaneous use of multiple ORB messaging and transport protocols.* To address the lack of support for multiple inter-ORB protocols in conventional ORBs, a pluggable protocols framework should support different messaging and transport protocols *simultaneously* within an ORB endsystem. The framework should configure inter-ORB protocols transparently, either *statically* during ORB initialization [11] or *dynamically* during ORB run-time [12].

4. *Support for multiple address representations.* This requirement addresses the lack of support for multiple Inter-Orb protocols and dynamic protocol configurations in conventional ORBs. For example, each pluggable protocol implementation can potentially have a different profile and object-addressing strategy. Therefore, a pluggable protocols framework should provide a general mechanism to represent these disparate address formats transparently, while also supporting standard IOR address representations efficiently.

5. *Support CORBA standard features and future enhancements.* A pluggable protocols framework should support standard CORBA [13] features, such as object reference forwarding, connection transparency, preserva-

tion of foreign IORs and profiles, and the GIOP 1.2 protocol, in a manner that does not degrade end-to-end performance and predictability. Moreover, a pluggable protocols framework should accommodate forthcoming enhancements to the CORBA specification, such as (1) *fault tolerance* [14, 15], which supports group communication, (2) *real-time properties* [11], which include features of reserve connection and threading resources on a per-object basis, (3) *asynchronous messaging* [16], which exports QoS policies to application developers, and (4) *wireless access and mobility* [6], which defines lighterweight Inter-ORB protocols for low-bandwidth links.

6. *Optimized Inter-ORB bridging.* A pluggable protocols framework should ensure that protocol implementators can create efficient, high-performance inter-ORB *in-line bridges.* An in-line bridge converts inter-ORB messages or requests from one type of IOP to another. This makes it possible to bridge disparate ORB domains efficiently without incurring unnecessary context switching, synchronization, or data movement.

7. *Provide common protocol optimizations and real-time features.* A pluggable protocols framework should support features required by real-time CORBA applications [11], such as resource pre-allocation and reservation, end-to-end priority propagation, and mechanisms to control properties specific to real-time protocols. These features should be implemented without modifying the standard CORBA programming APIs used by applications that do not possess real-time QoS requirements.

8. *Dynamic protocol bindings.* To address the limitations with static, inflexible protocol bindings in conventional ORBs, a pluggable protocols framework should support dynamic binding of specific ORB messaging protocols with specific instances of ORB transport protocols. This design permits efficient and predictable configuration for both standard and customized IOPs.

3.3 ARCHITECTURAL OVERVIEW OF TAO'S PLUGGABLE PROTOCOLS FRAMEWORK

To meet the requirements outlined in the preceding section, we identified logical communication component layers within TAO, factored out common features, defined general framework interfaces, and implemented components to support different concrete inter-ORB protocols. Higher-level services in the ORB, such as stubs, skeletons, and standard CORA pseudo-objects, are decoupled from the implementation details of particular protocols, as shown in Figure 19.2. This decoupling is essential to resolve several limitations of conventional ORBs outlined in Section 3.1, as well as to meet the requirements set forth in Section 3.2.

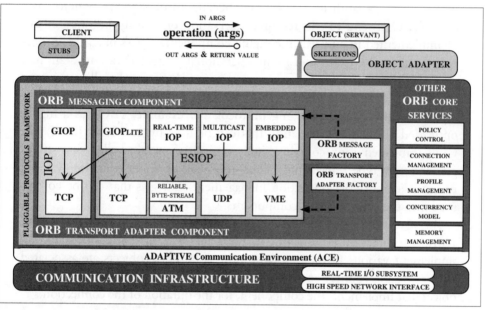

Figure 19.2. TAO's pluggable protocols framework architecture.

In general, the higher-level components and services of TAO use the Facade pattern [17] to access the mechanisms provided by its pluggable protocols framework. Thus, applications can (re)configure custom protocols without requiring global changes to the ORB. Moreover, because applications typically access only the standard CORBA APIs, TAO's pluggable protocols framework can be used transparently by CORBA application developers.

The key TAO pluggable protocols framework components illustrated in Figure 19.2 are described below.

3.3.1 ORB Messaging Component. This component is responsible for implementing ORB messaging protocols, such as the standard CORBA GIOP ORB messaging protocol, as well as custom ESIOPs. An ORB messaging protocol must define a data representation, an ORB message format, an ORB transport protocol or transport adapter, and an object addressing format. Within this framework, ORB protocol developers are free to implement optimized Inter-ORB protocols and enhanced transport adapters, as long as they respect the ORB interfaces.

Each ORB messaging protocol implementation inherits from a common base class that defines a uniform interface. This interface can be extended to include new capabilities needed by special protocol-aware policies. For example, ORB end-to-end resource reservation or priority negotiation can be implemented in an ORB messaging component. TAO's pluggable protocols framework ensures consistent operational characteristics and enforces general IOP syntax and semantic constraints, such as error handling.

When adding a new IOP, it may not be necessary to re-implement all aspects of the ORB's messaging protocol. For example, TAO has a highly optimized CDR implementation that can be used by new IOPs [7]. TAO's CDR implementation contains highly optimized memory allocation strategies and data type translations. Thus, protocol developers can simply identify new memory or connection management strategies that can be configured into the existing CDR components.

Message factories are another key part of TAO's ORB messaging component. During connection establishment, these factories instantiate objects that implement various ORB messaging protocols. These objects are associated with a specific connection and ORB transport adapter component, i.e., the object that implements the component, for the duration of the connection.

3.3.2 ORB Transport Adapter Component.
This component maps a specific ORB messaging protocol, such as GIOP or DCE-CIOP, onto a specific instance of an underlying transport protocol, such as TCP or ATM. Figure 19.2 shows an example in which TAO's transport adapter maps the GIOP messaging protocol onto TCP – this standard mapping is called IIOP. In this case, the ORB transport adapter combined with TCP corresponds to the transport layer in the Internet reference model. However, if ORBs are communicating over an embedded interconnect, such as a VME bus, the bus driver and DMA controller provide the "transport layer" in the communication infrastructure.

TAO's ORB transport component accepts a byte stream from the ORB messaging component, provides any additional processing required, and passes the resulting data unit to the underlying commercial infrastructure. Additional processing that can be implemented by protocol developers includes (1) concurrency strategies, (2) endsystem/network resource reservation protocols, (3) high-performance techniques, such as zero-copy I/O, shared memory pools, periodic I/O, and interface pooling, (4) enhancement of underlying communications protocols, e.g., provision of a reliable byte stream protocol over ATM, and (5) tight coupling between the ORB and efficient user-space protocol implementations, such as Fast Messages [18].

3.3.3 ORB Policy Control Component. It is not possible to determine a priori all attributes defined by all protocols. Therefore, TAO's pluggable protocols framework provides an extensible *policy control* component, which implements the QoS framework defined in the CORBA Messaging [16] and Real-Time CORBA [11] specifications. This component allows applications to control the QoS attributes of configured ORB transport protocols.

In general, the CORBA QoS framework allows applications to specify various *policies* to control the QoS attributes in the ORB. The CORBA specification uses policies to define semantic properties of ORB features precisely without (1) over-constraining ORB implementations or (2) increasing interface complexity for common use-cases. Example policies relevant for pluggable protocols include buffer pre-allocations, fragmentation, bandwidth reservation, and maximum transport queue sizes.

Policies in CORBA can be set at the ORB, thread, or object level. Thus, application developers can set global policies that take effect for any request issued in a particular ORB. Moreover, these global settings can be overridden on a per-thread basis, a per-object basis, or even before a particular request. In general, CORBA's Policy framework provides very fine-grained control over the ORB behavior, while providing simplicity for the common case.

Certain policies, such as timeouts, can be shared between multiple protocols. Other policies, such as ATM virtual circuit bandwidth allocation, may apply to a single protocol. Each configured protocol can query TAO's policy control component to determine its policies and use them to configure itself for user needs. Moreover, protocol implementations can simply ignore policies that do not apply to it.

TAO's policy control component enables applications to select their protocol(s). This choice can be controlled by the `ClientProtocolPolicy` defined in the Real-Time CORBA specification [11]. Using this policy, an application can indicate its preferred protocol(s) and TAO's policy control component, then attempt to match that preference with its set of available protocols. TAO provides other policies that control the behavior of the

ORB if an application's preferences cannot be satisfied. For example, an exception can be raised or another available protocol can be selected transparently.

3.3.4 Connection Management Services.

Connection management services are a fundamental component of TAO's pluggable protocols framework. These services are responsible for creating ORB protocol objects dynamically and associating them with specific connections. They also interpret profiles and create object references on the server. By employing patterns and leveraging TAO's real-time features [19], protocol implementators can design high-performance IOPs that enforce stringent QoS properties.

The connection management services are implemented with *connectors, acceptors, reactors,* and *registries* that keep track of available protocols, create protocol objects, and interpret profiles and object addresses. Acceptors and connectors implement the *Acceptor-Connector* pattern [3], which decouples the task of connection establishment and connection handler initialization from subsequent IOP message processing. The connectors and acceptors register themselves with their corresponding registries. The registries in turn keep track of available ORB message and transport protocols and are responsible for interpreting object references.

TAO's connection management services behave differently depending on whether the ORB plays the role of a client or a server, as outlined below.

Client ORB components. In the client ORB, the `Connector_Registry` and `Connector` establish connections to server objects and link the constituent objects together statically or dynamically. When a client application invokes an operation, it uses the list of profiles derived from the object's IOR.

For each inter-ORB and transport protocol combination available in the ORB, there is a corresponding `Connector` object responsible for performing the connection. The registry will cycle through the list of profiles for an object, requesting the appropriate connector to attempt a connection. If a connect succeeds, then the search is concluded and the successful profile is returned to the client. If no connect succeeds, the ORB throws a `transient` exception to the client.

Server ORB components. In the server ORB, an `Acceptor` waits passively for a connection event using a `Reactor` in accordance with the Reactor pattern [3]. Different concurrency architectures may be used, such as single-threaded, thread-per-connection, or thread-per-priority [20]. The actual concurrency strategy used is provided as a service by TAO's ORB

Core and the pluggable protocols framework. Regardless of the threading and connection concurrency strategy, the basic steps are the same:

1. An `Acceptor` listens to endpoints and waits for connection requests.
2. When a connection is accepted, a connection handler object and IOP object are created.

The `Acceptor_Registry` creates object references for registered server objects. When an object is advertised, the registry will request each registered `Acceptor` to create a profile for this object. The `Acceptor` will place in this profile the host address, the corresponding transport service access point (for example, port number for TCP/IP), and object key. All profiles are then bundled by the `Acceptor` into an IOR, which clients can use to access the object.

3.3.5 Multiple Profiles and Location Forwarding. As explained earlier, clients obtain interoperable object references (IORs), which are used to locate the objects upon which invocations are performed. An object reference includes at least one profile, which contains information for accessing an object through different network interfaces, shared memory, security restrictions, or QoS parameters. Multiple profiles could be used in a situation where an object resides on a server with multiple interfaces, e.g., ATM and Ethernet. A profile will then be created for each of the two interfaces.

TAO's multiple profiles implementation incorporates support for *location forwarding*, which occurs when an ORB sends a request to a server object, and the server responds with a location forward reply. The location forward reply will include an IOR that the client decodes to get the list of forwarding profiles. The forwarding profiles will then replace the forwarded profile in the original profile list. Each new profile will then be tried in turn until one succeeds, is itself forwarded, or until all fail. If all forwarding profiles fail, the forwarding list is removed and the ORB continues with the next profile after the one that was forwarded initially.

There is no pre-defined limit on the number of location-forward messages that an ORB may receive. For example, if an invocation using a profile from the list of forwarding profiles should also be forwarded, the process will repeat recursively until the operation succeeds or all profiles have been tried. In practice, however, it is advantageous to limit the depth of recursion in case forwarding loops occur.

Multiple profiles can be used for other purposes, such as fault-tolerance [14, 15]. For example, consider an object that is replicated in three locations, e.g., on different hosts, processes, or CPU boards in an embedded system. The IOR for this object would contain three profiles, one for each object location. If an invocation fails using the first profile, TAO's pluggable protocols framework will transparently retry the invocation using the second profile that corresponds to the replicated object at a different location. By using some form of checkpointing or reliable multicast the state of these object instances can be synchronized.

Location forwarding can also be used for load balancing. For example, if one server becomes overloaded, it can migrate some of its objects to another server. Subsequent requests on the relocated object will then result in a location-forward reply message. The message contains the new IOR for the relocated object. In the client ORB, TAO's pluggable protocols framework will then retry the object operation invocation using the new IOR transparently to the application. When system loads return to normal, the object can migrate back to the original server, and if the client performs another operation invocation, the forwarded server can reply with an exception indicating the object is no longer there. The client then retries at the original location transparently to the application.

3.4 PLUGGABLE PROTOCOLS SCENARIOS

To illustrate how TAO's pluggable protocols framework has been applied in practice, we now describe two scenarios that require performance-sensitive and real-time CORBA support. These scenarios are based on our experience developing high-bandwidth, low-latency audio/video streaming applications [21] and avionics mission computing [22] systems. In previous work [20], we address the network interface and I/O system and how to achieve predictable, real-time performance. In the discussion below, we focus on ORB support for alternate protocols.

3.4.1 Low-Latency, High-Bandwidth Multimedia Streaming

Multimedia applications running over high-speed networks require optimizations to utilize available link bandwidth, while still meeting application deadlines. For example, consider Figure 19.3, where network interfaces supporting 1.2 Mbps or 2.4 Mbps link speeds are used for a CORBA-based studio quality audio/video (A/V) application [21].

In this example, we use TAO's pluggable protocols framework to replace

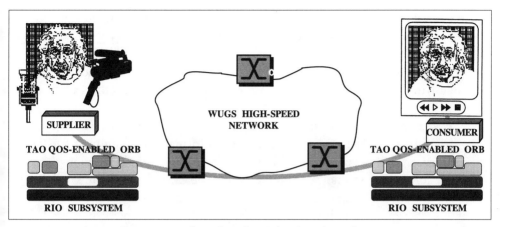

Figure 19.3. Example CORBA-based audio/video (A/V) application.

GIOP/IIOP with a custom ORB messaging and transport protocol that transmits A/V frames using TAO's real-time I/O (RIO) subsystem [20]. At the core of RIO is the high-speed ATM port interconnector controller (APIC) [23]. APIC is a high-performance ATM interface card that supports standard ATM host interface features, such as AAL5 (SAR). In addition, the APIC supports (1) shared memory pools between user and kernel space, (2) per-VC pacing, (3) two levels of priority queues, and (4) interrupt disabling on a per-VC basis.

We have leveraged the APIC features and the underlying ATM network to support end-to-end QoS guarantees for TAO middleware. In particular, pluggable ORB message and transport protocols can be created to provide QoS services to applications, while the ORB middleware encapsulates the actual resource allocation and QoS enforcement mechanisms. Leveraging the underlying APIC hardware requires the resolution of the following two design challenges:

Custom protocols. The first challenge is to create custom ORB messaging and transport protocols that can exploit high-speed ATM network interface hardware. A careful examination of the system requirements along with the hardware and communication infrastructure is required to determine (1) the set of optimizations required and (2) the best partitioning of the solution into ORB messaging, transport, and policy components.

The A/V streaming application is primarily concerned with (1) pushing data to clients via one-way method invocations and (2) meeting a specific set of latency and jitter requirements. Considering this, a simple frame sequencing protocol can be used as the ORB's ESIOP. Moreover, because multimedia data has diminishing value over time, a reliable protocol like TCP is not required. The overhead of full GIOP is not required, therefore, nor are the underlying assumptions that require a transport protocol with the semantics of TCP.

A key goal of this scenario is to simplify the ORB messaging and transport protocol, while adding QoS-related information to support timely delivery of the video frames and audio. For example, a CORBA request could correspond to one video frame or audio packet. To facilitate synchronization between endpoints, a timestamp and sequence number can be sent with each request. The Inter-ORB messaging protocol can perform a similar function as the real-time protocol (RTP) and real-time control protocols (RTCP) [24].

The ORB messaging protocol can be mapped onto an ORB transport protocol using AAL5. The transport adapter is then responsible for exploiting any local optimizations to hardware or the endsystem. For example, conventional ORBs copy user parameters into internal buffers used for marshaling. These buffers may be allocated from global memory or possibly from a memory pool maintained by the ORB. In either case, at least one system call is required to obtain mutexes, allocate buffers, and copy the data. Thus, not only is an additional data copy incurred, but this scenario is rife with opportunities for priority inversion and jitter while waiting to acquire shared ORB endsystem resources.

Optimized protocol implementations. The second challenge is to implement an optimized pluggable protocol that implements the design described above. For example, memory can be shared throughout the ORB endsystem, i.e., between the application, ORB middleware, OS kernel, and network interface, by allocating memory from a common buffer pool [23, 7]. This optimization eliminates memory copies between user- and kernel-space when data is sent or received. Moreover, the ORB endsystem can manage this memory, thereby relieving application developers from this responsibility. In addition, the ORB endsystem can manage the APIC interface driver, interrupt rates, and pacing parameters, as outlined in [20].

Figure 19.4 illustrates a buffering strategy where the ORB manages multiple pools of buffers to be used by applications sending multimedia data to remote nodes. These ORB buffers are shared between the ORB and APIC driver in the kernel. The transport adapter implements this shared buffer pool on a per-connection and possibly per-thread basis to minimize or reduce the use of resource locks. For example, in the strategy depicted in Figure 19.4, each active connection is assigned its own send and receive queues. Likewise, there are two free buffer pools per connection, one for receive and one for send.

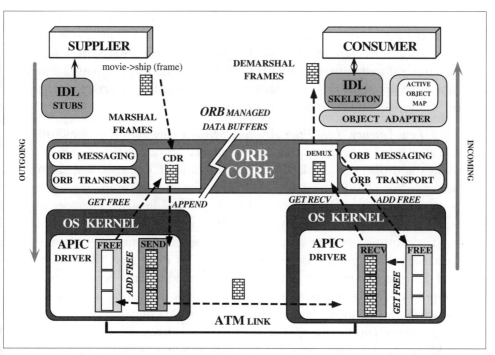

Figure 19.4. Shared buffer strategy.

An ORB can guarantee that only one application thread will be active within the send or receive operation of the transport adapter. Therefore, buffer allocation and de-allocation can be performed without locking. A similar buffer management strategy is described in [23].

User applications can interact with the buffering strategy described above as follows:

- *Zero-copy.* The application requests a set of send buffers from the ORB that it uses for video and audio data. In this case, application developers must not reuse a buffer after it has been given to the ORB. When the original set of buffers is exhausted, the application must request additional buffers.

- *Single-copy.* The ORB copies application data into the ORB managed buffers. While this strategy incurs one data copy, the application developer need not be concerned with how or when buffers are used in the ORB.

Well-designed ORBs can be strategized to allow applications to decide whether data are copied into ORB buffers or not. For instance, it may be more efficient to copy relatively small request data into ORB buffers, rather than using shared buffers within the ORB endsystem. By using TAO's policy control component, this decision can be configured on a per-connection, per-thread, per-object, or per-operation basis.

3.4.2 Low-Latency, Low-Jitter Avionics Mission Computing.

Avionics mission computing applications [22] are real-time embedded systems that manage sensors and operator displays, navigate the aircraft's course, and control weapon release. CORBA middleware for avionics mission computing applications must support deterministic real-time QoS requirements interoperating over shared memory, I/O buses, and traditional network interfaces. Support for deterministic real-time requirements is essential for mission computing tasks, such as weapon release and navigation, that must meet all their deadlines. Likewise, avionics software must support tasks, such as built-in-test and low-priority display queues, that can tolerate minor fluctuations in scheduling and reliability guarantees, but nonetheless require QoS support [25].

To enforce end-to-end application QoS guarantees, mission computing middleware must reduce overall inter-ORB communication latencies, maximize I/O efficiency, and increase overall system utilization [8, 26]. A particularly important optimization point is the inter-ORB protocol itself, and the selection of an optimal transport protocol implementation for a particular platform.

For example, Figure 19.5 depicts an embedded avionics configuration with three CPU boards, each with an ORB instance. Each board is connected via a VME bus, which enables the ORBs on each CPU board to communicate using optimized inter-board communication, such as DMA between the individual board address spaces. CPU board 1 has a 1553 bus interface to communicate with so-called remote terminals, such as aircraft sensors for determining global position and forward-looking infrared radar [22]. This configuration allows ORB A to provide a bridging service that forwards ORB requests between ORBs B and C and remote terminals connected with board 1.

The scenario in Figure 19.5 motivates the need for multiple ORB mes-

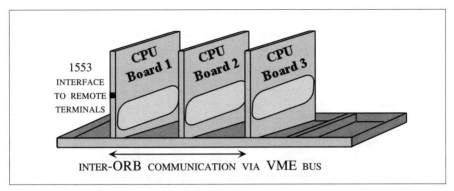

Figure 19.5. Example avionics embedded ORB platform.

saging and transport protocols that can be added seamlessly to an ORB without affecting the standard CORBA programming API. For instance, ORB A could use a 1553 transport protocol adapter to communicate with remote terminals. Likewise, custom ORB messaging and transport protocols can be used to leverage the underlying VME bus hardware and eliminate sources of unbounded priority inversion. Leveraging the underlying bus hardware requires the resolution of the following two design challenges:

Custom protocols. With TAO's pluggable protocols framework, we can create optimized VME-based and 1553-based inter-ORB messaging and transport protocols. Moreover, by separating the IOP messaging from a transport-specific mapping, we can adapt TAO's pluggable protocols framework to different transmission technologies, such as CompactPCI or Fibrechannel, by changing only the transport-specific mapping of the associated inter-ORB messaging protocol.

Consider an embedded application that must periodically process sensor data. The sensor data is collected and forwarded aperiodically to a central, although redundant, processor. The sensor data is sent/received aperiodically. Therefore, the resulting bus transfers, interrupts, and driver processing can reduce the overall utilization of the system. For example, a DMA transfer between two CPU boards requires that the VMEBus, the source PCI bus, and the destination PCI bus be acquired and data copied.

A more efficient protocol could buffer these one-way data transfers until a predetermined byte count or timeout value is reached. Thus the time required to acquire the different buses could be amortized over a larger data transfer. Additionally, given the periodic nature of the transfers rate, monotonic analysis could be used to better predict system performance.

Optimized protocol implementation. To optimize the on-the-wire protocol message footprint we use a lightweight version of GIOP, called GIOPlite. GIOPlite is a streamlined version of GIOP that removes ≥15 extraneous bytes from the standard GIOP message and request headers.[4] These bytes include the GIOP magic number (4 bytes), GIOP version (2 bytes), flags (1 byte), Request Service Context (at least 4 bytes), and Request Principal (at least 4 bytes). GIOPlite reduces the number of bytes transferred across the backplane per operation.

Another optimization that pertains to avionics mission computing involves the use of buffered one-way operations [19]. TAO's pluggable protocols framework has been optimized to send a series of queued one-way requests in a smaller number of ORB messages. For example, Figure 19.6 depicts the case where one-way CORBA invocations are buffered in the ORB for later delivery. In this case, a series of one-way invocations to the same object and for the same operation are queued in the same buffer and sent via a single ORB message. This results in an overall increase in throughput between CPU boards by amortizing key sources of communication overhead, such as context switching, synchronization, and DMA initialization.

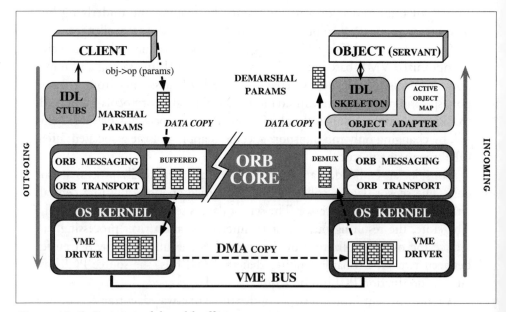

Figure 19.6. One-way delayed buffering strategy.

---

[4]The request header size is variable. Therefore, it is not possible to precisely pinpoint the proportional savings represented by these bytes. In many cases, however, the reduction is as large as 25%.

4 Key Design Challenges and Pattern-Based Resolutions

Section 3.3 described *how* TAO's pluggable protocols framework is designed. It does not, however, motivate *why* this particular design was selected. In this section, we explore each feature in TAO's pluggable protocols framework and show how they achieves the goals described earlier. To clarify and generalize our approach, the discussion below focuses on the patterns [17] we applied to resolve the key design challenges we faced during the development process.

4.1 Adding New Protocols Transparently

Context. The QoS requirements of many applications can be supported solely by using default static protocol configurations, i.e., GIOP/IIOP, described in Section 3.1. However, applications with more stringent QoS requirements often require custom protocol configurations. Implementations of these custom protocols requires several related classes, such as `Connectors`, `Acceptors`, `Transports`, and `Profiles`. To form a common framework, these classes must all be created consistently.

In addition, many embedded and deterministic real-time systems require protocols to be configured a priori, with no additional protocols required once the application is configured statically. These types of systems cannot afford the footprint overhead associated with dynamic protocol configurations.

Problem. It must be possible to add new protocols to TAO's pluggable protocols framework without making *any* changes to the rest of the ORB. Thus, the framework must be open for extensions, but closed to modifications, i.e., the Open-Closed principle [27]. Ideally, creating a new protocol and configuring it into the ORB is all that should be required.

Solution. Use a *registry* to maintain a collection of *abstract factories*. In the Abstract Factory pattern [17], a single class defines an interface for creating families of related objects, without specifying their concrete types. Subclasses of an abstract factory are responsible for creating concrete classes that collaborate among themselves. In the context of pluggable protocols, each abstract factory can create the `Connector`, `Acceptor`, `Profile`, and `Transport` classes for a particular protocol.

Applying the Solution in TAO. In TAO, the role of the protocol registry is played by the `Connector_Registry` on the client and the `Acceptor_Registry` on the server. This registry is created by TAO's `Resource_Factory`, which is an abstract factory that creates all the ORB's strategies and policies [28]. Figure 19.7 depicts the `Connector_Registry` and its relation to the abstract factories.

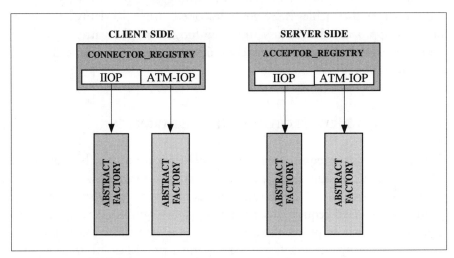

Figure 19.7. TAO connector and acceptor registries.

Note that TAO does not use abstract factories directly, however. Instead, these factories are accessed via the *Facade* [17] pattern to hide the complexity of manipulating multiple factories behind a simpler interface. The registry described above plays the role of a facade. As shown below, these patterns provide sufficient flexibility to add new protocols transparently to the ORB.

Establishing connections, manipulating profiles, and creating endpoints are delegated to the `Connector` and `Acceptor` registries respectively. Clients will simply provide the `Connector_Registry` with an opaque profile, which corresponds to an object address for a particular protocol instance. The registry is responsible for locating the correct concrete factory, to which it then delegates the responsibility for establishing the connection. The concrete factory establishes the connection using the corresponding protocol-specific instance, notifying the client of its success or failure. Thereafter, the client simply invokes CORBA operations using the selected protocol.

The server delegates endpoint creation to the `Acceptor_Registry` in a similar manner. The registry is passed an opaque endpoint representation, which it provides to the corresponding concrete factory for the indicated protocol instance. The concrete `Acceptor` factory creates the endpoint and enables the ORB to receive requests of the new endpoint.

4.2 ADDING NEW PROTOCOLS DYNAMICALLY

Context. When developing new pluggable protocols, it is inconvenient to recompile the ORB and applications just to validate a new protocol implementation. Moreover, it is often useful to experiment with different protocols, e.g., systematically compare their performance, footprint size, and QoS guarantees. Moreover, in 24×7 systems with high availability requirements, it is important to configure protocols dynamically, even while the system is running. This level of flexibility helps simplify upgrades and protocol enhancements.

Problem. How to populate the registry with the correct objects *dynamically.*

1. The Component Configurator pattern [3] can be used to dynamically load the registry class. This facade knows how to configure a particular set of protocols. To add new protocols, we must either implement a new registry class or derive from an existing one.

   This alternative is well-suited for embedded systems with tight memory footprint constraints since it minimizes the number of objects that are loaded dynamically. Implementations of the Component Configurator pattern can optimize for use-cases where objects are configured statically. Embedded systems can exploit these optimizations to eliminate the need for loading objects into the pluggable protocols framework dynamically.
2. Use the Component Configurator pattern to load the set of entries in a registry dynamically. For instance, a registry can simply parse a configuration script and link the services listed in it dynamically. This design is the most flexible strategy, but it requires more code, e.g., to parse the configuration script and load the objects dynamically.

Applying the Solution in TAO. TAO implements a class that maintains all parameters specified in a configuration script. Adding a new parameter to represent the list of protocols is straightforward, i.e., the default registry simply examines this list and links the services into the address-space of the application, using the Component Configurator pattern implementation provided by ACE [29].[5] Figure 19.8 depicts the `Connector_Registry` and its relation to the ACE Component Configurator implementation.

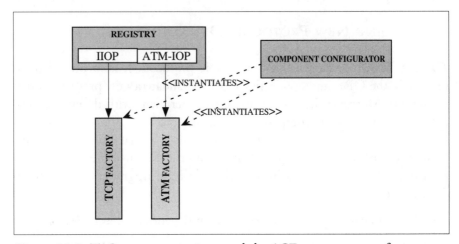

Figure 19.8. TAO connector registry and the ACE component configurator implementation.

4.3 PROFILE CREATION

Context. The contents of a profile must be parsed to determine an object's location. In general, the format and semantics of the profile contents are protocol-specific. Therefore, a completely generic component for it cannot be written. Parsing the data is a relatively expensive operation that should be avoided whenever possible. It is also useful to support multiple protocols, each one potentially using a different address representation.

Problem. As new protocols are added to the system, new profile formats are introduced. It is essential that the correct parsing function be used for each profile format.

Solution. We use the Factory Method pattern [17] to create the right `Profile` class for each protocol. This pattern defines a fixed interface to create

---

[5]ACE provides a rich set of reusable and efficient components for high-performance, real-time communication, and forms the portability layer of TAO.

an object, while allowing subclasses the flexibility to create the correct type of object. Two of our classes play the *Creator* role in this pattern: (1) the `Connector`, using the `Profile`'s CDR representation for initialization, and (2) the `Acceptor`, using the object key for initialization.

These two approaches are based on the two use-cases in which a `Profile` object must be maintained. In the `Connector` case TAO interprets a `Profile` received remotely, whereas in the `Acceptor` it builds a `Profile` for a local object. As usual, the `Connector_Registry` and the `Acceptor_Registry` are used as facades [17] that locate the appropriate `Connector` or `Acceptor` and delegate the job of building the object to it.

Applying the Solution in TAO. The `Profile` class is used to represent a protocol-specific profile. This class provides an abstract interface for parsing, marshaling, hashing, and comparing profiles. In addition, it provides a unit of encapsulation to maintain information about forwarding and caching connections established to a particular server.

4.4 Decoupling ORB Messaging and Transport Protocol Implementation

Context. It is desirable to support alternative mappings between different ORB messaging protocols and ORB transport adapters. For example, a single ORB messaging protocol, such as GIOP, can be mapped to any reliable, connection-oriented transport protocol, such as TCP. Alternatively, a single transport protocol can be the basis for alternative instantiations of ORB messaging protocols, e.g., different versions of GIOP differing in the number and types of messages, as well as in the format of those messages.

An ORB messaging protocol imposes requirements on any underlying network transport protocols. For instance, the transport requirements assumed by GIOP described in Section 2 require the underlying network transport protocol to support a reliable, connection-oriented byte-stream. These requirements are fulfilled by TCP, thus leading to the direct mapping of GIOP onto this transport protocol. However, alternative network transport protocols, such as ATM with AAL5 encapsulation, may be more appropriate in some environments. In this case, the messaging implementation must provide the missing semantics, such as reliability, to use GIOP.

Problem. The ORB Messaging protocol implementations must be independent of the adaptation layer needed for transports that do not satisfy all their requirements. Otherwise, the same messaging protocol may be re-implemented needlessly for each transport, which is time-consuming, error-prone, and time/space inefficient. Likewise, for those transports that can support multiple ORB Messaging protocols, it must be possible to isolate them from the details of the ORB messaging implementation. Care must be taken, however, because not all ORB Messaging protocols can be used with all transport protocols, i.e., some mechanism is needed to ensure that only semantically compatible protocols are configured [30].

Solution. Use the Layers architectural pattern [4], which decomposes the system into groups of components, each one at a different level of abstraction.[6] The Layers architectural pattern can be implemented differently, depending on whether the ORB plays the role of a client or a server, as outlined below.

- *Client ORB.* For the client, the ORB uses a particular ORB messaging protocol to send a request. This ORB messaging protocol delegates part of the work to the transport adapter component that completes the message and sends it to the server. If the low-level transport in use, such as ATM, UDP, or TCP/IP, does not satisfy the requirements of the ORB messaging protocol, the ORB transport adapter component can implement them.

- *Server ORB.* In the server, the transport adapter component receives data from the underlying communication infrastructure, such as sockets or shared memory, and it passes the message up to the ORB messaging layer. As with the client, this layer can be very lightweight if the requirements imposed by the ORB messaging layer are satisfied by the underlying network transport protocol. Otherwise, it must implement those missing requirements by building them into the concrete transport adapter component.

Applying the Solution in TAO. As shown in Figure 19.9, TAO implements the messaging protocol and the transport protocol in separate components. The client ORB uses the current profile to find the right transport and ORB messaging implementations. The creation and initialization of these classes is

---

[6]Protocol stacks based on the Internet or ISO OSI reference models are common examples of the Layers architectural pattern.

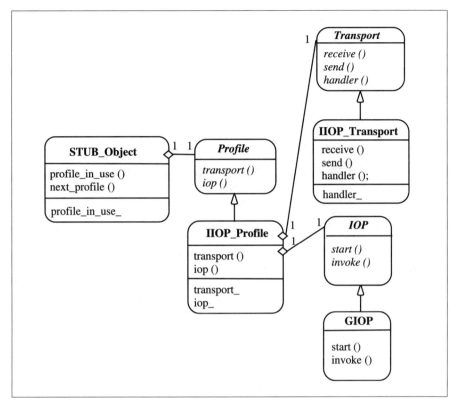

Figure 19.9. Client inter-ORB and transport class diagram.

controlled by the `Connector` (described later), with each `Connector` instance handling a particular ORB messaging/transport tuple.

Figure 19.10 illustrates how the server's implementation uses the same transport classes, but with a different relationship. In particular, the transport class calls back the messaging class when data is received from the IPC mechanism. As with the client, a factory – in this case the `Acceptor` – creates and initializes these objects.

4.5 EXCEPTION PROPAGATION AND ERROR DETECTION

Context. The server and client use the same exceptions to inform the application of failures in the communication media. The ORB must be able to

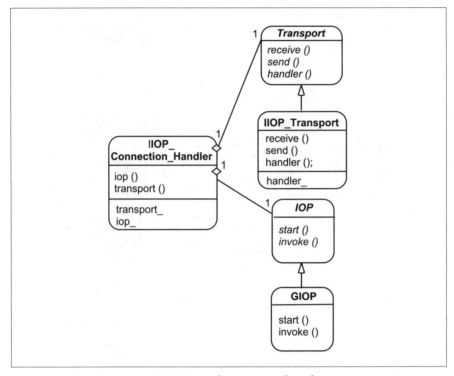

Figure 19.10. Server inter-ORB and transport class diagram.

ignore certain communication errors selectively and re-issue the request transparently using alternative addresses or resources.

Problem. Using the lower-level ACE IPC wrapper facade components directly is infeasible because ACE avoids polymorphism at this level to eliminate the overhead of virtual methods by non-optimizing compilers [22]. Thus, the ACE connectors for UNIX-domain sockets and Internet-domain sockets have no common ancestor that can be used to dispatch methods in subclasses polymorphically. However, a pluggable protocols framework must be able to establish connections using any protocol.

Solution. Use the External Polymorphism pattern [31] to encapsulate ACE components behind their TAO counterparts. This pattern enables classes that are not related by inheritance, or have no virtual methods, to be treated polymorphically.

Applying the Solution in TAO. A TAO `Acceptor` contains an ACE `Acceptor`, which is registered with an ACE `Reactor` that the ORB uses to demultiplex IOP events to the appropriate transport handlers. Eventually, the ACE IPC components accept a connection and create an ACE `Service Handler` to handle the communication. Our TAO-level `Acceptor` encapsulates that `Service Handler` in a `Transport` adapter object and passes it up to the ORB. As a practical consequence of this solution, there exist two sublayers within TAO's `Transport` object.

4.7 MULTIPLE PROFILES AND LOCATION FORWARDING

Context. Object references may contain multiple profiles, and servers may specify alternate object references in response to a client's request. In addition, a CORBA-compliant ORB is required to try all object references and profiles until one succeeds *without* any client intervention.

Problem. Retries must occur transparently to the client application, even though profiles for different ORB protocols may be dissimilar and profile lists may be altered dynamically as a result of forwarding.

Solution. Apply the Proxy pattern [17] and use polymorphism and an efficient list processing strategy.

Applying the Solution in TAO. Figure 19.11 depicts the class diagram for the solution. A `STUB_Object` is a client's local proxy for the (potentially) remote object. All communication with the server object is done through the stub proxy. While the server does not require a `STUB_Object`, the `Acceptor_Registry` will initialize an object's IOR using the `MProfile` and `Profile` classes.

Profile lists are maintained by an `MProfile` object. The profile list is stored as a simple array of pointers to `Profile` objects. All instances of IOP profiles are derived from this common `Profile` class. By relying on dynamic binding of objects, the base class can be used for both referencing and performing common method invocations on the concrete profile instances. The `MProfile` object can therefore maintain a list of `Profile` proxies to the actual concrete profile instances.

The `MProfile` object keeps track of the current profile and allows a user only to increment and decrement this reference. If the current profile is forwarded, a reference is kept in that profile to the forwarding `MProfile` object. Likewise, the forwarding `MProfile` contains a back pointer to the `MProfile` object that was forwarded. In this way, a list of `MProfiles` is maintained, corresponding to the initial and all forwarding profile lists.

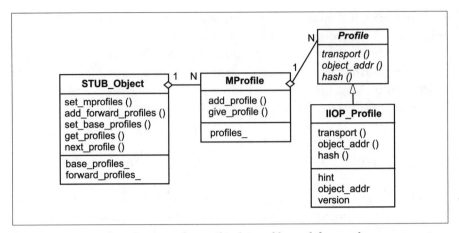

Figure 19.11. Class diagram for multiple profile and forwarding support in TAO's pluggable protocols framework.

When a client decodes the initial IOR, the resulting profile list is stored in an MProfile object. If the client receives a location forward, either as a result of a Locate_Request GIOP message or in a LOCATION_FORWARD reply, the received IOR is decoded and added to the STUB_Object using its add_forward_profiles method. The MProfile object that was forwarded keeps track of the current profile, marks it as being a FORWARDING state, and sets a reference to the forwarding profile list. The STUB_Object maintains a reference to the initial profile list and to the current forwarding profile list, i.e., the MProfile object, because the forwarding MProfile objects each contain a back pointer to the forwarded MProfile object.

Figure 19.12 illustrates how forwarding is represented using the MProfile objects. Not shown is the STUB_Object, which maintains references to the initial or unforwarded profile list, the current profile in use, and the last forwarding profile list. In effect, the STUB_Object and MProfile present the ordered profile list – P1, P2, P5, P6, P7, P8, P9, P3, P4 – to the Connection_Registry.

4.8 ESTABLISHING CONNECTIONS ACTIVELY

Context. When a client references an object, the ORB must obtain the corresponding profile list, which is derived from the IOR and a profile ordering policy, and establish a connection to the server transparently.

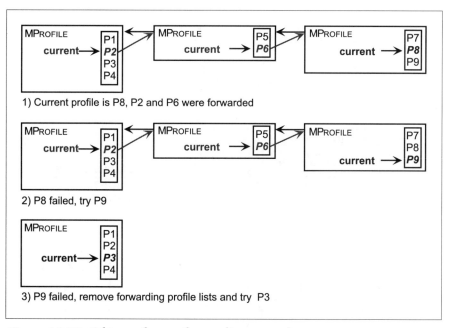

Figure 19.12. Object reference forwarding example.

Problem. There can be one or more combinations of inter-ORB and transport protocols available in an ORB. For a given profile, the ORB must verify the presence of the associated IOP and transport protocol, if available. It must then locate the applicable `Connector` and delegate to it to establish the connection.

Solution. We use the `Connector` component in the Acceptor-Connector pattern [3] to actively establish a connection to a remote object. This pattern decouples the connection establishment from the processing performed after the connection is successful. Figure 19.13 shows how multiple profiles may be used during connection establishment in both the client and server. This figure shows a connection to `Object A` being requested of the `Connector_Registry`. The registry will in turn try the profiles listed in the `supplied profile_list` for `Object A`. In this figure, the first profile is for an IIOP connection to `Host A` at `port 1`. Assuming the connect fails for some reason, the registry will try the second profile automatically. This profile contains a reference to the same host via ATM interface using an ESIOP.

Assuming the connect on the second profile succeeds, the `Connector`

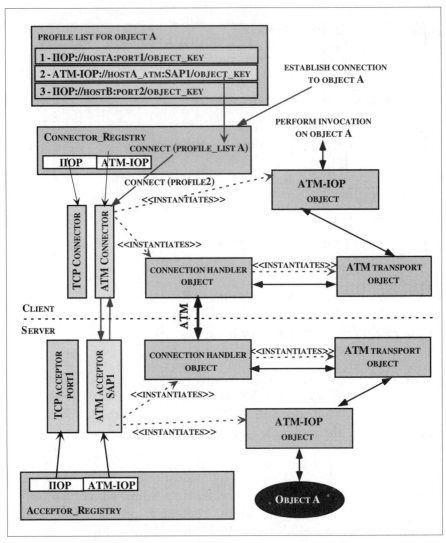

Figure 19.13. Connection establishment using multiple pluggable protocols.

and `Acceptor` create their corresponding connection handlers and ATM-IOP transport objects. The connection handlers then create transport objects, which provide the mapping from the chosen transport protocol to a transport-independent interface used by the IOP messaging component. The connection handler is considered part of the ORB transport adapter component.

Applying the Solution in TAO. As described earlier, `Connectors` are adapters for the ACE implementation of the Acceptor-Connector pattern. Thus, they are lightweight objects that simply delegate to a corresponding ACE component. Figure 19.15 shows the base classes and their relations for IIOP. This figure shows an explicit co-variance between the `Profile` and the `Connectors` for each protocol. In general, a `Connector` must downcast the `Profile` to its specific type. This downcast is safe because profile creation is limited to the `Connector` and `Acceptor` registries. In both cases, the profile is created with a matching tag. The tag is used by the `Connector_Registry` to choose the `Connector` that can handle each profile.

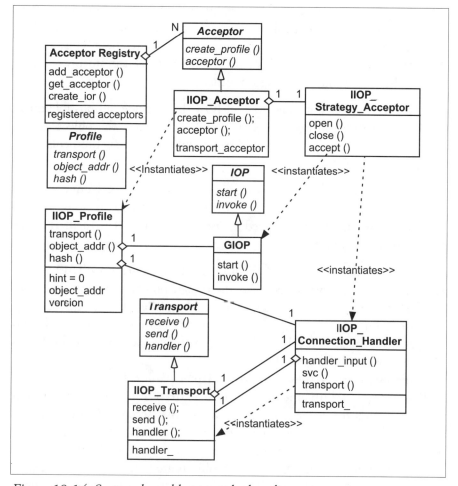

Figure 19.14. Server pluggable protocols class diagram.

473

As shown in the same figure, the `Connector_Registry` manipulates only the base classes. Therefore, new protocols can be added without requiring any modification to the existing pluggable protocols framework. When a connection is established successfully, the `Profile` is passed a pointer to the particular IOP object and to the `Transport` objects that were created.

4.9 ACCEPTING CONNECTIONS PASSIVELY

Context. A server can accept connections at one or more endpoints, potentially using the same protocol for all endpoints. The set of protocols that an ORB uses to play the client role need not match the set of protocols used for the server role. Moreover, the ORB can even be a "pure client," i.e., a client that only makes requests. In this case it can use several protocols to make requests, but receive no requests from other clients.

Problem. The server must generate an IOR that includes all possible inter-ORB and transport-protocol-specific profiles for which the object can be assessed. As with the client, it should be possible to add new protocols without changing the ORB.

Solution. Use the `Acceptor` component in the Acceptor-Connector pattern [3] to accept the connections. An `Acceptor` accepts a connection *passively*, rather than being initiated *actively*, as with the `Connector` component described above.

Applying the Solution to TAO. Figure 19.14 illustrates how TAO's pluggable protocols framework leverages the design presented earlier. The concrete ACE `Service Handler` created by the ACE `Acceptor` is responsible for implementing the External Polymorphism pattern [31] and encapsulating itself behind the `Transport` interface defined in TAO's pluggable protocols framework.

As discussed earlier, TAO uses the Adapter pattern [17] to leverage the ACE `Acceptor` implementation. This pattern also permits a seamless integration with lower levels of the ORB. In the Acceptor-Connector pattern, the `Acceptor` object is a factory that creates `Service Handlers`, which perform I/O with their connected peers. In TAO's pluggable protocols framework, the `Transport` objects are `Service Handlers` implemented as abstract classes. This design shields the ORB from variations

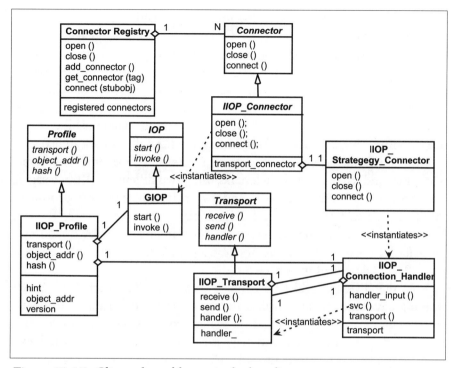

Figure 19.15. Client pluggable protocols class diagram.

in the `Acceptors`, `Connectors`, and `Service Handlers` for each particular protocol.

When a connection is established, the concrete `Acceptor` creates the appropriate `Connection Handler` and IOP objects. The `Connection Handler` also creates a `Transport` object that functions as the implementation role in the Bridge pattern [17]. As with the `Connector`, the `Acceptor` also acts as the interface role in the Bridge pattern, hiding the transport- and strategy-specific details of the `Acceptor`.

5 THE PERFORMANCE OF TAO'S PLUGGABLE PROTOCOLS FRAMEWORK

Despite the growing demand for off-the-shelf middleware in many application domains, a widespread belief persists that OO techniques are not suitable for real-time systems due to performance penalties [22]. In particular, the dynamic binding properties of OO programming languages and the indirection implied in OO designs seem antithetical to real-time systems, which require low latency and jitter. The results presented in this section are significant, therefore, because they illustrate empirically how the choice of patterns described in Section 4 enabled us to meet non-functional requirements, such as portability, flexibility, reusability, and maintainability, without compromising overall system efficiency, predictability, or scalability.

To quantify the benefits and costs of TAO's pluggable protocols framework, we conducted several benchmarks using two different ORB messaging protocols, GIOP and GIOPlite, and two different transport protocols, POSIX local IPC (also known as UNIX-domain sockets) and TCP/IP. These benchmarks are based on our experience developing CORBA middleware for avionics mission computing applications [22] and multimedia applications [21], as described in Section 3.4.

Note that POSIX local IPC is not a traditional high-performance networking environment. However, it does provide the opportunity to obtain an accurate measure of ORB and pluggable protocols framework overhead. Based on these measurements, we have isolated the overhead associated with each component, which provides a baseline for future work on high-performance protocol development and experimentation.

5.1 HARDWARE/SOFTWARE BENCHMARKING PLATFORM

All benchmarks in this section were run on a Quad-CPU Intel Pentium II Xeon 400 MHz workstation, with one gigabyte of RAM. The operating system used for the benchmarking was Debian GNU/Linux "potato" (glibc 2.1) with Linux kernel version 2.2.10. GNU/Linux is an open-source operating system that supports true multi-tasking, multi-threading, and symmetric multiprocessing.

For these experiments, we used the GIOP and GIOPlite [7] messaging protocols. GIOPlite is a streamlined version of GIOP that removes ≥15 extraneous bytes from the standard GIOP message and request headers.[7]

---

[7] The request header size is variable. Therefore, it is not possible to precisely pinpoint the proportional savings represented by these byes. In many cases, however, the reduction is as large as 25%.

These bytes include the GIOP magic number (4 bytes), GIOP version (2 bytes), flags (1 byte), Request Service Context (at least 4 bytes), and Request Principal (at least 4 bytes).

Our benchmarks were run using the standard GIOP ORB messaging protocol, as well as TAO's GIOPlite messaging protocol. For the TCP/IP tests, the GIOP and GIOPlite ORB messaging protocols were run using the standard CORBA IIOP transport adapter along with the Linux TCP/IP socket library and the loopback interface.

For the local IPC tests, GIOP and GIOPlite were used along with the optimized local IPC transport adapter. This resulted in the following four different Inter-ORB Protocols: (1) GIOP over TCP (IIOP), (2) GIOPlite over TCP, (3) GIOP over local IPC[8] (UIOP), and (4) GIOPlite over local IPC. No changes were required to our standard CORBA benchmarking tool, called `IDL_Cubit` [32], for either of the ORB messaging and transport protocol implementations.

5.2 BLACKBOX BENCHMARKS

Blackbox benchmarks measure the end-to-end performance of a system from an external application perspective. In our experiments, we used blackbox benchmarks to compute the average two-way response time incurred by clients sending various types of data using the four different Inter-ORB transport protocols.

Measurement Technique. A single-threaded client is used in the `IDL_Cubit` benchmark to issue two-way IDL operations at the fastest possible rate. The server performs the operation, which cubes each parameter in the request. For two-way calls, the client thread waits for the response and checks that it is correct. Interprocess communication is performed over the selected IOPs, as described above.

We measure throughput for operations using a variety of IDL data types, including `void`, `sequence`, and `struct` types. The `void` data type instructs the server not to perform any processing other than that necessary to prepare and send the response, i.e., it does not cube any input parameters.

---

[8]For historical reasons, TAO retains the expression "UNIX-domain" in its local IPC pluggable protocol implementation, which is what the name "UIOP" derives from.

The `sequence` and `struct` data types exercise TAO's (de)marshaling engine. The `struct` contains an `octet`, a `long`, and a `short`, along with padding necessary to align those fields. We also measure throughput using long and short sequences of the `long` and `octet` types. The `long` sequences contain 4,096 bytes (1,024 four byte `long`s or 4,096 `octet`s) and the short sequences are 4 bytes (one four byte `long` or four `octet`s).

Blackbox Results. The blackbox benchmark results are shown in Figure 19.16. All blackbox benchmarks were averaged over 100,000 two-way operation calls for each data type, as shown in the figure.

UIOP performance surpassed IIOP performance for all data types. The benchmark results show how UIOP improves performance from 20% to 50% depending on the data type and size. For smaller data sizes and basic types, such as `octet` and `long`, the performance improvement is approximately 50%. For larger data payload sizes and more complex data types, however, the performance improvements are reduced. This result occurs due to the increasing cost of both the data copies associated with performing I/O and the increasing complexity of marshaling structures other than the basic data types.

For certain data types, additional improvements are obtained by reducing the number of data copies required. Such a situation exists when marshaling and demarshaling data of type `octet` and `long`. For complicated data types, such as a large `sequence` of `struct`s, ORB overhead is particularly prevalent. Large ORB overhead implies lower efficiency, which accounts for the smaller performance improvement gained by UIOP over IIOP for complex data types.

GUIPlite outperformed GIOP by a small margin. For IIOP, GIOPlite performance increases over GIOP ranged from 0.36% to 4.74%, with an average performance increase of 2.74%. GIOPlite performance improvements were slightly better over UIOP due to the fact that UIOP is more efficient than IIOP. GIOPlite over UIOP provided improvements ranging from 0.37% to 5.29%, with an average of 3.26%.

Our blackbox results suggest that more substantial changes to the GIOP message protocol are required to achieve significant performance improvements. However, these results also illustrate that the GIOP message footprint has a relatively minor performance impact over high-speed networks and embedded interconnects. Naturally, the impact of the GIOP message footprint for lower-speed links, such as second-generation wireless systems or low-speed modems, is more significant.

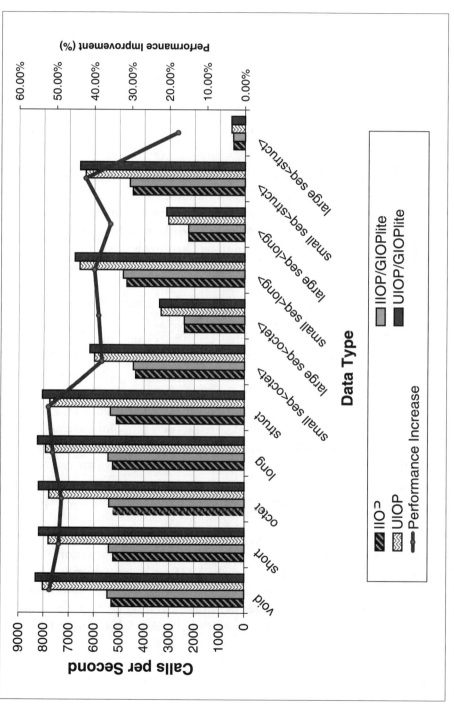

Figure 19.16. TAO's pluggable protocols framework performance over local IPC and TCP/IP.

5.3 WHITEBOX BENCHMARKS

Whitebox benchmarks measure the performance of specific components or layers in a system from an internal perspective. In our experiments, we used whitebox benchmarks to pinpoint the time spent in key components in TAO's client and server ORBs. The ORB's logical layers, or components, are shown in Figure 19.17 along with the timeprobe locations used for these benchmarks.

5.3.1 *Measurement Techniques.* One way to measure performance overhead of operations in complex CORBA middleware is to use a profiling tool, such as Quantify [33]. Quantify instruments an applications binary instruction and then analyzes performance bottlenecks by identifying sections of code that dominate execution time. Quantify is useful because it can measure the overhead of system calls and third-party libraries without requiring the source code.

Unfortunately, Quantify is not available for Linux kernel-based operating systems on which whitebox measurement of TAO's performance was performed. Moreover, Quantify modifies the binary code to collect timing information. It is most useful, therefore, to measure the *relative* overhead of different operations in a system, rather than measuring *absolute* run-time performance.

To avoid the limitations of Quantify, we therefore used a lightweight timeprobe mechanism provided by ACE to precisely pinpoint the amount of time spent in various ORB components and layers. The ACE timeprobe mechanism provides highly accurate, low-cost timestamps that record the time spent between regions of code in a software system. These timeprobes have minimal performance impact, e.g., 1–2 μsec overhead per timeprobe, and no binary code instrumentation is required.

Depending on the underlying platform, ACE's timeprobes are implemented either by high-resolution OS timers or by high-precision timing hardware. An example of the latter is the VMEtro board, which is a VME bus monitor. VMEtro writes unique ACE timeprobe values to an otherwise unused VME address. These values record the duration between timeprobe markers across multiple processors using a single clock. This enables TAO to collect synchronized timestamps and measure communication delays end-to-end accurately across distributed CPUs.

Below, we examine the client and server whitebox performance in detail.

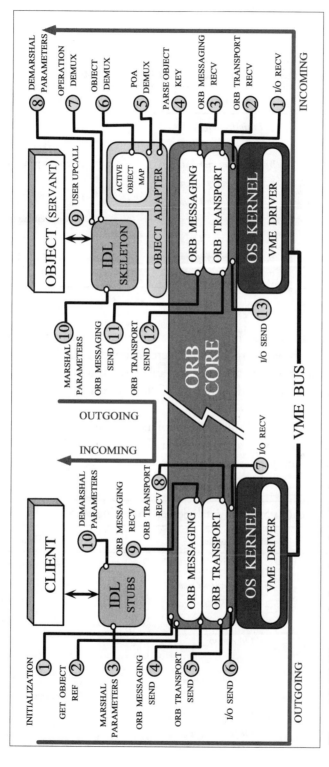

Figure 19.17. Timeprobe locations for whitebox experiment.

Table 19.1. μseconds Spent in Each Client Processing Step

Direction	Client Activities	Absolute time (μs)
Outgoing	1. *Initialization*	6.30
	2. *Get object reference*	15.6
	3. *Parameter marshal*	0.74 (param. dependent)
	4. *ORB messaging send*	7.78
	5. *ORB transport send*	1.02
	6. *I/O*	8.70 (op. dependent)
	7. *ORB transport recv*	50.7
	8. *ORB messaging recv*	9.25
	9. *Parameter demarshal*	op. dependent

5.3.2 Whitebox Results. Figure 19.17 shows the points in a two-way operation request path where timeprobes were inserted. Each labeled number in the figure corresponds to an entry in Table 19.1 and Table 19.2. The results presented in the tables and figures that follow were averaged over 1,000 samples.

Client performance. Table 19.1 depicts the time in microseconds (μs) spent in each sequential activity that a TAO client performs to process an outgoing operation request and its reply.

Table 19.2. μseconds Spent in Each Server Processing Step

Direction	Server Activities	Absolute Time (μs)
Incoming	1. *I/O*	7.0 (op. dependent)
	2. *ORB transport recv*	24.8
	3. *ORB messaging recv*	4.5
	4. *Parsing object key*	4.6
	5. *POA demux*	1.39
	6. *Servant demux*	4.6
	7. *Operation demux*	4.52
	8. *User upcall*	3.84 (op. dependent)
Outgoing	9. *ORB messaging send*	4.56
	10. *ORB transport send*	93.6

Each client outgoing step is outlined below:

1. In the *initialization* step, the client invocation is created and constructors are called for the input and output Common Data Representation (CDR) stream objects, which handle marshaling and demarshaling of operation parameters.
2. TAO's connector caches connections, so even though its `connect` method is called for every operation, existing connections are reused for repeated calls. For statically configured systems, such as avionics mission computing, TAO pre-establishes connections, so the initial connection setup overhead can be avoided entirely.
3. In the *parameter marshal* step, the outgoing `in` and `inout` parameters are marshaled. The overhead of this processing depends on the operation signature, i.e., the number of data parameters and their type complexity.
4. In the `send` operation in the *ORB messaging* layer, the client creates a request header and frames the message. The messaging layer then passes the message to the ORB transport component for transmission to the server. If the request is a synchronous two-way operation, the transport component waits for and processes the response.
5. The `send` operation in the *ORB transport* component implements the connection concurrency strategy and invokes the appropriate ACE I/O operation. TAO maintains a linked list of CDR buffers [7], which allows it to use "gather-write" OS calls, such as `writev`. Thus, multiple buffers can be written automatically without requiring multiple system calls or unnecessary memory allocation and data copying.
6. The *I/O* operation represents the time the client spends in the receive system call. This time is generally dominated by the cost of copying data from the kernel to user-supplied buffers.

Each client incoming step is outlined below:

7. The *I/O receive* operation copies the data from a kernel buffer to a receive CDR stream and returns control to the ORB transport component.
8. The `recv` operation in the *ORB transport* layer delegates the reading of the received messages header and body to the ORB messaging component. If the message header is valid, then the remainder of the message is read. This also includes time when the client is blocked waiting for the server to read the supplied data.

9. The `recv` operation in the *ORB messaging* layer checks the message type of the reply, and either raises an appropriate exception, initiates a location forward, or returns the reply to the calling application.

10. In the *parameter demarshal* step, the incoming reply `out` and `inout` parameters are demarshaled. The overhead of this step depends, as it does with the server, on the operation signature.

Server performance. Table 19.2 depicts the time in microseconds (μs) spent in each activity as a TAO server processes a request.

Each incoming server step is outlined below:

1. The *I/O* operation represents the time the server spends in the `read` system call.

2. The `recv` operation in the *ORB transport* layer delegates the reading of the received message header to the ORB messaging component. If it is a valid message the remaining data is read and passed to the ORB messaging component.

3. The `recv` operation in the *ORB messaging* layer checks the type of the message and forwards it to the POA. Otherwise, it handles the message or reports an error back to the client.

4. The *Parsing object key* step comes before any other POA activity. The time in the table includes the acquisition of a lock that is held through all POA activities, i.e., *POA demux, servant demux,* and *operation demux.*

5. The *POA demux* step locates the POA where the servant resides. The time in this table is for a POA that is one level deep, although in general, POAs can be many levels deep [7].

6. The *servant demux* step looks up a servant in the target POA. The time shown in the table for this step is based on TAO's active demultiplexing strategy [7], which locates a servant in constant time regardless of the number of objects in a POA.

7. The skeleton associated with the operation resides in the *operation demux* step. TAO uses perfect hashing [7] to locate the appropriate operation.

8. In the *parameter demarshal* step, the incoming request `in` and `inout` parameters are demarshaled. As with the client, the overhead of this step depends on the operation signature.

9. The time for the *user upcall* step depends upon the actual implementation of the operation in the servant.

Each outgoing server step is outlined below:

10. In the *return value marshal* step, the `return`, `inout`, and `out` parameters are marshaled. This time also depends on the signature of the operation.
11. The `send` operation in the *ORB messaging* layer passes the marshaled return data down to the ORB transport layer.
12. The `send` operation in the *ORB transport* layer adds the appropriate IOP header to the reply, sends the reply, and closes the connection if it detects an error. Also included in the category is the time the server is blocked in the `send` operation while the client runs.
13. The I/O `send` operation gets the peer I/O handle from the server connection handler and calls the appropriate `send` operation. The server uses a gather-write I/O call, just like the client-side I/O `send` operation described above.

Depending on the type and number of operation parameters, the *ORB transport recv* step often requires the most ORB processing time. This time is dominated by the required data copies. These costs can be reduced significantly by using a transport adapter that implements a shared buffer strategy.

Component costs. Figure 19.18 compares the relative overhead attributable to the ORB messaging component, transport adaptor, ORB and OS for two-way `IDL_Cubit` calls to the `cube_void` operation for each possible protocol combination. This figure shows that when using IIOP the I/O and OS overhead accounts for just over 50% of the total round trip latency. It also shows that the difference in performance between IIOP and UIOP is due primarily to the larger OS and I/O overhead of TCP/IP, compared with the local IPC.

The only overhead that depends on size is *(de)marshaling,* which depends on the type complexity, number, and size of operation parameters, and *data copying,* which depends on the size of the data. In our whitebox experiment, only the parameter size changes, i.e., the `sequences` vary in length. Moreover, TAO's (de)marshaling optimizations [8] incur minimal overhead when running between homogeneous ORB endsystems.

In Figure 19.19, the parameter size is varied as the above test is repeated. It shows that as the size of the operation parameters increases, I/O overhead grows faster than the overall ORB overhead, including messaging and transport. This result illustrates that the overall ORB overhead is largely independent of the request size. In particular, demultiplexing a request, creating

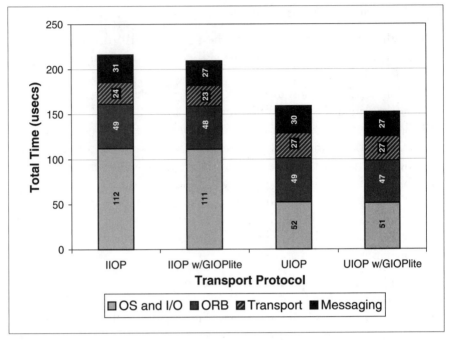

Figure 19.18. Comparison of ORB and transport/OS overhead using timeprobes.

message headers, and invoking an operation upcall are not affected by the size of the request.

TAO employs standard buffer size and data copy tradeoff optimizations. This optimization is demonstrated in Figure 19.19 by the fact that there is a slight increase in the time spent both in the transport component and in the ORB itself when the sequence size is greater than 256 bytes. The data copy tradeoff optimization is fully configurable via run-time command line options, so it is possible to configure TAO to further improve performance above the 256 byte data copy threshold.

For the operations tested in the `IDL_Cubit` benchmark, the overhead of the ORB is dominated by memory bandwidth limitations. Both the loop-back driver and local IPC driver copy data within the same host. Therefore, memory bandwidth limitations should essentially be the same for both IIOP and UIOP. This result is illustrated in Figure 19.18 by the fact that the time spent in the ORB is generally constant for the four protocol combinations shown.

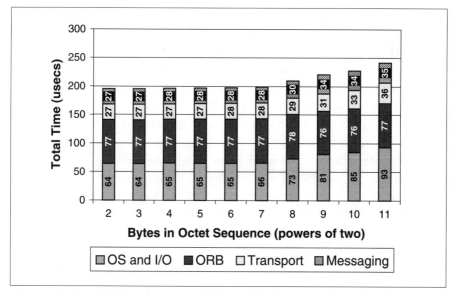

Figure 19.19. ORB and transport/OS overhead vs. parameter size.

In general, the use of UIOP demonstrates the advantages of TAO's pluggable protocols framework and how optimized, domain-specific protocols can be employed.

6 RELATED WORK

We have used TAO to research many dimensions of high-performance and real-time ORB endsystems, including static [2] and dynamic [25] scheduling, request demultiplexing [7], dispatching [34], event processing [22], ORB Core connection [32] and concurrency architectures [35], IDL compiler stub/skeleton optimizations for synchronous [8] and asynchronous [36] communication, I/O subsystem integration [20], evaluation Real-Time CORBA [11] features [19], fault tolerance features [14, 15], reflective QoS techniques, the CORBA Component Model [37], multimedia streaming support [21], systematic benchmarking of multiple ORBs [38], and patterns for ORB extensibility [28] and optimization [7]. The design of TAO's pluggable protocols framework is influenced by prior research on the design and optimization of protocol frameworks for communication subsystems. This section outlines that research and compares it with our work.

Configurable Communication Frameworks. The *x*-kernel [39], Conduit+ [30], System V STREAMS [40], ADAPTIVE [41], and F-CSS [42] are all configurable communication frameworks that provide a protocol backplane consisting of standard, reusable services that support network protocol development and experimentation. These frameworks support flexible composition of modular protocol processing components, such as connection-oriented and connectionless message delivery and routing, based on uniform interfaces.

The frameworks for communication subsystems listed above focus on implementing various protocol layers beneath relatively low-level programming APIs, such as sockets. In contrast, TAO's pluggable protocols framework focuses on implementing and/or adapting to transport protocols beneath a higher-level CORBA middleware API, i.e., the standard CORBA programming API. Therefore, existing communication subsystem frameworks can provide building block protocol components for TAO's pluggable protocols framework.

Patterns-Based Communication Frameworks. An increasing number of communication frameworks are being designed and documented using patterns [28, 30]. In particular, Conduit+ [30] is an OO framework for configuring network protocol software to support ATM signaling. Key portions of the Conduit+ protocol framework, e.g., demultiplexing, connection management, and message buffering, were designed using patterns like Strategy, Visitor, and Composite [17]. Likewise, the concurrency, connection management, and demultiplexing components in TAO's ORB Core and Object Adapter also have been explicitly designed using patterns such as Reactor, Acceptor-Connector, and Active Object [3].

CORBA Pluggable Protocols Frameworks. The architecture of TAO's pluggable protocols framework is inspired by the ORBacus [43] Open Communications Interface (OCI) [44]. The OCI framework provides a flexible, intuitive, and portable interface for pluggable protocols. The framework interfaces are defined in IDL, with a few special rules to map critical types, such as data buffers.

Defining pluggable protocols interfaces with IDL permits developers to familiarize themselves with a single programming model that can be used to implement protocols in different languages. In addition, the use of IDL makes it possible to write pluggable protocols that are portable among different ORB implementations and platforms.

However, using IDL also limits the degree to which various optimizations can be applied at the ORB and transport protocol levels. For example, efficiently handling locality constrained objects, optimizing profile handling, strategized buffer allocation, or interfacing with optimized OS abstraction layers/libraries is not generally supported by existing IDL compilers. Additionally, changes to an IDL compiler's mapping rules on a per-protocol basis is prohibitive.

In our approach we use C++ classes and optimized framework interfaces to allow protocol developers to exploit new strategies or available libraries. TAO uses the ACE framework [29] to isolate itself from non-portable aspects of underlying operating systems. This design leverages the testing, optimizations, implemented by ACE, enabling us to focus on the particular problems of developing a high-performance, real-time ORB.

Our framework allows each protocol implementation to represent a profile as it sees fit. Since these profiles are only created in a few instances, it is possible for them to parse the octet stream representation and store it in a more convenient format. The parsing can be also done on demand to minimize startup time. The protocol implementator is free to choose the strategy that best fits the application.

TAO implements a highly optimized pluggable protocols framework that is tuned for high-performance and real-time application requirements. For example, TAO's pluggable protocols framework can be integrated with zero-copy high-speed network interfaces [23, 45, 20, 9], embedded systems [8], or high-performance communication infrastructures like Fast Messages [18].

7 CONCLUDING REMARKS

To be an effective development platform for performance-sensitive applications, CORBA middleware must preserve end-to-end application QoS properties across the communication layer. It is essential, therefore, to define a pluggable protocols framework that allows custom inter-ORB messaging and transport protocols to be configured flexibly and transparently by CORBA applications.

This chapter identifies the protocol-related limitations of current ORBs and describes a CORBA-based pluggable protocols framework we developed and integrated with TAO to address these limitations. TAO's pluggable protocols framework contains two main components: an ORB messaging component and an ORB transport adapter component. These two components allow applications developers and end-users to extend their communication infrastructure transparently to support the dynamic and/or static binding of new ORB messaging and transport protocols. Moreover, TAO's patterns-oriented OO design makes it straightforward to develop custom inter-ORB protocol stacks that can be optimized for particular application requirements and endsystem/network environments.

This chapter illustrates the performance of TAO's pluggable protocols framework empirically when running CORBA applications over high-speed interconnects, such as VME. Our benchmarking results demonstrate that applying appropriate optimizations and patterns to CORBA middleware can yield highly efficient and predictable implementations, without sacrificing flexibility or reuse. These results support our contention that CORBA middleware performance is largely an implementation issue. Thus, well-tuned, standard-based CORBA middleware like TAO can replace ad hoc and proprietary solutions that are still commonly used in traditional distributed applications and real-time systems.

Most of the performance overhead associated with pluggable protocols framework described in this chapter stem from "out-of-band" creation operations, rather operations in the critical path. We have shown how patterns can resolve key design forces to flexibly create and control the objects in the framework. Simple and efficient wrapper facades can then be used to isolate the rest of the application from low-level implementation details, without significantly affecting end-to-end performance.

REFERENCES

1. M. Henning and S. Vinoski, *Advanced CORBA Programming with C++*. Addison-Wesley Longman, 1999.
2. D.C. Schmidt, D.L. Levine, and S. Mungee, "The Design and Performance of Real-Time Object Request Brokers," *Computer Communications*, vol. 21, pp. 294–324, April 1998.
3. D.C. Schmidt, M. Stal, H. Rohnert, and F. Buschmann, *Pattern-Oriented Software Architecture: Patterns for Concurrency and Distributed Objects*, volume 2. New York, NY: Wiley & Sons, 2000.
4. F. Buschmann, R. Meunier, H. Rohnert, P. Sommerlad, and M. Stal, *Pattern-Oriented Software Architecture – A System of Patterns*. Wiley and Sons, 1996.

5. Object Management Group, *The Common Object Request Broker: Architecture and Specification,* 2.2 ed., February 1998.

6. Object Management Group, *Telecom Domain Task Force Request for Information Supporting Wireless Access and Mobility in CORBA – Request for Information,* OMG Document telecom/98-06-04 ed., June 1998.

7. I. Pyarali, C. O'Ryan, D.C. Schmidt, N. Wang, V. Kachroo, and A. Gokhale, "Using Principle Patterns to Optimize Real-Time ORBs," *Concurrent Magazine,* vol. 8, no. 1, 2000.

8. A. Gokhale and D.C. Schmidt, "Optimizing a CORBA IIOP Protocol Engine for Minimal Footprint Multimedia Systems," *Journal of Selected Areas in Communication (Special Issue on Service Enabling Platforms for Networked Multimedia Systems),* vol. 17, September 1999.

9. R.S. Madukkarumukumana, H.V. Shah, and C. Pu, "Harnessing User-Level Networking Architectures for Distributed Object Computing over High-Speed Networks," in *Proceedings of the 2nd Usenix Windows NT Symposium,* August 1998.

10. Compaq, Intel, and Microsoft, "Virtual Interface Architecture, Version 1.0." http://www.viarch.org, 1997.

11. Object Management Group, *Realtime CORBA Joint Revised Submission,* OMG Document orbos/99-02-12 ed., March 1999.

12. F. Kon and R.H. Campbell, "Supporting Automatic Configuration of Component-Based Distributed Systems," in *Proceedings of the 5th Conference on Object-Oriented Technologies and Systems* (San Diego, CA), USENIX, May 1999.

13. Object Management Group, *The Common Object Request Broker: Architecture and Specification,* 2.3 ed., June 1999.

14. B. Natarajan, A. Gokhale, D.C. Schmidt, and S. Yajnik, "DOORS: Towards High-Performance Fault-Tolerant CORBA," in *Proceedings of the 2nd International Symposium on Distributed Objects and Applications (DOA 2000)* (Antwerp, Belgium), OMG, September 2000.

15. B. Natarajan, A. Gokhale, D.C. Schmidt, and S. Yajnik, "Applying Patterns to Improve the Performance of Fault-Tolerant CORBA," in *Proceedings of the 7th International Conference on High Performance Computing (HiPC 2000)* (Bangalore, India), ACM/IEEE, December 2000.

16. Object Management Group, *CORBA Messaging Specification,* OMG Document orbos/98-05-05 ed., May 1998.

17. E. Gamma, R. Helm, R. Johnson, and J. Vlissides, *Design Patterns: Elements of Reusable Object-Oriented Software.* Reading, MA: Addison-Wesley, 1995.

18. M. Lauria, S. Pakin, and A. Chien, "Efficient Layering for High Speed Communi-

cation: Fast Messages 2.x.," in *Proceedings of the 7th High Performance Distributed Computing (HPDC7) Conference* (Chicago, IL), July 1998.

19. C. O'Ryan, D.C. Schmidt, F. Kuhns, M. Spivak, J. Parsons, I. Pyarali, and D. Levine, "Evaluating Policies and Mechanisms for Supporting Embedded, Real-Time Applications with CORBA 3.0," in *Proceedings of the 6th IEEE Real-Time Technology and Applications Symposium* (Washington, DC), IEEE, May 2000.

20. F. Kuhns, D.C. Schmidt, C. O'Ryan, and D. Levine, "Supporting High-Performance I/O in QoS-Enabled ORB Middleware," *Cluster Computing: The Journal on Networks, Software, and Applications,* 2000.

21. S. Mungee, N. Surendran, and D.C. Schmidt, "The Design and Performance of a CORBA Audio/Video Streaming Service," in *Proceedings of the Hamilton International Conference on System Science,* January 1999.

22. T.H. Harrison, D.L. Levine, and D.C. Schmidt, "The Design and Performance of a Real-Time CORBA Event Service," in *Proceedings of OOPSLA '97* (Atlanta, GA), ACM, October 1997.

23. Z.D. Dittia, G.M. Parulkar, and J.R. Cox, Jr., "The APIC Approach to High Performance Network Interface Design: Protected DMA and Other Techniques," in *Proceedings of INFOCOM '97* (Kobe, Japan), pp. 179–187, IEEE, April 1997.

24. H. Schulzrinne, S. Casner, R. Frederick, and V. Jacobson, "Rtp: A Transport Protocol for Real-Time Applications," *Network Information Center RFC 1889,* January 1996.

25. C.D. Gill, D.L. Levine, and D.C. Schmidt, "The Design and Performance of a Real-Time CORBA Scheduling Service," *The International Journal of Time-Critical Computing Systems (Special Issue on Real-Time Middleware),* to appear 2001.

26. C. O'Ryan and D.C. Schmidt, "Applying a Real-Time CORBA Event Service to Large-Scale Distributed Interactive Simulation," in *5th International Workshop on Object-Oriented Real-Time Dependable Systems* (Monterey, CA), IEEE, November 1999.

27. B. Meyer, *Object-Oriented Software Construction,* second edition, Englewood Cliffs, NJ: Prentice Hall, 1997.

28. D.C. Schmidt and C. Cleeland, "Applying a Pattern Language to Develop Extensible ORB Middleware." See this volume, Chapter 18.

29. D.C. Schmidt, "Applying Design Patterns and Frameworks to Develop Object-Oriented Communication Software," in *Handbook of Programming Languages* (P. Salus, ed.), Macmillan Computer Publishing, 1997.

30. H. Hueni, R. Johnson, and R. Engel, "A Framework for Network Protocol Software," in *Proceedings of OOPSLA '95* (Austin, TX), ACM, October 1995.

31. C. Cleeland, D.C. Schmidt, and T. Harrison, "External Polymorphism – An Object Structural Pattern for Transparently Extending Concrete Data Types," in *Pattern Languages of Program Design 3* (R. Martin, F. Buschmann, and D. Riehle, eds.), Reading, MA: Addison-Wesley, 1997.

32. D.C. Schmidt, S. Mungee, S. Flores-Gaitan, and A. Gokhale, "Software Architectures for Reducing Priority Inversion and Non-determinism in Real-Time Object Request Brokers," *Journal of Real-Time Systems (Special Issue on Real-Time Computing in the Age of the Web and the Internet),* to appear 2001.

33. P.S. Inc., *Quantify User's Guide.* PureAtria Software Inc., 1996.

34. I. Pyarali, C. O'Ryan, and D.C. Schmidt, "A Pattern Language for Efficient, Predictable, Scalable, and Flexible Dispatching Mechanisms for Distributed Object Computing Middleware," in *Proceedings of the International Symposium on Object-Oriented Real-Time Distributed Computing (ISORC)* (Newport Beach, CA), IEEE/IFIP, March 2000.

35. D.C. Schmidt, "Evaluating Architectures for Multi-Threaded CORBA Object Request Brokers," *Communications of the ACM (Special Issue on CORBA),* vol. 41, October 1998.

36. A.B. Arulanthu, C. O'Ryan, D.C. Schmidt, M. Kircher, and J. Parsons, "The Design and Performance of a Scalable ORB Architecture for CORBA Asynchronous Messaging," in *Proceedings of the Middleware 2000 Conference,* ACM/IFIP, April 2000.

37. N. Wang, D.C. Schmidt, K. Parameswaran, and M. Kircher, "Applying Reflective Middleware Techniques to Optimize a QoS-Enabled CORBA Component Model Implementation," in *24th Computer Software and Applications Conference* (Taipei, Taiwan), IEEE, October 2000.

38. A. Gokhale and D.C. Schmidt, "Measuring the Performance of Communication Middleware on High-Speed Networks," in *Proceedings of SIGCOMM '96* (Stanford, CA), pp. 306–317, ACM, August 1996.

39. N.C. Hutchinson and L.L. Peterson, "The x-kernel: An Architecture for Implementing Network Protocols," *IEEE Transactions on Software Engineering,* vol. 17, pp. 64–76, January 1991.

40. D. Ritchie, "A Stream Input-Output System," *AT&T Bell Labs Technical Journal,* vol. 63, pp. 311–324, October 1984.

41. D.C. Schmidt, D.F. Box, and T. Suda, "ADAPTIVE: A Dynamically Assembled Protocol Transformation, Integration, and eValuation Environment," *Journal of Concurrency: Practice and Experience,* vol. 5, pp. 269–286, June 1993.

42. M. Zitterbart, B. Stiller, and A. Tantawy, "A Model for High-Performance Commu-

nication Subsystems," *IEEE Journal of Selected Areas in Communication,* vol. 11, pp. 507–519, May 1993.

43. I. Object-Oriented Concepts, "ORBacus." www.ooc.com/ob.

44. I. Object-Oriented Concepts, "ORBacus User Manual – Version 3.1.2." www.ooc.com/ob, 1999.

45. T.V. Eicken, A. Basu, V. Buch, and W. Vogels, "U-Net: A User-Level Network Interface for Parallel and Distributed Computing," in *15th ACM Symposium on Operating System Principles,"* ACM, December 1995.

20

OBJECT LIFETIME MANAGER
A COMPLEMENTARY PATTERN FOR
CONTROLLING OBJECT CREATION
AND DESTRUCTION

David L. Levine, Christopher D. Gill,
and Douglas C. Schmidt

1 INTRODUCTION

Creational patterns such as Singleton and Factory Method [1] address object construction and initialization, but do not consider object destruction. In some applications, however, object destruction is as important as object construction. The *Object Lifetime Manager* pattern addresses issues associated with object destruction. Object Lifetime Manager is also an example of a *complementary pattern,* which completes or extends other patterns. In particular, the Object Lifetime Manager pattern completes creational patterns by considering the entire lifetime of objects.

This chapter is organized as follows: Section 2 describes the Object Lifetime Manager pattern in detail using the Siemens format [2], and Section 3 presents concluding remarks.

Based on "Object Lifetime Manager," by David L. Levine, Christopher D. Gill, and Douglas Schmidt, which appeared in *C++ Report* 12(1), January 2000, pp. 31–40, 44. ©101 Communications. Used with permission from the authors.

2 THE OBJECT LIFETIME MANAGER PATTERN

2.1 INTENT

The *Object Lifetime Manager* pattern can be used to govern the entire life-time of objects, from creating them prior to their first use to ensuring they are destroyed properly at program termination. In addition, this pattern can be used to replace static object creation/destruction with dynamic object preallocation/deallocation that occurs automatically during application initialization/termination.

2.2 EXAMPLE

Singleton [1] is a common creational pattern that provides a global point of access to a unique class instance and defers creation of the instance until it is first accessed. If a singleton is not needed during the lifetime of a program, it will not be created. The Singleton pattern does not address the issue of when its instance is destroyed, however, which is problematic for certain applications and operating systems.

To illustrate why it is important to address destruction semantics, consider the following logging component that provides a client programming API to a distributed logging service [3]. Applications use the logging component as a front-end to the distributed logging service to report errors and generate debugging traces.

```
class Logger
{
public:
  // Global access point to Logger singleton.
  static Logger *instance (void) {
    if (instance_ == 0)
      instance_ = new Logger;
    return instance_;
  }

  // Write some information to the log.
  int log (const char *format, ...);

protected;
```

```
// Default constructor (protected to
// ensure Singleton pattern usage).
Logger (void);

static Logger *instance_;
// Contained Logger singleton instance.

// . . . other resources that are
//        held by the singleton . . .
};
// Initialize the instance pointer.
Logger *Logger::instance_ = 0;
```

The Logger constructor, which is omitted for brevity, allocates various OS endsystem resources, such as socket handles, shared memory segments, and/or system-wide semaphores, that are used to implement the logging service client API.

To reduce the size and improve the readability of its logging records, an application may choose to log certain data, such as timing statistics, in batch mode rather than individually. For instance, the following statistics class batches timing data for individual identifiers:

```
class Stats
{
public:
  // Global access point to the
  // statistics singleton.
  static Stats *instance (void) {
    if (instance_ == 0)
      instance_ = new Stats;
    return instance ;
  }

  // Record a timing data point.
  int record (int id,
              const timeval &tv);

  // Report recorded statistics
  // to the log.
  void report (int id) {
    Logger::instance ()->
      log ("Avg timing %d: "
           "%ld sec %ld usec\n",
```

497

```
                id,
                average_i (id).tv_sec,
                average_i (id).tv_usec);
      }

    protected:
      // Default constructor.
      Stats (void);

      // Internal accessor for an average.
      const timeval &average_i (void);

      // Contained Stats singleton instance.
      static Stats *instance_;

      // . . . other resource that are
      //         held by the instance . . .
    };

    // Initialize the instance pointer.
    Stats *Stats::instance_ = 0;
```

After recording various statistics, a program calls the `Stats::report` method, which uses the `Logger` singleton to report average timing statistics for an identifier.

Both the `Logger` and `Stats` classes provide distinct services to the application: the `Logger` class provides general logging capabilities, whereas the `Stats` class provides specialized batching and logging of time statistics. These classes are designed using the Singleton pattern, so that a single instance of each is used in an application process.

The following example illustrates how an application might use the `Logger` and `Stats` singletons.

```
    int main (int argc, char *argv[])
    {
      // Interval timestamps.
      timeval start_tv, stop_tv;

      // Logger, Stats singletons
      // do not yet exist.

      // Logger and Stats singletons created
```

```
    // during the first iteration.
    for (int i = 0; i < argc; ++i) {
      ::gettimeofday (&start_tv);
      // do some work between timestamps . . .
      ::gettimeofdday (&stop_tv);
      // then record the stats . . .
      timeval delta_tv;
      delta_tv.sec = stop_tv.sec - start_tv.sec;
      delta_tv.usec = stop_tv.usec - start_tv.usec;
      Stats::instance ()->record (i, delta_tv);

      // . . . and log some output.
      Logger::instance ()->
        log ("Arg %d [%s]\n", i, argv[i]);
      Stats::instance()->report (i);
    }

    // Logger and Stats singletons are not
    // cleaned up when main returns.
    return 0;
  }
```

Note that the `Logger` and `Stats` singletons are not constructed or destroyed explicitly by the application, i.e., their lifetime management is decoupled from the application logic. It is common practice to not destroy singletons at program exit [4].

Several drawbacks arise, however, from the fact that the Singleton pattern only addresses the *creation* of singleton instances and does not deal with their destruction. In particular, when the `main` program above terminates, neither the `Logger` nor the `Stats` singletons are cleaned up. At best, this can lead to false reports of leaked memory. At worst, important system resources may not be released and destroyed properly.

For instance, problems can arise if the `Logger` and/or `Stats` singletons hold OS resources, such as system-scope semaphores, I/O buffers, or other allocated OS resources. Failure to clean up these resources gracefully during program shutdown can cause deadlocks and other synchronization hazards. To alleviate this problem, each singleton's destructor should be called before the program exits.

One way of implementing the Singleton pattern that attempts to ensure singleton destruction is to employ the Scoped Locking C++ idiom [3] that declares a static instance of the class at file scope [4]. For example, the following `Singleton Destroyer` template provides a destructor that deletes the singleton:

```
template <class T>
Singleton_Destroyer
{
public:
  Singleton_Destroyer (void): t_ (0) {}
  void register (T *) { t_ = t; }
  ~Singleton_Destroyer (void) { delete t_; }
private:
  T *t_; // Holds the singleton instance.
};
```

To use this class, all that's necessary is to modify the `Logger` and `Stats` classes by defining a static instance of the `Singleton Destroyer`, such as the following example for `Logger`:

```
static Singleton_Destroyer<Logger>
  logger_destroyer;

// Global access point to the
// Logger singleton.
static Logger *instance (void) {
  if (instance_ == 0) {
    instance_ = new Logger;
    // Register the singleton so it will be
    // destroyed when the destructor of
    // logger_destroyer is run.
    logger_destroyer.register (instance_);
  }
  return instance_;
}


// . . . similar changes to Stats class . . .
```

Note how `logger_destroyer` class holds the singleton and deletes it when the program exists. A similar `Singleton_Destroyer` could be used by the `Stats` singleton, as well.

Unfortunately, there are several problems with explicitly instantiating static `Singleton_Destroyer` instances. In C++, for example, each `Singleton_Destroyer` could be defined in a different compilation unit.

In this case, there is no guaranteed order in which their destructors will be called, which can lead to undefined program behavior. In particular, if singletons in different compilation units share resources, such as socket handles, shared memory segments, and/or system-wide semaphores, the program may fail to exit cleanly. The undefined order of singleton destruction in C++ makes it hard to ensure these resources are released by the OS before (1) the last singleton using the resource is completely destroyed, but not before (2) a singleton that is still alive uses the resource(s).

In summary, the key forces that are not resolved in these examples above are: (1) resources allocated by a singleton must ultimately be released when a program exists, (2) unconstrained creation and destruction order of static instances can result in serious program errors, and (3) shielding software developers from responsibility for details of object lifetime management can make systems less error-prone.

2.3 CONTEXT

An application or system where full control over the lifetime of the objects it creates is necessary for correct operation.

2.4 PROBLEM

Many applications do not handle the entire lifetime of their objects properly. In particular, applications that use creational patterns, such as Singleton, often fail to address object destruction. Similarly, applications that use static objects to provide destruction often suffer from inconsistent initialization and termination behavior. These problems are outlined below.

Problems with Singleton Destruction. Singleton instances may be created dynamically.[1] A dynamically allocated singleton instance becomes a resource leak if it is not destroyed, however. Often, singleton leaks are ignored

---

[1]Singleton is used as an example in much of this pattern description because (1) it is a popular creational pattern and (2) it highlights challenging object destruction issues nicely. However, Object Lifetime Manager can complement other creational patterns, such as Factory Method, and does not assume that its managed objects are singletons or of homogeneous types.

because (1) they aren't significant in many applications and (2) on most multi-user general-purpose operating systems, such as UNIX or Windows NT, they are cleaned up when a process terminates.

Unfortunately, resource leaks can be troublesome in the following contexts:

- *When grateful shutdown is required [4].* Singletons may be responsible for system resources, such as system-wide locks, open network connections, and shared memory segments. Explicit destruction of these singletons may be desirable to ensure these resources are destroyed at a well-defined point during program termination. For instance, if the `Logger` class requires system-wide locks or shared memory, then it should release these resources after they are no longer needed.

- *When singletons maintain references to other singletons.* Explicitly managing the order of destruction of singletons may be necessary to avoid problems due to dangling references during program termination. For example, if the `Stats` class in the example above uses the `Logger` instance in its `report` method, this method could be invoked during the `Stats` instance destruction, which renders the behavior of the program undefined. Likewise, to support useful behaviors, such as logging previously unreported values during program shutdown, the termination ordering of these singletons must be controlled.

- *When checking for memory leaks.* Memory leak detection tools, e.g., NuMega BoundsCheck, ParaSoft Insure++, and Rational Purify, are useful for languages such as C and C++ that require explicit allocation and deallocation of dynamic memory. These tools identify singleton instances as leaked memory, reports of which obscure important memory leaks.

  For instance, if many identifiers are used to record `Stats` data in our running example, it may appear that a sizable amount of memory is leaking during program operation. In large-scale applications, these "leaks" can result in numerous erroneous warnings, thereby obscuring real memory leaks and hindering system debugging.

- *Dynamic memory allocation may be from a global pool.* Some real-time operating systems, such as VxWorks [5] and pSOS [6], have only a single, global heap for all applications. Therefore, application tasks must release dynamically allocated memory upon task termination; otherwise, it cannot be reallocated to other applications until the OS is rebooted. Failure to explicitly release memory that was allocated dynamically by the `Logger` and `Stats` singletons in our running example represents real resource leaks on such platforms.

Problems with Static Object Lifetime. Some objects must be created prior to use. In C++, such instances traditionally have been created as *static objects*, which are intended to be constructed prior to invocation of the main program entry point and destroyed at program termination. However, there are several important drawbacks to static objects:

- *Unspecified order of construction/destruction.* C++ only specifies the order of construction/destruction of state objects *within* a compilation unit (file); the construction order matches the declaration order and destruction is the reverse order [7]. However, there is no constraint specified on the order of construction/destruction *between* static objects in different files. Therefore, construction/destruction ordering is implementation-dependent. For example, the versions of the `Logger` and `Stats` classes that use the `Singleton Destroyer` illustrate problems that arise from the undefined order of destruction of the `Stats` and `Logger` singleton instances.

   It is hard to write portable C++ code that uses static objects processing initialization dependencies. Often, it is simpler to avoid using static objects altogether, rather than trying to analyze for, and protect against, such dependencies. This approach is particularly appropriate for reusable components and frameworks [8], which should avoid unnecessary constraints on how they are used and/or initialized.

   Explicit singleton management is necessary for correct program operation on some platforms because they destroy singletons prematurely. For instance, the garbage collector in older Java Development Kits (JDKs) may destroy an object when there are no longer any references to it, even if the object was intended to be a singleton [9]. Though this deficiency has been fixed in later JDKs, the Object Lifetime Manager could solve it, under application control, by maintaining singleton references.

Another problem in Java applications is the sharing of namespaces, which allow sharing (intended or otherwise) between singletons in separate applets [10]. Again, the Object Lifetime Manager can be used to register singleton instances. Applets would then access their singletons from this registry.

- *Poor support by embedded systems.* Embedded systems have historically used C. Therefore, they do not always provide seamless support for OO programming language features. For instance, the construction/destruction of static objects in C++ is one such feature that often complicates embedded systems programming. The embedded OS may have support for explicit invocation of static constructor/destructor calls, but this is not optimal from a programmer's perspective.

  Some embedded operating systems do not support the notion of a *program* that has a unique entry point. For example, VxWorks supports multiple *tasks,* which are similar to threads because they all share one address space. However, there is no designated *main* task for each application. Therefore, these embedded systems platforms can be configured to call static constructors/destructors at module (object file) load/unload time, respectively. On such platforms, it is not otherwise necessary to unload and load between repeated executions. To properly destroy and construct static objects, however, the static object destructors/constructors either must be called manually, or the module unloaded and loaded again, which hinders repeated testing.

  In addition, placement of data in read-only memory (ROM) complicates the use of static objects [11]. The data must be placed in ROM prior to run-time; however, static constructors are called at run-time. Therefore, embedded systems sometimes do not support calls of static constructors and destructors. Moreover, if they are supported it may be under explicit application control, instead of by implicit arrangement of the compiler and run-time system.

- Static objects extend application startup time. Static objects may be considered at application startup time, prior to invocation of the main entry point. If these objects are not used during a specific execution, then application construction (and destruction) times are needlessly extended. One way to eliminate this waste is to replace each such static object with one that is allocated on demand, e.g., by using the Singleton pattern.

Replacement of a static object with a singleton also can be used to delay construction until the first use of the object. Again, this reduces startup time. Some real-time applications may find it advantageous to construct the singletons at a specific time, after the main entry point has been entered, but before the objects are needed.

One or more of these drawbacks of static objects typically provides sufficient motivation for removing them from a program. Often, it is better not to use them in the first place, but to apply the following solution instead.

2.5 SOLUTION

Define an *Object Lifetime Manager,* which is a singleton that contains a collection of *Preallocated Objects* and *Managed Objects.* The Object Lifetime Manager is responsible for constructing and destructing the Preallocated Objects at program initialization and termination, respectively. It is further responsible for ensuring all of its Managed Objects are destroyed properly at program termination.

2.6 APPLICABILITY

Use Object Lifetime Manager when:

Singletons and other dynamically created objects must be removed without application intervention at program termination. Singleton and other creational patterns do not typically address the question of when the objects they create should be removed, or who should remove them. In contrast, Object Lifetime Manager provides a convenient, global object that deletes dynamically created objects. Creational pattern objects can then register with the Object Lifetime Manager for deletion, which usually occurs at program termination.

Static objects must be removed from the application. As described in Section 2.4, static objects can be troublesome, especially in some languages and on some platforms. Object Lifetime Manager provides a mechanism to replace static objects with Preallocated Objects. Preallocated Objects are dynamically allocated before the application uses them, and deallocated at program termination.

The platform does not support static object construction/destruction. Some embedded platforms, such as VxWorks and pSOS, do not always construct static objects at program initialization and destroy them at program termination.[2] In general, it is best to remove all static objects, e.g., to support repeated testing of a program. Another situation where static objects can cause difficulty is when they are placed in ROM. Objects in ROM cannot be initialized at run-time, because they cannot be modified at all.

The underlying platform does not provide a notion of a main program, although the application needs it. The lack of support for static object construction/destruction on some platforms stems from their lack of support for the notion of a program, as discussed in Section 2.4. The Object Lifetime Manager pattern can be used to emulate programs by partitioning this address space. The scope of each Object Lifetime Manager delineates a program, from an application's perspective.

Destruction order must be specified by the application. Dynamically created objects can be *registered* with the Object Lifetime Manager for destruction. The Object Lifetime Manager can be implemented to destroy objects in any desired order.

The application requires explicit singleton management. As described in Section 2.4, singletons may be destroyed prematurely, for example, on earlier Java platforms. The Object Lifetime Manager delays singleton destruction until program termination.

---

[2]On VxWorks and pSOS, static objects can be constructed when the module is loaded and destroyed when it is unloaded. After loading, an entry point can be called more than once before unloading. Therefore, a *program* can be run more than once after constructing static objects, without ever destroying them. Conversely, static object constructors and destructors can be invoked explicitly.

2.7 Structure and Participants

The structure and participants of the Object Lifetime Manager pattern are shown using UML in the following figure and described below.

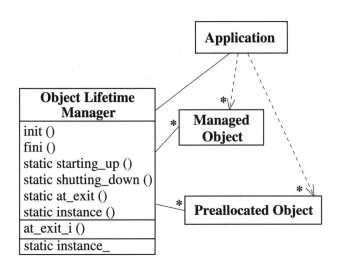

Object Lifetime Manager. Each Object Lifetime Manager is a singleton that contains collections of Managed Objects and Preallocated Objects.

Managed Objects. Any object may be *registered* with an Object Lifetime Manager, which is responsible for destroying the object. Object destruction occurs when the Object Lifetime Manager itself is destroyed, typically at program termination.

Preallocated Objects. An object may be hard-coded for construction and destruction by an Object Lifetime Manager. Preallocated Objects have the same lifetime as the Object Lifetime Manager, i.e., the lifetime of the process that executes the program.

Application. The Application initializes and destroys its Object Lifetime Managers, either implicitly or explicitly. In addition, the Application registers its Managed Objects with an Object Lifetime Manager, which may also contain Preallocated Objects.

2.8 DYNAMICS

The dynamic collaborations among participants in the Object Lifetime Manager pattern are shown in the following figure. The diagram depicts four separate activities:

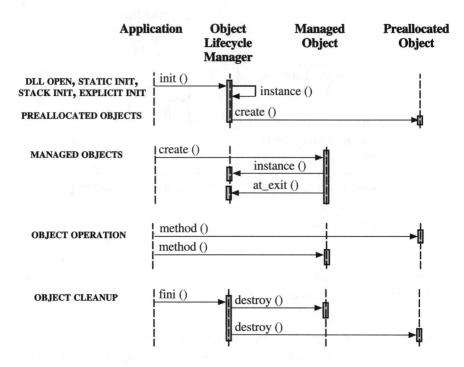

1. Object Lifetime Manager creation and initialization, which in turn creates the Preallocated Objects;
2. Managed Object creation by the Application, and registration with the Object Lifetime Manager;
3. Use of Preallocated and Managed Objects by the Application; and
4. Destruction of the Object Lifetime Manager, which includes destruction of all the Managed and Preallocated Objects it controls.

Within each activity, time increases down the vertical axis.

2.9 IMPLEMENTATION

The Object Lifetime Manager pattern can be implemented using the steps presented below. This implementation is based on the `Object Manager` provided in the ACE framework [8], which motivates many interesting issues discussed in this section. Some of the steps discussed below are language-specific because ACE is written in C++. The appendix illustrates even more concretely how the Object Lifetime Manager pattern has been implemented in ACE.

1. *Define the Object Lifetime Manager component.* This componenprovides applications with an interface with which to register objects whose lifetime must be managed to ensure proper destruction upon program termination. In addition, this component defines a repository that ensures proper destruction of its managed objects. The `Object Lifetime Manager` is a container for the `Preallocated Objects` and for the `Managed Objects` that are registered to be destroyed at program termination.

The following substeps can be used to implement the `Object Lifetime Manager`.

- *Define an interface for registering Managed Objects.* One way to register `Managed Objects` with the `Object Lifetime Manager` would be to use the C-library `atexit` function to invoke the termination functions at program exit. However, not all platforms support `atexit`. Furthermore, `atexit` implementations usually have a limit of 32 registered termination functions. Therefore, the `Object Lifetime Manager` should support the following two techniques for registered `Managed Objects` with a container that holds these objects and cleans them up automatically at program exit:

  1. *Define a cleanup function interface* – The `Object Lifetime Manager` allows applications to register arbitrary types of objects. When a program is shut down, the `Object Lifetime Manager` cleans up these objects automatically.

     The following C++ class illustrates a specialized `CLEANUP_FUNC` used in ACE to register an object or array for cleanup:

```
typedef void (*CLEANUP_FUNC) (void *object,
                              void *param);

class Object_Lifetime_Manager
{
public:
  // . . .
  static int at_exit (void *object,
                      CLEANUP_FUNC cleanup_hook,
                      void *param);
  // . . .
};
```

The static `at_exit` method registers an object or array of objects for cleanup at process termination. The `cleanup_hook` argument points to a global function or static method that is called at cleanup time to destroy the object or array. At destruction time, the `Object Lifetime Manager` passes the `object` and `param` arguments to the `cleanup_hook` function. The `param` argument contains any additional information needed by the `cleanup_hook` function, such as the number of objects in the array.

2. *Define a cleanup base class interface* – This interface allows applications to register for destruction with the `Object Lifetime Manager` any object whose class derives from a `Cleanup` base class. The `Cleanup` base class should have a virtual destructor and a `cleanup` method that simply calls `delete this`, which in turn invokes all derived class destructors. The following code fragment illustrates how this class is implemented in ACE:

```
class Cleanup
{
public:
  // . . .

  // Destructor.
  virtual ~Cleanup (void);

  // By default, simply deletes this.
  virtual void cleanup (void *param = 0);
};
```

The following code fragment illustrates the `Object Life-time Manager` interface used to register objects derived from the `Cleanup` base class in ACE:

```
class Object_Lifetime_Manager
{
public:
  // . . .
    static int at_exit (Clean *object,
                        void *param = 0);
  // . . .
};
```

This static `at_exit` method registers a `Cleanup` object for cleanup at process termination. At destruction time, the `Object Lifetime Manager` calls the `Cleanup` object's `cleanup` method, passing in the `param` argument. The `param` argument contains any additional information needed by the `cleanup` method.

- *Define a singleton adapter.* Although it is possible to explicitly code singletons to use `Object Lifetime Manager` methods defined above, this approach is tedious and error-prone. Therefore, it is useful to define a `Singleton` adapter class template that encapsulates the details of creating singleton objects and registering them with the `Object Life-time Manager`. In addition, the `Singleton` adapter can ensure the thread-safe Double-Checked Locking Optimization pattern [3] is used to construct and access an instance of the type-specific `Singleton`.

  The following code fragment illustrates how a singleton adapter is implemented in ACE:

```
template <class TYPE>
class Single : public Cleanup
{
public:
  // Global access point to the
  // wrapped singleton.
  static TYPE *instance (void) {
    // Details of Double Checked
    // Locking Optimization omitted . . .
    if (singleton_ == 0) {
      singleton_ = new Singleton<TYPE>;
```

```
      // Register with the Object Lifetime
      // Manager to control destruction.
      Object_Lifetime_Manager::
        at_exit (singleton_);
    }
    return &singleton_->instance_;
  }

protected:
  // Default constructor.
  Singleton (void);

  // Contained instance.
  TYPE instance_;

  // Instance of the singleton adapter.
  static Singleton<TYPE> *singleton_;
};
```

The Singleton class template is derived from the Cleanup class. This allows the Singleton instance to register itself with the Object Lifetime Manager. The Object Lifetime Manager then assumes responsibility for dynamically deallocating the Singleton instance and with it the adapted TYPE instance.

- *Define an interface for registering Preallocated Objects.* Preallocated Objects must always be created before the application's main processing begins. For instance, in some applications, synchronization locks must be created before their first use in order to avoid race conditions. Thus, these objects must be hard-coded into each Object Lifetime Manager class. Encapsulating their creation with the Object Lifetime Manager's own initialization phase ensures this will occur, without adding complexity to application code.

  The Object Lifetime Manager should be able to preallocate objects or arrays. The Object Lifetime Manager can perform these preallocations either statically in global data or dynamically on the heap. An efficient implementation is to store each Preallocated Object in an array. Certain languages, such as C++, do not support arrays of heterogeneous objects, however. Therefore, in these languages pointers must be stored instead of the objects themselves. The actual objects are allocated dynamically by the `Object Lifetime Manager` when it is instantiated, and destroyed by the `Object Lifetime Manager` destructor.

The following substeps should be used to implement `Preallocated Objects`:

1. *Limit exposure* – To minimize the exposure of header files, identify the Preallocated Objects by macros or enumerated literals, e.g.,

```
enum Preallocated_Object_ID
   {
     ACE_FILECACHE_LOCK,
     ACE_STATIC_OBJECT_LOCK,
     ACE_LOG_MSG_INSTANCE_LOCK,
     ACE_DUMP_LOCK,
     ACE_SIG_HANDLER_LOCK,
     ACE_SINGLETON_NULL_LOCK,
     ACE_SINGLETON_RECURSIVE_THREAD_LOCK,
     ACE_THREAD_EXIT_LOCK,
   };
```

The use of an enumerated type is appropriate when all preallocated objects are known *a priori*.

2. *Use cleanup adapters* – The `Cleanup Adapter` class template is derived from the `Cleanup` base class and wraps types not derived from the `Cleanup` base class so that they can be managed by the `Object Lifetime Manager`. Use template functions or macros for allocation/deallocation, e.g.,

```
#define PREALLOCATE_OBJECT(TYPE, ID) {\
   Cleanup_Adapter<TYPE> *obj_p;\
   obj_p = new Cleanup_Adapter<TYPE>;\
   preallocated_object[ID] = obj_p;\
 }

#define DELETE_PREALLOCATED_OBJECT(TYPE, ID)\
   cleanup_destroyer (\
     static_cast<Cleanup_Adapter<TYPE> *>\
       (preallocated_object[ID]), 0);\
   preallocated_object[ID] = 0;
```

The Cleanup Adapter adapts any object to use the simpler Object Lifetime Manager registration interface, as discussed in Appendix A. Similarly, Cleanup Destroyer uses the Cleanup Adapter to destroy the object.

An analogous array, enum, and macro pair can be supplied for preallocated arrays, if necessary.

3. *Define an accessor interface to the Preallocated Objects* – Applications need a convenient and typesafe interface to access preallocated objects. Because the Object Lifetime Manager supports preallocated objects of different types, it is necessary to provide a separate class template adapter with a member function that takes the id under which the object was preallocated in the Object Lifetime Manager, and returns a correctly typed pointer to the preallocated object.

The following code fragment illustrates how this interface is provided via a class template adapter in ACE:

```
template <class TYPE>
class Preallocated_Object_Interface
{
public:
  static TYPE *
  get_preallocated_object
    (Object_Lifetime_Manager::
      Preallocated_Object_ID id)
  {
    // Cast the return type of the object
    // pointer based on the type of the
    // function template parameter.
    return
      &(static_cast<Cleanup_Adapter<TYPE> *>
        (Object_Lifetime_Manager::
          preallocated_object[id]))->object ();
  }
  // . . . other methods omitted.
};
```

• *Determine the destruction order of registered objects.* As noted earlier, the Object Lifetime Manager can be implemented to destroy registered objects in any desired order. For example, priority levels could be assigned and destruction could proceed in decreasing order of priority. An interface could be provided for objects to set and change their destruction priority.

We have found that destruction in reverse order of registration has been a sufficient policy for ACE applications. An application can, in effect, specify destruction order by controlling the order in which it registers objects with the `Object Lifetime Manager`

- *Define a termination function interface.* Lifetime management functionality has been discussed so far in terms of destruction of objects at program termination. However, the `Object Lifetime Manager` can provide a more general capability – the ability to call a function at program termination – using the same internal implementation mechanism.

  For example, to ensure proper cleanup of open Win32 WinSock sockets at program termination, the `WSACleanup` function must be called. A variation of the Scoped Locking C++ idiom [3] could be applied, by creating a special wrapper facade [3] class whose constructor calls the API initialization functions, and whose destructor calls the API cleanup functions. The application can then register an instance of this class with the `Object Lifetime Manager` so that the object is destroyed and API termination methods are called during `Object Lifetime Manager` termination.

  However, this design may be overkill for many applications. Moreover, it can be error-prone because the application must ensure the class is used only as a singleton so that the API functions are only called once. Finally, this design may increase the burden on the application to manage object destruction order, so that the singleton is not destroyed before another object that uses the API in its destructor.

  Instead, the API termination functions can be called as part of the termination method of the `Object Lifetime Manager` itself. This latter approach is illustrated by the `socket_fini` call in the `Object_Lifetime_Manager::fini` method in Appendix A. The `socket_fini` function provides a platform-specific implementation that calls WSACleanup on Win32 platforms, and does nothing on other platforms.

- *Migrate common interfaces and implementation details into a base class.*

Factoring common internal details into an `Object Lifetime Manager Base` class can make the `Object Lifetime Manager` implementation simpler and more robust. Defining an `Object Lifetime Manager Base` class also supports the creation of multiple `Object Lifetime Managers`, each of a separate type. To simplify our discussion, we only touch on the use of multiple `Object Lifetime Managers` briefly. They do not add consequences to the pattern, but are useful for partitioning libraries and applications.

2. *Determine how to manage the lifetime of the* `Object Lifetime Manager`. The `Object Lifetime Manager` is responsible for initializing other global and static objects in a program. However, that begs the important bootstrapping question of how this singleton initializes and destroys itself. The following are the alternatives for initializing the `Object Lifetime Manager` singleton instance:

- *Static initialization.* If an application has no static objects with constraints on their order of construction or destruction, it's possible to create the `Object Lifetime Manager` as a static object. For example, ACE's `Object Lifetime Manager` can be created as a static object. The ACE library has no other static objects that have constraints on order of construction or destruction.

- *Stack initialization.* When there is a main program thread with well-defined points of program entry and termination, creating the `Object Lifetime Manager` on the stack of the main program thread can simplify program logic for creating and destroying the `Object Lifetime Manager`. This approach to initializing the `Object Lifetime Manager` assumes that there is one unique main thread per program. This thread defines the program: i.e., it is *running* if, and only if, the main thread is alive. This approach has a compelling advantage: the `Object Lifetime Manager` instance is automatically destroyed via any path out of `main`.[3]

---

[3]On platforms such as VxWorks and pSOS that have no designated `main` function, the main thread can be simulated by instantiating the `Object Lifetime Manager` on the stack of one thread, which is denoted by convention as *the* `main` thread.

Stack initialization is implemented transparently in ACE via a preprocessor macro named `main`. The macro renames the `main` program entry point to another, configurable name, such as `main_i`. It provides a `main` function that creates the `Object Lifetime Manager` instance as a local object (on the run-time stack) and then calls the renamed application entry point.

There are two drawbacks to the Stack initialization approach:

1. `main (int, char *[])` must be declared with arguments, even if they're not used. All of ACE uses this convention, so only applications must be concerned with it.

2. If there are any static objects depending on those that are destroyed by the `Object Lifetime Manager`, their destructors might attempt to access the destroyed objects. Therefore, the application developer is responsible for ensuring that no static objects depend on those destroyed by the `Object Lifetime Manager`.

- *Explicit initialization.* In this approach, create the `Object Lifetime Manager` explicitly under application control. The `Object Lifetime Manager init` and `fini` methods allow the application to create and destroy the `Object Lifetime Manager` when desired. This option alleviates complications that arise when using dynamic link libraries (DLLs).

- *Dynamic link library initialization.* In this approach, create and destroy the `Object Lifetime Manager` when its DLL is loaded and unloaded, respectively. Most dynamic library facilities include the ability to call (1) an initialization function when the library is loaded and (2) a termination function when the library is unloaded. However, see Section 2.13 for a discussion of the consequences of managing singletons from an `Object Lifetime Manager` in different DLLs.

2.10 EXAMPLE RESOLVED

The preceding discussion demonstrates how the Object Lifetime Manager pattern can be used to resolve key design forces related to managing object lifetimes. In particular, the unresolved forces described in Section 2.2 can be satisfied by applying the Object Lifetime Manager pattern.

The following example shows how the Object Lifetime Manager pattern can be applied to the original Logger and Stats examples from Section 2.2. Using the Singleton adapter template described in Section 2.9 greatly simplifies managed object implementations by encapsulating key implementation details, such as registration with the Object Lifetime Manager. For instance, the original Stats class can be replaced by a managed Stats class, as follows.

```
class Stats
{
public:
  friend class Singleton<Stats>;

  // Destructor: frees resources.
  ~Stats (void);

  // Record a timing data point.
  int record (int id,
              const timeval &tv);

  // Report recorded statistics
  // to the log.
  void report (int id) {
    Singleton<Logger>::instance ()->
      log ("Avg timing %d: "
           "%ld sec %ld usec\n",
           id,
           average_i (id).tv_sec,
           average_i (id).tv_usec);
  }

protected:
  // Default constructor.
  Stats (void)
  {
    // Ensure the Logger instance
    // is registered first, and will be
    // cleaned up after, the Stats
    // instance.
    Singleton<Logger>::instance ();
  }
```

```
    // Internal accessor for an average.
    const timeval &average_i (void);

    // . . . other resources that are
    //         held by the instance . . .
  };
```

Notice that the singleton aspects have been factored out of the original Stats class and are now provided by the Singleton adapter template. Similar modifications can be made to the original Logger class so that it uses the Singleton adapter template.

Finally, the following example shows how an application might use the Logger and Stats classes.

```
    int main (int argc, char *argv[])
    {
      // Interval timestamps.
      timeval start_tv, stop_tv;

      // Logger and Stats singletons
      // do not yet exist.

      // Logger and then Stats singletons
      // are created and registered on the first
      // iteration.
      for (int i = 0; i < argc; ++i) {
        ::gettimeofday (&start_tv);
        // do some work between timestamps ...
        ::gettimeofday (&stop_tv);
        // then record the stats ...
        timeval delta_tv;
        delta_tv.sec = stop_tv.sec - start_tv.sec;
        delta_tv.usec = stop_tv.usec - start_tv.usec;
        Singleton<Stats>::instance ()->
          record (i, delta_tv);

        // . . . and log some output.
        Singleton<Logger>::instance ()->
          log ("Arg %d [%s]\n", i, argv[i]);
        Singleton<Stats>::instance()->report (i);
      }

      // Logger and Stats singletons are
      // cleaned up by Object Lifetime Manager
```

```
    // upon program exit.
    return 0;
}
```

The following key forces are resolved in this example: (1) ensuring resources allocated by an instance are subsequently released, (2) managing the order of creation and destruction of singletons, and (3) providing a framework that encapsulates these details within a well-defined interface.

2.11 KNOWN USES

Object Lifetime Manager is used in the Adaptive Communication Environment (ACE) [8] to ensure destruction of singletons at program termination and to replace static objects with dynamically allocated, managed objects. ACE is used on many different OS platforms, some of which do not support static object construction/destruction for every program invocation. ACE can be configured to not contain any objects whose initialization is necessary prior to program invocation.

Gabrilovich [12] argumented the Singleton pattern to permit applications to specify destruction order. A local static `auto_ptr`[4] is responsible for the destruction of each singleton instance. Destruction of singleton instances proceeds by application-defined phases; an application may optionally register its singleton instances for destruction in a specific phase.

An interesting example of a "small" Object Lifetime Manager is the *strong pointer* [13, 14].[5] A strong pointer manages just one object; it destroys the object when its scope is exited, either normally or via an exception. There can be many strong pointers in a program, behaving as Function-as-Owner (or Block-as-Owner). Moreover, the strong pointers themselves have transient lifetimes, i.e., that of their enclosing blocks.

In contrast, there is typically just one Object Lifetime Manager per program (or per large-scale component). And Object Lifetime Managers live for the duration of the program invocation. This reflects the specific intent of the Object Lifetime Manager to destroy objects at program termination, but not sooner. Such objects may be used after the current block or function has been exited, and destruction/creation cycles are not possible or desired.

---

[4]The `auto_ptr` is a local static object in the singleton instance accessor method.

[5]A C++ `auto_ptr` is an implementation of a strong pointer.

2.12 SEE ALSO

The Object Lifetime Manager pattern is related to the Manager [15] pattern. In both patterns, a client application uses a collection of objects, relying upon a manager to encapsulate the details of how the objects themselves are managed. This separation of concerns makes the application more robust, because management aspects that are potentially error-prone are hidden behind a type-safe interface. Using these managers also makes the application more extensible, because certain details of the managed objects can be varied independent of the manager implementation. For example, a manager for a certain class can be used to manage objects of classes derived from that base class.

The Object Lifetime Manager pattern differs from the Manager pattern in the types of the managed objects. Whereas the Manager pattern requires that the managed objects have a common base type, the Object Lifetime Manager pattern allows objects of unrelated types to be managed. The Manager pattern relies on inheritance for variations in the manager and managed object classes. In contrast, the Object Lifetime Manager relies on object composition and type parameterization to achieve greater decoupling of the manager from the managed objects.

The Object Lifetime Manager pattern further differs from the Manager pattern in the details of the object management services it provides to applications. The Manager pattern provides both key-based and query-based search services, e.g., ISBN lookup or finding a list of books by an author [15], while the Object Lifetime Manager pattern supports a simpler, more generic key-based lookup service. The Manager pattern supports fine-grained control of object creation and destruction by the application, while the Object Lifetime Manager pattern only supports destruction of its registered objects at the end of the program.

The application can *register* a pre-existing object with the Object Lifetime Manager, which then assumes responsibility for the remaining lifetime of the managed object. The Manager pattern only allows on-demand creation of objects, so that the lifetime of objects is managed in an all-or-none manner.

These distinctions in object types and services details reflect the different intents of the two patterns. Fundamentally, the Manager pattern focuses on the search structure aspects of object management, whereas the Object Lifetime Manager pattern emphasizes the lifetime aspects instead. The Manager pattern should be used to provide tailored object lifetime services for a well-defined collection of related objects. The Object Lifetime Manager pattern should be used to *complement* creational patterns, providing more generic object lifetime services for a wider collection of possibly unrelated objects.

Object Lifetime Manager complements creational patterns, such as Singleton, by managing object instance destruction. Singleton addresses only part of the object lifetime because it just manages instance creation. However, destruction is usually not an important issue with Singleton because it does not retain *ownership* of created objects [4]. Ownership conveys the responsibility for managing the object, including its destruction. Singleton is the prototypical example of a creational pattern that does not explicitly transfer ownership, yet does not explicitly arrange for object destruction. Object Lifetime Manager complements Singleton by managing the destruction portion of the object lifetime.

Object Lifetime Manager can complement other creational patterns, such as Abstract Factory and Factory Method. Implementations of these patterns could register dynamically allocated objects for deletion at program termination. Alternatively (or additionally), they could provide interfaces for object destruction, corresponding to those for object creation.

Cargill presented a taxonomy of the dynamic C++ object lifetime [16]. The Localized Ownership pattern language includes patterns, such as Creator-as-Owner, Sequence-of-Owners, and Shared Ownership, which primarily address object ownership. Ownership conveys the responsibility for destruction.

Creator-as-Owner is further subdivided into Function-as-Owner, Object-as-Owner, and Class-as-Owner. The Singleton destruction capability of Object Lifetime Manager may be viewed as a new category of Creator-as-Owner: Program-as-Owner. It is distinct from Function-as-Owner, because static objects outlive the program entry point (`main`). Object Lifetime Manager's Preallocated Objects similarly can be viewed logically, at least, as outliving the main program function.

When Singleton is used on multi-threaded platforms, a mutex should be used to serialize access to the instance pointer. Double-Checked Locking [3] greatly reduces the use of this mutex by only requiring it prior to creation of the singleton. However, the mutex is still required, and it must be initialized.[6] Object Lifetime Manager solves the chicken-and-egg problem of initialization of the mutex by preallocating one for each singleton, or group of singletons.

---

[6]POSIX 1003.1c [17] mutexes can be initialized without calling a static constructor. However, they are not available on all platforms.

Object Lifetime Manager uses Adapter for type-safe storage of objects of any class. By using inline functions, the Managed Object Adapter should have no size/performance overhead. We confirmed this with the GreenHills 1.8.9 compiler for VxWorks on Intel targets. However, some compilers do not inline template member functions. Fortunately, the size overhead of Managed Object is very small, i.e., we measured 40 to 48 bytes with g++ on Linux and LynxOS. The ACE Cleanup Adapter template class has slightly higher size overhead, about 160 bytes per instantiation.

2.13 CONSEQUENCES

The *benefits* of using Object Lifetime Manager include:

Destruction of Singletons and other Managed Objects at program termination. The Object Lifetime Manager pattern allows a program to shut down cleanly, releasing memory for Managed Objects, along with the resources they hold at program termination. All heap-allocated memory can be released by the application. This supports repeated testing on platforms where heap allocations outlive the program.[7] It also eliminates the memory-in-use warnings reported for singletons by memory access checkers at program termination.

Specification of destruction order. The order of destruction of objects can be specified. The order specification mechanism can be as simple or as complex as desired. As noted earlier, simple mechanisms are generally sufficient in practice.

Removal of static objects from libraries and applications. Static objects can be replaced by preallocated Objects. This prevents applications from relying on the order in which static objects are constructed/destroyed. Moreover, it allows code to target embedded systems, which sometimes have little or no support for constructing/destroying static objects.

However, the following *liabilities* must be considered when using the Object Lifetime Manager pattern:

---

[7]On some operating systems, notably some real-time operating systems, there is no concept of a *program*. There are tasks, i.e., threads, but no one task has any special, main identity. Thus, there is no cleanup of dynamically allocated memory, open files, etc., at task termination.

Lifetime of the manager itself. The application must ensure that it respects the lifetime of the Object Lifetime Manager, and does not attempt to use its services outside that lifetime. For example, the application must not attempt to access `Preallocated Objects` prior to the complete initialization of the `Object Lifetime Manager`. Similarly, the application must not destroy the `Object Lifetime Manager` prior to the application's last use of a `Managed` or `Preallocated Object`. Finally, the implementation of the `Object Lifetime Manager` is simplified if it can assume that it will be initialized by only one thread. This precludes the need for a static lock to guard its initialization.

Use with shared libraries. On platforms that support loading and unloading shared libraries at run-time, the application must be *very* careful of platform-specific issues that impact the lifetime of the `Object Lifetime Manager` itself. For example, on Windows NT, the `Object Lifetime Manager` should be initialized by the application or by a DLL that contains it. This avoids a potential deadlock situation due to serialization within the OS when it loads DLLs.

A related issue arises with singletons that are created in DLLs, but managed by an `Object Lifetime Manager` in the main application code. If the DLL is unloaded before program termination, the `Object Lifetime Manager` would try to destroy it using code that is no longer linked into the application. For this reason, we have added an unmanaged Singleton class to ACE. An unmanaged Singleton is of the conventional design, i.e., it does not provide implicit destruction. ACE uses a managed Singleton by default because we found the need for unmanaged Singletons to be very unusual.

CONCLUDING REMARKS

Many creational patterns specifically address only object *creation*. They do not consider when or how to *destroy* objects that are no longer needed. The Object Lifetime Manager pattern provides mechanisms for object destruction at program termination. Thus, it complements many creational patterns by covering the entire object lifetime.

The Singleton pattern provides a notable example where coordinated object lifetime management is important. In particular, deletion at program termination ensures that programs have no memory leaks of singleton objects. Moreover, applications that employ the Object Lifetime Manager pattern do not require use of static object constructors and destructors, which is important for embedded systems. In addition, the Object Lifetime Manager pattern supports replacement of static objects with dynamically Preallocated Objects, which is useful on embedded platforms and with OO languages, such as C++.

One of the Object Lifetime Manager pattern's more interesting aspects is that it addresses weaknesses of another pattern, at least in some contexts. Our initial motivation was to remedy these weaknesses by registering and deleting singletons at program termination. The utility, applicability, novelty, and complexity of the ACE `Object Lifetime Manager` class seemed to be on a par with those of the ACE `Singleton` adapter template class, so we felt that it deserved consideration as a pattern. Because it can address just part of the object lifetime, however, we consider Object Lifetime Manager to be a *complementary* pattern.

Another interesting question was: "How do we categorize Object Lifetime Manager?" It was not (originally) a Creational pattern, because it handled only object destruction, not creation. Again, it seemed appropriate to refer to the Object Lifetime Manager pattern as complementing the Singleton pattern.

In addition, we realized that `Object Lifetime Manager` had another use that was related to destroying singletons. Static objects create problems similar to those of singletons, i.e., destruction, especially on operating systems that have no notion of a program, and order of creation/destruction. `Preallocated Objects` were added to support removal of static objects. Our first `Preallocated Object` was the mutex used for Double-Checked Locking [3] in the ACE implementation of . . . the `Singleton` adapter template.

Current development efforts include breaking the one instance into multiple `Object Lifetime Managers`, to support subsetting. Each layer of ACE, e.g., OS, logging, threads, connection management, sockets, interprocess communication, service configuration, streams, memory management, and utilities, will have its own `Object Lifetime Manager`. When any `Object Lifetime Manager` is instantiated, it will instantiate each dependent `Object Lifetime Manager`, if not already done. And similar, configured-in cooperation will provide graceful termination.

A highly portable implementation of the Object Lifetime Manager pattern and the `Singleton` adapter template is freely available and can be downloaded from `www.cs.wustl.edu/~schmidt/ACE-obtain.html`.

ACKNOWLEDGMENTS

Thanks to Matthias Kerkhoff, Per Andersson, Steve Huston, Elias Sreih, and Liang Chen for many helpful discussions on the design and implementation of ACE's `Object Manager`. Thanks to Brad Appleton, our PLoP '99 shepherd and C++ Report Patterns++ section editor, Evgeniy Gabrilovich, Kevlin Henney, and our PLoP '99 workshop group for many helpful suggestions on the content and presentation of the Object Lifetime Manager pattern. And thanks to Bosko Zivaljevic for pointing out that static object construction can extend application startup time.

REFERENCES

1. E. Gamma, R. Helm, R. Johnson, and J. Vlissides, *Design Patterns: Elements of Reusable Object-Oriented Software.* Reading, MA: Addison-Wesley, 1995.

2. F. Buschmann, R. Meunier, H. Rohnert, P. Sommerlad, and M. Stal, *Pattern-Oriented Software Architecture – A System of Patterns.* Wiley & Sons, 1996.

3. D.C. Schmidt, M. Stal, H. Rohnert, and F. Buschmann, *Pattern-Oriented Software Architecture: Patterns for Concurrency and Distributed Objects,* volume 2. New York, NY: Wiley & Sons, 2000.

4. J. Vlissides, *Pattern Hatching: Design Patterns Applied.* Reading, MA: Addison-Wesley, 1998.

5. Wind River Systems, "VxWorks 5.3." http://www.wrs.com/products/html/vxworks.html.

6. Integrated Systems, Inc., "pSOSystem." http://www.isi.com/products/psosystem/.

7. Bjarne Stroustrup, *The C++ Programming Language,* 3rd Edition. Addison-Wesley, 1998.

8. D.C. Schmidt, "ACE: An Object-Oriented Framework for Developing Distributed Applications," in *Proceedings of the 6th USENIX C++ Technical Conference* (Cambridge, MA), USENIX Association, April 1994.

9. E. Shea, "Java Singleton," June 7, 2000. http://www.c2.com/cgi/wiki?JavaSingleton.

10. D. McNicol, "Another Java Singleton Problem," June 7, 2000. http://www.c2.com/cgi/wiki?AnotherJavaSingletonProblem.

11. D. Saks, "Ensuring Static Initialization in C++," *Embedded Systems Programming,* vol. 12, pp. 109–111, March 1999.

12. E. Gabrilovich, "Destruction-Managed Singleton: A Compound Pattern for Reliable Deallocation of Singletons," *C++ Report,* vol. 12, January 2000.

13. B. Milewski, "Strong Pointers and Resources Management in C++," *C++ Report,* vol. 10, pp. 23–27, September 1998.

14. B. Milewski, "Strong Pointers and Resource Management in C++, Part 2," *C++ Report,* vol. 11, pp. 36–39, 50, February 1999.

15. P. Sommerland, "Manager," in *Pattern Languages of Program Design 3*, R. Martin, D. Riehle, F. Buschmann, eds., Reading, MA: Addison-Wesley, 1998, pp. 19–28.

16. T. Cargill, "Localized Ownership: Managing Dynamic Objects in C++," in *Pattern Languages of Program Design* 2 J.M. Vlissides, J.O. Coplien, and N.L. Kerth, eds., Reading, MA: Addison-Wesley, 1996.

17. "Information Technology – Portable Operating System Interface (POSIX) – Part 1: System Application: Program Interface (API) [C Language]," 1995.

Appendix A: Detailed Implementation

This section provides an example of a concrete Object Lifetime Manager implementation in C++ described in Section 2.9. It is based on the ACE [8] Object Lifetime Manager implementation. The ACE implementation reveals some interesting design issues. Its most visible purpose is to manage cleanup of singletons at program termination, and create/destroy Preallocated Objects. In addition, it performs other cleanup actions, such as shutdown of services provided by the ACE library, at program termination.

The Object Lifetime Manager Base abstract base class, shown in Figure 20.1, provides the initialization and finalization mechanisms for an Object Lifetime Manager. Subclasses must specialize and provide implementations, described below.

In addition, Object Lifetime Manager Base supports chaining of Object Lifetime Managers. Object Lifetime Managers are Singletons, each with its own locus of interest. An application may have a need for more than one Object Lifetime Manager, e.g., one per major component. Chaining permits ordered shutdown of the separate components.

Figure 20.2 shows an example of Object Lifetime Manager class. It is a Singleton, so it provides a static instance accessor. In addition, it provides static starting_up and shutting_down state accessors. An enumeration lists identifiers for the Preallocated Objects that it owns.

An interesting detail is the (boolean) reference count logic provided by the derived class `init` and `fini` methods. There are several alternatives for constructing an Object Lifetime Manager, discussed in Section 2.9. The reference count ensures that an Object Lifetime Manager is only constructed once, and destroyed once.

The implementation of the `instance`, `init`, and `fini` methods are shown in Figures 20.3 and 20.4. The `instance` method is typical of Singleton instance accessors, but includes logic to support static placement instead of dynamic allocation. In addition, it is not thread safe, requiring construction before the program spawns any threads. This avoids the need for a lock to guard the allocation.

The `init` and `fini` methods show creation and destruction of Preallocated Objects, respectively. They show application-specific startup and shutdown code. Finally, they show maintenance of the Object Lifetime Manager state.[8]

---

[8]This should be moved up to the base class.

Figure 20.1. Object Lifetime Manager base class.

```
class Object_Lifetime_Manager_Base
{
public:
  virtual int init (void) = 0;
  // Explicitly initialize. Returns 0 on success,
  // -1 on failure due to dynamic allocation
  // failure (in which case errno is set to
  / ENOMEM), or 1 if it had already been called.

  virtual int fini (void) = 0;
  // Explicitly destroy. Returns 0 on success,
  // -1 on failure because the number of <fini>
  // calls hasn't reached the number of <init>
  // calls, or 1 if it had already been called.

  enum Object_Lifetime_Manager_State {
    OBJ_MAN_UNINITIALIZED,
    OBJ_MAN_INITIALIZING,
    OBJ_MAN_INITIALIZED,
    OBJ_MAN_SHUTTING_DOWN,
    OBJ_MAN_SHUT_DOWN
  };
```

```
protected:
  Object_Lifetime_Manager_Base (void) :
    object_manager_state_ (OBJ_MAN_UNINITIALIZED),
    dynamically_allocated_ (0),
    next_ (0) {}

  virtual ~Object_Lifetime_Manager_Base (void) {
    // Clear the flag so that fini
    // doesn't delete again.
    dynamically_allocated_ = 0;
  }

  int starting_up_i (void) {
    return object_manager_state_ <
      OBJ_MAN_INITIALIZED;
  }
  // Returns 1 before Object_Lifetime_Manager_Base
  // has been constructed. This flag can be used
  // to determine if the program is constructing
  // static objects. If no static object spawns
  // any threads, the program will be
  // single-threaded when this flag returns 1.

  int shutting_down_i (void) {
    return object_manager_state_ >
      OBJ_MAN_INITIALIZED;
  }
  // Returns 1 after Object_Lifetime_Manager_Base
  // has been destroyed.

  Object_Lifetime_Manager_State
    object_manager_state;
  // State of the Object_Lifetime_Manager;

  u_int dynamically_allocated_;
  // Flag indicating whether the
  // Object_Lifetime_Manager instance was
  // dynamically allocated by the library.
  // (If it was dynamically allocated by the
  // application, then the application is
  // responsible for deleting it.)

  Object_Lifetime_Manager_Base *next_;
  // Link to next Object_Lifetime_Manager,
  // for chaining.
};
```

Figure 20.2. Object Lifetime Manager class.

```cpp
class Object_Lifetime_Manager :
  public Object_Lifetime_Manager_Base
{
public:
  virtual int init (void);

  virtual int fini (void);

  static int starting_up (void) {
    return instance_ ?
      instance_->starting_up_i () : 1;
  }

  static int shutting_down (void) {
    return instance_ ?
      instance_->shutting_down_i () : 1;
  }

  enum Preallocated_Object
    {
# if defined (MT_SAFE) && (MT_SAFE ! = 0)
      OS_MONITOR_LOCK,
      TSS_CLEANUP_LOCK,
# else
      // Without MT_SAFE. There are no
      // preallocated objects. Make
      // sure that the preallocated_array
      // size is at least one by declaring
      // this dummy.
      EMPTY_PREALLOCATED_OBJECT,
# endif /* MT_SAFE */
      // This enum value must be last!
      PREALLOCATED_OBJECTS
    };
  // Unique identifiers for Preallocated Objects.

  static Object_Lifetime_Manager *instance (void);
  // Accessor to singleton instance.

public:
  // Application code should not use these
  // explicitly, so they're hidden here. They're
```

```
  // public so that the Object_Lifetime_Manager
  // can be constructed/destroyed in main, on
  // the stack.
  Object_Lifetime_Manager (void) {
    // Make sure that no further instances are
    // created via instance.
    if (instance_ == 0)
      instance_ = this;
    init ();
   }

  ~Object_Lifetime_Manager (void) {
    // Don't delete this again in fini.
    dynamically_allocated_ = 0;
    fini ();
  }

private:
  static Object_Lifetime_Manager *instance_;
  // Singleton instance pointer.

  static void *
    preallocated_object[PREALLOCATED_OBJECTS];
  // Array of Preallocated Objects.
};
```

Figure 20.3. Object lifetime method implementation.

```
Object_Lifetime_Manager *
Object_Lifetime_Manager::instance_ = 0;
// Singleton instance pointer.

Object_Lifetime_Manager *
Object_Lifetime_Manager::instance (void)
{
  // This function should be called during
  // construction of static instances, or
  // before any other threads have been created
  // in the process. So, it's not thread safe.
  if (instance_ == 0) {
    Object_Lifetime_Manager *instance_pointer =
      new Object_Lifetime_Manager;
```

```
    // instance_ gets set as a side effect of the
    // Object_Lifetime_Manager allocation, by
    // the default constructor. Verify that . . .
    assert (instance_pointer == instance_);

    instance_pointer->dynamically_allocated_ = 1;
  }
  return instance_;
}

int
Object_Lifetime_Manager::init (void)
{
  if (starting_up_i ()) {
    // First, indicate that this
    // Object_Lifetime_Manager instance
    // is being initialized.
    object_manager_state = OBJ_MAN_INITIALIZING;

    if (this == instance_) {
# if defined (MT_SAFE) && (MT_SAFE != 0)
      PREALLOCATE_OBJECT (mutex_t,
        OS_MONITOR_LOCK)
      // Mutex initialization omitted.

      PREALLOCATE_OBJECT (recursive_mutex_t,
        TSS_CLEANUP_LOCK)
      // Recursive mutex initialization omitted.
# endif /* MT_SAFE */

    // Open Winsock (no-op on other
    // platforms).
    socket_init (/* WINSOCK_VERSION */);

    // Other startup code omitted.
    }

  // Finally, indicate that the
  // Object_Lifetime_Manager instance
  // has been initialized.
    object_manager_state_ = OBJ_MAN_INITIALIZED;
    return 0;
```

```
  } else {
    // Had already initialized.
    return 1;
  }
}
```

Figure 20.4. Object lifetime method implementations.

```
int
Object_Lifetime_Manager::fini (void)
{
  if (shutting_down_i ())
    // Too late. Or, maybe too early. Either
    // <fini> has already been called, or
    // <init> was never called.
    return object_manager_state_ ==
      OBJ_MAN_SHUT_DOWN  ?  1  :  -1;

  // Indicate that the Object_Lifetime_Manager
  // instance is being shut down.
  // This object manager should be the last one
  // to be shut down.
  object_manager_state_ = OBJ_MAN_SHUTTING_DOWN;

  // If another Object_Lifetime_Manager has
  // registered for termination, do it.
  if (next_) {
    next_->fini ();
    // Protect against recursive calls.
    next_ = 0;
  }

  // Only clean up Preallocated Objects when
  // the singleton Instance is being destroyed.
  if (this == instance_) {
    // Close down Winsock (no-op on other
    // platforms).
    socket_fini ();

    // Cleanup the dynamically preallocated
    // objects.
# if defined (MT_SAFE) && (MT_SAFE != 0)
    // Mutex destroy not shown . . .
```

```
        DELETE_PREALLOCATED_OBJECT (mutex_t,
          MONITOR_LOCK)

        // Recursive mutex destroy not shown . . .
        DELETE_PREALLOCATED_OBJECT (
          recursive_mutex_t,
          TSS_CLEANUP_LOCK)
# endif /* MT_SAFE */
      }

    // Indicate that this Object_Lifetime_Manager
    // instance has been shut down.
    object_manager_state_ = OBJ_MAN_SHUT_DOWN;

    if (dynamically_allocated_)
      delete this;

    if (this == instance_)
      instance_ = 0;

    return 0;
}
```

INDEX